D1256713

309

ENGLISH VERSE
VOLUME II

Oxford University Press, Ely House, London W. 1

GLASGOW NEW YORK TORONTO MELBOURNE WELLINGTON
CAPE TOWN SALISBURY IBADAN NAIROBI DAR ES SALAAM LUSAKA ADDIS ABABA
BOMBAY CALCUTTA MADRAS KARACHI LAHORE DACCA
KUALA LUMPUR SINGAPORE HONG KONG TOKYO

ENGLISH VERSE

Chosen and edited by
W. PEACOCK

In five volumes
VOLUME II
CAMPION
TO THE BALLADS

LONDON
OXFORD UNIVERSITY PRESS

*The second volume of these Selections of English Verse
was published in* The World's Classics *in 1929 and
reprinted in 1932, 1936, 1940, 1947, 1950, 1952,
1955, 1958, 1961, 1964, 1967, and 1971*

S B N 19 250309 X

PRINTED IN GREAT BRITAIN

CONTENTS

CONTENTS

CONTENTS

CONTENTS

THOMAS CAMPION

1567(?)–1619

WHEN TO HER LUTE CORINNA SINGS

WHEN to her lute Corinna sings,
Her voice revives the leaden strings,
And doth in highest notes appear,
As any challenged echo clear;
But when she doth of mourning speak,
E'en with her sighs the strings do break.

And as her lute doth live or die,
Led by her passion, so must I,
For when of pleasure she doth sing,
My thoughts enjoy a sudden spring,
But if she doth of sorrow speak,
E'en from my heart the strings do break.

CHERRY-RIPE

THERE is a garden in her face,
Where roses and white lilies grow;
A heavenly paradise is that place,
Wherein all pleasant fruits do flow.
    There cherries grow, which none may buy
    Till Cherry-ripe themselves do cry.

Those cherries fairly do enclose
Of orient pearl a double row;
Which when her lovely laughter shows,
They look like rose-buds filled with snow.
    Yet them nor peer nor prince can buy,
    Till Cherry-ripe themselves do cry.

Her eyes like angels watch them still;
Her brows like bended bows do stand,
   Threat'ning with piercing frowns to kill
All that attempt with eye or hand
      Those sacred cherries to come nigh,
      Till Cherry-ripe themselves do cry.

FOLLOW YOUR SAINT

FOLLOW your saint, follow with accents sweet;
Haste you, sad notes, fall at her flying feet:
There, wrapped in cloud of sorrow pity move,
And tell the ravisher of my soul I perish for her
   love.
But if she scorns my never-ceasing pain,
Then burst with sighing in her sight and ne'er re-
   turn again.

All that I sang still to her praise did tend,
Still she was first; still she my songs did end.
Yet she my love and music both doth fly,
The music that her echo is and beauty's sympathy;
Then let my notes pursue her scornful flight:
It shall suffice that they were breathed and died for
   her delight.

LOVE ME OR NOT

LOVE me or not, love her I must or die;
Leave me or not, follow her needs must I.
O that her grace would my wished comforts give.
How rich in her, how happy should I live!

All my desire, all my delight should be,
Her to enjoy, her to unite to me:

Envy should cease, her would I love alone:
Who loves by looks, is seldom true to one.

Could I enchant, and that it lawful were,
Her would I charm softly that none should hear.
But love enforced rarely yields firm content;
So would I love that neither should repent.

NOW WINTER NIGHTS ENLARGE

Now winter nights enlarge
    The number of their hours;
And clouds their storms discharge
    Upon the airy towers.
Let now the chimneys blaze
    And cups o'erflow with wine,
Let well-tuned words amaze
    With harmony divine.
Now yellow waxen lights
    Shall wait on honey love
While youthful revels, masques, and courtly sights,
    Sleep's leaden spells remove.

This time doth well dispense
    With lovers' long discourse;
Much speech hath some defence,
    Though beauty no remorse.
All do not all things well;
    Some measures comely tread;
Some knotted riddles tell;
    Some poems smoothly read.
The summer hath his joys,
    And winter his delights;
Though Love and all his pleasures are but toys,
    They shorten tedious nights.

BLAME NOT MY CHEEKS

BLAME not my cheeks, though pale with love they
 be;
The kindly heat unto my heart is flown,
To cherish it that is dismayed by thee,
Who art so cruel and unsteadfast grown:
For nature, called for by distressèd hearts,
Neglects and quite forsakes the outward parts.

But they whose cheeks with careless blood are
 stained,
Nurse not one spark of love within their hearts,
And, when they woo, they speak with passion
 feigned,
For their fat love lies in their outward parts:
But in their breasts, where love his court should
 hold,
Poor Cupid sits and blows his nails for cold.

LAURA

ROSE-CHEEKED Laura, come
Sing thou smoothly with thy beauty's
Silent music, either other
  Sweetly gracing.

Lovely forms do flow
From consent divinely framèd;
Heaven is music, and thy beauty's
  Birth is heavenly.

These dull notes we sing
Discords need for helps to grace them;
Only beauty purely loving
  Knows no discord,

But still moves delight,
Like clear springs renewed by flowing,
Ever perfect, ever in them-
    selves eternal.

THE MAN OF LIFE UPRIGHT

THE man of life upright,
    Whose guiltless heart is free
From all dishonest deeds,
    Or thought of vanity,

The man whose silent days
    In harmless joys are spent,
Whom hopes cannot delude,
    Nor sorrow discontent;

That man needs neither towers
    Nor armour for defence,
Nor secret vaults to fly
    From thunder's violence.

He only can behold
    With unaffrighted eyes
The horrors of the deep
    And terrors of the skies.

Thus, scorning all the cares
    That fate, or fortune brings,
He makes the heaven his book,
    His wisdom heavenly things,

Good thoughts his only friends,
    His wealth a well-spent age,
The earth his sober inn
    And quiet pilgrimage.

WERE MY HEART AS SOME MEN'S ARE

WERE my heart as some men's are, thy errors
    would not move me;
But thy faults I curious find and speak because I
    love thee:
Patience is a thing divine and far, I grant, above
    me.

Foes sometimes befriend us more, our blacker
    deeds objecting,
Than th'obsequious bosom-guest, with false respect
    affecting,
Friendship is the glass of Truth, our hidden stains
    detecting.

While I use of eyes enjoy and inward light of reason,
Thy observer will I be and censor, but in season:
Hidden mischief to conceal in State and Love is
    treason.

JACK AND JOAN THEY THINK NO ILL

JACK and Joan they think no ill,
But loving live, and merry still;
Do their week-day's work, and pray
Devoutly on the holy day:
Skip and trip it on the green,
And help to choose the summer queen:
Lash out, at a country feast,
Their silver penny with the best.

Well can they judge of nappy ale,
And tell at large a winter tale;

nappy] frothy.

Climb up to the apple loft,
And turn the crabs till they be soft.
Tib is all the father's joy,
And little Tom the mother's boy.
All their pleasure is content;
And care, to pay their yearly rent.

Joan can call by name her cows,
And deck her windows with green boughs;
She can wreaths and tutties make,
And trim with plums a bridal cake.
Jack knows what brings gain or loss;
And his long flail can stoutly toss:
Make the hedge, which others break,
And ever thinks what he doth speak.

Now, you courtly dames and knights,
That study only strange delights;
Though you scorn the home-spun gray,
And revel in your rich array:
Though your tongues dissemble deep,
And can your heads from danger keep;
Yet, for all your pomp and train,
Securer lives the silly swain.

AWAKE, AWAKE, THOU HEAVY SPRITE

AWAKE, awake, thou heavy sprite,
That sleep'st the deadly sleep of sin,
  Rise now and walk the ways of light;
'Tis not too late yet to begin.
    Seek heaven early, seek it late:
    True faith still finds an open gate.

crabs] crab apples.   tutties] nosegays.

Get up, get up, thou leaden man:
　　Thy track to endless joy or pain
　　　Yields but the model of a span;
　　Yet burns out thy life's lamp in vain.
　　　　One minute bounds thy bane, or bliss,
　　　　Then watch and labour, while time is.

AND WOULD YOU SEE MY MISTRESS' FACE

AND would you see my Mistress' face?
　　It is a flowery garden place,
Where knots of beauties have such grace
　　That all is work and nowhere space.

It is a sweet delicious morn,
　　Where day is breeding, never born,
It is a meadow yet unshorn,
　　Which thousand flowers do adorn.

It is the heaven's bright reflex,
　　Weak eyes to dazzle and to vex,
It is th' idea of her sex,
　　Envy of whom doth world perplex.

It is a face of death that smiles,
　　Pleasing, though it kills the whiles,
Where death and love in pretty wiles
　　Each other mutually beguiles.

It is fair beauty's freshest youth,
　　It is the feign'd Elysium's truth:
The spring that winter'd hearts renew'th;
　　And this is that my soul pursu'th.

NOW HATH FLORA ROBBED HER BOWERS

Now hath Flora robbed her bowers
To befriend this place with flowers:
    Strew about, strew about.
The sky rained never kindlier showers.
Flowers with bridals well agree,
Fresh as brides and bridegrooms be:
    Strew about, strew about,
And mix them with fit melody.
    Earth hath no princelier flowers
Than roses white, and roses red,
But they must still be mingled:
And as a rose new plucked from Venus' thorn,
So doth a bride her bridegroom's bed adorn.

Divers divers flowers affect
For some private dear respect:
    Strew about, strew about.
Let every one his own protect;
But he's none of Flora's friend
That will not the rose commend.
    Strew about, strew about;
Let princes princely flowers defend:
    Roses, the garden's pride,
Are flowers for love and flowers for kings,
In courts desirèd and weddings:
And as a rose in Venus' bosom worn,
So doth a bridegroom his bride's bed adorn.

O SWEET DELIGHT

O SWEET delight, O more than human bliss,
With her to live that ever loving is;
To hear her speak, whose words so well are placed,
That she by them, as they in her are graced:
  Those looks to view, that feast the viewer's
   eye,
  How blest is he that may so live and die!

Such love as this the golden times did know,
When all did reap, yet none took care to sow:
Such love as this an endless summer makes,
And all distaste from frail affection takes.
  So loved, so blest, in my beloved am I;
  Which till their eyes do ache, let iron men
   envy.

THOMAS NASHE

1567–1601

SPRING

SPRING, the sweet Spring, is the year's pleasant
  king,
Then blooms each thing, then maids dance in a
  ring,
Cold doth not sting, the pretty birds do sing,
  Cuckoo, jug-jug, pu-we, to-witta-woo.

The palm and may make country houses gay;
Lambs frisk and play, the shepherds pipe all day;
And we hear aye birds tune this merry lay,
  Cuckoo, jug-jug, pu-we, to-witta-woo.

The fields breathe sweet, the daisies kiss our feet,
Young lovers meet, old wives a-sunning sit;
In every street these tunes our ears do greet,
  Cuckoo, jug-jug, pu-we, to-witta-woo.
  Spring, the sweet Spring!

AMBITION

I NEVER loved ambitiously to climb,
Or thrust my hand too far into the fire.
To be in heaven sure is a blessed thing;
But, Atlas-like, to prop heaven on one's back
Cannot but be more labour than delight.
Such is the state of men in honour placed:
They are gold vessels made for servile uses;
High trees that keep the weather from low houses,
But cannot shield the tempest from themselves.
I love to dwell betwixt the hills and dales,
Neither to be so great as to be envied,
Nor yet so poor the world should pity me.

A LAMENT IN TIME OF PESTILENCE

ADIEU, farewell, earth's bliss!
This world uncertain is:
Fond are life's lustful joys,
Death proves them all but toys.
None from his darts can fly;
I am sick, I must die—
    Lord, have mercy on us!

Rich men, trust not in wealth,
Gold cannot buy you health;
Physic himself must fade;
All things to end are made;

The plague full swift goes by;
I am sick, I must die—
Lord, have mercy on us!

Beauty is but a flower
Which wrinkles will devour;
Brightness falls from the air;
Queens have died young and fair;
Dust hath closed Helen's eye;
I am sick, I must die—
Lord, have mercy on us!

Strength stoops unto the grave,
Worms feed on Hector brave;
Swords may not fight with fate;
Earth still holds ope her gate;
Come, come! the bells do cry;
I am sick, I must die—
Lord, have mercy on us!

Wit with his wantonness
Tasteth death's bitterness;
Hell's executioner
Hath no ears for to hear
What vain art can reply;
I am sick, I must die—
Lord, have mercy on us!

Haste therefore each degree,
To welcome destiny;
Heaven is our heritage,
Earth but a player's stage.
Mount we unto the sky;
I am sick, I must die—
Lord, have mercy on us!

SIR WILLIAM ALEXANDER, EARL OF STIRLING

1567(?)–1640

TO AURORA

i

I SWEAR, Aurora, by thy starry eyes,
And by those golden locks whose lock none slips,
And by the coral of thy rosy lips,
And by the naked snows which beauty dyes,
I swear by all the jewels of thy mind,
Whose like yet never worldly treasure bought,
Thy solid judgement and thy generous thought,
Which in this darkened age have clearly shined:
I swear by those, and by my spotless love,
And by my secret yet most fervent fires,
That I have never nursed but chaste desires,
And such as modesty might well approve.
  Then since I love those virtuous parts in thee,
  Shouldst thou not love this virtuous mind in me?

ii

O if thou knew'st how thou thyself dost harm,
And dost prejudge thy bliss, and spoil my rest;
Then thou would'st melt the ice out of thy breast
And thy relenting heart would kindly warm.
O if thy pride did not our joys control,
What world of loving wonders should'st thou see!
For if I saw thee once transform'd in me,
Then in thy bosom I would pour my soul;

Then all thy thoughts should in my visage shine,
And if that aught mischanced thou should'st not
   moan
Nor bear the burthen of thy griefs alone;
No, I would have my share in what were thine:
  And whilst we thus should make our sorrows one,
  This happy harmony would make them none.

SIR HENRY WOTTON

1568–1639

THE CHARACTER OF A HAPPY LIFE

How happy is he born and taught
That serveth not another's will;
Whose armour is his honest thought,
And simple truth his utmost skill!

Whose passions not his masters are;
Whose soul is still prepared for death;
Untied unto the world by care
Of public fame or private breath;

Who hath his life from rumours freed;
Whose conscience is his strong retreat;
Whose state can neither flatterers feed,
Nor ruin make oppressors great;

Who envieth none whom chance doth raise,
Or vice; who never understood
How deepest wounds are given by praise;
Nor rules of state, but rules of good;

Who God doth late and early pray
More of His grace than gifts to lend;

if that] archaic for *if*.

And entertains the harmless day
With a religious book or friend;

—This man is freed from servile bands
Of hope to rise or fear to fall:
Lord of himself, though not of lands,
And having nothing, yet hath all.

ON A BANK AS I SAT A-FISHING

A DESCRIPTION OF THE SPRING

AND now all nature seemed in love;
The lusty sap began to move;
New juice did stir th' embracing vines,
And birds had drawn their valentines;
The jealous trout that low did lie,
Rose at a well-dissembled fly:
There stood my friend with patient skill,
Attending of his trembling quill.
Already were the eaves possessed
With the swift pilgrims' daubèd nest:
The groves already did rejoice
In Philomel's triumphing voice.
The showers were short, the weather mild,
The morning fresh, the evening smiled.
Joan takes her neat-rubbed pail, and now
She trips to milk the sand-red cow;
Where, for some sturdy football swain,
Joan strokes a sillabub, or twain.
The field and gardens were beset
With tulip, crocus, violet;
And now, though late, the modest rose
Did more than half a blush disclose.
Thus all looked gay, all full of cheer,
To welcome the new-liveried year!

HYMN MADE BY SIR H. WOTTON

WHEN HE WAS AN AMBASSADOR AT VENICE, IN THE TIME OF A GREAT SICKNESS THERE

ETERNAL Mover, whose diffusèd glory,
  To show our grovelling reason what Thou art,
Unfolds itself in clouds of nature's story,
  Where Man, Thy proudest creature, acts his
    part;
Whom yet, alas, I know not why, we call
The world's contracted sum, the little all;

For what are we but lumps of walking clay?
  Why should we swell? whence should our spirits
    rise?
Are not brute beasts as strong, and birds as gay,—
  Trees longer lived, and creeping things as wise?
Only our souls was left an inward light,
To feel our weakness, and confess Thy might.

Thou then, our strength, Father of life and death,
  To whom our thanks, our vows, ourselves we
    owe,
From me, Thy tenant of this fading breath,
  Accept those lines which from Thy goodness
    flow;
And Thou, that wert Thy regal Prophet's muse,
Do not Thy praise in weaker strains refuse.

Let these poor notes ascend unto Thy throne,
  Where majesty doth sit with mercy crown'd,
Where my Redeemer lives, in Whom alone
  The errors of my wandering life are drown'd:
Where all the Quire of Heaven resound the same,
That only Thine, Thine is the saving Name.

Well, then, my soul, joy in the midst of pain;
  Thy Christ, that conquer'd Hell, shall from above
With greater triumph yet return again,
  And conquer His own justice with His love;
Commanding earth and seas to render those
Unto His bliss, for whom He paid his woes.

Now have I done; now are my thoughts at peace;
  And now my joys are stronger than my grief:
I feel those comforts that shall never cease,
  Future in hope, but present in belief;
Thy words are true, Thy promises are just,
And Thou wilt find Thy dearly-bought in dust.

UPON THE DEATH OF SIR ALBERT MORTON'S WIFE

HE first deceased; she for a little tried
To live without him: liked it not, and died.

OF A WOMAN'S HEART

O faithless world, and thy more faithless part,
          a woman's heart!
The true shop of variety, where sits
          nothing but fits
And fevers of desire, and pangs of love,
          which toys remove.
Why was she born to please, or I to trust
          words writ in dust?
Suffering her eyes to govern my despair,
          my pain for air;
And fruit of time rewarded with untruth,
          the food of youth?

Untrue she was; yet I believed her eyes
        (instructed spies),
Till I was taught that love was but a school
        to breed a fool.
Or sought she more, by triumphs of denial,
        to make a trial
How far her smiles commanded my weakness?
        yield and confess!
Excuse no more thy folly; but, for cure,
        blush and endure
As well thy shame as passions that were vain;
        and think, 'tis gain,
To know, that love lodged in a woman's breast
        is but a guest.

ELIZABETH OF BOHEMIA

You meaner beauties of the night,
  That poorly satisfy our eyes
More by your number than your light,
    You common people of the skies;
    What are you when the sun shall rise?

You curious chanters of the wood,
  That warble forth Dame Nature's lays,
Thinking your voices understood
    By your weak accents; what's your praise
    When Philomel her voice shall raise?

You violets, that first appear,
  By your pure purple mantles known,
Like the proud virgins of the year,
    As if the spring were all your own;
    What are you when the rose is blown?

So, when my mistress shall be seen
  In form and beauty of her mind,
By virtue first, then choice a queen,
  Tell me, if she were not design'd
  Th' eclipse and glory of her kind.

SIR JOHN DAVIES

1569-1626

From *Nosce Teipsum* (*Of the Soul of Man and the Immortality thereof*) (1599)

OF HUMAN KNOWLEDGE

Why did my parents send me to the schools,
  That I with knowledge might enrich my mind,
Since the desire to know first made men fools,
  And did corrupt the root of all mankind?

For when God's hand had written in the hearts
  Of our first parents all the rules of good,
So that their skill infus'd did pass all arts
  That ever were, before, or since the flood;

And when their reason's eye was sharp and clear,
  And (as an eagle can behold the sun),
Could have approach'd th' eternal light as near
  As th' intellectual Angels could have done;

Even then to them the Spirit of lies suggests,
  That they were blind, because they saw not ill;
And breathes into their incorrupted breasts
  A curious wish, which did corrupt their will.

For that same ill they straight desir'd to know;
  Which ill, being naught but a defect of good,
In all God's works the devil could not show,
  While man, their lord, in his perfection stood:

So that themselves were first to do the ill,
   Ere they thereof the knowledge could attain;
Like him that knew not poison's power to kill,
   Until (by tasting it) himself was slain.

Ev'n so, by tasting of that fruit forbid,
   Where they sought knowledge, they did error
    find;
Ill they desir'd to know, and ill they did;
   And, to give Passion eyes, made Reason blind;

For then their minds did first in passion see
   Those wretched shapes of misery and woe,
Of nakedness, of shame, of poverty,
   Which then their own experience made them
    know.

But then grew reason dark, that she no more
   Could the fair forms of good and truth discern;
Bats they became that eagles were before,
   And this they got by their desire to learn.

But we, their wretched offspring, what do we?
   Do not we still taste of the fruit forbid,
While with fond fruitless curiosity,
   In books profane we seek for knowledge hid?

What is this knowledge, but the sky-stol'n fire,
   For which the thief still chain'd in ice doth sit?
And which the poor rude satyr did admire,
   And needs would kiss, but burnt his lips with it?

What is it, but the cloud of empty rain,
   Which when Jove's guest embrac'd he monsters
    got?
Or the false pails, which oft being fill'd with pain,
   Receiv'd the water, but retain'd it not?

Shortly, what is it? but the fiery coach,
    Which the youth sought, and sought his death
      withal?
Or the boy's wings, which when he did approach
    The sun's hot beams, did melt and let him fall?

And yet, alas! when all our lamps are burn'd,
    Our bodies wasted and our spirits spent;
When we have all the learned volumes turn'd,
    Which yield men's wits both help and orna-
      ment;

What can we know? or what can we discern,
    When error clouds the windows of the mind?
The diverse forms of things how can we learn,
    That have been ever from our birth-day blind?

When reason's lamp, which (like the sun in sky)
    Throughout man's little world her beams did
      spread,
Is now become a sparkle, which doth lie
    Under the ashes, half extinct, and dead;

How can we hope that through the eye and ear,
    This dying sparkle, in this cloudy place,
Can recollect these beams of knowledge clear,
    Which were infus'd in the first minds by grace?

So might the heir, whose father hath in play
    Wasted a thousand pounds of ancient rent,
By painful earning of one groat a day,
    Hope to restore the patrimony spent.

The wits that div'd most deep, and soar'd most high,
    Seeking man's powers, have found his weakness
      such:
Skill comes so slow, and life so fast doth fly;
    We learn so little, and forget so much:

For this the wisest of all moral men
 Said *he knew naught, but that he naught did know;*
And the great mocking master mock'd not then,
 When he said, *Truth was buried deep below.*

For how may we to others' things attain,
 When none of us his own soul understands?
For which the devil mocks our curious brain,
 When *Know thyself* his oracle commands.

For why should we the busy soul believe,
 When boldly she concludes of that or this;
When of herself she can no judgement give,
 Nor how, nor whence, nor where, nor what she
  is?

All things without, which round about we see,
 We seek to know, and have therewith to do:
But that whereby we reason, live, and be,
 Within ourselves, we strangers are thereto.

We seek to know the moving of each sphere,
 And the strange cause of th' ebbs and floods of
  Nile;
But of that clock which in our breasts we bear,
 The subtle motions we forget the while.

We that acquaint ourselves with every zone,
 And pass both tropics, and behold both poles;
When we come home, are to ourselves unknown,
 And unacquainted still with our own souls.

We study speech, but others we persuade;
 We leech-craft learn, but others cure with it:
We interpret laws, which other men have made,
 But read not those which in our hearts are writ.

Is it because the mind is like the eye,
  (Through which it gathers knowledge by de-
    grees,)
Whose rays reflect not, but spread outwardly;
  Not seeing itself, when other things it sees?

No, doubtless; for the mind can backward cast,
  Upon herself, her understanding light;
But she is so corrupt, and so defac'd,
  As her own image doth herself affright.

As is the fable of that lady fair,
  Which for her lust was turn'd into a cow;
When thirsty to a stream she did repair,
  And saw herself transform'd she wist not how,

At first she startles, then she stands amaz'd;
  At last with terror she from thence doth fly,
And loathes the wat'ry glass wherein she gaz'd,
  And shuns it still, though she for thirst do die.

Ev'n so man's soul, which did God's image bear,
  And was at first fair, good, and spotless pure,
Since with her sins her beauties blotted were,
  Doth of all sights, her own sight least endure;

For ev'n at first reflection she espies
  Such strange chimeras, and such monsters there;
Such toys, such antics, and such vanities,
  As she retires, and shrinks from shame and fear.

And as the man loves least at home to be,
  That hath a sluttish house, haunted with sprites;
So she, impatient her own faults to see,
  Turns from herself, and in strange things de-
    lights.

For this, few *know themselves*: for merchants broke,
  View their estate with discontent and pain;
As seas are troubled, when they do revoke
  Their flowing waves into themselves again.

And while the face of outward things we find,
  Pleasing, and fair, agreeable, and sweet,
These things transport, and carry out the mind,
  That with herself herself can never meet.

Yet if affliction once her wars begin,
  And threat the feebler sense with sword and fire,
The mind contracts herself and shrinketh in,
  And to herself she gladly doth retire;

As spiders touch'd, seek their web's inmost part;
  As bees in storms unto their hives return;
As blood in danger gathers to the heart,
  As men seek towns when foes the country burn.

If aught can teach us aught, affliction's looks,
  (Making us look into ourselves so near)
Teach us to *know ourselves*, beyond all books,
  Or all the learned schools that ever were.

This mistress lately pluck'd me by the ear,
  And many a golden lesson hath me taught;
Hath made my senses quick, and reason clear,
  Reform'd my will, and rectified my thought.

So do the winds and thunders cleanse the air;
  So working lees settle and purge the wine;
So lopp'd and pruned trees do flourish fair;
  So doth the fire the drossy gold refine.

Neither Minerva, nor the learned muse,
  Nor rules of art, nor precepts of the wise,

Could in my brain those beams of skill infuse,
    As but the glance of this dame's angry eyes.

She within lists my ranging mind hath brought,
    That now beyond myself I list not go;
Myself am centre of my circling thought,
    Only *myself* I study, learn, and *know*:

I know my body's of so frail a kind,
    As force without, fevers within can kill;
I know the heavenly nature of my mind,
    But 'tis corrupted both in wit and will.

I know my soul hath power to know all things,
    Yet is she blind and ignorant in all;
I know I am one of nature's little kings,
    Yet to the least and vilest things am thrall.

I know my life's a pain, and but a span;
    I know my sense is mock'd with ev'ry thing;
And, to conclude, *I know* myself a man,
    Which is a proud and yet a wretched thing.

THE IMMORTALITY OF THE SOUL

ALL moving things to other things do move,
    Of the same kind, which shows their nature such:
So earth falls down, and fire doth mount above,
    Till both their proper elements do touch.

And as the moisture which the thirsty earth
    Sucks from the sea, to fill her empty veins,
From out her womb at last doth take a birth,
    And runs a nymph along the grassy plains;

Long doth she stay, as loth to leave the land,
    From whose soft side she first did issue make:

She tastes all places, turns to ev'ry hand,
   Her flow'ry banks unwilling to forsake;

Yet nature so her streams doth lead and carry,
   As that her course doth make no final stay,
Till she herself unto the ocean marry,
   Within whose wat'ry bosom first she lay:

Ev'n so the soul, which in this earthy mould
   The Spirit of God doth secretly infuse,
Because at first she doth the earth behold,
   And only this material world she views,—

At first our mother earth she holdeth dear,
   And doth embrace the world and worldly things;
She flies close by the ground, and hovers here,
   And mounts not up with her celestial wings:

Yet under heaven she cannot light on aught,
   That with her heavenly nature doth agree;
She cannot rest, she cannot fix her thought,
   She cannot in this world contented be.

For who did ever yet, in honour, wealth,
   Or pleasure of the sense, contentment find?
Who ever ceas'd to wish, when he had health?
   Or having wisdom, was not vex'd in mind?

Then as a bee, which among weeds doth fall,
   Which seem sweet flow'rs, with lustre fresh and
      gay;
She lights on that, and this, and tasteth all,
   But pleas'd with none, doth rise and soar away;

So, when the soul finds here no true content,
   And, like Noah's dove, can no sure footing take,
She doth return from whence she first was sent,
   And flies to him that first her wings did make.

SIR ROBERT AYTON

1570–1638

I'LL LOVE NO MORE

I LOVED thee once; I'll love no more—
  Thine be the grief, as is the blame;
Thou art not what thou wast before,
  What reason I should be the same?
    He that can love unloved again,
    Hath better store of love than brain:
God send me love my debts to pay,
  While unthrifts fool their love away!

Nothing could have my love o'erthrown
  If thou had still continued mine;
Yea, if thou hadst remain'd thy own,
  I might perchance have yet been thine.
    But thou thy freedom did recall
    That it thou might elsewhere enthral:
And then how could I but disdain
A captive's captive to remain?

When new desires had conquer'd thee
  And changed the object of thy will,
It had been lethargy in me,
  Not constancy, to love thee still.
    Yea, it had been a sin to go
    And prostitute affection so:
Since we are taught no prayers to say
To such as must to others pray.

Yet do thou glory in thy choice—
  Thy choice of his good fortune boast;
I'll neither grieve nor yet rejoice
  To see him gain what I have lost:

The height of my disdain shall be
  To laugh at him, to blush for thee;
To love thee still, but go no more
A-begging at a beggar's door.

THE INCONSTANT MISTRESS

I DO confess thou'rt smooth and fair,
  And I might ha' gone near to love thee,
Had I not found the slightest prayer
  That lip could speak, had power to move thee;
But I can let thee now alone
As worthy to be loved by none.

I do confess thou'rt sweet; yet find
  Thee such an unthrift of thy sweets,
Thy favours are but like the wind
  Which kisseth everything it meets:
And since thou canst love more than one,
Thou'rt worthy to be kiss'd by none.

The morning rose, that untouch'd stands,
  Arm'd with her briars, how sweet she smells!
But pluck'd, and strain'd through ruder hands,
  Her sweets no longer with her dwells:
But scent and beauty both are gone,
And leaves fall from her one by one.

Such fate ere long will thee betide
  When thou hast handled been awhile,
With sere flowers to be thrown aside,
  And I shall sigh, when some will smile,
To see thy love to every one
Hath brought thee to be loved by none!

Attributed to Ayton in *Playford's Select Ayres*, 1659.

JOHN DONNE
1571(?)–1631

HAIL, BISHOP VALENTINE

HAIL, Bishop Valentine, whose day this **is**,
    All the air is thy diocese,
    And all the chirping choristers
And other birds are thy parishoners,
      Thou marryest every year
The lyric lark, and the grave whispering **dove,**
The sparrow that neglects his life for love,
The household bird, with the red stomacher;
    Thou makest the blackbird speed as soon,
As doth the goldfinch, or the halcyon;
The husband cock looks out, and straight is sped,
And meets his wife, which brings her feather-bed.
This day more cheerfully than ever shine,
This day, which might inflame thyself, old Valentine.

A LECTURE UPON THE SHADOW

STAND still, and I will read to thee
A lecture, Love, in love's philosophy.
    These three hours that we have spent,
    Walking here, two shadows went
Along with us, which we ourselves produced;
But, now the sun is just above our head,
    We do those shadows tread;
    And to brave clearness all things are reduced.
    So whilst our infant loves did grow,
    Disguises did, and shadows, flow,
From us, and our cares; but now 'tis not so.

That love hath not attained the highest degree,
Which is still diligent lest others see.

Except our loves at this noon stay,
We shall new shadows make the other way.
    As the first were made to blind
    Others; these which come behind
Will work upon ourselves, and blind our eyes.
If our loves faint, and westwardly decline,
    To me thou, falsely, thine,
    And I to thee mine actions shall disguise.
The morning shadows wear away,
But these grow longer all the day,
But oh, love's day is short, if love decay.

Love is a growing, or full constant light;
And his first minute, after noon, is night.

THE BLOSSOM

    LITTLE think'st thou, poor flower,
    Whom I have watchèd six or seven days,
And seen thy birth, and seen what every hour
Gave to thy growth, thee to this height to raise,
        And now dost laugh and triumph on this bough,
            Little think'st thou
That it will freeze anon, and that I shall
To-morrow find thee fallen, or not at all.

    Little think'st thou, poor heart,
    That labour'st yet to nestle thee,
And think'st by hovering here to get a part
In a forbidden or forbidding tree,
    And hop'st her stiffness by long siege to bow:
          Little think'st thou,
That thou to-morrow, ere that sun doth wake,
Must with this sun, and me, a journey take.

    But thou which lov'st to be
    Subtle to plague thyself, wilt say,

Alas, if you must go, what's that to me?
Here lies my business, and here I will stay:
You go to friends, whose love and means present
       Various content
To your eyes, ears, and tongue, and every part.
If then your body go, what need you a heart?

  Well then, stay here; but know,
    When thou hast stayed and done thy most,
A naked thinking heart, that makes no show,
Is to a woman, but a kind of ghost;
How shall she know my heart; or having none,
      Know thee for one?
Practice may make her know some other part,
But take my word, she doth not know a heart.

  Meet me at London, then,
    Twenty days hence, and thou shalt see
Me fresher, and more fat, by being with men,
Than if I had stayed still with her and thee.
For God's sake, if you can, be you so too:
      I would give you
There, to another friend, whom we shall find
As glad to have my body, as my mind.

SONG

  Go, and catch a falling star,
    Get with child a mandrake root,
Tell me, where all past years are,
    Or who cleft the Devil's foot,
Teach me to hear mermaids singing,
Or to keep off envy's stinging,
      And find
      What wind
Serves to advance an honest mind.

If thou beest born to strange sights,
  Things invisible to see,
Ride ten thousand days and nights,
  Till age snow white hairs on thee,
Thou, when thou return'st, wilt tell me
All strange wonders that befell thee,
        And swear
        No where
Lives a woman true, and fair.

If thou find'st one, let me know,
  Such a pilgrimage were sweet;
Yet do not, I would not go,
  Though at next door we might meet,
Though she were true, when you met her,
And last, till you write your letter,
        Yet she
        Will be
False, ere I come, to two, or three.

RESIGNATION TO GOD (HOLY SONNET II)

As due by many titles I resign
Myself to thee, O God, first I was made
By thee, and for thee, and when I was decayed
Thy blood bought that, the which before was thine;
I am thy son, made with thyself to shine,
Thy servant, whose pains thou hast still repaid,
Thy sheep, thine image, and, till I betrayed
Myself, a temple of thy Spirit divine;
Why doth the devil then usurp on me?
Why doth he steal, nay ravish that's thy right?
Except thou rise and for thine own work fight,
Oh I shall soon despair, when I do see
That thou lov'st mankind well, yet wilt not choose me,
And Satan hates me, yet is loth to lose me.

A HYMN TO GOD THE FATHER

Wilt Thou forgive that sin where I begun,
   Which was my sin, though it were done before?
Wilt Thou forgive that sin through which I run,
   And do run still though still I do deplore?
When Thou hast done, Thou hast not done,
     For I have more.

Wilt Thou forgive that sin which I have won
   Others to sin? and, made my sin their door?
Wilt Thou forgive that sin which I did shun
   A year, or two, but wallowed in, a score?
When Thou hast done, Thou hast not done,
     For I have more.

I have a sin of fear, that when I have spun
   My last thread, I shall perish on the shore;
But swear by Thyself, that at my death Thy Son
   Shall shine as He shines now, and heretofore;
And, having done that, Thou hast done,
     I fear no more.

ABSENCE

That Time and Absence proves
Rather helps than hurts to loves

Absence, hear my protestation
    Against thy strength,
    Distance and length,
Do what thou canst for alteration:
    For hearts of truest mettle
    Absence doth join, and time doth settle.

Who loves a mistress of right quality,
    His mind hath found
    Affection's ground

Beyond time, place, and all mortality:
    To hearts that cannot vary
    Absence is present, time doth tarry:

My senses want their outward motion
    Which now within
    Reason doth win,
Redoubled by her secret notion:
    Like rich men that take pleasure
    In hiding more than handling treasure.

By absence this good means I gain
    That I can catch her
    Where none can watch her
In some close corner of my brain:
    There I embrace and there kiss her,
    And so enjoy her, and so miss her.

SONG

SWEETEST love, I do not go,
    For weariness of thee,
Nor in hope the world can show
    A fitter love for me;
      But since that I
Must die at last, 'tis best,
To use my self in jest
    Thus by feign'd deaths to die;

Yesternight the sun went hence,
    And yet is here to-day,
He hath no desire nor sense,
    Nor half so short a way:
      Then fear not me,
But believe that I shall make
Speedier journeys, since I take
    More wings and spurs than he.

O how feeble is man's power,
    That if good fortune fall,
Cannot add another hour,
    Nor a lost hour recall!
      But come, bad chance,
And we join to it our strength,
And we teach it art and length,
    Itself o'er us to advance.

When thou sigh'st, thou sigh'st not wind,
    But sigh'st my soul away,
When thou weep'st, unkindly kind,
    My life's blood doth decay.
      It cannot be
That thou lov'st me, as thou say'st.
If in thine my life thou waste:
    Thou art the best of me.

Let not thy divining heart
    Forethink me any ill,
Destiny may take thy part,
    And may thy fears fulfil;
      But think that we
Are but turned aside to sleep;
They who one another keep
    Alive, ne'er parted be.

THE CANONIZATION

For God sake hold your tongue, and let me love,
    Or chide my palsy, or my gout,
My five gray hairs, or ruined fortune flout,
    With wealth your state, your mind with arts
        improve,
    Take you a course, get you a place,
    Observe his honour, or his grace,

Or the king's real, or his stampèd face
    Contemplate, what you will approve,
    So you will let me love.

Alas, alas, who's injured by my love?
    What merchant's ships have my sighs drowned?
Who says my tears have overflowed his ground?
    When did my colds a forward spring remove?
        When did the heats which my veins fill
        Add one more to the plaguey bill?
Soldiers find wars, and lawyers find out still
    Litigious men, which quarrels move,
    Though she and I do love.

Call us what you will, we are made such by love;
    Call her one, me another sly,
We are tapers too, and at our own cost die,
    And we in us find the eagle and the dove.
        The phoenix riddle hath more wit
        By us, we two being one, are it.
So to one neutral thing both sexes fit,
    We die and rise the same, and prove
    Mysterious by this love.

We can die by it, if not live by love,
    And if unfit for tombs and hearse
Our legend be, it will be fit for verse;
    And if no piece of chronicle we prove,
        We'll build in sonnets pretty rooms;
        As well a well-wrought urn becomes
The greatest ashes, as half-acre tombs,
    And by these hymns, all shall approve
    Us *canonized* for love:

And thus invoke us; you whom reverend love
    Made one another's hermitage;

You, to whom love was peace, that now is rage;
  Who did the whole world's soul contract, and
    drove
      Into the glasses of your eyes
      (So made such mirrors, and such spies,
That they did all to you epitomize),
  Countries, towns, courts: beg from above
  A pattern of your love!

LOVE'S DEITY

I LONG to talk with some old lover's ghost,
  Who died before the god of love was born:
I cannot think that he, who then loved most,
  Sunk so low, as to love one which did scorn.
But since this god produced a destiny,
And that vice-nature, custom, lets it be;
  I must love her, that loves not me.

Sure, they which made him god, meant not so
    much,
  Nor he in his young godhead practised it;
But when an even flame two hearts did touch,
  His office was indulgently to fit
Actives to passives. Correspondency
Only his subject was; it cannot be
  Love, till I love her, that loves me.

But every modern god will now extend
  His vast prerogative, as far as Jove.
To rage, to lust, to write to, to commend,
  All is the purlieu of the god of love.
Oh were we wakened by this tyranny
To ungod this child again, it could not be
  I should love her, who loves not me.

Rebel and atheist too, why murmur I,
  As though I felt the worst that love could do?
Love might make me leave loving, or might try
  A deeper plague, to make her love me too,
Which, since she loves before, I am loath to see;
Falsehood is worse than hate; and that must be,
  If she whom I love, should love me.

THE GOOD MORROW

I WONDER by my troth, what thou and I
Did, till we loved? were we not weaned till then?
But sucked on country pleasures, childishly?
Or snorted we in the seven sleepers' den?
'Twas so; but this, all pleasures fancies be.
If ever any beauty I did see,
Which I desired, and got, 'twas but a dream of
    thee.

And now good-morrow to our waking souls,
Which watch not one another out of fear;
For love all love of other sights controls,
And makes one little room an everywhere.
Let sea-discoverers to new worlds have gone,
Let maps to other, worlds on worlds have shown,
Let us possess one world, each hath one, and
    is one.

My face in thine eye, thine in mine appears,
And true plain hearts do in the faces rest,
Where can we find two better hemispheres
Without sharp North, without declining West?
Whatever dies, was not mixed equally;
If our two loves be one, or thou and I
Love so alike that none do slacken, none can die.

THE FUNERAL

WHOEVER comes to shroud me, do not harm
      Nor question much
That subtle wreath of hair, which crowns my arm;
The mystery, the sign you must not touch,
      For 'tis my outward soul,
Viceroy to that, which, then to heaven being gone,
      Will leave this to control,
And keep these limbs, her provinces, from dis-
    solution.

For if the sinewy thread my brain lets fall
      Through every part,
Can tie those parts, and make me one of all;
These hairs which upward grew, and strength and
    art
      Have from a better brain,
Can better do it; except she meant that I
      By this should know my pain,
As prisoners then are manacled, when they're con-
    demned to die.

Whate'er she meant by it, bury it with me,
      For since I am
Love's martyr, it might breed idolatry,
If into other hands these relics came,
      As 'twas humility
To afford to it all that a soul can do,
      So, 'tis some bravery,
That since you would save none of me, I bury some
    of you.

THE EXPIRATION

So, so, break off this last lamenting kiss,
  Which sucks two souls, and vapours both away,
Turn, thou ghost, that way, and let me turn this,
  And let our selves benight our happiest day,
We asked none leave to love; nor will we owe
  Any, so cheap a death, as saying, go;

Go; and if that word have not quite killed thee,
  Ease me with death, by bidding me go too.
Oh, if it have, let my word work on me,
  And a just office on a murderer do.
Except it be too late, to kill me so,
  Being double dead, going, and bidding go.

DEATH
i (Holy Sonnet X)

Death, be not proud, though some have callèd thee
Mighty and dreadful, for thou art not so,
For those, whom thou think'st thou dost over-
    throw,
Die not, poor death, nor yet canst thou kill me.
From rest and sleep, which but thy pictures be,
Much pleasure, then from thee much more, must
    flow,
And soonest our best men with thee do go,
Rest of their bones, and souls' delivery.
Thou art slave to fate, chance, kings, and des-
    perate men,
And dost with poison, war, and sickness dwell,
And poppy, or charms, can make us sleep as well,
And better than thy stroke; Why swell'st thou
    then?

One short sleep past, we wake eternally,
    And death shall be no more; death, thou shalt
      die.

ii (Holy Sonnet VII)

At the round earth's imagined corners, blow
Your trumpets, angels, and arise, arise
From death, you numberless infinities
Of souls, and to your scattered bodies go,
All whom the flood did, and fire shall o'erthrow,
All whom war, dearth, age, agues, tyrannies,
Despair, law, chance, hath slain, and you whose
    eyes
Shall behold God, and never taste death's woe.
But let them sleep, Lord, and me mourn a space,
For, if above all these, my sins abound,
'Tis late to ask abundance of thy grace,
When we are there; here on this lowly ground,
Teach me how to repent; for that's as good
As if thou had'st sealed my pardon with thy blood.

A HYMN TO CHRIST, AT THE AUTHOR'S LAST GOING INTO GERMANY

In what torn ship soever I embark,
    That ship shall be my emblem of Thy ark;
What sea soever swallow me, that flood
Shall be to me an emblem of Thy blood;
Though Thou with clouds of anger do disguise
Thy face; yet through that mask I know those eyes,
    Which, though they turn away sometimes,
      They never will despise.

I sacrifice this island unto Thee,
And all whom I loved there, and who loved me;
When I have put our seas twixt them and me,
Put Thou Thy sea betwixt my sins and Thee.

As the tree's sap doth seek the root below
In winter, in my winter now I go,
  Where none but thee, th'Eternal root
    Of true Love I may know.

Nor Thou nor Thy religion dost control
The amorousness of an harmonious soul,
But Thou would'st have that love Thyself: as Thou
Art jealous, Lord, so I am jealous now,
Thou lov'st not, till from loving more, Thou free
My soul: whoever gives, takes liberty:
  O, if thou car'st not whom I love
    Alas, Thou lov'st not me.

Seal then this bill of my divorce to all,
On whom those fainter beams of love did fall;
Marry those loves, which in youth scattered be
On fame, wit, hopes, false mistresses, to Thee,
Churches are best for prayer, that have least light:
To see God only, I go out of sight:
  And to 'scape stormy days, I choose
    An everlasting night.

BEN JONSON

1573–1637

SONG TO CELIA

DRINK to me only with thine eyes,
  And I will pledge with mine;
Or leave a kiss but in the cup
  And I'll not look for wine.
The thirst that from the soul doth rise
  Doth ask a drink divine;
But might I of Jove's nectar sup,
  I would not change for thine.

I sent thee late a rosy wreath,
   Not so much honouring thee
As giving it a hope that there
   It could not wither'd be;
But thou thereon didst only breathe
   And sent'st it back to me;
Since when it grows, and smells, I swear,
   Not of itself but thee!

THE TRIUMPH OF CHARIS

SEE the chariot at hand here of Love,
   Wherein my lady rideth!
Each that draws is a swan or a dove,
   And well the car Love guideth.
As she goes, all hearts do duty
         Unto her beauty;
And enamour'd do wish, so they might
         But enjoy such a sight,
That they still were to run by her side,
Through swords, through seas, whither she would
   ride.

Do but look on her eyes, they do light
   All that Love's world compriseth!
Do but look on her hair, it is bright
   As Love's star when it riseth!
Do but mark, her forehead's smoother
         Than words that soothe her;
And from her arched brows such a grace
         Sheds itself through the face,
As alone there triumphs to the life
All the gain, all the good, of the elements' strife.

Have you seen but a bright lily grow
   Before rude hands have touch'd it?

Have you mark'd but the fall o' the snow
    Before the soil hath smutch'd it?
Have you felt the wool of the beaver,
        Or swan's down ever?
Or have smelt o' the bud o' the brier,
        Or the nard in the fire?
Or have tasted the bag of the bee?
O so white, O so soft, O so sweet is she!

Underwoods.

THE NOBLE NATURE

    It is not growing like a tree
    In bulk, doth make man better be;
Or standing long an oak, three hundred year,
To fall a log at last, dry, bald, and sere:
        A lily of a day
        Is fairer far in May,
    Although it fall and die that night;
    It was the plant and flower of light.
In small proportions we just beauties see;
And in short measures life may perfect be.

A Pindaric Ode to the Memory of
Sir L. Carey and Sir H. Morison.

HYMN TO DIANA

Queen and Huntress, chaste and fair,
    Now the sun is laid to sleep,
Seated in thy silver chair
    State in wonted manner keep:
        Hesperus entreats thy light,
        Goddess excellently bright.

Earth, let not thy envious shade
    Dare itself to interpose;

Cynthia's shining orb was made
    Heaven to clear when day did close:
        Bless us then with wishéd sight,
        Goddess excellently bright.

Lay thy bow of pearl apart
    And thy crystal-shining quiver;
Give unto the flying hart
    Space to breathe, how short soever:
        Thou that mak'st a day of night,
        Goddess excellently bright!

Cynthia's Revels.

AN ODE: TO HIMSELF

WHERE dost thou careless lie
    Buried in ease and sloth?
Knowledge, that sleeps, doth die;
And this security,
    It is the common moth,
That eats on wits, and arts, and destroys them
    both.

Are all th' Aonian springs
    Dried up? lies Thespia waste?
Doth Clarius' harp want strings,
That not a nymph now sings!
    Or droop they as disgraced,
To see their seats and bowers by chatt'ring pies
    defaced?

If hence thy silence be,
    As 'tis too just a cause;
Let this thought quicken thee—
Minds that are great and free,
    Should not on fortune pause,
'Tis crown enough to virtue still, her own applause.

What though the greedy fry
   Be taken with false baits
Of worded balladry,
And think it poësy?
   They die with their conceits,
And only piteous scorn upon their folly waits.

Then take in hand thy lyre,
   Strike in thy proper strain,
With Japhet's line, aspire
Sol's chariot for new fire,
   To give the world again:
Who aided him, will thee, the issue of Jove's brain.

And since our dainty age,
   Cannot endure reproof,
Make not thyself a page,
To that strumpet the stage,
   But sing high and aloof,
Safe from the wolf's black jaw, and the dull ass's hoof.

Underwoods.

SIMPLICITY AND SWEET NEGLECT

STILL to be neat, still to be drest,
As you were going to a feast;
Still to be powdered, still perfumed:
Lady, it is to be presumed,
Though art's hid causes are not found,
All is not sweet, all is not sound.

Give me a look, give me a face,
That makes simplicity a grace;
Robes loosely flowing, hair as free:
Such sweet neglect more taketh me,
Than all th' adulteries of art.
They strike mine eyes, but not my heart.

The Silent Woman.

SONG: THE KISS

O THAT joy so soon should waste!
    Or so sweet a bliss
    As a kiss
Might not for ever last!
So sugared, so melting, so soft, so delicious,
    The dew that lies on roses,
    When the morn herself discloses,
Is not so precious.
O, rather than I would it smother
Were I to taste such another,
It should be my wishing
That I might die with kissing.

Cynthia's Revels.

ECHO'S LAMENT FOR NARCISSUS

SLOW, slow, fresh fount, keep time with my salt
        tears:
    Yet slower, yet; O faintly, gentle springs:
List to the heavy part the music bears,
    Woe weeps out her division, when she sings.
            Droop, herbs and flowers,
            Fall grief in showers,
            Our beauties are not ours;
                O, I could still,
Like melting snow upon some craggy hill,
            Drop, drop, drop, drop,
Since Nature's pride is now a withered daffodil.

Cynthia's Revels.

TO JAMES WARRE,

ON HIS BOOK, *The Touchstone of Truth*, 1630

TRUTH is the trial of itself,
    And needs no other touch;
And purer than the purest gold,
    Refine it ne'er so much.
It is the life and light of love,
    The sun that ever shineth,
And spirit of that special grace,
    That faith and love defineth.
It is the warrant of the word,
    That yields a scent so sweet,
As gives a power to faith, to tread
    All falsehood under feet.
It is the sword that doth divide
    The marrow from the bone,
And in effect of heavenly love
    Doth show the Holy One.
This, blessèd Warre, thy blessèd book
    Unto the world doth prove;
A worthy work, and worthy well
    Of the most worthy love.

Underwoods.

TO CELIA

COME, my Celia, let us prove,
While we can, the sports of love,
Time will not be ours for ever,
He, at length, our good will sever;
Spend not then his gifts in vain;
Suns that set may rise again:
But if once we lose this light,
'Tis with us perpetual night.
Why should we defer our joys?
Fame and rumour are but toys.

Cannot we delude the eyes
Of a few poor household spies?
Or his easier ears beguile,
Thus removèd by our wile?—
'Tis no sin love's fruits to steal;
But the sweet thefts to reveal,
To be taken, to be seen,
These have crimes accounted been.

Volpone.

O, DO NOT WANTON

O, DO not wanton with those eyes,
   Lest I be sick with seeing;
Nor cast them down, but let them rise,
   Lest shame destroy their being:
O, be not angry with those fires,
   For then their threats will kill me;
Nor look too kind on my desires,
   For then my hopes will spill me;
O, do not steep them in thy tears,
   For so will sorrow slay me;
Nor spread them as distract with fears,
   Mine own enough betray me.

Underwoods.

TO THE MEMORY OF MY BELOVED, THE AUTHOR, MR. WILLIAM SHAKESPEARE: AND WHAT HE HATH LEFT US

To draw no envy, Shakespeare, on thy name,
Am I thus ample to thy book and fame;
While I confess thy writings to be such,
As neither man, nor muse, can praise too much,

distract] distraught.

'Tis true, and all men's suffrage. But these ways
Were not the paths I meant unto thy praise;
For seeliest ignorance on these may light,
Which, when it sounds at best, but echoes right;
Or blind affection, which doth ne'er advance
The truth, but gropes, and urgeth all by chance;
Or crafty malice might pretend this praise,
And think to ruin, where it seemed to raise.
These are, as some infàmous bawd, or whore,
Should praise a matron; what could hurt her
    more?
But thou art proof against them, and, indeed,
Above the ill fortune of them, or the need.
I therefore will begin : Soul of the age!
The applause, delight, the wonder of our stage,
My Shakespeare, rise! I will not lodge thee by
Chaucer, or Spenser, or bid Beaumont lie
A little further, to make thee a room:
Thou art a monument without a tomb,
And art alive still, while thy book doth live,
And we have wits to read, and praise to give.
That I not mix thee so my brain excuses;
I mean, with great but disproportioned Muses.
For, if I thought my judgement were of years,
I should commit thee, surely, with thy peers.
And tell how far thou didst our Lyly outshine
Or sporting Kyd, or Marlowe's mighty line.
And though thou hadst small Latin and less
    Greek,
From thence, to honour thee, I will not seek
For names, but call forth thundering Aeschylus,
Euripides, and Sophocles to us,
Pacuvius, Accius, him of Cordova dead
To life again, to hear thy buskin tread,

And shake a stage; or when thy socks were on,
Leave thee alone, for the comparison
Of all that insolent Greece or haughty Rome
Sent forth; or since did from their ashes come.
Triumph, my Britain! Thou hast one to show
To whom all scenes of Europe homage owe.
He was not of an age, but for all time!
And all the Muses still were in their prime,
When, like Apollo, he came forth to warm
Our ears, or, like a Mercury to charm.
Nature herself was proud of his designs,
And joyed to wear the dressing of his lines,
Which were so richly spun, and woven so fit
As, since, she will vouchsafe no other wit.
The merry Greek, tart Aristophanes,
Neat Terence, witty Plautus, now not please;
But antiquated and deserted lie,
As they were not of Nature's family.
Yet must I not give Nature all! Thy art,
My gentle Shakespeare, must enjoy a part.
For though the poet's matter Nature be
His art doth give the fashion. And that he
Who casts to write a living line, must sweat
(Such as thine are), and strike the second heat
Upon the Muses' anvil, turn the same
(And himself with it), that he thinks to frame;
Or for the laurel he may gain a scorn!
For a good poet's made as well as born;
And such wert thou! Look how the father's face
Lives in his issue; even so, the race
Of Shakespeare's mind and manners brightly shines
In his well-turnèd and true-filèd lines;
In each of which he seems to shake a lance
As brandished at the eyes of ignorance.

Sweet Swan of Avon! what a sight it were
To see thee in our waters yet appear,
And make those flights upon the banks of Thames
That so did take Eliza, and our James!
But stay, I see thee in the hemisphere
Advanced, and made a constellation there!
Shine forth, thou star of poets, and with rage,
Or influence, chide or cheer the drooping stage;
Which, since thy flight from hence, hath mourn'd
    like night,
And despairs day, but for thy volume's light.

First Folio of Shakespeare, 1623.

ON THE PORTRAIT OF SHAKESPEARE

THIS figure that thou here seest put,
It was for gentle Shakespeare cut,
Wherein the graver had a strife
With Nature, to outdo the life.

Oh, could he but have drawn his wit
As well in brass, as he has hit
His face, the print would then surpass
All that was ever writ in brass.

But, since he cannot, reader, look
Not on his picture, but his book.

First Folio of Shakespeare, 1623.

A HYMN TO GOD THE FATHER

HEAR me, O God!
A broken heart
Is my best part:
Use still thy rod,
That I may prove
Therein, thy love.

If thou hadst not
   Been stern to me,
   But left me free,
I had forgot
   Myself and thee.

For sin's so sweet,
   As minds ill bent
   Rarely repent,
Until they meet
   Their punishment.

Who more can crave
   Than thou hast done:
   That gav'st a Son,
To free a slave?
   First made of nought;
   With all since bought.

Sin, Death, and Hell,
   His glorious Name
   Quite overcame;
Yet I rebel,
   And slight the same.

But I'll come in,
   Before my loss,
   Me farther toss,
As sure to win
   Under His Cross.

Underwoods.

A HYMN ON THE NATIVITY OF MY SAVIOUR

I SING the birth was born to-night,
The Author both of life and light;
     The angels so did sound it,
And like the ravished shepherds said,
Who saw the light, and were afraid,
     Yet searched, and true they found it.

The Son of God, th' Eternal King,
That did us all salvation bring,
     And freed the soul from danger;
He whom the whole world could not take,
The Word, which heaven and earth did make,
     Was now laid in a manger.

The Father's wisdom willed it so,
The Son's obedience knew no No,
     Both wills were in one stature;
And as that wisdom had decreed,
The Word was now made Flesh indeed,
     And took on Him our nature.

What comfort by Him do we win,
Who made Himself the price of sin,
     To make us heirs of glory!
To see this Babe, all innocence,
A martyr born in our defence;
     Can man forget this story?

Underwoods.

AN ODE

HIGH-SPIRITED friend,
  I send nor balms nor cor'sives to your wound:
     Your fate hath found
A gentler and more agile hand to tend
     take] contain.

The cure of that which is but corporal;
And doubtful days, which were named critical,
Have made their fairest flight
And now are out of sight.
Yet doth some wholesome physic for the mind
Wrap't in this paper lie,
Which in the taking if you misapply,
You are unkind.

Your covetous hand,
Happy in that fair honour it hath gain'd,
Must now be rein'd.
True valour doth her own renown command
In one full action; nor have you now more
To do, than be a husband of that store.
Think but how dear you bought
This fame which you have caught:
Such thoughts will make you more in love with truth.
'Tis wisdom, and that high,
For men to use their fortune reverently,
Even in youth.

RICHARD BARNEFIELD

1574–1627

THE NIGHTINGALE

As it fell upon a day
In the merry month of May,
Sitting in a pleasant shade
Which a grove of myrtles made,
Beasts did leap and birds did sing,
Trees did grow and plants did spring,
Everything did banish moan
Save the Nightingale alone.

She, poor bird, as all forlorn,
Lean'd her breast up-till a thorn,
And there sung the dolefull'st ditty
That to hear it was great pity.
Fie, fie, fie, now would she cry;
Tereu, tereu, by and by:
That to hear her so complain
Scarce I could from tears refrain;
For her griefs so lively shown
Made me think upon mine own.
—Ah, thought I, thou mourn'st in vain,
None takes pity on thy pain:
Senseless trees, they cannot hear thee,
Ruthless beasts, they will not cheer thee;
King Pandion, he is dead,
All thy friends are lapp'd in lead:
All thy fellow birds do sing
Careless of thy sorrowing:
Even so, poor bird, like thee
None alive will pity me.

JOSEPH HALL
1574–1656
THE TRENCHER CHAPLAIN

A GENTLE squire would gladly entertain
Into his house some trencher-chapelain;
Some willing man that might instruct his sons,
And that would stand to good conditions.
First, that he lie upon the truckle-bed,
While his young master lieth o'er his head.
Secondly, that he do, on no default,
Ever presume to sit above the salt.

up-till] up to.   lively] vividly.

Third, that he never change his trencher twice.
Fourth, that he use all comely courtesies;
Sit bare at meals, and one half rise and wait.
Last, that he never his young master beat,
But he must ask his mother to define
How many jerks she would his breech should line.
All these observed, he could contented be
To give five marks and winter livery.

THE COXCOMB

FIE on all courtesy, and unruly winds,
Two only foes that fair disguisement finds.
　Strange curse! But fit for such a fickle age,
When scalps are subject to such vassalage.
Late travelling along in London way,
Me met, as seemed by his disguised array,
A lusty courtier whose curlèd head,
With abron locks was fairly furnishèd.
I him saluted in our lavish wise:
He answers my untimely courtesies.
His bonnet railed, ere ever he could think,
Th' unruly wind blows off his periwink,
He lights, and runs, and quickly hath him sped,
To overtake his over-running head.
The sportful wind, to mock the headless man,
Tosses apace his pitched Rogerian:
And straight it to a deeper ditch hath blown:
There must my younker fetch his waxen crown.
I looked and laughed, whiles in his raging mind,
He curst all courtesy, and unruly wind.
I looked, and laughed, and much I marvellèd
To see so large a causeway in his head,

　　jerks] stripes.　　　abron] auburn.　　　railed] arranged.
Rogerian] false scalp.　　younker] youngster.

And me bethought, that when it first begun,
'Twas some shrewd autumn, that so bared the bone.
Is't not sweet pride, when men their crowns must
    shade,
With that which irks the hams of every jade,
Or floor-strewed locks from off the barber's shears?
But waxen crowns well 'gree with borrowed hairs.

THOMAS HEYWOOD

1575–1650

MATIN SONG

PACK, clouds, away, and welcome day,
    With night we banish sorrow;
Sweet air blow soft, mount lark aloft
    To give my Love good-morrow!
Wings from the wind to please her mind
    Notes from the lark I'll borrow;
Bird prune thy wing, nightingale sing,
    To give my Love good-morrow;
        To give my Love good-morrow
        Notes from them all I'll borrow.

Wake from thy nest Robin Red-breast,
    Sing birds in every furrow;
And from each bill let music shrill
    Give my fair Love good-morrow!
Blackbird and thrush in every bush,
    Stare, linnet, and cock-sparrow,
You pretty elves, amongst yourselves
    Sing my fair Love good-morrow!
        To give my Love good-morrow
        Sing birds in every furrow!

Stare] starling.

YE PRETTY WANTONS, WARBLE

YE little birds that sit and sing
  Amidst the shady valleys,
And see how Phillis sweetly walks
  Within her garden-alleys;
Go, pretty birds, about her bower;
Sing, pretty birds, she may not lower;
Ah me! methinks I see her frown!
    Ye pretty wantons, warble.

Go tell her through your chirping bills,
  As you by me are bidden,
To her is only known my love;
  Which from the world is hidden.
Go, pretty birds, and tell her so,
See that your notes strain not too low,
For still methinks I see her frown;
    Ye pretty wantons, warble.

Go tune your voices' harmony
  And sing, I am her lover;
Strain loud and sweet, that every note
  With sweet content may move her:
And she that hath the sweetest voice,
Tell her I will not change my choice:
Yet still methinks I see her frown!
    Ye pretty wantons, warble.

O fly! make haste! see, see, she falls
  Into a pretty slumber!
Sing round about her rosy bed
  That waking she may wonder:

Say to her, 'tis her lover true
That sendeth love to you, to you!
And when you hear her kind reply,
    Return with pleasant warblings.

JOHN CHALKHILL

15—(?)–16—(?)

CORIDON'S SONG

OH, the sweet contentment
The countryman doth find.
    High trolollie lollie loe,
    High trolollie lee,
That quiet contemplation
Possesseth all my mind:
    Then care away,
    And wend along with me.

For courts are full of flattery,
As hath too oft been tried;
    High trolollie lollie loe,
    High trolollie lee,
The city full of wantonness,
And both are full of pride.
    Then care away,
    And wend along with me.

But oh, the honest countryman
Speaks truly from his heart,
    High trolollie lollie loe,
    High trolollie lee,
His pride is in his tillage,
His horses and his cart:
    Then care away,
    And wend along with me.

Our clothing is good sheepskins,
Grey russet for our wives,
   High trolollie lollie loe,
   High trolollie lee,
'Tis warmth and not gay clothing
That doth prolong our lives;
   Then care away,
   And wend along with me.

The ploughman, though he labour hard,
Yet on the holiday,
   High trolollie lollie loe,
   High trolollie lee,
No emperor so merrily
Does pass his time away;
   Then care away,
   And wend along with me.

To recompense our tillage
The heavens afford us showers;
   High trolollie lollie loe,
   High trolollie lee,
And for our sweet refreshments
The earth affords us bowers:
   Then care away,
   And wend along with me.

The cuckoo and the nightingale
Full merrily do sing,
   High trolollie lollie loe,
   High trolollie lee,
And with their pleasant roundelays
Bid welcome to the spring:
   Then care away,
   And wend along with me.

This is not half the happiness
The countryman enjoys;
   High trolollie lollie loe,
   High trolollie lee,
Though others think they have as much
Yet he that says so lies:
   Then come away, turn
   Countryman with me.

THOMAS DEKKER

1575–1641

O SWEET CONTENT

ART thou poor, yet hast thou golden slumbers?
   O sweet content!
Art thou rich, yet is thy mind perplexed?
   O punishment!
Dost thou laugh to see how fools are vexed
To add to golden numbers, golden numbers?
O sweet content! O sweet, O sweet content!
  Work apace, apace, apace, apace;
  Honest labour bears a lovely face;
Then hey nonny nonny, hey nonny nonny!

Canst drink the waters of the crispèd spring?
   O sweet content!
Swimm'st thou in wealth, yet sink'st in thine own
       tears?
   O punishment!
Then he that patiently want's burden bears
No burden bears, but is a king, a king!

crispèd] ruffled, bracing.

O sweet content! O sweet, O sweet content!
  Work apace, apace, apace, apace;
    Honest labour bears a lovely face;
Then hey nonny nonny, hey nonny nonny!

A PORTRAIT

My Infelice's face, her brow, her eye,
The dimple on her cheek; and such sweet skill
Hath from the cunning workman's pencil flown,
These lips look fresh and lovely as her own.
False colours last after the true be dead.
Of all the roses grafted on her cheeks,
Of all the graces dancing in her eyes,
Of all the music set upon her tongue,
Of all that was past woman's excellence
In her white bosom; look, a painted board
Circumscribes all.

GOLDEN SLUMBERS

    GOLDEN slumbers kiss your eyes,
    Smiles awake you when you rise:
    Sleep, pretty wantons, do not cry,
    And I will sing a lullaby.
    Rock them, rock them, lullaby.

    Care is heavy, therefore sleep you.
    You are care, and care must keep you:
    Sleep, pretty wantons, do not cry,
    And I will sing a lullaby.
    Rock them, rock them, lullaby.

THE FIRST THREE-MAN'S SONG

O, THE month of May, the merry month of May,
  So frolick, so gay, and so green, so green, so
    green!
O, and then did I unto my true love say:
  'Sweet Peg, thou shalt be my summer's queen!

'Now the nightingale, the pretty nightingale,
  The sweetest singer in all the forest's choir,
Entreats thee, sweet Peggy, to hear thy true love's
    tale;
  Lo, yonder she sitteth, her breast against a brier,

'But O, I spy the cuckoo, the cuckoo, the cuckoo;
  See where she sitteth: come away, my joy;
Come away, I prithee: I do not like the cuckoo
  Should sing where my Peggy and I kiss and toy.'

O, the month of May, the merry month of May,
  So frolick, so gay, and so green, so green, so green!
And then did I unto my true love say:
  'Sweet Peg, thou shalt be my summer's queen!'

THE SECOND THREE-MAN'S SONG

COLD's the wind, and wet's the rain,
  Saint Hugh be our good speed:
Ill is the weather that bringeth no gain,
  Nor helps good hearts in need.

Troll the bowl, the jolly nut-brown bowl,
  And here, kind mate, to thee:
Let's sing a dirge for Saint Hugh's soul,
  And down it merrily.

troll] pass round.

Down a down hey down a down,
Hey derry derry, down a down!
Ho, well done; to let me come!
    Ring compass gentle joy.

Troll the bowl, the nut brown bowl,
    And here kind mate to thee: &c.

Cold's the wind, and wet's the rain,
    Saint Hugh be our good speed;
Ill is the weather that bringeth no gain,
    Nor helps good hearts in need.

                  The Shoemaker's Holiday.

SONG

HAYMAKERS, rakers, reapers, and mowers,
    Wait on your summer queen.
Dress up with musk-rose her eglantine bowers,
    Daffodils strew the green.
        Sing, dance, and play,
        'Tis holiday.
    The sun does bravely shine

        On our ears of corn.
          Rich as a pearl,
          Comes every girl,
    This is mine, this is mine, this is mine;
Let us die, ere away they be borne.

Bow to the sun, to our queen, and that fair one,
    Come to behold our sports.
Each bonny lass here is counted a rare one,
    As those in princes' courts.

These and we
   With country glee,
Will teach the woods to resound
And the hills with echoes hollow;
    Skipping lambs
    Their bleating dams
'Mongst kids shall trip it round;
For joy thus our wenches we follow.

Wind, jolly huntsmen, your neat bugles shrilly,
   Hounds make a lusty cry;
Spring up, you falconers, the partridges freely,
   Then let your brave hawks fly.
    Horses amain
    Over ridge, over plain,
The dogs have the stag in chase;
    So, ho! ho! through the skies
    How the proud bird flies,
And sousing, kills with a grace.
Now the deer falls; hark! how they ring.

The Sun's Darling.

sousing] swooping, pouncing.

JOHN FLETCHER

1579–1625

MELANCHOLY

HENCE, all you vain delights,
As short as are the nights
   Wherein you spend your folly:
There's nought in this life sweet,
If man were wise to see 't,
   But only melancholy,
   O sweetest melancholy!
Welcome, folded arms, and fixèd eyes,
A sigh that piercing mortifies,
A look that 's fasten'd to the ground,
A tongue chain'd up without a sound!
Fountain heads and pathless groves,
Places which pale passion loves!
Moonlight walks, when all the fowls
Are warmly housed, save bats and owls!
   A midnight bell, a parting groan—
   These are the sounds we feed upon;
Then stretch our bones in a still gloomy valley;
Nothing's so dainty sweet as lovely melancholy.

                    The Nice Valour.

WEEP NO MORE

WEEP no more, nor sigh, nor groan,
Sorrow calls no time that 's gone:
Violets pluck'd, the sweetest rain
Makes not fresh nor grow again.
Trim thy locks, look cheerfully;
Fate's hid ends eyes cannot see.

still gloomy] always gloomy.

Joys as wingèd dreams fly fast,
Why should sadness longer last?
Grief is but a wound to woe;
Gentlest fair, mourn, mourn no moe.

The Queen of Corinth.

THE DEAD HOST'S WELCOME

'TIS late and cold; stir up the fire;
Sit close, and draw the table nigher;
Be merry, and drink wine that's old,
A hearty medicine 'gainst a cold:
Your beds of wanton down the best,
Where you shall tumble to your rest;
I could wish you wenches too,
But I am dead, and cannot do.
Call for the best the house may ring,
Sack, white, and claret, let them bring,
And drink apace, while breath you have;
You'll find but cold drink in the grave:
Plover, partridge, for your dinner,
And a capon for the sinner,
You shall find ready when you're up,
And your horse shall have his sup:
Welcome, welcome, shall fly round,
And I shall smile, though under ground.

The Lover's Progress.

SLEEP

CARE-CHARMING Sleep, thou easer of all woes,
Brother to Death, sweetly thyself dispose
On this afflicted prince; fall like a cloud
In gentle showers; give nothing that is loud,
Or painful to his slumbers; easy, sweet,
And as a purling stream, thou son of night,

Pass by his troubled senses, sing his pain,
Like hollow murmuring wind, or silver rain.
Into this prince gently, O gently slide,
And kiss him into slumbers like a bride.

Valentinian.

THE SATYR

HERE be grapes, whose lusty blood
Is the learned poet's good,
Sweeter yet did never crown
The head of Bacchus; nuts more brown
Than the squirrel's teeth that crack them;
Deign, oh, fairest fair, to take them.
For these black-eyed Driope
Hath oftentimes commanded me
With my clasped knee to climb:
See how well the lusty time
Hath decked their rising cheeks in red,
Such as on your lips is spread.
Here be berries for a queen,
Some be red, some be green;
These are of that luscious meat,
The great god Pan himself doth eat:
All these, and what the woods can yield,
The hanging mountain or the field,
I freely offer, and ere long
Will bring you more, more sweet and strong;
Till when humbly leave I take,
Lest the great Pan do awake,
That sleeping lies in a deep glade,
Under a broad beech's shade:
I must go, I must run
Swifter than the fiery sun.

The Faithful Shepherdess.

SONG TO PAN

ALL ye woods and trees and bowers,
All ye virtues and ye powers
That inhabit in the lakes,
In the pleasant springs or brakes,
  Move your feet
   To our sound
  Whilst we greet
   All this ground
With his honour and his name
That defends our flocks from blame.

He is great, and he is just,
He is ever good, and must
Thus be honoured. Daffadillies,
Roses, pinks, and lovèd lilies,
   Let us fling,
   Whilst we sing
   'Ever holy,
   Ever holy,
Ever honoured, ever young!'
Thus great Pan is ever sung.

       The Faithful Shepherdess.

MORNING SONG

SHEPHERDS, rise, and shake off sleep!
See the blushing morn doth peep
Through the windows, whilst the sun
To the mountain tops is run,
Gilding all the vales below
With his rising flames, which grow
Greater by his climbing still.
Up, ye lazy grooms, and fill

Bag and bottle for the field!
Clasp your cloaks fast, lest they yield
To the bitter north-east wind.
Call the maidens up, and find
Who lay longest, that she may
Go without a friend all day;
Then reward your dogs, and pray
Pan to keep you from decay:
So unfold, and then away!

The Faithful Shepherdess.

EVENING SONG

SHEPHERDS all, and maidens fair,
Fold your flocks up, for the air
'Gins to thicken, and the sun
Already his great course hath run.
See the dewdrops how they kiss
Every little flower that is;
Hanging on their velvet heads
Like a rope of crystal beads.
See the heavy clouds low falling,
And bright Hesperus down calling
The dead night from under ground,
At whose rising mists unsound,
Damps, and vapours fly apace,
Hovering o'er the wanton face
Of these pastures, where they come,
Striking dead both bud and bloom;
Therefore from such danger lock
Everyone his lovèd flock,
And let your dogs lie loose without,
Lest the wolf come as a scout

From the mountain, and ere day
Bear a lamb or kid away;
Or the crafty thievish fox
Break upon your simple flocks.
So secure yourselves from these,
Be not too secure in ease;
Let one eye his watches keep,
Whilst the t'other eye doth sleep;
So you shall good shepherds prove,
And for ever hold the love
Of our great god. Sweetest slumbers
And soft silence fall in numbers
On your eyelids; so farewell,
Thus I end my evening's knell.

The Faithful Shepherdess.

JOY OF BATTLE

Arm, arm, arm, arm, the scouts are all come in.
Keep your ranks close, and now your honours win.
Behold from yonder hill the foe appears,
Bows, bills, glaives, arrows, shields and spears,
Like a dark wood he comes, or tempest pouring;
O view the wings of horse the meadows scouring:
The vanguard marches bravely; hark the drums
    —dub, dub.
    They meet, they meet, now the battle comes:
        See how the arrows fly,
        That darken all the sky!
        Hark how the trumpets sound,
        Hark how the hills rebound—tara, tara,
        tara.
Hark how the horses charge; in boys, in boys, in—
    tara, tara.

glaives] swords.

The battle totters; now the wounds begin;
 O how they cry,
 O how they die!
Room for the valiant Memnon armed with thunder!
 See how he breaks the ranks asunder!
They fly, they fly, Eumenes has the chase,
And brave Polybius makes good his place.
 To the plains, to the woods,
 To the rocks, to the floods,
They fly for succour. Follow, follow, follow,
 hey, hey.
 Hark how the soldiers hollo!
 Brave Diocles is dead,
 And all his soldiers fled,
 The battle's won, and lost,
 That many a life hath cost.

MAN HIS OWN STAR

Man is his own star; and the soul that can
Render an honest and a perfect man
Commands all light, all influence, all fate;
Nothing to him falls early, or too late.
Our acts our angels are, or good or ill,
Our fatal shadows that walk by us still.

      The Honest Man's Fortune.

THE SONG OF THE RIVER-GOD TO AMORET

Do not fear to put thy feet
Naked in the river, sweet;
Think not leech, or newt, or toad,
Will bite thy foot, when thou hast trod;

Nor let the water rising high,
As thou wad'st in, make thee **cry**
And sob; but ever live with me,
And not a wave shall trouble thee.

The Faithful Shepherdess.

SONG TO BACCHUS

GOD Lyaeus, ever young,
Ever honoured, ever sung;
Stained with blood of lusty grapes,
In a thousand lusty shapes
Dance upon the mazer's brim,
In the crimson liquor swim;
From thy plenteous hand divine
Let a river run with wine:
    God of Youth, let this day here
    Enter neither care nor fear.

Valentinian.

FRANCIS BEAUMONT
1586-1616
ON THE TOMBS IN WESTMINSTER ABBEY

MORTALITY, behold and fear!
What a change of flesh is here!
Think how many royal bones
Sleep within this heap of stones:
Here they lie had realms and lands,
Who now want strength to stir their hands:
Where from their pulpits seal'd with dust
They preach, 'In greatness is no trust.'

Lyaeus] Bacchus, the god of wine.   mazer] hard
wood used as material for drinking-cups.

Here's an acre sown indeed
With the richest, royal'st seed
That the earth did e'er suck in
Since the first man died for sin:
Here the bones of birth have cried—
'Though gods they were, as men they died.'
Here are sands, ignoble things,
Dropt from the ruin'd sides of kings;
Here's a world of pomp and state,
Buried in dust, once dead by fate.

SHAKE OFF YOUR HEAVY TRANCE

Shake off your heavy trance!
    And leap into a dance
Such as no mortals use to tread:
    Fit only for Apollo
To play to, for the moon to lead,
    And all the stars to follow!

BEAUMONT AND FLETCHER

ASPATIA'S SONG

Lay a garland on my hearse
    Of the dismal yew:
Maidens, willow branches bear;
    Say, I dièd true.

My love was false, but I was firm
    From my hour of birth.
Upon my buried body lie
    Lightly, gentle earth!

The Maid's Tragedy.

use] are accustomed.

DIRGE

COME, you whose loves are dead,
  And, whiles I sing,
   Weep and wring
Every hand, and every head
Bind with cypress and sad yew,
Ribands black and candles blue
For him that was of men most true!

Come with heavy moaning,
  And on his grave
   Let him have
Sacrifice of sighs and groaning;
Let him have fair flowers enow,
White and purple, green and yellow,
For him that was of men most true!

      The Knight of the Burning Pestle

JOHN WEBSTER

1580(?)–1625

DIRGES

(1) *Call for the robin-redbreast and the wren.*

CALL for the robin-redbreast and the wren,
Since o'er shady groves they hover,
And with leaves and flowers do cover
The friendless bodies of unburied men.
Call unto his funeral dole
The ant, the field-mouse, and the mole,

To rear him hillocks that shall keep him warm,
And (when gay tombs are robb'd) sustain no harm;
But keep the wolf far thence, that's foe to men,
For with his nails he'll dig them up again.

The White Devil.

(2) *All the flowers of the Spring*

ALL the flowers of the spring
Meet to perfume our burying;
These have but their growing prime,
And man does flourish but his time.
Survey our progress from our birth;
We are set, we grow, we turn to earth.
Courts adieu, and all delights,
All bewitching appetites;
Sweetest breath and clearest eye,
Like perfumes, go out and die;
And consequently this is done
As shadows wait upon the sun.
Vain the ambition of kings
Who seek by trophies and dead things
To leave a living name behind,
And weave but nets to catch the wind.

The Devil's Law Case.

(3) *Hark! Now everything is still*

HARK! Now everything is still,
The screech-owl and the whistler shrill,
Call upon our dame aloud,
And bid her quickly don her shroud!
Much you had of land and rent;
Your length in clay's now competent:
A long war disturb'd your mind;
Here your perfect peace is sign'd.

Of what is't fools make such vain keeping:
Sin their conception, their birth weeping,
Their life a general mist of error,
Their death a hideous storm of terror.
Strew your hair with powders sweet,
Don clean linen, bathe your feet,
And (the foul fiend more to check!)
A crucifix let bless your neck!
'Tis now full tide 'tween night and day;
End your groan, and come away!

The Duchess of Malfi.

PHINEAS FLETCHER

1580–1650

DROP, DROP, SLOW TEARS

Drop, drop, slow tears,
   And bathe those beauteous feet
Which brought from Heaven
   The news and Prince of peace:
Cease not, wet eyes,
   His mercies to entreat;
To cry for vengeance
   Sin doth never cease.
In your deep floods
   Drown all my faults and fears;
Nor let His eye
   See sin, but through my tears.

Piscatory Eclogues.

PARTHENIA

WITH her, her sister went, a warlike maid,
Parthenia, all in steel, and gilded arms;
In needle's stead a mighty spear she swayed,
With which in bloody fields and fierce alarms
    The boldest champion she down would bear,
    And like a thunderbolt wide passage tear,
Flinging all to the earth with her enchanted spear.

Her goodly armour seemed a garden green,
Where thousand spotless lilies freshly blew;
And on her shield the 'lone bird might be seen,
Th' Arabian bird, shining in colours new:
    Itself unto itself was only mate;
    Ever the same, but new in newer date:
And underneath was writ, 'Such is chaste single
    state.'

Thus hid in arms, she seemed a goodly knight,
And fit for any warlike exercise:
And when she list lay down her armour bright,
And back resume her peaceful maiden's guise;
    The fairest maid she was, that ever yet
    Prisoned her locks within a golden net,
Or let them waving hang, with roses fair beset.

Choice nymph, the crown of chaste Diana's train,
Thou beauty's lily, set in heavenly earth;
Thy fairs, unpatterned, all perfections stain:
Sure heaven with curious pencil at thy birth
    In thy rare face her own full picture drew:
    It is a strong verse here to write but true:
Hyperboles in others are but half thy due.

                    The Purple Island.

    Parthenia] Chastity in the single state.
    Th' Arabian bird] The phoenix (a virgin bird).

GILES FLETCHER

1588(?)–1623

DESCRIPTION OF MERCY

IF any ask why roses please the sight?
Because their leaves upon thy cheeks do bower:
If any ask why lilies are so white?
Because their blossoms in thy hand do flower:
Or why sweet plants so grateful odours shower?
    It is because thy breath so like they be:
    Or why the orient sun so bright we see?
What reason can we give, but from thine eyes, and
    thee?

Rosed all in lively crimson are thy cheeks,
Where beauties indeflourishing abide,
And, as to pass his fellow either seeks,
Seems both do blush at one another's pride;
And on thine eyelids, waiting thee beside,
    Ten thousand graces sit, and when they move
    To earth their amorous belgards from above
They fly from heaven, and on their wings convey
    thy love.

Christ's Victory and Triumph.

WOOING SONG

LOVE is the blossom where there blows
Every thing that lives or grows:
Love doth make the Heav'ns to move,
And the Sun doth burn in love:
Love the strong and weak doth yoke,
And makes the ivy climb the oak,

belgards] kind, loving looks.

Under whose shadows lions wild,
Soften'd by love, grow tame and mild:
Love no med'cine can appease,
He burns the fishes in the seas:
Not all the skill his wounds can stench,
Not all the sea his fire can quench.
Love did make the bloody spear
Once a leavy coat to wear,
While in his leaves there shrouded lay
Sweet birds, for love that sing and play
And of all love's joyful flame
I the bud and blossom am.

 Only bend thy knee to me,
 Thy wooing shall thy winning be!

See, see the flowers that below
Now as fresh as morning blow;
And of all the virgin rose
That as bright Aurora shows;
How they all unleavèd die,
Losing their virginity!
Like unto a summer shade,
But now born, and now they fade.
Everything doth pass away;
There is danger in delay:
Come, come, gather then the rose,
Gather it, or it you lose!
All the sand of Tagus' shore
Into my bosom casts his ore:
All the valleys' swimming corn
To my house is yearly borne:
Every grape of every vine
Is gladly bruised to make me wine:

  stench] stanch. leavy] leafy.

While ten thousand kings, as proud,
   To carry up my train have bow'd,
And a world of ladies send me
   In my chambers to attend me:
All the stars in Heav'n that shine,
And ten thousand more, are mine:
     Only bend thy knee to me,
     Thy wooing shall thy winning be!

         Christ's Victory and Triumph.

LORD HERBERT OF CHERBURY

1581–1648

NOW THAT THE APRIL OF YOUR YOUTH

Now that the April of your youth adorns
   The garden of your face,
Now that for you each knowing lover mourns,
   And all seek to your grace:
Do not repay affection with scorns.

What though you may a matchless beauty vaunt,
   And that all hearts can move,
By such a power, as seemeth to enchant;
   Yet, without help of love,
Beauty no pleasure to itself can grant.

Then think each minute that you lose a day,
   The longest youth is short,
The shortest age is long; Time flies away,
   And makes us but his sport,
And that which is not Youth's is Age's prey.

See but the bravest horse, that prideth most,
   Though he escape the war,
Either from master to the man is lost,
   Or turned into the car,
Or else must die with being ridden post.

Then lose not beauty, lovers, time and all,
    Too late your fault you see,
When that in vain you would these days recall;
    Nor can you virtuous be,
When without these you have not wherewithall.

BREAKING FROM UNDER THAT THY CLOUDY VEIL

BREAKING from under that thy cloudy veil,
    Open and shine yet more, shine out more clear
    Thou glorious golden-beam-darting hair,
Even till my wonder-stricken senses fail.

Shoot out in light, and shine those rays on far,
    Thou much more fair than is the Queen of Love,
    When she doth comb her in her sphere above,
And from a planet turns a blazing-star.

Nay, thou art greater too, more destiny
    Depends on thee, than on her influence,
    No hair thy fatal hand doth now dispense,
But to some one a thread of life must be.

While gracious unto me, thou both dost sunder
    Those glories which, if they united were,
    Might have amazed sense, and shew'st each hair,
Which if alone had been too great a wonder.

And now spread in their goodly length, she appears
    No creature which the earth might call her own,
    But rather one, that in her gliding down,
Heav'n's beams did crown, to show us she was theirs.

And come from thence, how can they fear time's rage
    Which in his power else on earth most strange
    Such golden treasure doth to silver change
By that improper alchemy of Age?

But stay, methinks new beauties do arise,
   While she withdraws these glories which were
      spread.
   Wonder of beauties, set thy radiant head,
And strike out day from thy yet fairer eyes.

RICHARD CORBET
1582-1635
FAREWELL, REWARDS AND FAIRIES

FAREWELL, rewards and fairies,
   Good housewives now may say,
For now foul sluts in dairies
   Do fare as well as they.
And though they sweep their hearths no less
   Than maids were wont to do
Yet who of late for cleanliness
   Finds sixpence in her shoe?

Lament, lament, old abbeys,
   The fairies' lost command!
They did but change priests' babies,
   But some have changed your land.
And all your children, sprung from thence,
   Are now grown puritans,
Who live as changelings ever since
   For love of your demesnes.

At morning and at evening both
   You merry were and glad,
So little care of sleep or sloth
   These pretty ladies had;
When Tom came home from labour,
   Or Cis to milking rose,
Then merrily went their tabor,
   And nimbly went their toes.

Witness those rings and roundelays
   Of theirs, which yet remain,
Were footed in Queen Mary's days
   On many a grassy plain;
But since of late Elizabeth,
   And later James came in,
They never danced on any heath
   As when the time hath been.

By which we note the fairies
   Were of the old profession;
Their songs were 'Ave Mary's',
   Their dances were procession.
But now, alas, they all are dead;
   Or gone beyond the seas;
Or farther for religion fled;
   Or else they take their ease.

A tell-tale in their company
   They never could endure!
And whoso kept not secretly
   Their mirth, was punished, sure;
It was a just and christian deed
   To pinch such black and blue.
Oh how the commonwealth doth want
   Such Justices as you!

TO HIS SON VINCENT CORBET

WHAT I shall leave thee, none can tell,
But all shall say I wish thee well:
I wish thee, Vin, before all wealth,
Both bodily and ghostly health;
Nor too much wealth nor wit come to thee,
So much of either may undo thee.

I wish thee learning, not for show,
Enough for to instruct and know;
Not such as gentleness require
To prate at table or at fire.
I wish thee all thy mother's graces
Thy father's fortunes and his places.
I wish thee friends, and one at court,
Not to build on, but support;
To keep thee not in doing many
Oppressions, but from suffering any.
I wish thee peace in all thy ways,
Nor lazy nor contentious days;
And, when thy soul and body part,
As innocent as now thou art.

DREAMS

THE damask meadows and the crawling streams
  Sweeten and make soft thy dreams;
The purling springs, groves, birds, and well-weaved
    bowers,
  With fields enamellèd with flowers,
Present thee shapes, while phantasy discloses
  Millions of lilies mixt with roses.
Then dream thou hear'st the lambs with many a
    bleat
  Wooed to come suck the milky teat;
Whilst Faunus in the vision vows to keep
  From ravenous wolf the woolly sheep;
With thousand such enchanting dreams, which
    meet
  To make sleep not so sound as sweet.
Nor can these figures so thy rest endear,
  As not to up when chanticleer

Speaks the last watch, but with the dawn dost rise
　　To work, but first to sacrifice:
Making thy peace with Heaven for some late fault
　　With holy meal, and crackling salt.

SIR JOHN BEAUMONT

1582–1628

ON MY DEAR SON, GERVASE BEAUMONT

CAN I, who have for others oft compiled
The songs of death, forget my sweetest child,
Which, like a flower crushed, with a blast is dead,
And ere full time hangs down his smiling head,
Expecting with clear hope to live anew,
Among the angels fed with heavenly dew?
We have this sign of joy, that many days,
While on the earth his struggling spirit stays,
The name of Jesus in his mouth contains,
His only food, his sleep, his ease from pains.
O may that sound be rooted in my mind,
Of which in him such strong effect I find.
Dear Lord, receive my son, whose winning love
To me was like a friendship, far above
The course of nature, or his tender age;
Whose looks could all my bitter griefs assuage;
Let his pure soul—ordained seven years to be
In that frail body, which was part of me—
Remain my pledge in heaven, as sent to show
How to this port at every step I go.

PHILIP MASSINGER

1583–1640

SONG

Why art thou slow, thou rest of trouble, Death,
 To stop a wretch's breath,
That calls on thee, and offers her sad heart
 A prey unto thy dart?
I am nor young nor fair; be therefore bold:
 Sorrow hath made me old,
Deformed, and wrinkled; all that I can crave
 Is quiet in my grave.
Such as live happy, hold long life a jewel;
 But to me thou art cruel,
If thou end not my tedious misery;
 And I soon cease to be.
Strike, and strike home then; pity unto me,
 In one short hour's delay, is tyranny.

The Emperor of the East.

WILLIAM DRUMMOND OF HAWTHORNDEN

1585–1649

JERUSALEM

Jerusalem, that place divine,
The vision of sweet peace is named;
In heaven her glorious turrets shine,
Her walls of living stones are framed;
While Angels guard her on each side,
Fit company for such a bride.

She, deck'd in new attire from heaven,
Her wedding chamber, now descends,
Prepared in marriage to be given
To Christ, on whom her joy depends.

Her walls, wherewith she is enclosed,
And streets are of pure gold composed.

The gates adorn'd with pearls most bright
The way to hidden glory show,
And thither by the blessèd might
Of faith in Jesus' merits go
All those who are on earth distress'd,
Because they have Christ's name profess'd.

These stones the workmen dress and beat
Before they throughly polished are;
Then each is in his proper seat
Establish'd by the Builder's care,
In this fair frame to stand for ever,
So join'd that them no force can sever.

To God, who sits in highest seat,
Glory and power given be;
To Father, Son, and Paraclete,
Who reign in equal dignity;
Whose boundless power we still adore,
And sing their praise for evermore.

REDEEM TIME PAST

MORE oft than once Death whispered in mine ear,
Grave what thou hear'st in diamond and gold,
I am that monarch whom all monarchs fear,
Who hath in dust their far-stretch'd pride up-
　　roll'd;

All, all is mine beneath moon's silver sphere,
And nought, save virtue, can my power withhold:
This, not believed, experience true thee told,
By danger late when I to thee came near.

As bugbear then my visage I did show,
That of my horrors thou right use might'st make,
And a more sacred path of living take:—
Now still walk armèd for my ruthless blow:

Trust flattering life no more, redeem time past
And live each day as if it were thy last.

OF THIS FAIR VOLUME

OF this fair volume which we World do name
  If we the sheets and leaves could turn with care,
Of Him who it corrects, and did it frame,
  We clear might read the art and wisdom rare:

Find out His power which wildest powers doth
    tame,
  His providence extending everywhere,
  His justice which proud rebels doth not spare,
In every page, no period of the same.

But silly we, like foolish children, rest
  Well pleased with colour'd vellum, leaves of gold,
Fair dangling ribbands, leaving what is best,
  On the great Writer's sense ne'er taking hold;

Or if by chance we stay our minds on aught,
It is some picture on the margin wrought.

DOTH THEN THE WORLD GO THUS

DOTH then the world go thus, doth all thus move?
  Is this the justice which on Earth we find?
  Is this that firm decree which all doth bind?
Are these your influences, Powers above?

Those souls which vice's moody mists most blind,
Blind Fortune, blindly, most their friend doth prove;
And they who thee, poor idol, Virtue! love,
    Ply like a feather toss'd by storm and wind.

Ah! if a Providence doth sway this all,
    Why should best minds groan under most distress?
Or why should pride humility make thrall,
    And injuries the innocent oppress?

Heavens! hinder, stop this fate; or grant a time
When good may have, as well as bad, their prime.

MADRIGAL

    LIKE the Idalian queen,
    Her hair about her eyne,
With neck and breast's ripe apples to be seen,
    At first glance of the morn
In Cyprus' gardens gathering those fair flow'rs
    Which of her blood were born,
I saw, but fainting saw, my paramours.
The Graces naked danced about the place,
    The winds and trees amazed
    With silence on her gazed,
The flowers did smile, like those upon her face;
And as their aspen stalks those fingers band,
    That she might read my case,
A hyacinth I wish'd me in her hand.

INVOCATION TO LOVE

    PHŒBUS, arise!
    And paint the sable skies
With azure, white, and red;
Rouse Memnon's mother from her Tithon's bed,

ply] go to and fro.

That she thy càriere may with roses spread;
The nightingales thy coming each-where sing;
Make an eternal spring!
Give life to this dark world which lieth dead;
Spread forth thy golden hair
In larger locks than thou wast wont before,
And emperor-like decore
With diadem of pearl thy temples fair:
Chase hence the ugly night
Which serves but to make dear thy glorious light.
This is that happy morn,
That day, long wishèd day
Of all my life so dark
(If cruel stars have not my ruin sworn
And fates not hope betray),
Which, only white, deserves
A diamond for ever should it mark:
This is the morn should bring unto this grove
My Love, to hear and recompense my love.
Fair King, who all preserves,
But show thy blushing beams,
And thou two sweeter eyes
Shalt see than those which by Penèus' streams
Did once thy heart surprise:
Nay, suns, which shine as clear
As thou when two thou did to Rome appear.
Now, Flora, deck thyself in fairest guise:
If that ye, winds, would hear
A voice surpassing far Amphion's lyre,
Your stormy chiding stay;
Let zephyr only breathe
And with her tresses play,
Kissing sometimes these purple ports of death.

càriere] career. course.   decore] decorate.

The winds all silent are;
And Phœbus in his chair
Ensaffroning sea and air
Makes vanish every star:
Night like a drunkard reels
Beyond the hills to shun his flaming wheels:
The fields with flowers are deck'd in every hue,
The clouds bespangle with bright gold their blue:
Here is the pleasant place—
And everything, save Her, who all should grace.

LOOK HOW THE FLOWER

Look how the flower, which ling'ringly doth fade,
The morning's darling late, the summer's queen,
Spoiled of that juice which kept it fresh and green,
As high as it did raise, bows low the head:
Right so my life, contentments being dead,
Or in their contraries but only seen,
With swifter speed declines than erst it spread,
And, blasted, scarce now shows what it hath been.
As doth the pilgrim therefore, whom the night
By darkness would imprison on his way,
Think on thy home, my soul, and think aright
Of what yet rests thee of life's wasting day:
    Thy sun posts westward, passèd is thy morn,
    And twice it is not given thee to be born.

TO HIS LUTE

My lute, be as thou wert when thou didst grow
    With thy green mother in some shady grove,
    When immelodious winds but made thee move,
And birds their ramage did on thee bestow.

Ensaffroning] painting yellow. erst] at first. ramage]
warbling, singing.

Since that dear Voice which did thy sounds
        approve,
Which wont in such harmonious strains to flow,
    Is reft from Earth to tune those spheres above
What art thou but a harbinger of woe?

Thy pleasing notes be pleasing notes no more,
        But orphans' wailings to the fainting ear;
        Each stroke a sigh, each sound draws forth a
            tear;
For which be silent as in woods before:

Or if that any hand to touch thee deign,
Like widow'd turtle still her loss complain.

SWEET SPRING, THOU TURN'ST

Sweet Spring, thou turn'st with all thy goodly train,
Thy head with flames, thy mantle bright with
        flow'rs:
The zephyrs curl the green locks of the plain,
The clouds for joy in pearls weep down their
        show'rs.
Thou turn'st, sweet youth, but ah! my pleasant
        hours
And happy days with thee come not again;
The sad memorials only of my pain
Do with thee turn, which turn my sweets in sours.
Thou art the same which still thou wast before,
Delicious, wanton, amiable, fair;
But she, whose breath embalm'd thy wholesome air,
Is gone—nor gold nor gems her can restore.
    Neglected virtue, seasons go and come,
    While thine forgot lie closèd in a tomb.

wont] was accustomed.   turtle] turtle-dove.
        still] always, continually.

MADRIGAL

DEAR night, the ease of care,
　　Untroubled seat of peace,
Time's eldest child, which oft the blind do see,
　　On this our hemisphere.
What makes thee now so sadly dark to be?
Com'st thou in funeral pomp her grave to grace,
Or do those stars which should thy horror clear
　　　In Jove's high hall advise
　　　In what part of the skies
With them or Cynthia she shall appear?
Or, ah, alas! because those matchless eyes
Which shone so fair below thou dost not find,
Striv'st thou to make all other eyes look blind?

A SOLITARY LIFE

THRICE happy he, who by some shady grove,
Far from the clamorous world, doth live his own;
Though solitary, who is not alone,
But doth converse with that eternal love.
O how more sweet is bird's harmonious moan,
Or the hoarse sobbings of the widowed dove,
Than those smooth whisperings near a prince's
　　　throne,
Which good make doubtful, do the evil approve!
O how more sweet is Zephyr's wholesome breath,
And sighs embalmed, which newborn flowers un-
　　　fold,
Than that applause vain honour doth bequeath!
How sweet are streams to poison drunk in gold!
　　The world is full of horrors, troubles, slights,
　　Woods' silent shades have only true delights.

AS IN A DUSKY AND TEMPESTUOUS NIGHT

As in a dusky and tempestuous night
   A star is wont to spread her locks of gold,
   And while her pleasant rays abroad are roll'd,
Some spiteful cloud doth rob us of her sight,
Fair soul, in this black age so shin'd thou bright,
   And made all eyes with wonder thee behold,
Till ugly Death, depriving us of light,
   In his grim misty arms thee did enfold.

Who more shall vaunt true beauty here to see?
   What hope doth more in any heart remain
   That such perfection shall his reason reign
If Beauty, with thee born, too died with thee?
   World, 'plain no more of Love, nor count his
     harms;
   With his pale trophies Death hath hung his
     arms.

MADRIGAL

The ivory, coral, gold,
Of breast, of lips, of hair,
So lively Sleep doth show to inward sight,
That wake I think I hold
No shadow, but my fair:
Myself so to deceive,
With long-shut eyes I shun the irksome light.
Such pleasure thus I have,
Delighting in false gleams,
If Death Sleep's brother be,
   And souls relieved of sense have so sweet dreams,
   That I would wish me thus to dream and die.

MADRIGAL

THIS Life, which seems so fair,
Is like a bubble blown up in the air
    By sporting children's breath,
    Who chase it everywhere
And strive who can most motion it bequeath.
And though it sometime seem of its own might,

    Like to an eye of gold, to be fix'd there,
And firm to hover in that empty height,
That only is because it is so light.
    —But in that pomp it doth not long appear;
For, when 'tis most admirèd, in a thought,
Because it erst was nought, it turns to nought.

TO THE NIGHTINGALE

(1)

SWEET bird, that sing'st away the early hours
Of winters past or coming void of care,
Well pleasèd with delights which present are,
Fair seasons, budding sprays, sweet-smelling
    flowers;
To rocks, to springs, to rills, from leavy bowers
Thou thy Creator's goodness dost declare,
And what dear gifts on thee he did not spare,
A stain to human sense in sin that lowers.
What soul can be so sick which by thy songs,
Attired in sweetness, sweetly is not driven
Quite to forget earth's turmoils, spites, and wrongs,
And lift a reverent eye and thought to heaven?
    Sweet artless songster, thou my mind dost raise
    To airs of spheres, yes, and to angels' lays.

in a thought] quick as thought.

(2)

DEAR quirister, who from those shadows sends,
Ere that the blushing dawn dare show her light,
Such sad lamenting strains, that night attends
(Become all ear), stars stay to hear thy plight;
If one whose grief even reach of thought trans-
    cends,
Who ne'er (not in a dream) did taste delight,
May thee importune who like case pretends,
And seems to joy in woe, in woe's despite;
Tell me (so may thou fortune milder try,
And long, long sing) for what thou thus complains,
Sith, winter gone, the sun in dappled sky
Now smiles on meadows, mountains, woods, and
    plains?
  The bird, as if my questions did her move,
    With trembling wings sobbed forth, I love, I
    love.

SAINT JOHN BAPTIST

THE last and greatest herald of heaven's King,
Girt with rough skins, hies to the deserts wild,
Among that savage brood the woods forth bring,
Which he than man more harmless found and mild:
His food was locusts, and what there doth spring,
With honey that from virgin hives distilled;
Parched body, hollow eyes, some uncouth thing
Made him appear, long since from earth exiled.
Then burst he forth: 'All ye, whose hopes rely
On God, with me amidst these deserts mourn;
Repent, repent, and from old errors turn.'
Who listened to his voice, obeyed his cry?
  Only the echoes, which he made relent,
    Rung from their marble caves, 'Repent, repent!'

MADRIGAL

My thoughts hold mortal strife,
I do detest my life,
And with lamenting cries,
Peace to my soul to bring,
Oft call that prince which here doth monarchize:
—But he, grim grinning King,
Who caitiffs scorns, and doth the blest surprise,
Late having deck'd with beauty's rose his tomb,
Disdains to crop a weed, and will not come.

JOHN FORD

1586-1639

MATIN SONG

FLY hence, shadows, that do keep
Watchful sorrows charmed in sleep!
Tho' the eyes be overtaken,
Yet the heart doth ever waken
Thoughts, chained up in busy snares
Of continual woes and cares:
Love and griefs are so exprest
As they rather sigh than rest.
    Fly hence, shadows, that do keep
    Watchful sorrows charmed in sleep!

The Lover's Melancholy, 1629.

DIRGE

GLORIES, pleasures, pomps, delights,
    and ease,
        Can but please
    Outward senses, when the mind
Is untroubled, or by peace refined.

First Voice. Crowns may flourish and decay,
     Beauties shine, but fade away,
Second „   Youth may revel, yet it must
     Lie down in a bed of dust.
Third „   Earthly honours flow and waste,
     Time alone doth change and last.
Chorus.   Sorrows mingled with contents prepare
         Rest for care;
     Love only reigns in death; though art
     Can find no comfort for a broken heart.

The Broken Heart, 1633.

WILLIAM BROWNE, OF TAVISTOCK

1588–1643

THE SIRENS' SONG

STEER hither, steer, your wingèd pines,
     All beaten mariners!
Here lie Love's undiscover'd mines,
     A prey to passengers;
Perfumes far sweeter than the best
Which make the Phœnix' urn and nest.
     Fear not your ships,
Nor any to oppose you save our lips;
     But come on shore,
Where no joy dies till Love hath gotten more.

For swelling waves our panting breasts,
     Where never storms arise,
Exchange and be awhile our guests:
     For stars gaze on our eyes.
The compass Love shall hourly sing,
And as he goes about the ring,

We will not miss
To tell each point he nameth with a kiss.
   —Then come on shore,
Where no joy dies till Love hath gotten more.

SHALL I TELL YOU WHOM I LOVE

SHALL I tell you whom I love?
   Hearken then awhile to me;
And if such a woman move
   As I now shall versify,
Be assured 'tis she or none
That I love, and love alone.

Nature did her so much right,
   As she scorns the help of Art;
In as many virtues dight
   As e'er yet embraced a heart.
So much good so truly tried,
Some for less were deified.

Wit she hath without desire
   To make known how much she hath;
And her anger flames no higher
   Than may fitly sweeten wrath.
Full of pity as may be,
Though perhaps not so to me.

Reason masters every sense,
   And her virtues grace her birth:
Lovely as all excellence,
   Modest in her most of mirth:
Likelihood enough to prove,
Only worth could kindle love.

      dight] arrayed, adorned.

Such she is: and if you know
  Such a one as I have sung;
Be she brown, or fair, or so,
  That she be but somewhile young;
Be assured, 'tis she, or none,
That I love, and love alone.

A WELCOME

WELCOME, welcome! do I sing,
  Far more welcome than the spring;
He that parteth from you never
Shall enjoy a spring for ever.

He that to the voice is near
  Breaking from your iv'ry pale,
Need not walk abroad to hear
  The delightful nightingale.
      Welcome, welcome, then . . .

He that looks still on your eyes,
  Though the winter have begun
To benumb our arteries,
  Shall not want the summer's sun.
      Welcome, welcome, then . . .

He that still may see your cheeks,
  Where all rareness still reposes,
Is a fool if e'er he seeks
  Other lilies, other roses.
      Welcome, welcome, then . . .

He to whom your soft lip yields,
  And perceives your breath in kissing,
All the odours of the fields
  Never, never shall be missing.
      Welcome, welcome, then . . .

He that question would anew
    What fair Eden was of old,
Let him rightly study you,
    And a brief of that behold.
        Welcome, welcome, then . . .

MEMORY

So shuts the marigold her leaves
    At the departure of the sun;
So from the honeysuckle sheaves
    The bee goes when the day is done;
So sits the turtle when she is but one,
    And so all woe, as I since she is gone.

To some few birds kind Nature hath
    Made all the summer as one day:
Which once enjoy'd, cold winter's wrath
    As night they sleeping pass away.
Those happy creatures are, that know not **yet**
    The pain to be deprived or to forget.

I oft have heard men say there be
    Some that with confidence profess
The helpful Art of Memory:
    But could they teach Forgetfulness,
I'd learn; and try what further art could **do**
    To make me love her and forget her too.

ON THE COUNTESS DOWAGER OF PEMBROKE

UNDERNEATH this sable herse
Lies the subject of all verse:
Sidney's sister, Pembroke's mother:
Death, ere thou hast slain another,
Fair, and learn'd, and good as she,
Time shall throw a dart at thee.

Marble piles let no man raise
To her name: for after days
Some kind woman born as she,
Reading this, like Niobe
Shall turn marble, and become
Both her mourner and her tomb.

THE ROSE

A ROSE, as fair as ever saw the North,
Grew in a little garden all alone;
A sweeter flower did Nature ne'er put forth,
Nor fairer garden yet was never known:
The maidens danced about it morn and noon,
And learnèd bards of it their ditties made;
The nimble fairies by the pale-faced moon
Water'd the root and kiss'd her pretty shade.
But well-a-day!—the gardener careless grew;
The maids and fairies both were kept away,
And in a drought the caterpillars threw
Themselves upon the bud and every spray.
    God shield the stock! If heaven send no supplies,
    The fairest blossom of the garden dies.

HAIL, THOU MY NATIVE SOIL

HAIL, thou my native soil! thou blessed plot
Whose equal all the world affordeth not!
Show me who can so many crystal rills,
Such sweet-cloth'd valleys or aspiring hills;
Such wood-ground, pastures, quarries, wealthy
      mines;
Such rocks in whom the diamond fairly shines;
And if the earth can show the like again,
Yet will she fail in her sea-ruling men.

Time never can produce men to o'ertake
The fames of Greenvil, Davies, Gilbert, Drake,
Or worthy Hawkins, or of thousands more
That by their power made the Devonian shore
Mock the proud Tagus; for whose richest spoil
The boasting Spaniard left the Indian soil
Bankrupt of store, knowing it would quit cost
By winning this, though all the rest were lost.

PRAISE OF SPENSER

    ALL their pipes were still,
And Colin Clout began to tune his quill
With such deep art, that every one was given
To think Apollo, newly slid from heaven,
Had ta'en a human shape to win his love,
Or with the western swains for glory strove.
He sung th' heroic knights of fairyland
In lines so elegant, of such command,
That had the Thracian played but half so well,
He had not left Eurydice in hell.
But ere he ended his melodious song
An host of angels flew the clouds among,
And rapt this swan from his attentive mates
To make him one of their associates
In heaven's fair choir: where now he sings the
    praise
Of him that is the first and last of days.
Divinest Spenser, heaven-bred, happy Muse!
Would any power into my brain infuse
Thy worth, or all that poets had before,
I could not praise till thou deserv'st no more.

         Britannia's Pastorals, Book II, Song I.

NIGHT

The sable mantle of the silent night
Shut from the world the ever-joysome light;
Care fled away, and softest slumbers please
To leave the court for lowly cottages;
Wild beasts forsook their dens on woody hills,
And sleightful otters left the purling rills;
Rooks to their nests in high woods now were flung,
And with their spread wings shield their naked
　　　young;
When thieves from thickets to the cross-ways stir,
And terror frights the lonely passenger;
When nought was heard but now and then the
　　　howl
Of some vile cur, or whooping of the owl.

GEORGE WITHER

1588–1667

SHALL I, WASTING IN DESPAIR

Shall I, wasting in despair,
Die because a woman's fair?
Or make pale my cheeks with care
'Cause another's rosy are?
Be she fairer than the day
Or the flowery meads in May—
　　　If she think not well of me,
　　　What care I how fair she be?

Shall my silly heart be pined
'Cause I see a woman kind;
Or a well disposèd nature
Joinèd with a lovely feature?

Be she meeker, kinder, than
Turtle-dove or pelican,
 If she be not so to me,
 What care I how kind she be?

Shall a woman's virtues move
Me to perish for her love?
Or her well-deservings known
Make me quite forget mine own?
Be she with that goodness blest
Which may merit name of Best;
 If she be not such to me,
 What care I how good she be?

'Cause her fortune seems too high,
Shall I play the fool and die?
She that bears a noble mind,
If not outward helps she find,
Thinks what with them he would do
That without them dares her woo;
 And unless that mind I see,
 What care I how great she be?

Great or good, or kind or fair,
I will ne'er the more despair;
If she love me, this believe,
I will die ere she shall grieve;
If she slight me when I woo,
I can scorn and let her go;
 For if she be not for me,
 What care I for whom she be?

Fidelia.

THE MISTRESS OF PHILARETE

I. HER FAIRNESS

THERE's her hair with which Love angles
And beholders' eyes entangles;
For in these fair curlèd snares
They are hampered unawares,
And compelled to swear a duty
To her sweet, enthralling beauty.
In my mind 'tis the most fair
That was ever callèd hair;
Somewhat brighter than a brown,
And her tresses waving down
At full length, and so dispread,
Mantles her from foot to head.
   If you saw her archèd brow,
Tell me, pray, what art knows how
To have made it in a line
More exact or more divine.
Beauty there may be descried
In the height of all her pride,
'Tis a meanly rising plain,
Whose pure white hath many a vein
Interlacing, like the springs
In the earth's enamellings.
If the tale be not a toy
Of the little wingèd boy,—
When he means to strike a heart,
Thence he throws the fatal dart;
Which of wounds still makes a pair,
One of love, one of despair. . . .
   Short her chin is, and yet so
As it is just long enow;

                    meanly] moderately. fairly.

Loveliness doth seem to glory
In that circling promontory.
Pretty moving features skip
'Twixt that hillock and the lip,
If you note her but the while
She is pleased to speak or smile.

And her lips, that show no dullness
Full are in the meanest fulness;
Those the leaves be, whose unfolding
Brings sweet pleasures to beholding
For such pearls they do disclose
Both the Indies match not those;
Yet are so in order placed.
As their whiteness is more graced.
Each part is so well disposed,
And her dainty mouth composed,
So as there is no distortion
Misbeseems that sweet proportion.

When her ivory teeth she buries
Twixt her two enticing cherries,
There appears such pleasures hidden
As might tempt, what were forbidden.
If you look again, the whiles
She doth part those lips in smiles,
'Tis as when a flash of light
Breaks from heaven to glad the night.

Other parts my pencil crave,
But those lips I cannot leave;
For methinks if I should go,
And forsake those cherries so,
There's a kind of excellence
Would hold me from departing hence.
I would tell you what it were,

E

But my cunning fails me there.
They are like in their discloses
To the morning's dewy roses,
That beside the name of fair
Cast perfumes that sweet the air.
Melting-soft her kisses be,
And had I now two or three,
More inspirèd by their touch,
I had praised them twice as much.

But, sweet Muses, mark ye, how
Her fair eyes do check me now,
That I seemed to pass them so,
And their praises overgo:
And yet blame me not, that I
Would so fain have passed them by.
For I fearèd to have seen them
Lest there were some danger in them.
Yet such gentle looks they lend
As might make her foe a friend
And by their allurings move
All beholders unto love.
Such a power is also there,
As will keep those thoughts in fear
And command enough I saw
To hold impudence in awe.
There may he, that knows to love,
Read contents which are above
Their ignoble aims, who know
Nothing that so high doth grow.
Whilst she me beholding is,
My heart dare not think amiss,
For her sight most piercing clear,
Seems to see what's written there. . . .

Then, almost obscured, appears
Those her jewel-gracing ears,
Whose own beauties more adorn
Than the richest pearl that's worn
By the proudest Persian dames,
Or the best that Nature frames.
There the voice in love's meanders,
Those their pretty circlings, wanders,
Whose rare turnings will admit
No rude speech to enter it.

Stretching from mount Forehead lies
Beauty's cape betwixt her eyes;
Which two crystal-passing lakes
Love's delightful isthmus makes.
Neither more or less extending
Than most meriteth commending. . . .

On the either side of this,
Love's most lovely prospect is;
Those her smiling cheeks whose colour
Comprehends true beauty fuller
Than the curious't mixtures can
That are made by art of man;
It is beauty's garden-plot,
Where, as in a true-love-knot,
So the snowy lily grows
Mixèd with the crimson rose,
That as friends they joinèd be;
Yet they seem to disagree
Whether of the two shall reign;
And the lilies oft obtain
Greatest sway, unless a blush
Help the roses at a push
Hollow fallings none there are

There's no wrinkle, there's no scar;
Only there's a little mole
Which from Venus' cheek was stole. . . .

But descend awhile, mine eye,
See if polished ivory,
Or the finest fleecèd flocks,
Or the whitest Albion rocks,
For comparisons may stand
To express that snowy hand.
When she draws it from her glove,
It hath virtue to remove,
Or disperse 't, if there be aught
Cloudeth the beholder's thought.
If that palm but toucheth your,
You shall feel a secret power
Cheer your heart, and glad it more,
Though it drooped with grief before.
Through the veins, disposèd true,
Crimson yields a sapphire hue,
Which adds grace and more delight
By embracing with the white.
Smooth and moist and soft and tender
Are her palms; the fingers slender,
Tipt with mollifièd pearl:
As if that transformèd girl,
Whose much cunning made her dare
With Jove's daughter to compare,
Had that hand worn, maugre spite,
She had shamed the goddess quite;
For there is in every part
Nature perfecter than art.

II. HER VIRTUE

THIS a servant made me sworn
Who before-time held in scorn
To yield vassalage, or duty,
Though unto the queen of beauty.
Yet that I her servant am
It shall more be to my fame
Than to own these woods and downs
Or be lord of fifty towns;
And my mistress to be deemed
Shall more honour be esteemed
Than those titles to acquire
Which most women most desire.
Yea, when you a woman shall
Countess or a duchess call
That respect it shall not move,
Neither gain her half such love
As to say, lo! this is she
That supposèd is to be
Mistress to Philareté:
And that lovely nymph, which he,
In a pastoral poem famed,
And *Fair Virtue* there hath named.....

ME so oft my fancy drew
Here and there, that I ne'er knew
Where to place desire before
So that range it might no more;
But as he that passeth by
Where, in all her jollity,
Flora's riches in a row
Doth in seemly order grow,
And a thousand flowers stand
Bending as to kiss his hand;

Out of which delightful store
One he may take and no more.
Long he pausing doubted whether
Of those fair ones he should gather.
 First the primrose courts his eyes,
Then the cowslip he espies;
Next the pansy seems to woo him,
Then carnations bow unto him;
Which whilst that enamoured swain
From the stalk intends to strain,
As half fearing to be seen
Prettily her leaves between
Peeps the violet, pale to see
That her virtues slighted be;
Which so much his liking wins,
That to seize her he begins.
Yet before he stooped so low
He his wanton eye did throw
On a stem that grew more high
And the rose did there espy,
Who besides her precious scent.
To procure his eyes content
Did display her goodly breast,
Where he found at full exprest
All the good that nature showers
On a thousand other flowers;
Wherewith he affected takes it,
His beloved flower he makes it,
And without desire of more
Walks through all he saw before.
 So I wandering but erewhile
Through the garden of this isle,
Saw rich beauties, I confess,
And in number numberless.

Yea, so differing lovely too,
That I had a world to do,
Ere I could set up my rest,
Where to choose and choose the best. . . .

Thus I fondly fared, till Fate,
(Which I must confess in that
Did a greater favour to me
Than the world can malice do me)
Showed to me that matchless flower,
Subject for this song of our;
Whose perfection having eyed,
Reason instantly espied
That desire, which ranged abroad
There would find a period,
And no marvel if it might,
For it there hath all delight,
And in her hath nature placed
What each several fair one graced. . . .

Let who list for me advance
The admirèd flowers of France;
Let who will praise and behold
The reservèd Marigold;
Let the sweet-breathed Violet now
Unto whom she pleaseth bow;
And the fairest Lily spread
Where she will her golden head;
I have such a flower to wear,
That for those I do not care. . . .

Let the young and happy swains,
Playing on the Britain' plains,
Court unblamed their shepherdesses,
And with their gold-curlèd tresses

Toy uncensured, until I
Grutch at their prosperity.
   Let all times, both present, past,
And the age that shall be last,
Vaunt the beauties they bring forth.
I have found in one such worth,
That, content, I neither care
What the best before me were;
Nor desire to live and see
Who shall fair hereafter be.
For I know the hand of nature
Will not make a fairer creature.

OLD CHRISTMAS

So now is come our joyful'st feast,
   Let every man be jolly;
Each room with ivy leaves is drest,
   And every post with nolly.
Though some churls at our mirth repine,
Round your foreheads garlands twine;
Drown sorrow in a cup of wine,
   And let us all be merry.

Now all our neighbours' chimneys smoke,
   And Christmas blocks are burning;
Their ovens they with baked meats choke,
   And all their spits are turning.
Without the door let sorrow lie;
And, if for cold it hap to die,
We'll bury 't in a Christmas pie,
   And evermore be merry.

grutch] murmur, complain.

Now every lad is wondrous trim,
  And no man minds his labour;
Our lasses have provided them
  A bag-pipe and a tabour;
Young men and maids, and girls and boys,
Give life to one another's joys;
And you anon shall by their noise
  Perceive that they are merry.

Rank misers now do sparing shun;
  Their hall of music soundeth;
And dogs thence with whole shoulders run,
  So all things there aboundeth.
The country folks themselves advance,
For crowdy-mutton's come out of France;
And Jack shall pipe, and Jill shall dance,
  And all the town be merry.

Ned Swash hath fetched his bands from pawn,
  And all his best apparel;
Brisk Nell hath bought a ruff of lawn,
  With droppings of the barrel.
And those that hardly all the year
Had bread to eat or rags to wear,
Will have both clothes and dainty fare,
  And all the day be merry.

Now poor men to the justices
  With capons make their arrants,
And if they hap to fail of these,
  They plague them with their warrants.
But now they feed them with good cheer,
And what they want they take in beer;
For Christmas comes but once a year,
  And then they shall be merry.

crowdy-mutton] a fiddler

Good farmers in the country nurse
    The poor that else were undone;
Sour landlords spend their money worse
    On lust and pride at London.
There the roysters they do play,
Drab and dice their lands away,
Which may be ours another day;
    And therefore let's be merry.

The client now his suit forbears,
    The prisoner's heart is easèd;
The debtor drinks away his cares,
    And for the time is pleasèd.
Though other purses be more fat,
Why should we pine or grieve at that?
Hang sorrow! care will kill a cat,
    And therefore let's be merry.

Hark, how the wags abroad do call
    Each other forth to rambling:
And you 'll see them in the hall
    For nuts and apples scrambling.
Hark, how the roofs with laughter sound!
Anon they 'll think the house goes round:
For they the cellar's depth have found,
    And there they will be merry.

The wenches with their wassail-bowls
    About the streets are singing;
The boys are come to catch the owls,
    The wildmare in is bringing.
Our kitchen-boy hath broke his box,
And to the dealing of the ox
    Our honest neighbours come by flocks,
    And here they will be merry.

Now kings and queens poor sheep-cotes have,
  And mate with everybody:
The honest now may play the knave,
  And wise men play at noddy.
Some youths will now a-mumming go,
Some others play at Rowland-ho,
And twenty other gameboys mo,
  Because they will be merry.

Then wherefore in these merry days,
  Should we, I pray, be duller?
Ho, let us sing some roundelays,
  To make our mirth the fuller.
And whilest thus inspired we sing,
Let all the streets with echoes ring,
Woods and hills and everything,
  Bear witness we are merry.

I LOVED A LASS

I LOVED a lass, a fair one,
  As fair as e'er was seen;
She was indeed a rare one,
  Another Sheba Queen:
But, fool as then I was,
  I thought she loved me too:
But now, alas! sh' 'as left me,
  Falero, lero, loo!

Her hair like gold did glister,
  Each eye was like a star,
She did surpass her sister,
  Which passed all others far;
She would me honey call,
  She'd, O she'd kiss me too!
But now, alas! sh' 'as left me,
  Falero, lero, loo!

In summer time to Medley,
  My love and I would go;
The boatmen there stood ready,
  My love and I to row
For cream there would we call,
  For cakes and for prunes too;
But now, alas! sh' 'as left me,
  Falero, lero, loo!

Many a merry meeting
  My love and I have had;
She was my only sweeting,
  She made my heart full glad.
The tears stood in her eyes
  Like to the morning dew;
But now, alas! sh' 'as left me,
  Falero, lero, loo! . . .

Her cheeks were like the cherry,
  He skin was white as snow;
When she was blithe and merry
  She angel-like did show;
Her waist exceeding small,
  The fives did fit her shoe:
But now, alas! sh' 'as left me,
  Falero, lero, loo!

In summer time or winter
  She had her heart's desire;
I still did scorn to stint her
  From sugar, sack, or fire.
The world went round about,
  No cares we ever knew;
But now, alas! sh' 'as left me,
  Falero, lero, loo! . . .

To maidens' vows and swearing
    Henceforth no credit give;
You may give them the hearing,
    But never them believe.
They are as false as fair,
    Unconstant, frail, untrue;
For mine, alas! has left me,
    Falero, lero, loo! . . .

No riches now can raise me,
    No want make me despair;
No misery amaze me,
    Nor yet for want I care.
I have lost a world itself,
    My earthly heaven, adieu,
Since she, alas! hath left me,
    Falero, lero, loo!

A LULLABY

SWEET baby, sleep! what ails my dear,
    What ails my darling thus to cry?
Be still, my child, and lend thine ear
    To hear me sing thy lullaby:
My pretty lamb, forbear to weep;
Be still, my dear; sweet baby, sleep.

.   .   .   .

The King of kings, when He was born,
    Had not so much for outward ease;
By Him such dressings were not worn,
    Nor such like swaddling-clothes as these.
Sweet baby, then forbear to weep;
Be still, my babe; sweet baby, sleep.

Within a manger lodged thy Lord,
    Where oxen lay, and asses fed:

Warm rooms we do to thee afford,
   An easy cradle or a bed.
Sweet baby, then forbear to weep;
Be still, my babe; sweet baby, sleep.

ON THE MUSE OF POETRY

IN my former days of bliss,
Her divine skill taught me this,
That from everything I saw,
I could some invention draw,
And raise pleasure to her height
Through the meanest object's sight;
By the murmur of a spring,
Or the least bough's rusteling,
By a daisy whose leaves spread
Shut when Titan goes to bed,
Or a shady bush or tree,
She could more infuse in me
Than all nature's beauties can
In some other wiser man.
By her help I also now
Make this churlish place allow
Some things that may sweeten gladness
In the very gall of sadness.
The dull loneness, the black shade
That these hanging vaults have made.
The strange music of the waves
Beating on these hollow caves,
This black den which rocks emboss,
Overgrown with eldest moss,
The rude portals that give light
More to terror than delight,
This my chamber of neglect,
Walled about with disrespect,

From all these and this dull air,
A fit object for despair,
She hath taught me, by her might,
To draw comfort and delight.
Therefore, thou best earthly bliss,
I will cherish thee for this.
Poesy; thou sweet'st content
That ere Heaven to mortals lent,
Though they as a trifle leave thee
Whose dull thoughts cannot conceive thee;
Though thou be to them a scorn
That to nought but earth are born:
Let my life no longer be
Than I am in love with thee.
Though our wise ones call it madness.
Let me never taste of gladness.
If I love thy maddest fits
Above all their greatest wits.
And though some too seeming holy
Do account thy raptures folly
Thou dost teach me to contemn
What makes knaves and fools of them.

ROBERT HERRICK

1591–1674

A CHRISTMAS CAROL, SUNG TO THE KING IN THE PRESENCE AT WHITEHALL

Chor. WHAT sweeter music can we bring,
      Than a Carol for to sing
      The birth of this our heavenly King?
      Awake the voice! Awake the string!
      Heart, ear, and eye, and everything

Awake! the while the active finger
Runs division with the singer.

From the flourish they came to the song.

1. Dark and dull night, fly hence away,
   And give the honour to this day,
   That sees December turned to May.
2. If we may ask the reason, say;
   The why, and wherefore all things here
   Seem like the Spring-time of the year?
3. Why does the chilling winter's morn
   Smile, like a field beset with corn?
   Or smell, like to a mead new-shorn,
   Thus, on the sudden? 4. Come and see
   The cause, why things thus fragrant be:
   'Tis He is born whose quickening birth
   Gives life and lustre, public mirth,
   To Heaven, and the under-earth.

Chor. We see Him come, and know Him ours,
   Who with His sunshine and His showers,
   Turns all the patient ground to flowers.

1. The Darling of the world is come,
   And fit it is, we find a room
   To welcome Him. 2. The nobler part
   Of all the house here is the heart,

Chor. Which we will give Him; and bequeath
   This holly, and this ivy wreath,
   To do Him honour; who's our King,
   And Lord of all this revelling.

A CHILD'S GRACE

HERE a little child I stand,
Heaving up my either hand;
Cold as paddocks though they be,
Here I lift them up to Thee,
For a benison to fall
On our meat, and on us all. Amen.

ANOTHER GRACE FOR A CHILD

WHAT God gives, and what we take,
'Tis a gift for Christ His sake:
Be the meal of beans and peas,
God be thanked for those, and these:
Have we flesh, or have we fish,
All are fragments from His dish.
He His Church save, and the King,
And our peace here, like a Spring,
Make it ever flourishing.

CHERRY-RIPE

CHERRY-RIPE, ripe, ripe, I cry,
Full and fair ones; come and buy:
If so be, you ask me where
They do grow? I answer, There,
Where my Julia's lips do smile;
There's the land, or cherry-isle:
Whose plantations fully show
All the year, when cherries grow.

paddocks] toads

DELIGHT IN DISORDER

A SWEET disorder in the dress
Kindles in clothes a wantonness:
A lawn about the shoulders thrown
Into a fine distraction:
An erring lace, which here and there
Enthrals the crimson stomacher:
A cuff neglectful, and thereby
Ribbands to flow confusedly:
A winning wave, deserving note,
In the tempestuous petticoat:
A careless shoe-string, in whose tie
I see a wild civility:
Do more bewitch me than when art
Is too precise in every part.

TO THE VIRGINS, TO MAKE MUCH OF TIME

GATHER ye rosebuds while ye may,
    Old Time is still a-flying:
And this same flower that smiles to-day,
    To-morrow will be dying.

The glorious lamp of heaven, the sun,
    The higher he's a-getting;
The sooner will his race be run,
    And nearer he's to setting.

That age is best, which is the first,
    When youth and blood are warmer;
But being spent, the worse, and worst
    Times still succeed the former.

Then be not coy, but use your time,
    And while ye may, go marry:
For having lost but once your prime,
    You may for ever tarry.

TO ANTHEA, WHO MAY COMMAND HIM
ANYTHING

Bid me to live, and I will live
    Thy Protestant to be:
Or bid me love, and I will give
    A loving heart to thee.

A heart as soft, a heart as kind,
    A heart as sound and free
As in the whole world thou canst find,
    That heart I'll give to thee.

Bid that heart stay, and it will stay,
    To honour thy decree:
Or bid it languish quite away,
    And't shall do so for thee.

Bid me to weep, and I will weep,
    While I have eyes to see:
And having none, yet I will keep
    A heart to weep for thee.

Bid me despair, and I'll despair,
    Under that cypress tree:
Or bid me die, and I will dare
    E'en death to die for thee.

Thou art my life, my love, my heart,
    The very eyes of me:
And hast command of every part
    To live and die for thee.

THE BRACELET: TO JULIA

WHY I tie about thy wrist,
Julia, this my silken twist;
For what other reason is't
But to show thee how in part,
Thou my pretty captive art?
But thy bond slave is my heart:
'Tis but silk that bindeth thee,
Knap the thread, and thou art free:
But 'tis otherwise with me;
I am bound, and fast bound so,
That from thee I cannot go;
If I could, I would not so.

TO VIOLETS

WELCOME, maids of honour!
    You do bring
    In the spring;
And wait upon her.

She has virgins many,
    Fresh and fair;
    Yet you are
More sweet than any.

You're the maiden posies,
    And so graced,
    To be placed,
'Fore damask roses.

Yet though thus respected,
    By-and-by
    Ye do lie,
Poor girls, neglected.

TO DAFFODILS

FAIR daffodils, we weep to see
　　You haste away so soon;
As yet the early-rising sun
　　Has not attained his noon.
　　　　Stay, stay,
　　Until the hasting day
　　　　Has run
　　But to the evensong;
And, having prayed together, we
　　Will go with you along.

We have short time to stay, as you,
　　We have as short a spring;
As quick a growth to meet decay,
　　As you, or anything.
　　　　We die,
　　As your hours do, and dry
　　　　Away,
　　Like to the summer's rain;
Or as the pearls of morning's dew
　　Ne'er to be found again.

TO BLOSSOMS

FAIR pledges of a fruitful tree;
　　Why do ye fall so fast?
　　Your date is not so past;
But you may stay yet here awhile,
　　To blush and gently smile;
　　　　And go at last.

What, were ye born to be
　　An hour or half's delight;
　　And so to bid good night?

'Twas pity Nature brought ye forth
　　Merely to show your worth,
　　　　And lose you quite.

But you are lovely leaves, where we
　　May read how soon things have
　　Their end, though ne'er so brave:
And after they have shown their pride,
　　Like you awhile: they glide
　　　　Into the grave.

A THANKSGIVING TO GOD FOR HIS HOUSE

LORD, Thou hast given me a cell
　　　　Wherein to dwell,
A little house, whose humble roof
　　　　Is weather-proof;
Under the spars of which I lie
　　　　Both soft, and dry;
Where Thou my chamber for to ward
　　　　Hast set a guard
Of harmless thoughts, to watch and keep
　　　　Me, while I sleep.
Low is my porch, as is my fate,
　　　　Both void of state;
And yet the threshold of my door
　　　　Is worn by the poor,
Who thither come, and freely get
　　　　Good words, or meat;
Like as my parlour, so my hall
　　　　And kitchen's small;
A little buttery, and therein
　　　　A little bin,
Which keeps my little loaf of bread
　　　　Unchipt, unflead:

Some brittle sticks of thorn or briar
    Make me a fire,
Close by whose living coal I sit,
    And glow like it.
Lord, I confess, too, when I dine,
    The pulse is Thine,
And all those other bits, that be
    There placed by Thee;
The worts, the purslain, and the mess
    Of water-cress,
Which of Thy kindness Thou hast sent;
    And my content
Makes those, and my beloved beet,
    To be more sweet.
'Tis Thou that crown'st my glittering hearth
    With guiltless mirth;
And giv'st me wassail bowls to drink,
    Spiced to the brink.
Lord, 'tis Thy plenty-dropping hand,
    That soils my land;
And giv'st me, for my bushel sown,
    Twice ten for one.
Thou mak'st my teeming hen to lay
    Her egg each day:
Besides my healthful ewes to bear
    Me twins each year:
The while the conduits of my kine
    Run cream (for wine).
All these, and better Thou dost send
    Me, to this end,
That I should render, for my part,
    A thankful heart;

soils] manures

Which, fired with incense, I resign,
        As wholly Thine;
But the acceptance, that must be,
            My Christ, by Thee.

TO DIANEME

Sweet, be not proud of those two eyes,
Which star-like sparkle in their skies:
Nor be you proud, that you can see
All hearts your captives; yours, yet free:
Be you not proud of that rich hair,
Which wantons with the love-sick air:
Whenas that ruby, which you wear,
Sunk from the tip of your soft ear,
Will last to be a precious stone,
When all your world of beauty's gone.

UPON JULIA'S CLOTHES

Whenas in silks my Julia goes,
Then, then methinks, how sweetly flows
That liquefaction of her clothes!

Next, when I cast mine eyes and see
That brave vibration each way free;
O how that glittering taketh me!

TO ELECTRA

I dare not ask a kiss;
    I dare not beg a smile;
Lest having that, or this,
    I might grow proud the while.
No, no, the utmost share
    Of my desire, shall be
Only to kiss that air
    That lately kissèd thee.

THE WHITE ISLAND: OR PLACE OF THE BLEST

In this world, the Isle of Dreams,
While we sit by sorrow's streams,
Tears and terrors are our themes
   Reciting:

But when once from hence we fly,
More and more approaching nigh
Unto young eternity
   Uniting:

In that whiter Island, where
Things are evermore sincere;
Candour here, and lustre there
   Delighting:

There no monstrous fancies shall
Out of hell an horror call,
To create, or cause at all,
   Affrighting.

There in calm and cooling sleep
We our eyes shall never steep;
But eternal watch shall keep,
   Attending

Pleasures, such as shall pursue
Me immortalized, and you;
And fresh joys, as never too
   Have ending.

HIS LITANY TO THE HOLY SPIRIT

In the hour of my distress,
When temptations me oppress,
And when I my sins confess,
  Sweet Spirit, comfort me!

When I lie within my bed,
Sick in heart and sick in head,
And with doubts discomforted,
    Sweet Spirit, comfort me!

When the house doth sigh and weep,
And the world is drowned in sleep,
Yet mine eyes the watch do keep,
    Sweet Spirit, comfort me!

When the artless doctor sees
No one hope, but of his fees,
And his skill runs on the lees;
    Sweet Spirit, comfort me!

When his potion and his pill,
Has, or none, or little skill,
Meet for nothing, but to kill;
    Sweet Spirit, comfort me!

When the passing bell doth toll,
And the Furies in a shoal
Come to fright a parting soul;
    Sweet Spirit, comfort me!

When the tapers now burn blue,
And the comforters are few,
And that number more than true;
    Sweet Spirit, comfort me!

When the priest his last hath prayed,
And I nod to what is said,
'Cause my speech is now decayed,
    Sweet Spirit, comfort me!

When, God knows, I'm toss'd about,
Either with despair or doubt;
Yet before the glass be out,
    Sweet Spirit, comfort me!

When the tempter me pursu'th
With the sins of all my youth,
And half damns me with untruth;
    Sweet Spirit, comfort me!

When the flames and hellish cries
Fright mine ears, and fright mine eyes,
And all terrors me surprise;
    Sweet Spirit, comfort me!

When the Judgement is revealed,
And that opened which was sealed,
When to Thee I have appealed;
    Sweet Spirit, comfort me!

OF LOVE

How Love came in, I do not know,
Whether by th' eye, or ear, or no:
Or whether with the soul it came,
At first, infusèd with the same:
Whether in part 'tis here or there,
Or, like the soul, whole everywhere:
This troubles me: but I as well
As any other, this can tell;
That when from hence she does depart,
The outlet then is from the heart.

HOW THE WALLFLOWER CAME FIRST AND WHY
SO CALLED

Why this flower is now called so,
List' sweet maids, and you shall know.
Understand, this firstling was
Once a brisk and bonny lass,
Kept as close as Danae was:

Who a sprightly springall loved,
And to have it fully proved,
Up she got upon a wall,
'Tempting down to slide withal:
But the silken twist untied,
So she fell, and bruis'd, she died.
Love, in pity of the deed,
And her loving-luckless speed,
Turned her to this plant, we call
Now, The Flower of the Wall.

TO DAISIES, NOT TO SHUT SO SOON

SHUT not so soon; the dull-eyed night
     Has not as yet begun
To make a seizure on the light,
     Or to seal up the sun.

No marigolds yet closèd are;
     No shadows great appear;
Nor doth the early shepherd's star
     Shine like a spangle here.

Stay but till my Julia close
     Her life-begetting eye;
And let the whole world then dispose
     Itself to live or die.

TO DEATH

THOU bidst me come away,
And I'll no longer stay,
Than for to shed some tears
For faults of former years;
And to repent some crimes,
Done in the present times:

And next, to take a bit
Of Bread, and Wine with it:
To d' on my robes of love,
Fit for the place above;
To gird my loins about
With charity throughout:
And so to travel hence
With feet of innocence:
These done, I'll only cry
God mercy; and so die.

CORINNA'S GOING A-MAYING

GET up, get up for shame! The blooming morn
Upon her wings presents the god unshorn.
    See how Aurora throws her fair
    Fresh-quilted colours through the air:
    Get up, sweet slug-a-bed, and see
    The dew bespangling herb and tree.
Each flower has wept, and bowed toward the east,
Above an hour since, yet you not drest;
    Nay! not so much as out of bed?
    When all the birds have matins said
    And sung their thankful hymns, 'tis sin,
    Nay, profanation, to keep in,
Whenas a thousand virgins on this day
Spring sooner than the lark, to fetch in May.

Rise and put on your foliage, and be seen
To come forth, like the spring-time, fresh and green;
    And sweet as Flora. Take no care
    For jewels for your gown or hair:
    Fear not; the leaves will strew
    Gems in abundance upon you:

        d' on] do on

Besides, the childhood of the day has kept,
Against you come, some orient pearls unwept.
 Come, and receive them while the light
 Hangs on the dew-locks of the night:
 And Titan on the eastern hill
 Retires himself, or else stands still
Till you come forth! Wash, dress, be brief in pray-
  ing:
Few beads are best when once we go a-Maying.

Come, my Corinna, come; and coming, mark
How each field turns a street, each street a park,
 Made green and trimmed with trees! see how
 Devotion gives each house a bough
 Or branch! each porch, each door, ere this,
 An ark, a tabernacle is,
Made up of white-thorn neatly interwove,
As if here were those cooler shades of love.
 Can such delights be in the street
 And open fields, and we not see't?
 Come, we'll abroad: and let's obey
 The proclamation made for May,
And sin no more, as we have done, by staying;
But, my Corinna, come, let's go a-Maying.

There's not a budding boy or girl this day
But is got up and gone to bring in May.
 A deal of youth ere this is come
 Back, and with white-thorn laden home.
 Some have despatched their cakes and cream,
 Before that we have left to dream:
And some have wept and wooed, and plighted
  troth,
And chose their priest, ere we can cast off sloth:

    beads] prayers.

Many a green-gown has been given,
Many a kiss, both odd and even:
Many a glance, too, has been sent
From out the eye, love's firmament:
Many a jest told of the keys betraying
This night, and locks pick'd: yet we're not a-
      Maying!

Come, let us go, while we are in our prime,
And take the harmless folly of the time!
We shall grow old apace, and die
Before we know our liberty.
Our life is short, and our days run
As fast away as does the sun.
And, as a vapour or a drop of rain,
Once lost, can ne'er be found again,
So when or you or I are made
A fable, song, or fleeting shade,
All love, all liking, all delight
Lies drowned with us in endless night.
Then, while time serves, and we are but decaying,
Come, my Corinna, come, let's go a-Maying.

THE COUNTRY LIFE

Sweet country life, to such unknown,
Whose lives are others', not their own!
But serving courts, and cities, be
Less happy, less enjoying thee.
Thou never plough'st the Ocean's foam
To seek, and bring rough pepper home:
Nor to the Eastern Ind dost rove
To bring from thence the scorchèd clove.
Nor, with the loss of thy loved rest,
Bring'st home the ingot from the West.

No, thy ambition's masterpiece
Flies no thought higher than a fleece:
Or how to pay thy hinds, and clear
All scores; and so to end the year:
But walk'st about thy own dear bounds,
Not envying others' larger grounds:
For well thou know'st, 'tis not th' extent
Of land makes life, but sweet content.
When now the cock (the ploughman's horn)
Calls forth the lily-wristed morn;
Then to thy corn-fields thou dost go,
Which though well soiled, yet thou dost know,
That the best compost for the lands
Is the wise master's feet and hands.
There at the plough thou find'st thy team,
With a hind whistling there to them:
And cheer'st them up, by singing how
The kingdom's portion is the plough.
This done, then to th' enamel'd meads
Thou go'st; and as thy foot then treads,
Thou see'st a present God-like power
Imprinted in each herb and flower:
And smell'st the breath of great-ey'd kine,
Sweet as the blossoms of the vine.
Here thou behold'st thy large sleek neat
Unto the dew-laps up in meat:
And, as thou look'st, the wanton steer,
The heifer, cow, and ox draw near
To make a pleasing pastime there.
These seen, thou go'st to view thy flocks
Of sheep (safe from the wolf and fox)
And find'st their bellies there as full
Of short sweet grass, as back with wool.
And leav'st them (as they feed and fill)

A shepherd piping on a hill.
For sports, for pageantry, and plays,
Thou hast thy eves and holidays:
On which the young men and maids meet,
To exercise their dancing feet:
Tripping the comely country round,
With daffodils and daisies crowned.
Thy wakes, thy quintels, here thou hast,
The may-poles too with garlands graced:
Thy morris-dance; thy Whitsun-ale;
Thy shearing-feast, which never fail.
Thy harvest home; thy wassail bowl,
That's tost up after fox i' th' hole.
Thy mummeries; thy Twelfth-tide kings
And queens; thy Christmas revellings:
Thy nut-brown mirth; thy russet wit;
And no man pays too dear for it.
To these, thou hast thy time to go
And trace the hare 'i the treacherous snow:
Thy witty wiles to draw, and get
The lark into the trammel net:
Thou hast thy cockrood, and thy glade
To take the precious pheasant made:
Thy lime-twigs, snares, and pit-falls then
To catch the pilfering birds, not men.
O happy life! if that their good
The husbandmen but understood!
Who all the day themselves do please,
And younglings, with such sport as these.
And, lying down, have naught t' affright
Sweet sleep, that makes more short the night.

Cætera desunt.

THE NIGHT-PIECE: TO JULIA

HER eyes the glow-worm lend thee,
    The shooting stars attend thee
      And the elves also,
      Whose little eyes glow
Like the sparks of fire, befriend thee.

No Will-o'-the-wisp mislight thee,
Nor snake or slow-worm bite thee;
      But on, on thy way
      Not making a stay,
Since ghost there's none to affright thee.

Let not the dark thee cumber:
What though the moon does slumber?
      The stars of the night
      Will lend thee their light
Like tapers clear without number.

Then, Julia, let me woo thee,
Thus, thus to come unto me;
      And when I shall meet
      Thy silv'ry feet,
My soul I'll pour into thee.

UPON MRS. ELIZ. WHEELER, UNDER THE NAME OF AMARILLIS

SWEET Amarillis, by a spring's
Soft and soul-melting murmurings,
Slept, and thus sleeping, thither flew
A Robin-Redbreast; who at view,
Not seeing her at all to stir,
Brought leaves and moss to cover her:

But while he, perking, there did pry
About the arch of either eye;
The lid began to let out day;
At which poor Robin flew away:
And seeing her not dead, but all disleaved,
He chirp't for joy, to see himself deceived.

THE MAD MAID'S SONG

GOOD-MORROW to the day so fair,
   Good-morning, sir, to you;
Good-morrow to mine own torn hair
   Bedabbled with the dew.

Good-morning to this primrose too,
   Good-morrow to each maid;
That will with flowers the tomb bestrew
   Wherein my love is laid.

Ah! woe is me, woe, woe is me!
   Alack and well-a-day!
For pity, sir, find out that bee
   Which bore my love away.

I'll seek him in your bonnet brave,
   I'll seek him in your eyes;
Nay, now I think they've made his grave
   I' th' bed of strawberries.

I'll seek him there; I know ere this
   The cold, cold earth doth shake him;
But I will go, or send a kiss
   By you, sir, to awake him.

Pray hurt him not; though he be dead,
   He knows well who do love him,
And who with green turfs rear his head,
   And who do rudely move him.

He's soft and tender (pray take heed);
   With bands of cowslips bind him,
And bring him home—but 'tis decreed
   That I shall never find him!

CEREMONIES FOR CHRISTMAS

COME, bring with a noise,
   My merry merry boys,
The Christmas log to the firing;
   While my good Dame, she
   Bids ye all be free;
And drink to your heart's desiring.

With the last year's brand
   Light the new block, and
For good success in his spending,
   On your psaltries play,
   That sweet luck may
Come while the boy is a-teending.

Drink now the strong beer,
   Cut the white loaf here,
The while the meat is a-shredding;
   For the rare mince-pie
   And the plums stand by
To fill the paste that's a-kneading.

CEREMONIES FOR CANDLEMASS EVE

DOWN with the rosemary and bays,
   Down with the mistletoe;
Instead of holly, now upraise
   The greener box, for show.

           teending] kindling

The holly hitherto did sway;
  Let box now domineer;
Until the dancing Easter-day,
  Or Easter's eve appear.

Then youthful box which now hath grace,
  Your houses to renew,
Grown old, surrender must his place,
  Unto the crispèd yew.

When yew is out, then birch comes in,
  And many flowers beside;
Both of a fresh, and fragrant kin
  To honour Whitsuntide.

Green bushes then, and sweetest bents,
  With cooler oaken boughs;
Come in for comely ornaments,
  To re-adorn the house.
Thus times do shift; each thing his turn does
    hold;
New things succeed, as former things grow old.

THE HOCK CART, OR HARVEST HOME

Come, sons of summer, by whose toil,
We are the lords of wine and oil:
By whose tough labours, and rough hands,
We rip up first, then reap our lands.
Crown'd with the ears of corn, now come,
And, to the pipe, sing harvest home.
Come forth, my lord, and see the cart
Drest up with all the country art.

See, here a maukin, there a sheet,
As spotless pure, as it is sweet:
The horses, mares, and frisking fillies
(Clad, all, in linen, white as lilies).
The harvest swains, and wenches bound
For joy, to see the hock-cart crowned.
About the cart, hear how the rout
Of rural younglings raise the shout;
Pressing before, some coming after,
Those with a shout, and these with laughter.
Some bless the cart; some kiss the sheaves;
Some prank them up with oaken leaves:
Some cross the fill-horse; some with great
Devotion, stroke the home-born wheat:
While other rustics, less attent
To prayers, than to merriment,
Run after with their breeches rent.
Well, on, brave boys, to your lord's hearth,
Glitt'ring with fire, where, for your mirth,
Ye shall see first the large and chief
Foundation of your feast, fat beef:
With upper stories, mutton, veal
And bacon (which makes full the meal)
With sev'ral dishes standing by,
As here a custard, there a pie,
And here all tempting frumenty
And for to make the merry cheer,
If smirking wine be wanting here,
There's that, which drowns all care, stout
        beer;
Which freely drink to your lord's health,
Then to the plough (the common-wealth),
Next to your flails, your fans, your vats;
Then to the maids with wheaten hats:

To the rough sickle, the crooked scythe,
Drink frolic boys, till all be blithe.
Feed, and grow fat; and as ye eat,
Be mindful, that the labouring neat
(As you) may have their fill of meat.
And know, besides, ye must revoke
The patient ox unto the yoke,
And all go back unto the plough
And harrow (though they're hang'd up now).
And, you must know, your lord's word 's true,
Feed him ye must, whose food fills you.
And that this pleasure is like rain,
Not sent ye for to drown your pain,
But for to make it spring again.

A TERNARY OF LITTLES, UPON A PIPKIN OF JELLY SENT TO A LADY

A LITTLE saint best fits a little shrine,
A little prop best fits a little vine,
As my small cruse best fits my little wine.

A little seed best fits a little soil,
A little trade best fits a little toil:
As my small jar best fits my little oil.

A little bin best fits a little bread,
A little garland fits a little head:
As my small stuff best fits my little shed.

A little hearth best fits a little fire,
A little chapel fits a little choir,
As my small bell best fits my little spire.

A little stream best fits a little boat:
A little lead best fits a little float;
As my small pipe best fits my little note.

A little meat best fits a little belly,
As sweetly, lady, give me leave to tell ye
This little pipkin fits this little jelly.

TO MUSIC, TO BECALM HIS FEVER

CHARM me asleep, and melt me so
  With thy delicious numbers,
That, being ravished, hence I go
    Away in easy slumbers.
      Ease my sick head,
      And make my bed,
Thou power that canst sever
      From me this ill,
      And quickly still,
      Though thou not kill
        My fever.

Thou sweetly canst convert the same
  From a consuming fire
Into a gentle licking flame,
  And make it thus expire.
      Then make me weep
      My pains asleep;
And give me such reposes
      That I, poor I,
      May think thereby
      I live and die
        'Mongst roses.

Fall on me like a silent dew,
  Or like those maiden showers,
Which, by the peep of day, do strew
  A baptism o'er the flowers.
      Melt, melt my pains,
      With thy soft strains;

That, having ease me given,
    With full delight
    I leave this light,
    And take my flight
      For Heaven.

TO HIS DYING BROTHER, MASTER WILLIAM HERRICK

LIFE of my life, take not so soon thy flight,
But stay the time till we have bade good night.
Thou hast both wind and tide with thee; thy way
As soon dispatched is by the night, as day.
Let us not then so rudely henceforth go
Till we have wept, kiss'd, sigh'd, shook hands, or so.
There's pain in parting; and a kind of hell,
When once true-lovers take their last farewell.
What? shall we two our endless leaves take here
Without a sad look, or a solemn tear?
He knows not love, that hath not this truth proved,
Love is most loth to leave the thing beloved.
Pay we our vows, and go; yet when we part,
Then, even then, I will bequeath my heart
Into thy loving hands: For I'll keep none
To warm my breast, when thou my pulse art gone.
No, here I'll last, and walk (a harmless shade)
About this urn, wherein thy dust is laid,
To guard it so, as nothing here shall be
Heavy, to hurt those sacred seeds of thee.

UPON TIME

TIME was upon
    The wing, to fly away;
      And I call'd on
    Him but a while to stay;

But he'd be gone,
For ought that I could say.

He held out then,
A writing, as he went;
    And ask'd me, when
False man would be content
    To pay again,
What God and Nature lent.

An hour glass,
In which were sands but few,
    As he did pass,
He shew'd, and told me too,
    Mine end near was,
And so away he flew.

THE WAKE

Come, Anthea, let us two
Go to feast, as others do.
Tarts and custards, creams and cakes,
Are the junkets still at wakes:
Unto which the tribes resort,
Where the business is the sport:
Morris-dancers thou shalt see,
Marian too in pageantry:
And a mimic to devise
Many grinning properties.
Players there will be, and those
Base in action as in clothes:
Yet with strutting they will please
The incurious villages.
Near the dying of the day,
There will be a cudgel-play,

Where a coxcomb will be broke,
Ere a good word can be spoke:
But the anger ends all here,
Drench'd in ale, or drown'd in beer.
Happy rustics, best content
With the cheapest merriment:
And possess no other fear,
Than to want the wake next year.

HIS DESIRE

Give me a man that is not dull,
When all the world with rifts is full:
But unamazed dares clearly sing,
When as the roof's a tottering:
And, though it falls, continues still
Tickling the cittern with his quill.

THE PRIMROSE

Ask me why I send you here
This sweet Infanta of the year?
Ask me why I send to you
This primrose, thus bepearl'd with dew?
I will whisper to your ears:—
The sweets of Love are mixed with tears.

Ask me why this flower does show
So yellow-green, and sickly too?
Ask me why the stalk is weak
And bending (yet it doth not break)?
I will answer, These discover
What fainting hopes are in a lover.

TO PRIMROSES FILLED WITH MORNING DEW

Why do ye weep, sweet babes? can tears
      Speak grief in you,
      Who were but born
    Just as the modest morn
    Teem'd her refreshing dew?
Alas you have not known that shower,
      That mars a flower;
      Nor felt th' unkind
    Breath of a blasting wind;
    Nor are ye worn with years;
      Or warped, as we,
    Who think it strange to see,
Such pretty flowers, (like to orphans young)
To speak by tears, before ye have a tongue.

Speak, whimp'ring younglings, and make known
      The reason why
      Ye droop and weep;
    Is it for want of sleep?
    Or childish lullaby?
Or that ye have not seen as yet
      The violet?
      Or brought a kiss
    From that sweetheart, to this?
    No, no, this sorrow shown
      By your tears shed,
      Would have this lecture read,
That things of greatest, so of meanest worth,
Conceived with grief are, and with tears brought
    forth.

THE FUNERAL RITES OF THE ROSE

THE Rose was sick and smiling died;
And, being to be sanctified,
About the bed there sighing stood
The sweet and flowery sisterhood:
Some hung the head, while some did bring,
To wash her, water from the spring;
Some laid her forth, while others wept,
But all a solemn fast there kept:
The holy sisters, some among,
The sacred dirge and trental sung.
But ah! what sweets smelt everywhere,
As Heaven had spent all perfumes there.
At last, when prayers for the dead
And rites were all accomplishèd,
They, weeping, spread a lawny loom,
And closed her up as in a tomb.

TO MEADOWS

YE have been fresh and green,
 Ye have been filled with flowers,
And ye the walks have been
 Where maids have spent their hours.

You have beheld how they
 With wicker arks did come
To kiss, and bear away
 The richer cowslips home.

You've heard them sweetly sing,
 And seen them in a round:
Each virgin, like a spring,
 With honeysuckles crowned.

trental] trentals are services for the dead, of thirty
masses on as many successive days.

But now we see none here,
   Whose silv'ry feet did tread,
And with dishevelled hair
   Adorned this smoother mead.

Like unthrifts, having spent,
   Your stock and needy grown,
You're left here to lament
   Your poor estates, alone.

A MEDITATION FOR HIS MISTRESS

You are a tulip seen to-day,
But, dearest, of so short a stay;
That where you grew scarce man can say.

You are a lovely July-flower,
Yet one rude wind or ruffling shower
Will force you hence, and in an hour.

You are a sparkling rose i' th' bud,
Yet lost ere that chaste flesh and blood
Can show where you or grew or stood.

You are a full-spread, fair-set vine,
And can with tendrils love entwine,
Yet dried ere you distil your wine.

You are like balm enclosèd well
In amber or some crystal shell,
Yet lost ere you transfuse your smell.

You are a dainty violet,
Yet wither'd ere you can be set
Within the virgin's coronet.

You are the queen all flowers among;
But die you must, fair maid, ere long,
As he, the maker of this song.

AN ODE FOR BEN JONSON

Ah Ben!
Say how, or when
Shall we, thy guests,
Meet at those lyric feasts,
Made at the Sun,
The Dog, the Triple Tun?
Where we such clusters had,
As made us nobly wild, not mad;
And yet each verse of thine
Out-did the meat, out-did the frolic wine.

My Ben!
Or come again,
Or send to us,
Thy wit's great overplus;
But teach us yet
Wisely to husband it,
Lest we that talent spend;
And having once brought to an end
That precious stock, the store
Of such a wit the world should have no more.

COMFORT TO A YOUTH THAT HAD LOST HIS LOVE

What needs complaints,
When she a place
Has with the race
   Of saints?

In endless mirth
She thinks not on
What's said or done
   In earth.

She sees no tears,
Or any tone
Of thy deep groan
    She hears:

Nor does she mind
Or think on't now
That ever thou
    Wast kind;

But changed above,
She likes not there,
As she did here,
    Thy love.

Forbear therefore,
And lull asleep
Thy woes, and weep
    No more.

EPITAPH
UPON A CHILD THAT DIED

HERE she lies, a pretty bud,
Lately made of flesh and blood:
Who as soon fell fast asleep
As her little eyes did peep.
Give her strewings, but not stir
The earth that lightly covers her.

TO HIS SAVIOUR, A CHILD
A PRESENT BY A CHILD

Go, pretty child, and bear this flower
Unto thy little Saviour;
And tell Him, by that bud now blown,
He is the Rose of Sharon known.

When thou hast said so, stick it there
Upon His bib or stomacher;
And tell Him, for good handsel too,
That thou hast brought a whistle new,
Made of a clean straight oaten reed,
To charm His cries at time of need.
Tell Him, for coral, thou hast none,
But if thou hadst, He should have one;
But poor thou art, and known to be
Even as moneyless as He.
Lastly, if thou canst win a kiss
From those mellifluous lips of His;
Then never take a second on,
To spoil the first impression.

FRANCIS QUARLES

1592–1644

THE WORLD'S FALLACIES

FALSE World! thou liest! thou canst not lend
    The least delight!
Thy favours cannot gain a friend;
    They are so slight!
Thy morning pleasures make an end
    To please, at night!
Poor are the wants that thou suppliest;
And yet thou vaunt'st! and yet thou viest
With heaven! fond earth, thou boast'st! false
    world, thou liest!

Thy babbling tongue tells golden tales
    Of endless treasure!
Thy bounty offers easy sales
    Of lasting pleasure!

Thou ask'st the conscience, what she ails?
        And swear'st to ease her!
There's none can want, where thou suppliest!
There's none can give, where thou deniest!
Alas, fond world! thou boast'st! false world, thou
    liest!

What well-advisèd ear regards
        What earth can say?
Thy words are gold; but thy rewards
        Are painted clay!
Thy cunning can but pack the cards;
        Thou canst not play!
Thy game, at weakest, still thou viest!
If seen, and then revied, deniest!
Thou are not what thou seem'st! false world,
    thou liest!

Thy tinsel bosom seems a mint
        Of new-coined treasure!
A paradise, that has no stint,
        No change, no measure!
A painted cask; but nothing in it,
        Nor wealth, nor pleasure!
Vain earth! that falsely thus compliest
With man! vain man! that thou reliest
On earth! vain man, thou doat'st! vain earth,
    thou liest!

What mean, dull souls! in this high measure
        To haberdash
In earth's base wares; whose greatest treasure
        Is dross and trash!

The height of whose enchanting pleasure
    Is but a flash!
Are these the goods that thou suppliest
Us mortals with? Are these the highest?
Can these bring cordial peace? False world, thou
    liest!

Emblems.

ON PSALM CXIX. 5

Where shall I seek a guide? where shall I meet
    Some lucky hand to lead my trembling paces?
What trusty lantern will direct my feet
    To scape the danger of these dangerous places?
      What hopes have I to pass without a guide?
Where one gets safely through, a thousand fall
    beside.

An unrequested star did gently slide
    Before the Wise Men to a greater Light;
Backsliding Israel found a double guide;
    A pillar, and a cloud; by day, by night:
      Yet in my desperate dangers, which be far
More great than theirs, I have nor pillar, cloud,
    nor star.

O that the pinions of a clipping dove
    Would cut my passage through the empty air;
Mine eyes being sealed, how would I mount above
    The reach of danger and forgotten care!
      My backward eyes should ne'er commit that
    fault,
Whose lasting guilt should build a monument of
    salt.

Great God, that art the flowing Spring of light,
 Enrich mine eyes with Thy refulgent ray:
Thou art my path; direct my steps aright;
 I have no other light, no other way:
  I'll trust my God, and Him alone pursue;
His Law shall be my path; His heavenly light my
 clue.

Emblems.

WHY DOST THOU SHADE THY LOVELY FACE

WHY dost Thou shade Thy lovely face? O why
Does that eclipsing hand so long deny
The sunshine of Thy soul-enliv'ning eye?

Without that light, what light remains in me?
Thou art my Life, my Way, my Light; in Thee
I live, I move, and by Thy beams I see.

Thou art my life; If Thou but turn away,
My life's a thousand deaths: Thou art my Way;
Without thee, Lord, I travel not, but stray.

My light Thou art; without Thy glorious sight,
Mine eyes are darkened with perpetual night.
My God, Thou art my Way, my Life, my Light.

Thou art my Way; I wander, if Thou fly:
Thou art my Light; If hid, how blind am I?
Thou art my Life; If Thou withdraw, I die.

Mine eyes are blind and dark; I cannot see;
To whom, or whither should my darkness flee,
But to the Light? and who's that Light but Thee?

My path is lost; my wandering steps do stray;
I cannot safely go, nor safely stay;
Whom should I seek but Thee, my Path, my Way?

O, I am dead: To whom shall I, poor I,
Repair? To whom shall my sad ashes fly
But Life? And where is Life but in Thine eye?

And yet thou turn'st away Thy face, and fly'st me;
And yet I sue for grace, and Thou deny'st me;
Speak, art Thou angry, Lord, or only try'st me?

Unscreen those heavenly lamps, or tell me why
Thou shadest Thy face; perhaps, Thou think'st
     no eye
Can view those flames, and not drop down and die.

If that be all, shine forth, and draw Thee nigher;
Let me behold and die; for my desire
Is Phœnix-like to perish in that fire.

Death-conquered Laz'rus was redeemed by Thee;
If I am dead, Lord, set death's prisoner free;
Am I more spent, or stink I worse than he?

If my puffed light be out, give leave to tine
My flameless snuff at that bright Lamp of Thine;
O what's Thy Light the less for lighting mine?

If I have lost my path, great Shepherd, say,
Shall I still wander in a doubtful way?
Lord, shall a lamb of Israel's sheepfold stray?

Thou art the pilgrim's path; the blind man's eye;
The dead man's life; on Thee my hopes rely;
If Thou remove, I err; I grope; I die.

Disclose Thy sunbeams; close Thy wings, and stay;
See, see, how I am blind, and dead, and stray,
O Thou, that art my Light, my Life, my Way.

Emblems.

to tine] to light or kindle.

HENRY KING, BISHOP OF CHICHESTER

1592-1669

THE DIRGE

WHAT is the existence of man's life
But open war, or slumbered strife?
Where sickness to his sense presents
The combat of the elements:
And never feels a perfect peace,
Till Death's cold hand signs his release.

It is a storm, where the hot blood
Outvies in rage the boiling flood;
And each loud passion of the mind
Is like a furious gust of wind,
Which beats his bark with many a wave,
Till he casts anchor in the grave.

It is a flower, which buds and grows,
And withers as the leaves disclose;
Whose spring and fall faint seasons keep,
Like fits of waking before sleep:
Then shrinks into that fatal mould
Where its first being was enrolled.

It is a dream, whose seeming truth
Is moralized in age and youth:
Where all the comforts he can share
As wandering ashes fancies are;
Till in a mist of dark decay
The dreamer vanish quite away.

It is a dial, which points out
The sunset as it moves about;

And shadows out in lines of night
The subtle stages of time's flight,
Till all obscuring earth hath laid
The body in perpetual shade.

It is a weary interlude
Which doth short joys, long woes, include.
The world the stage, the prologue tears,
The acts vain hope, and varied fears;
The scene shuts up with loss of breath,
And leaves no epilogue but death.

A CONTEMPLATION UPON FLOWERS

BRAVE flowers, that I could gallant it like you
    And be as little vain!
You come abroad and make a harmless show,
    And to your beds of earth again;
You are not proud, you know your birth,
For your embroidered garments are from earth.

You do obey your months and times, but I
    Would have it ever spring;
My fate would know no winter, never die,
    Nor think of such a thing.
Oh that I could my bed of earth but view,
And smile, and look as cheerfully as you!

Oh teach me to see death and not to fear,
    But rather to take truce;
How often have I seen you at a bier,
    And there look fresh and spruce.
You fragrant flowers then teach me that my breath
Like yours may sweeten and perfume my death.

EXEQUY ON HIS WIFE

ACCEPT, thou shrine of my dead saint,
Instead of dirges this complaint;
And for sweet flowers to crown thy hearse,
Receive a strew of weeping verse
From thy grieved friend, whom thou might'st see
Quite melted into tears for thee.

Dear loss! since thy untimely fate,
My task hath been to meditate
On thee, on thee; thou art the book,
The library, whereon I look,
Though almost blind. For thee, loved clay,
I languish out, nor live, the day,
Using no other exercise
But what I practise with mine eyes:
By which wet glasses, I find out
How lazily time creeps about
To one that mourns; this, only this,
My exercise and business is:
So I compute the weary hours
With sighs dissolvèd into showers.

Nor wonder, if my time go thus
Backward and most preposterous;
Thou hast benighted me; thy set
This eve of blackness did beget,
Who wast my day, (though overcast,
Before thou had'st thy noon-tide past),
And I remember must in tears,
Thou scarce had'st seen so many years
As day tells hours. By thy clear sun
My love and fortune first did run;
But thou wilt never more appear
Folded within my hemisphere,

Since both thy light and motion
Like a fled star is fallen, and gone,
And twixt me and my soul's dear wish
The earth now interposèd is,
Which such a strange eclipse doth make
As ne'er was read in almanack.

I could allow thee, for a time,
To darken me and my sad clime,
Were it a month, a year, or ten,
I would thy exile live till then;
And all that space my mirth adjourn,
So thou would'st promise to return;
And putting off thy ashy shroud,
At length disperse this sorrow's cloud.

But woe is me! the longest date
Too narrow is to calculate
These empty hopes: never shall I
Be so much blest as to descry
A glimpse of thee, till that day come,
When shall the earth to cinders doom,
And a fierce fever must calcine
The body of this world, like thine,
My little world! that fit of fire
Once off, our bodies shall aspire
To our souls' bliss: then we shall rise,
And view ourselves with clearer eyes
In that calm region, where no night
Can hide us from each other's sight.

Meantime thou hast her, earth: much good
May my harm do thee. Since it stood
With Heaven's will, I might not call
Her longer mine, I give thee all

My short-lived right and interest
In her, whom living I loved best:
With a most free and bounteous grief,
I give thee what I could not keep.
Be kind to her, and prithee look
Thou write into thy doomsday book
Each parcel of this rarity,
Which in thy casket shrined doth lie:
See that thou make thy reckoning straight,
And yield her back again by weight;
For thou must audit on thy trust
Each grain and atom of this dust,
As thou wilt answer Him that lent,
Not gave thee, my dear monument.

So close the ground, and 'bout her shade
Black curtains draw;—my bride is laid.

Sleep on, my love, in thy cold bed,
Never to be disquieted!
My last good night! Thou wilt not wake,
Till I thy fate shall overtake:
Till age, or grief, or sickness, must
Marry my body to that dust
It so much loves; and fill the room
My heart keeps empty in thy tomb.
Stay for me there; I will not fail
To meet thee in that hollow vale:
And think not much of my delay;
I am already on the way,
And follow thee with all the speed
Desire can make, or sorrows breed.
Each minute is a short degree,
And ev'ry hour a step towards thee.

At night, when I betake to rest,
Next morn I rise nearer my west
Of life, almost by eight hours' sail,
Than when sleep breathed his drowsy gale.

Thus from the sun my bottom steers,
And my day's compass downward bears:
Nor labour I to stem the tide,
Through which to thee I swiftly glide.

'Tis true, with shame and grief I yield,
Thou, like the van, first took'st the field,
And gotten hast the victory,
In thus adventuring to die
Before me, whose more years might crave
A just precedence in the grave.
But hark! My pulse, like a soft drum,
Beats my approach, tells thee I come;
And slow howe'er my marches be,
I shall at last sit down by thee.

The thought of this bids me go on,
And wait my dissolution
With hope and comfort. Dear (forgive
The crime), I am content to live
Divided, with but half a heart,
Till we shall meet and never part.

BARTEN HOLYDAY

1593–1661

DISTICHES

THE world's a prison; no man can get out:
Let th' atheist storm then; 'tis Heaven round about.
Heaven is the silk-worm's sphere: what art did
     spin it
Does at its pleasure choose to dwell within it. . . .

Was Paul more happy at the third heaven's sight,
Or more tormented to delay delight?

See how the eagle mounts towards Heaven: he's
    gone
Quite out of sight; right emblem of St. John . . .

The Nightingale's a choir, no single note:
Oh! various power of God in one small throat.

O mock of pride! man cannot change his shape,
Though, whiles unchanged, he is but like an ape.

The Egyptian thought the dog a god! He might
Make him a friend: he's safety or delight.

What shall I do to-day? I prayed to shun
All sin, but from my prayer 'tis I run.

How what was first, was first, exceeds all wonder!
Whisper has more proportion unto thunder.

What knowledge may of the first Being be,
Nature first learns of what's philosophy. . . .

How prudent Hesiod Laws of Plough rehearses,
Breaking the mould with a glad team of verses. . . .

Who gripes too much casts all upon the ground:
Too great a greatness greatness does confound.

Columbus was by his brave spirit so hurl'd,
He seem'd the sea-apostle of the world.

All things are wonder since the world began:
The World's a riddle, and the meaning's man.

Grave, wise, sweet Basil, free from fond desires
Was his own monastery, his thoughts the friars.

Father of Gifts, who to the dust did'st give
Life, say to these my meditations, *Live*.

GEORGE HERBERT

1593–1632

DISCIPLINE

THROW away Thy rod,
Throw away Thy wrath;
O my God,
Take the gentle path!

For my heart's desire
Unto Thine is bent:
I aspire
To a full consent.

Not a word or look
I affect to own,
But by book,
And Thy Book alone.

Though I fail, I weep;
Though I halt in pace,
Yet I creep
To the throne of grace.

Then let wrath remove;
Love will do the deed:
For with love
Stony hearts will bleed.

Love is swift of foot;
Love's a man of war,
And can shoot,
And can hit from far.

Who can 'scape his bow?
That which wrought on Thee,
Brought Thee low,
Needs must work on me.

Throw away Thy rod;
Though man frailties hath,
Thou art God:
Throw away Thy wrath!

THE COLLAR

I STRUCK the board, and cried, No more.
I will abroad.
What? shall I ever sigh and pine?
My lines and life are free; free as the road,
Loose as the wind, as large as store.
Shall I be still in suit?
Have I no harvest but a thorn
To let me blood, and not restore
What I have lost with cordial fruit?
Sure there was wine
Before my sighs did dry it: there was corn
Before my tears did drown it.
Is the year only lost to me?
Have I no bays to crown it?
No flowers, no garlands gay? all blasted?
All wasted?
Not so, my heart: but there is fruit,
And thou hast hands.
Recover all thy sigh-blown age
On double pleasures: leave thy cold dispute
Of what is fit and not; forsake thy cage,
Thy rope of sands,
Which petty thoughts have made, and made to
thee
Good cable, to enforce and draw,
And be thy law,
While thou didst wink and would not see.

Away; take heed:
I will abroad.
Call in thy death's-head there: tie up thy fears.
He that forbears
To suit and serve his need,
Deserves his load.
But as I rav'd and grew more fierce and wild
At every word,
Methought I heard one calling, *Child*;
And I replied, *My Lord*.

THE PULLEY

WHEN God at first made Man,
Having a glass of blessings standing by;
Let us (said He) pour on him all we can:
Let the world's riches, which dispersèd lie,
Contract into a span.

So strength first made a way;
Then beauty flow'd, then wisdom, honour, pleasure:
When almost all was out, God made a stay,
Perceiving that alone, of all His treasure,
Rest in the bottom lay.

For if I should (said He)
Bestow this jewel also on My creature,
He would adore My gifts instead of Me,
And rest in Nature, not the God of Nature:
So both should losers be.

Yet let him keep the rest,
But keep them with repining restlessness:
Let him be rich and weary, that at least,
If goodness lead him not, yet weariness
May toss him to My breast.

CONSTANCY

Who is the honest man?
He that doth still and strongly good pursue,
To God, his neighbour, and himself most true:
    Whom neither force nor fawning can
Unpin, or wrench from giving all their due.

    Whose honesty is not
So loose or easy, that a ruffling wind
Can blow away, or glittering look it blind:
    Who rides his sure and even trot,
While the world now rides by, now lags behind.

    Who when great trials come,
Nor seeks nor shuns them, but doth calmly stay,
Till he the thing and the example weigh:
    All being brought into a sum,
What place or person calls for, he doth pay.

    Whom none can work or woo
To use in anything a trick or sleight,
For above all things he abhors deceit:
    His words and works and fashion too
All of a piece, and all are clear and straight.

    Who never melts or thaws
At close temptations: when the day is done,
His goodness sets not, but in dark can run:
    The sun to others writeth laws,
And is their virtue; virtue is his sun.

    Who, when he is to treat
With sick folks, women, those whom passions
    sway,
Allows for that, and keeps his constant way:
    Whom others' faults do not defeat;
But though men fail him, yet his part doth play.

Whom nothing can procure,
When the wide world runs bias, from his will,
To writhe his limbs, and share, not mend the ill!
        This is the Mark-man, safe and sure,
Who still is right, and prays to be so still.

THE ODOUR. 2 Cor. 2.15

How sweetly doth *My Master* sound! *My Master!*
        As ambergris leaves a rich scent
                Unto the taster:
        So do these words a sweet content,
An oriental fragrancy, *My Master*.

With these all day I do perfume my mind,
        My mind ev'n thrust into them both:
                That I might find
        What cordials make this curious broth,
This broth of smells, that feeds and fats my mind.

My Master, shall I speak? O that to thee
        My servant were a little so,
                As flesh may be;
        That these two words might creep and grow
To some degree of spiciness to Thee!

Then should the pomander, which was before
        A speaking sweet, mend by reflection,
                And tell me more;
        For pardon of my imperfection
Would warm and work it sweeter than before.

For when *My Master*, which alone is sweet,
        And ev'n in my unworthiness pleasing,
                Shall call and meet,
        My servant, as *thee not displeasing*,
That call is but the breathing of the sweet.

                Mark-man] ? Marksman.

This breathing would with gains by sweetning me
 (As sweet things traffick when they meet)
  Return to Thee.
 And so this new commerce and sweet
Should all my life employ, and busy me.

JUDGE NOT THE PREACHER FOR HE IS THY JUDGE

Judge not the preacher; for He is thy Judge:
If thou mislike him, thou conceiv'st him not.
God calleth preaching folly. Do not grudge
To pick out treasures from an earthen pot.
 The worst speak something good: if all want
  sense,
 God takes a text, and preacheth patience.

IESU

Iesu is in my heart, His sacred name
Is deeply carvèd there: but th' other week
A great affliction broke the little frame,
Ev'n all to pieces: which I went to seek:
And first I found the corner, where was *I*,
After, where *ES*, and next where *U* was graved.
When I had got these parcels, instantly
I sat me down to spell them, and perceived
That to my broken heart he was *I ease you*,
  And to my whole is *IESU*.

THE QUIP

 The merry world did on a day
With his train-bands and mates agree
 To meet together, where I lay,
And all in sport to jeer at me.

First, Beauty crept into a rose,
Which when I pluck'd not, 'Sir,' said she,
'Tell me, I pray, whose hands are those.'
But thou shalt answer, Lord, for me.

Then Money came, and chinking still,
'What tune is this, poor man?' said he:
'I heard in Music you had skill':
But thou shalt answer, Lord, for me.

Then came brave Glory puffing by
In silks that whistled, who but he!
He scarce allowed me half an eye.
But thou shalt answer, Lord, for me.

Then came quick Wit and Conversation,
And he would needs a comfort be,
And, to be short, make an oration.
But thou shalt answer, Lord, for me.

Yet when the hour of thy design
To answer these fine things shall come;
Speak not at large, say, I am Thine:
And then they have their answer home.

THE FLOWER

How fresh, O, Lord, how sweet and clean
Are thy returns! ev'n as the flowers in spring;
To which, besides their own demean,
The late-past frosts tributes of pleasure bring.
Grief melts away
Like snow in May,
As if there were no such cold thing.

Who would have thought my shrivel'd heart
Could have recover'd greenness? It was gone
  Quite under ground, as flowers depart
To see their mother-root, when they have blown
      Where they together
      All the hard weather,
  Dead to the world, keep house unknown.

These are Thy wonders, Lord of power,
Killing and quick'ning, bringing down to hell,
  And up to heaven in an hour;
Making a chiming of a passing-bell.
      We say amiss
      This or that is:
  Thy word is all, if we could spell.

O that I once past changing were
Fast in Thy Paradise, where no flower can wither!
  Many a spring I shoot up fair,
Off'ring at Heav'n, growing and groaning thither:
      Nor doth my flower,
      Want a spring-shower,
  My sins and I joining together.

But while I grow in a straight line,
Still upwards bent, as if Heav'n were mine own,
  Thy anger comes, and I decline:
What frost to that? What pole is not the zone,
      Where all things burn,
      When Thou dost turn,
  And the least frown of Thine is shown?

And now in age I bud again,
After so many deaths I live and write;
  I once more smell the dew and rain,

And relish versing: O my only light,
    It cannot be
    That I am he
On whom Thy tempests fell all night.

 These are Thy wonders, Lord of Love,
To make us see we are but flowers that glide;
 Which when we once can find and prove,
Thou hast a garden for us, where to bide.
    Who would be more,
    Swelling through store,
Forfeit their Paradise by their pride.

DIALOGUE

  Sweetest Saviour, if my soul
   Were but worth the having,
  Quickly should I then control
   Any thought of waving.
  But when all my care and pains
  Cannot give the name of gains
  To Thy wretch so full of stains,
  What delight or hope remains?

  What, child, is the balance thine,
   Thine the poise and measure?
  If I say, 'Thou shalt be Mine,'
   Finger not My treasure.
  What the gains in having thee
  Do amount to, only He,
  Who for man was sold, can see;
  That transferr'd th' accounts to Me.

  But as I can see no merit,
   Leading to this favour:
  So the way to fit me for it,
   Is beyond my savour.

   savour] *savoir,* knowledge.

As the reason then is Thine;
So the way is none of mine:
I disclaim the whole design:
Sin disclaims and I resign.

That is all, if that I could
   Get without repining;
And My clay My creature would
   Follow My resigning.
That as I did freely part
With My glory and desert,
Left all joys to feel all smart——

Ah! no more: Thou break'st my heart.

SIN

Lord, with what care hast Thou begirt us round!
   Parents first season us; then schoolmasters
Deliver us to laws; they send us bound
   To rules of reason, holy messengers,

Pulpits and Sundays, sorrow dogging sin,
   Afflictions sorted, anguish of all sizes,
Fine nets and stratagems to catch us in,
   Bibles laid open, millions of surprises;

Blessings beforehand, ties of gratefulness,
   The sound of glory ringing in our ears:
Without, our shame; within, our consciences;
   Angels and grace, eternal hopes and fears.

Yet all these fences and their whole array
One cunning bosom-sin blows quite away.

EMPLOYMENT

Oh that I were an orange-tree,
          That busy plant!
Then should I ever laden be
          And never want
Some fruit for him that dresseth me.

But we are still too young or old;
          The man is gone,
Before we do our wares unfold;
          So we freeze on,
Until the grave increase our cold.

AFFLICTION

When first thou did'st entice to Thee my heart,
          I thought the service brave :
So many joys I writ down for my part,
          Besides what I might have
Out of my stock of natural delights,
Augmented with thy gracious benefits.

I lookèd on Thy furniture so fine,
          And made it fine to me:
Thy glorious household-stuff did me entwine,
          And 'tice me unto Thee;
Such stars I counted mine: both heav'n and earth
Paid me my wages in a world of mirth.

What pleasures could I want, whose King I served?
          Where joys my fellows were.
Thus argu'd into hopes, my thoughts reserved
          No place for grief or fear.
Therefore my sudden soul caught at the place,
And made her youth and fierceness seek Thy face.

At first thou gav'st me milk and sweetnesses;
        I had my wish and way;
My days were straw'd with flow'rs and happiness;
        There was no month but May.
But with my years sorrow did twist and grow,
And made a party unawares for woe.

My flesh began unto my soul in pain,
        Sicknesses cleave my bones;
Consuming agues dwell in ev'ry vein,
        And tune my breath to groans.
Sorrow was all my soul; I scarce believed,
Till grief did tell me roundly, that I lived.

When I got health, Thou took'st away my life,
        And more; for my friends die:
My mirth and edge was lost; a blunted knife
        Was of more use than I.
Thus thin and lean without a fence or friend,
I was blown through with ev'ry storm and wind.

Whereas my birth and spirit rather took
        The way that takes the town;
Thou did'st betray me to a ling'ring book,
        And wrap me in a gown.
I was entangled in the world of strife,
Before I had the power to change my life.

Yet, for I threatened oft the siege to raise,
        Not simp'ring all mine age,
Thou often didst with academic praise
        Melt and dissolve my rage.
I took Thy sweetened pill, till I came near;
I could not go away, nor persevere.

Yet lest perchance I should too happy be
        In my unhappiness,

Turning my purge to food, Thou throwest me
        Into more sicknesses.
Thus doth thy power cross-bias me, not making
Thine own gift good, yet me from my ways taking.

Now I am here, what Thou wilt do with me
        None of my books will show:
I read, and sigh, and wish I were a tree;
        For sure then I should grow
To fruit or shade: at least some bird would trust
Her household to me, and I should be just.

Yet, though Thou troublest me, I must be meek;
        In weakness must be stout.
Well, I will change the service, and go seek
        Some other master out.
Ah my dear God, though I am clean forgot,
Let me not love Thee, if I love Thee not.

CHRISTMAS

ALL after pleasures as I rid one day,
  My horse and I, both tir'd, body and mind,
With full cry of affections, quite astray,
  I took up in the next inn I could find.

There when I came, whom found I but my dear,
  My dearest Lord, expecting till the grief
Of pleasures brought me to Him, ready there
  To be all passengers' most sweet relief?

O Thou, whose glorious, yet contracted light,
  Wrapt in night's mantle, stole into a manger;
Since my dark soul and brutish is Thy right,
  To Man of all beasts be not Thou a stranger:

Furnish and deck my soul, that Thou mayst have
A better lodging than a rack or grave.

ANTIPHON

Cho. LET all the world in ev'ry corner sing,
　　　　　My God and King.
　Vers. The heav'ns are not too high,
　　　　His praise may thither fly:
　　　　The earth is not too low,
　　　　His praises there may grow.
Cho. Let all the world in ev'ry corner sing,
　　　　　My God and King.
　Vers. The church with psalms must shout.
　　　　No door can keep them out:
　　　　But above all, the heart
　　　　Must bear the longest part.
Cho. Let all the world in ev'ry corner sing,
　　　　　My God and King.

VIRTUE

　SWEET day, so cool, so calm, so bright,
　The bridal of the earth and sky,
　The dew shall weep thy fall to-night;
　　　　For thou must die.

Sweet rose, whose hue angry and brave
Bids the rash gazer wipe his eye,
Thy root is ever in its grave,
　　　　And thou must die.

Sweet spring, full of sweet days and roses,
A box where sweets compacted lie,
My music shows ye have your closes,
　　　　And all must die.

Only a sweet and virtuous soul,
Like season'd timber, never gives;
But though the whole world turn to coal,
　　　　Then chiefly lives.

He hath at will
More quaint and subtle ways to kill;
A smile or kiss, as he will use the art,
Shall have the cunning skill to break a heart.

Cupid and Death.

THOMAS CAREW

1595 ?–1639 ?

DISDAIN RETURNED

He that loves a rosy cheek,
  Or a coral lip admires,
Or from star-like eyes doth seek
  Fuel to maintain his fires:
As old Time makes these decay,
So his flames must waste away.

But a smooth and steadfast mind,
  Gentle thoughts and calm desires,
Hearts with equal love combined,
  Kindle never-dying fires.
Where these are not, I despise
Lovely cheeks or lips or eyes.

No tears, Celia, now shall win
  My resolved heart to return;
I have searched thy soul within,
  And find nought but pride and scorn;
I have learned thy acts, and now
Can disdain as much as thou.
Some power, in my revenge convey
That love to her I cast away.

quaint] ingenious.

A SONG

Ask me no more where Jove bestows,
When June is past, the fading rose;
For in your beauties' orient deep
These flowers, as in their causes, sleep.

Ask me no more whither do stray
The golden atoms of the day;
For in pure love heaven did prepare
Those powders to enrich your hair.

Ask me no more whither doth haste
The nightingale when May is past;
For in your sweet dividing throat
She winters, and keeps warm her note.

Ask me no more where those stars 'light
That downwards fall in dead of night;
For in your eyes they sit, and there
Fixèd become as in their sphere.

Ask me no more if east or west
The Phoenix builds her spicy nest;
For unto you at last she flies,
And in your fragrant bosom dies.

A PASTORAL DIALOGUE

(SHEPHERD—NYMPH—CHORUS)

Shep.   This mossy bank they pressed.
Nymph. That aged oak
         Did canopy the happy pair
         All night from the damp air.
Chor.   Here let us sit, and sing the words they
      spoke,
      Till the day breaking their embraces
      broke.

Shep. See, Love, the blushes of the morn appear,
And now she hangs her pearly store,
Robbed from the eastern shore,
I' th' cowslip's bell and roses rare;
Sweet, I must stay no longer here!

Nymph. Those streaks of doubtful light usher not
day,
But show my sun must set; no morn
Shall shine till thou return;
The yellow planets and the grey
Dawn shall attend thee on thy way.

Shep. If thine eyes gild my paths, they may
forbear
Their useless shine. *Nymph.* My tears will
quite
Extinguish their faint light.

Shep. Those drops will make their beams more
clear,
Love's frames will shine in every tear.

Cho. They kissed and wept, and from their lips
and eyes,
In a mixed dew of briny sweet
Their joys and sorrows meet:
But she cries out:—*Nymph.* Shepherd,
arise,
The sun betrays us else to spies.

Shep. The wingèd hours fly fast whilst we em-
brace,
But when we want their help to meet,
They move with leaden feet.

Nymph. Then let us pinion time and chase
The day for ever from this place.

Shep. Hark! *Nymph.* Ay me! stay! *Shep.* For
ever: *Nymph.* No! arise!

We must be gone! *Shep.* My nest of
spice!
Nymph My soul! *Shep.* My Paradise!

Cho.   Neither could say farewell, but through
their eyes
Grief interrupted speech with tears'
supplies.

TO MY WORTHY FRIEND MASTER GEORGE SANDYS ON HIS TRANSLATION OF THE PSALMS

I PRESS not to the choir, nor dare I greet
The holy place with my unhallowed feet:
My unwashed Muse pollutes not things divine,
Nor mingles her profaner notes with thine;
Here, humbly at the porch, she stays,
And with glad ears sucks in thy sacred lays.
So, devout penitents of old were wont,
Some without door, and some beneath the font,
To stand and hear the Church's liturgies,
Yet not assist the solemn exercise.
Sufficeth her, that she a lay-place gain,
To trim thy Vestments, or but bear thy train:
Though nor in tune, nor wing, she reach thy lark,
Her lyric feet may dance before the ark.
Who knows, but that Her wandering eyes, that run
Now hunting glow-worms, may adore the Sun.
A pure flame may, shot by Almighty power
Into her breast, the earthy flame devour:
My eyes, in penitential dew may steep
That brine, which they for sensual love did weep:
So (though 'gainst Nature's course) fire may be
quenched
With fire, and water be with water drenched.

Perhaps, my restless soul, tired with pursuit
Of mortal beauty, seeking without fruit
Contentment there; which hath not, when en-
   joyed,
Quenched all her thirst, nor satisfied, though
   cloyed;
Weary of her vain search below, above
In the first fair may find the immortal Love.
Prompted by thy example then, no more
In moulds of clay will I my God adore;
But tear those Idols from my heart, and write
What his blest spirit, not fond love, shall indite;
Then, I no more shall court the verdant bay,
But the dry leafless trunk on Golgotha:
And rather strive to gain from thence one thorn,
Than all the flourishing leaves by laureates worn.

CELIA THREATENED

Know, Celia, since thou art so proud,
   'Twas I that gave thee thy renown.
Thou hadst in the forgotten crowd
   Of common beauties lived unknown,
Had not my verse exhaled thy name,
And with it imp'd the wings of Fame.

That killing power is none of thine;
   I gave it to thy voice and eyes;
Thy sweets, thy graces, all are mine;
   Thou art my star, shin'st in my skies;
Then dart not from thy borrow'd sphere
Lightning on him that fix'd thee there.

Tempt me with such affrights no more,
   Lest what I made I uncreate;
Let fools thy mystic forms adore,

I'll know thee in thy mortal state.
Wise poets, that wrapt Truth in tales,
Knew her themselves through all her veils.

CELIA SINGS

You that think love can convey
        No other way
But through the eyes, into the heart,
        His fatal dart,
Close up those casements and but hear
        This siren sing,
        And on the wing
Of her sweet voice it shall appear
That love can enter at the ear.

Then unveil your eyes, behold
        The curious mould
Where that voice dwells, and as we know,
        When the cocks crow,
        We freely may
        Gaze on the day,
So may you, when the music's done,
Awake and see the rising sun.

EPITAPH ON THE LADY MARY VILLIERS

The Lady Mary Villiers lies
Under this stone; with weeping eyes
The parents that first gave her breath,
And their sad friends, laid her in earth.
If any of them, reader, were
Known unto thee, shed a tear,
Or if thyself possess a gem
As dear to thee, as this to them,

Though a stranger to this place,
Bewail in theirs thine own hard case:
   For thou perhaps at thy return
   May'st find thy darling in an urn.

TO MY INCONSTANT MISTRESS

WHEN thou, poor excommunicate
   From all the joys of love, shalt see
The full reward, and glorious fate,
   Which my strong faith shall purchase me,
   Then curse thine own inconstancy.

A fairer hand than thine shall cure
   That heart which thy false oaths did wound;
And to my soul a soul more pure
   Than thine shall by Love's hand be bound,
   And both with equal glory crown'd.

Then shalt thou weep, entreat, complain
   To Love, as I did once to thee;
When all thy tears shall be as vain
   As mine were then, for thou shalt be
   Damn'd for thy false apostasy.

CHLORIS IN THE SNOW

I SAW fair Chloris walk alone
When feathered rain came softly down,
Then Jove descended from his tower
To court her in a silver shower.
   The wanton snow flew to her breast,
Like little birds into their nest;
But overcome with whiteness there,
For grief it thawed into a tear;
Then falling down her garment hem,
To deck her froze into a gem.

TO A. L.

PERSUASIONS TO LOVE

THINK not, 'cause men flatt'ring say,
Y' are as fresh as April, sweet as May,
Bright as is the morning star,
That you are so; or though you are
Be not therefore proud, and deem
All men unworthy your esteem:
For being so, you lose the pleasure
Of being fair, since that rich treasure
Of rare beauty and sweet feature
Was bestowed on you by nature
To be enjoyed, and 'twere a sin,
There to be scarce, where she hath been
So prodigal of her best graces;
Thus common beauties and mean faces
Shall have more pastime and enjoy
The sport you lose by being coy. . . .
Starve not yourself, because you may
Thereby make me pine away;
Nor let brittle beauty make
You your wiser thoughts forsake:
For that lovely face will fail;
Beauty's sweet but beauty's frail;
'Tis sooner past, 'tis sooner done
Than summer's rain, or winter's sun;
Most fleeting, when it is most dear;
'Tis gone, while we but say 'tis here.
These curious locks so aptly twined,
Whose every hair a soul doth bind,
Will change their abroun hue, and grow
White, and cold as winter's snow.

abroun] auburn.

That eye which now is Cupid's nest
Will prove his grave, and all the rest
Will follow; in the cheek, chin, nose,
Nor lily shall be found, nor rose;
And what will then become of all
Those, whom now you servants call?
Like swallows, when your summer's done
They'll fly, and seek some warmer sun.
Then wisely choose one to your friend,
Whose love may (when your beauties end)
Remain still firm: be provident,
And think before the summer's spent
Of following winter; like the ant
In plenty hoard for time of scant,
Cull out amongst the multitude
Of lovers, that seek to intrude
Into your favour, one that may
Love for an age, not for a day; . . .
For when the storms of time have moved
Waves on that cheek which was beloved;
When a fair lady's face is pined,
And yellow spread where red once shined;
When beauty, youth, and all sweets leave her,
Love may return, but lover never: . . .
Oh love me then, and now begin it,
Let us not lose this present minute:
For time and age will work that wrack,
Which time and age shall ne'er call back.
The snake each year fresh skin resumes,
And eagles change their aged plumes;
The faded rose each spring receives
A fresh red tincture on her leaves:
But if your beauties once decay,
You never know a second May.

Oh, then be wise, and whilst your season
Affords you days for sport, do reason;
Spend not in vain your life's short hour,
But crop in time your beauty's flower:
Which will away, and doth together
Both bud and fade, both blow and wither.

BOLDNESS IN LOVE

MARK how the bashful morn in vain
  Courts the amorous marigold
With sighing blasts and weeping rain,
  Yet she refuses to unfold:
But when the planet of the day
Approacheth with his powerful ray
Then she spreads, then she receives
His warmer beams into her virgin leaves.

So shalt thou thrive in love, fond boy;
  If thy tears and sighs discover
Thy grief, thou never shalt enjoy
  The just reward of a bold lover.
But when with moving accents thou
Shalt constant faith and service vow,
Thy Celia shall receive those charms
With open ears, and with unfolded arms.

NOW THAT THE WINTER'S GONE

Now that the winter's gone, the earth hath lost
Her snow-white robes: and now no more the frost
Candies the grass, or casts an icy cream
Upon the silver lake or crystal stream:
But the warm sun thaws the benumbèd earth
And makes it tender: gives a sacred birth

To the dead swallow; wakes in hollow tree
The drowsy cuckoo and the humble-bee.
Now do a choir of chirping minstrels bring,
In triumph to the world, the youthful Spring;
The valleys, hills, and woods, in rich array,
Welcome the coming of the longed-for May.
Now all things smile—only my love doth lour:
Nor hath the scalding noon-day sun the power
To melt that marble ice which still doth hold
Her heart congealed, and makes her pity cold.
The ox which lately did for shelter fly
Into the stall, doth now securely lie
In open fields; and love no more is made
By the fireside; but in the cooler shade
Amyntas now doth with his Chloris sleep
Under a sycamore, and all things keep
Time with the season—only she doth carry
June in her eyes, in her heart January.

A DEPOSITION FROM LOVE

I was foretold, your rebel sex,
   Nor love, nor pity knew;
And with what scorn you use to vex
   Poor hearts that humbly sue;
Yet I believ'd, to crown our pain,
   Could we the fortress win,
The happy lover sure should gain
   A paradise within:
I thought love's plagues, like dragons sate,
Only to fright us at the gate.
But I did enter, and enjoy
   What happy lovers prove;
For I could kiss, and sport, and toy,
   And taste those sweets of love;

Which had they but a lasting state,
  Or if in Celia's breast
The force of love might not abate,
  Jove were too mean a guest.
But now her breach of faith, far more
Afflicts, than did her scorn before.

Hard fate to have been once possessed,
  As victor, of a heart
Achieved with labour, and unrest,
  And then forced to depart.
If the stout foe will not resign
  When I besiege a Town,
I lose, but what was never mine;
  But he that is cast down
From enjoy'd beauty, feels a woe,
Only deposèd Kings can know.

WILLIAM HABINGTON

1605–1654

EPISTLE TO A FRIEND

I HATE the country's dirt and manners, yet
I love the silence; I embrace the wit
And courtship, flowing here in a full tide;
But loathe the expense, the vanity, and pride.
No place each way is happy. Here I hold
Commerce with some, who to my ear unfold
(After a due oath ministered) the height
And greatness of each star shines in the state,
The brightness, the eclipse, the influence.
With others I commune, who tell me whence
The torrent doth of foreign discord flow;
Relate each skirmish, battle, overthrow,

Soon as they happen; and by rote can tell
Those German towns, even puzzle me to spell.
The cross or prosperous fate of Princes, they
Ascribe to rashness, cunning, or delay;
And on each action, comment with more skill
Than upon Livy did old Matchavill.

   O busy folly! Why do I my brain
Perplex with the dull policies of Spain,
Or quick designs of France? Why not repair
To the pure innocence o' th' country air;
And neighbour thee, dear friend? who so dost give
Thy thoughts to worth and virtue, that to live
Blest, is to trace thy ways. There might not we
Arm against passion with philosophy;
And by the aid of leisure, so control
Whate'er is earth in us, to grow all soul?

   Knowledge doth ignorance engender when
We study mysteries of other men
And foreign plots. Do but in thy own shade,
(Thy head upon some flow'ry pillow laid,
Kind Nature's housewifery) contemplate all
His stratagems who labours to enthral
The world to his great master; and you'll find
Ambition mocks itself, and grasps the wind!
Not conquest makes us great! Blood is too dear
A price for glory: Honour doth appear
To statesmen like a vision in the night,
And juggler-like works o' th' deluded sight.

   Th' unbusied only wise: for no respect
Endangers them to error; they affect
Truth in her naked beauty, and behold
Man with an equal eye, not bright in gold,
Or tall in title, so much him they weigh,

              Matchavill] Machiavel.

As Virtue raiseth him above his clay.

Thus let us value things: And since we find
Time bends us towards Death, let 's in our mind
Create new youth; and arm against the rude
Assaults of age; that no dull solitude
O' th' country dead our thoughts, nor busy care
O' th' town make us not think, where now we are
And whither we are bound. Time ne'er forgot
His journey, though his steps we numbered not!

TO ROSES IN THE BOSOM OF CASTARA

YE blushing virgins happy are
    In the chaste nunnery of her breasts—
For he 'd profane so chaste a fair,
    Whoe'er should call them Cupid's nests.

Transplanted thus how bright ye grow!
    How rich a perfume do ye yield!
In some close garden cowslips so
    Are sweeter than i' th' open field.

In those white cloisters live secure
    From the rude blasts of wanton breath!—
Each hour more innocent and pure,
    Till you shall wither into death.

Then that which living gave you room,
    Your glorious sepulchre shall be.
There wants no marble for a tomb
    Whose breast hath marble been to me.

TO CASTARA

OF THE KNOWLEDGE OF LOVE

WHERE sleeps the north wind when the south
 inspires
Life in the Spring, and gathers into quires
The scattered nightingales? whose subtle ears
Heard first th' harmonious language of the
 spheres?
Whence hath the stone magnetic force t' allure
Th' enamoured iron? from a seed impure
Or natural did first the mandrake grow?
What power i' th' ocean makes it ebb and flow?
What strange materials is the azure sky
Compacted of? of what its brightest eye,
The ever flaming sun? what people are
In th' unknown world? what worlds in every star?
    Let curious fancies at this secret rove:
    Castara, what we know, we'll practise—love.

TO CASTARA

THE REWARD OF INNOCENT LOVE

WE saw and wooed each other's eyes,
My soul contracted then with thine,
And both burnt in one sacrifice,
By which our marriage grew divine.

Let wilder youth, whose soul is sense,
Profane the temple of delight,
And purchase endless penitence
With the stol'n pleasure of one night.

Time's ever ours, while we despise
The sensual idol of our clay,

For though the sun doth set and rise,
　　We joy one everlasting day;

Whose light no jealous clouds obscure,
　　While each of us shine innocent;
The troubled stream is still impure;
　　With virtue flies away content.

And though opinion often err,
　　We'll court the modest smile of fame,
For sin's black danger circles her
　　Who hath infection in her name.

Thus when to one dark silent room
　　Death shall our loving coffins thrust,
Fame will build columns on our tomb,
　　And add a perfume to our dust.

NOX NOCTI INDICAT SCIENTIAM

When I survey the bright
　　　　Celestial sphere;
So rich with jewels hung, that night
　　Doth like an Æthiop bride appear:

My soul her wings doth spread
　　　　And heavenward flies,
Th' Almighty's mysteries to read
　　In the large volumes of the skies.

For the bright firmament
　　　　Shoots forth no flame
So silent, but is eloquent
　　In speaking the Creator's name.

No unregarded star
　　　　Contracts its light
Into so small a character,
　　Removed far from our human sight,

But if we steadfast look
　　　We shall discern
In it, as in some holy book,
　　How man may heavenly knowledge learn.

It tells the conqueror
　　　That far-stretch'd power,
Which his proud dangers traffic for,
　　Is but the triumph of an hour:

That from the farthest North,
　　　Some nation may,
Yet undiscover'd, issue forth,
　　And o'er his new-got conquest sway:

Some nation yet shut in
　　　With hills of ice
May be let out to scourge his sin,
　　Till they shall equal him in vice.

And then they likewise shall
　　　Their ruin have;
For as yourselves your empires fall,
　　And every kingdom hath a grave.

Thus those celestial fires,
　　　Though seeming mute,
The fallacy of our desires
　　And all the pride of life confute:—

For they have watch'd since first
　　　The World had birth:
And found sin in itself accurst,
　　And nothing permanent on Earth.

THOMAS RANDOLPH

1605–1635

TO A LADY ADMIRING HERSELF IN A LOOKING-GLASS

FAIR lady, when you see the grace
Of beauty in your looking-glass;
A stately forehead, smooth and high,
And full of princely majesty;
A sparkling eye, no gem so fair,
Whose lustre dims the Cyprian star;
A glorious cheek, divinely sweet,
Wherein both roses kindly meet;
A cherry lip that would entice
Even gods to kiss at any price;
You think no beauty is so rare
That with your shadow might compare;
That your reflection is alone
The thing that men most dote upon.
Madam, alas! your glass doth lie,
And you are much deceived; for I
A beauty know of richer grace—
Sweet, be not angry—'tis your face.
Hence, then, O learn more mild to be,
And leave to lay your blame on me:
If me your real substance move,
When you so much your shadow love,
Wise nature would not let your eye
Look on her own bright majesty;
Which had you once but gazed upon,
You could except yourself love none:
What then you cannot love, let me;
That face I can, you cannot see.

'Now you have what to love,' you'll say,
'What then is left for me, I pray?'
My face, sweet heart, if it please thee;
That which you can, I cannot see:
So either love shall gain his due,
Yours, sweet, in me, and mine in you.

AN ODE TO MR. ANTHONY STAFFORD TO HASTEN HIM INTO THE COUNTRY

COME, spur away,
I have no patience for a longer stay,
But must go down
And leave the chargeable noise of this great
    town:
I will the country see,
Where old simplicity,
Though hid in gray,
Doth look more gay
Than foppery in plush and scarlet clad.
Farewell, you city wits, that are
Almost at civil war—
'Tis time that I grow wise, when all the world grows
    mad.

More of my days
I will not spend to gain an idiot's praise;
Or to make sport
For some slight Puisne of the Inns of Court.
Then, worthy Stafford, say,
How shall we spend the day?
With what delights
Shorten the nights?
When from this tumult we are got secure,

Where mirth with all her freedom goes,
　　　Yet shall no finger lose;
Where every word is thought, and every thought
　　is pure?

　　　　　There from the tree
We'll cherries pluck, and pick the strawberry;
　　　　And every day
Go see the wholesome country girls make hay,
　　　Whose brown hath lovelier grace
　　　Than any painted face
　　　　That I do know
　　　Hyde Park can show:
Where I had rather gain a kiss than meet
　　　(Though some of them in greater state
　　　Might court my love with plate)
The beauties of the Cheap, and wives of Lombard
　　Street.

　　　　　But think upon
Some other pleasures: these to me are none.
　　　　Why do I prate
Of women, that are things against my fate?
　　　I never mean to wed
　　　That torture to my bed:
　　　　My Muse is she
　　　My love shall be.
Let clowns get wealth and heirs: when I am gone
　　And that great bugbear, grisly Death,
　　　Shall take this idle breath,
If I a poem leave, that poem is my son.

　　　　　Of this, no more!
We'll rather taste the bright Pomona's store.
　　　No fruit shall 'scape
Our palates, from the damson to the grape.

Then, full, we'll seek a shade,
And hear what music's made;
　　How Philomel
　　Her tale doth tell,
And how the other birds do fill the quire;
　　The thrush and blackbird lend their throats,
　　Warbling melodious notes;
We will all sports enjoy, which others but desire.

　　Ours is the sky,
Where at what fowl we please our hawk shall
　　fly:
　　Nor will we spare
To hunt the crafty fox or timorous hare;
　　But let our hounds run loose
　　In any ground they'll choose;
　　　The buck shall fall,
　　　The stag, and all.
Our pleasures must from their own warrants be,
　　For to my Muse, if not to me,
　　I'm sure all game is free:
Heaven, earth, are all but parts of her great royalty.

　　And when we mean
To taste of Bacchus' blessings now and then,
　　And drink by stealth
A cup or two to noble Barkley's health,
　　I'll take my pipe and try
　　The Phrygian melody;
　　　Which he that hears,
　　　Lets through his ears
A madness to distemper all the brain:
　　Then I another pipe will take
　　And Doric music make,
To civilize with graver notes our wits again.

POETRY DEFINED

From witty men and mad
All poetry conception had.

No sires but these will poetry admit:
Madness or wit.

This definition poetry doth fit:
It is witty madness, or mad wit.

Only these two poetic heat admits:
A witty man, or one that's out of's wits.

SIR THOMAS BROWNE

1605–1682

EVENING HYMN

The night is come like to the day,
Depart not Thou, great God, away;
Let not my sins, black as the night,
Eclipse the lustre of Thy light.
Keep still in my horizon, for to me
The sun makes not the day, but Thee.
Thou whose nature cannot sleep,
On my temples sentry keep;
Guard me 'gainst those watchful foes,
Whose eyes are open while mine close.
Let no dreams my head infest,
But such as Jacob's temples blest.
While I do rest, my soul advance,
Make my sleep a holy trance:
That I may, my rest being wrought,
Awake into some holy thought.
And with as active vigour run
My course, as doth the nimble sun.

Sleep is a death, O make me try
By sleeping what it is to die.
And as gently lay my head
On my grave, as now my bed.
Now ere I rest, great God, let me
Awake again at last with Thee.
And thus assured, behold I lie
Securely, or to wake or die.
These are my drowsy days, in vain
I do now wake to sleep again.
O come that hour, when I shall never
Sleep again, but wake for ever!

SIR WILLIAM DAVENANT

1606–1668

THE LARK NOW LEAVES HIS WATERY NEST

THE lark now leaves his watery nest,
   And climbing shakes his dewy wings.
He takes this window for the East,
   And to implore your light he sings—
Awake, awake, the morn will never rise
Till she can dress her beauty at your eyes.

The merchant bows unto the seaman's star,
   The ploughman from the sun his season takes;
But still the lover wonders what they are
   Who look for day before his mistress wakes.
Awake, awake! break through your veils of lawn!
Then draw your curtains, and begin the dawn!

THE SOLDIER GOING TO THE FIELD

PRESERVE thy sighs, unthrifty girl,
   To purify the air!
Thy tears to thread, instead of pearl,
   On bracelets of thy hair.

The trumpet makes the echo hoarse,
   And wakes the louder drum.
Expense of grief gains no remorse,
   When sorrow should be dumb.

For I must go where lazy Peace
   Will hide her drowsy head,
And, for the sport of kings, increase
   The number of the dead.

But, first, I'll chide thy cruel theft:
   Can I in war delight,
Who (being of my heart bereft)
   Can have no heart to fight?

Thou know't, the sacred laws of old
   Ordained a thief should pay,
To quit him of his theft, sevenfold
   What he had stol'n away.

Thy payment shall but double be,
   O then with speed resign
My own seducèd heart to me
   Accompanied with thine.

THE DREAM

No victor when in battle spent,
When he at night asleep doth lie
Rich in a conquered monarch's tent,
E'er had so vain a dream as I.

Methought I saw the earliest shade
And sweetest that the spring can spread
Of jesmin, briar, and woodbine made;
And there I saw Clorinda dead.

Though dead she lay, yet could I see
No cypress nor no mourning yew;
Nor yet the injured lover's tree,
No willow near her coffin grew.

But all showed unconcerned to be,
As if just Nature there did strive
To be as pitiless as she
Was to her lover when alive.

And now, methought, I lost all care,
In losing her; and was as free
As birds let loose into the air,
Or rivers that are got to sea.

Methought Love's monarchy was gone;
And whilst elective numbers sway,
Our choice and change makes power our own,
And those court us whom we obey.

Yet soon, now from my Princess free,
I rather frantic grew than glad,
For subjects, getting liberty,
Get but a licence to be mad.

Birds that are long in cages awed,
If they get out, awhile will roam;
But straight want skill to live abroad,
Then pine and hover near their home.

And to the ocean rivers run
From being pent in banks of flowers;
Not knowing that th' exhaling sun
Will send them back in weeping showers.

Soon thus for pride of liberty
I low desires of bondage found;
And vanity of being free
Bred the discretion to be bound.

But as dull subjects see too late
Their safety in monarchal reign,
Finding their freedom in a State
Is but proud strutting in a chain;

Then growing wiser, when undone,
In winter's nights sad stories sing
In praise of monarchs long since gone,
To whom their bells they yearly ring;

So now I mourned that she was dead,
Whose single power did govern me;
And quickly was by reason led
To find the harm of liberty. . . .

In Love's free state where many sway,
Number to change our hearts prepares,
And but one fetter takes away
To lay a world of handsome snares.

And I, Love's secretary now,
(Rayed in my dream to that grave style)
The dangers of Love's state to show
Wrote to the lovers of this isle.

For lovers correspond, and each
Though statesmanlike, he th' other hate,
Yet slily one another teach
By civil love to save the State.

And, as in interreign men draw
Power to themselves of doing right,
When generous reason, not the law,
They think restrains their appetite.

Even so the lovers of this land
(Love's empire in Clorinda gone)
Thought they were quit from Love's command,
And beauty's world was all their own.

But lovers, who are Nature's best
Old subjects, never long revolt;
They soon in passion's war contest,
Yet in their march soon make a halt.

And those, when by the mandates brought
Near dead Clorinda, ceased to boast
Of freedom found, and wept for thought
Of their delightful bondage lost.

And now the day to night was turned,
Or sadly night's close mourning wore;
All maids for one another mourned,
That lovers now could love no more.

All lovers quickly did perceive
They had on earth no more to do
But civilly to take their leave,
As worthies that to dying go.

And now all quires her dirges sing,
In shades of cypress and of yew;
The bells of every temple ring,
Where maids their withered garlands strew.

To such extremes did sorrow rise,
That it transcended speech and form,
And was so lost to ears and eyes
As seamen sinking in a storm.

My soul, in sleep's soft fetters bound,
Did now for vital freedom strive;
And straight, by horror waked, I found
The fair Clorinda still alive.

Yet she's to me but such a light,
As are the stars to those who know
We can at most but guess their height,
And hope they mind us here below.

EDMUND WALLER

1606–1687

SONG

Go, lovely Rose!
Tell her, that wastes her time and me,
    That now she knows,
When I resemble her to thee,
How sweet and fair she seems to be.

    Tell her that's young
And shuns to have her graces spied,
    That hadst thou sprung
In deserts, where no men abide,
Thou must have uncommended died.

    Small is the worth
Of beauty from the light retired:
    Bid her come forth,
Suffer herself to be desired,
And not blush so to be admired.

    Then die! that she
The common fate of all things rare
    May read in thee:
How small a part of time they share
That are so wondrous sweet and fair!

resemble] liken.

ON A GIRDLE

THAT which her slender waist confined
Shall now my joyful temples bind:
No monarch but would give his crown
His arms might do what this has done.

It was my Heaven's extremest sphere,
The pale which held that lovely deer:
My joy, my grief, my hope, my love
Did all within this circle move.

A narrow compass! and yet there
Dwelt all that's good, and all that's fair:
Give me but what this ribband bound,
Take all the rest the Sun goes round.

TO A LADY SINGING A SONG OF HIS COMPOSING

CHLORIS, yourself you so excel,
    When you vouchsafe to breathe my thought,
That, like a spirit, with this spell
    Of my own teaching, I am caught.

That eagle's fate and mine are one,
    Which, on the shaft that made him die,
Espied a feather of his own,
    Wherewith he wont to soar so high.

Had Echo, with so sweet a grace,
    Narcissus' loud complaints returned,
Not for reflection of his face,
    But of his voice, the boy had mourned

FROM 'A PANEGYRIC TO MY LORD PROTECTOR,'
1655

WHILST with a strong and yet a gentle hand
You bridle faction, and our hearts command,
Protect us from ourselves, and from the foe,
Make us unite, and make us conquer too;

Let partial spirits still aloud complain,
Think themselves injured that they cannot
    reign,
And own no liberty, but when they may
Without control upon their fellows prey.

Above the waves, as Neptune showed his face,
To chide the winds, and save the Trojan race,
So has your Highness, raised above the rest,
Storms of ambition tossing us repressed.

Your drooping country, torn with civil hate,
Restored by you, is made a glorious state;
The seat of Empire, where the Irish come,
And the unwilling Scotch, to fetch their doom.

The sea's our own; and now all nations greet
With bending sails each vessel of our fleet;
Your power extends as far as winds can blow,
Or swelling sails upon the globe may go.

Heaven, that hath placed this island to give law
To balance Europe, and its states to awe,
In this conjunction doth on Britain smile,
The greatest leader, and the greatest isle!

Whether this portion of the world were rent
By the rude ocean from the continent,
Or thus created, it was sure designed
To be the sacred refuge of mankind:

Hither th' oppressèd shall henceforth resort,
Justice to crave, and succour at your court;
And then your Highness, not for ours alone,
But for the world's Protector shall be known.

Fame swifter than your wingèd navy flies
Through every land that near the ocean lies,
Sounding your name, and telling dreadful news
To all that piracy and rapine use.

With such a chief the meanest nation blest
Might hope to lift her head above the rest.
What may be thought impossible to do
By us, embracèd by the seas and you,

Lord of the world's great waste, the Ocean? we
Whole forests send to reign upon the sea,
And every coast may trouble or relieve,
But none can visit us without your leave.

Angels and we have this prerogative,
That none can at our happy seas arrive,
While we descend at pleasure to invade
The bad with vengeance, and the good to aid.

Our little world the image of the great,
Like that amidst the boundless ocean set,
Of her own growth hath all that Nature craves,
And all that's rare, as tribute from the waves.

As Egypt does not on the clouds rely
But to the Nile owes more than to the sky,
So what our earth and what our Heaven denies,
Our ever-constant friend the sea supplies.

The taste of hot Arabia's spice we know,
Free from the scorching sun that makes it grow,
Without the worm in Persian silks we shine,
And without planting drink of every vine.

To dig for wealth we weary not our limbs,
Gold (though the heaviest metal) hither swims:
Ours is the harvest where the Indians mow,
We plough the deep, and reap what others sow.

Things of the noblest kind our own soil breeds;
Stout are our men, and warlike are our steeds;
Rome, though her eagle through the world had
    flown,
Could never make this island all her own.

TO MY YOUNG LADY LUCY SIDNEY

Why came I so untimely forth
Into a world which, wanting thee,
Could entertain us with no worth
Or shadow of felicity,
That time should me so far remove
From that which I was born to love?

Yet, fairest blossom! do not slight
That eye which you may know so soon;
The rosy morn resigns her light
And milder glory, to the noon:
And then what wonders shall you do
Whose dawning beauty warms us so?

Hope waits upon the flowery prime;
And summer, though it be less gay,
Yet is not looked on as a time
Of declination or decay;
For with a full hand that does bring
All that was promised by the spring.

FROM 'DIVINE POEMS'

The seas are quiet when the winds give o'er;
So calm are we when passions are no more;
For then we know how vain it was to boast
Of fleeting things so certain to be lost.
Clouds of affection from our younger eyes
Conceal that emptiness which age descries.

The soul's dark cottage, battered and decayed,
Lets in new light through chinks that time hath
    made;
Stronger by weakness, wiser men become
As they draw near to their eternal home:
Leaving the Old, both worlds at once they view
That stand upon the threshold of the New.

JOHN MILTON

1608–1674

HYMN ON THE MORNING OF CHRIST'S NATIVITY

It was the winter wild,
    While the heaven-born child,
    All meanly wrapt in the rude manger lies;
Nature in awe to him
Had doffed her gaudy trim,
    With her great Master so to sympathize:
It was no season then for her
To wanton with the sun her lusty paramour.

Only with speeches fair
She woos the gentle air
    To hide her guilty front with innocent snow,
And on her naked shame,
Pollute with sinful blame,

The saintly veil of maiden white to throw,
Confounded, that her Maker's eyes
Should look so near upon her foul deformities.

But he her fears to cease,
Sent down the meek-eyed Peace,
    She crowned with olive green, came softly sliding
Down through the turning sphere
His ready harbinger,
    With turtle wing the amorous clouds dividing,
And waving wide her myrtle wand,
She strikes a universal peace through sea and land.

No war, or battle's sound
Was heard the world around,
    The idle spear and shield were high uphung;
The hookèd chariot stood
Unstained with hostile blood,
    The trumpet spake not to the armèd throng,
And kings sat still with awful eye,
As if they surely knew their sovereign Lord was by.

But peaceful was the night
Wherein the Prince of light
    His reign of peace upon the earth began:
The winds with wonder whist,
Smoothly the waters kissed,
    Whispering new joys to the mild ocean,
Who now hath quite forgot to rave,
While birds of calm sit brooding on the charmèd
    wave.

The stars with deep amaze
Stand fixed in steadfast gaze,
    Bending one way their precious influence,

whist] hushed, silenced.

And will not take their flight,
For all the morning light,
  Or Lucifer that often warned them thence;
But in their glimmering orbs did glow,
Until their Lord himself bespake, and bid them go.

And though the shady gloom
Had given day her room,
  The sun himself withheld his wonted speed,
And hid his head for shame,
As his inferior flame
  The new enlightened world no more should need;
He saw a greater sun appear
Than his bright throne or burning axletree could
    bear.

The shepherds on the lawn,
Or ere the point of dawn,
  Sat simply chatting in a rustic row;
Full little thought they than,
That the mighty Pan
  Was kindly come to live with them below;
Perhaps their loves, or else their sheep,
Was all that did their silly thoughts so busy keep.

When such music sweet
Their hearts and ears did greet,
  As never was by mortal finger strook,
Divinely-warbled voice
Answering the stringèd noise,
  As all their souls in blissful rapture took:
The air such pleasure loth to lose,
With thousand echoes still prolongs each heavenly
    close.

    Lucifer] Morning Star.   than] then.   strook] struck.

Nature that heard such sound
Beneath the hollow round
  Of Cynthia's seat, the airy region thrilling,
Now was almost won
To think her part was done,
  And that her reign had here its last fulfilling;
She knew such harmony alone
Could hold all heaven and earth in happier union.

At last surrounds their sight
A globe of circular light,
  That with long beams the shame-faced night
    arrayed,
The helmèd Cherubim
And sworded Seraphim,
  Are seen in glittering ranks with wings displayed,
Harping in loud and solemn choir,
With unexpressive notes to Heaven's new-born
    Heir.

Such music (as 'tis said)
Before was never made,
  But when of old the sons of morning sung,
While the Creator great
His constellations set,
  And the well-balanced world on hinges hung,
And cast the dark foundations deep,
And bid the wel'tring waves their oozy channel
    keep.

Ring out, ye crystal spheres,
Once bless our human ears,
  (If ye have power to touch our senses so)
And let your silver chime
Move in melodious time;

Cynthia] the Moon.   unexpressive] inexpressible.

And let the base of heaven's deep organ blow,
And with your ninefold harmony
Make up full consort to the angelic symphony.

For if such holy song
Enwrap our fancy long,
 Time will run back, and fetch the age of gold,
And speckled vanity
Will sicken soon and die,
 And leprous sin will melt from earthly mould,
And hell itself will pass away,
And leave her dolorous mansions to the peering
  day.

Yea, truth and justice then
Will down return to men,
 The enamelled arras of the rainbow wearing,
And mercy set between,
Throned in celestial sheen,
 With radiant feet the tissued clouds down steer-
  ing,
And heaven as at some festival,
Will open wide the gates of her high palace hall.

But wisest fate says no,
This must not yet be so,
 The Babe lies yet in smiling infancy,
That on the bitter cross
Must redeem our loss;
 So both himself and us to glorify:
Yet first to those ychained in sleep,
The wakeful trump of doom must thunder through
  the deep,

   consort] harmony, singing together.

With such a horrid clang
As on mount Sinai rang
   While the red fire, and smouldering clouds out-
     brake:
The agèd earth aghast
With terror of that blast,
   Shall from the surface to the centre shake;
When at the world's last session,
The dreadful Judge in middle air shall spread his
    throne.

And then at last our bliss
Full and perfect is,
   But now begins; for from this happy day
The old dragon under ground
In straiter limits bound,
   Not half so far casts his usurpèd sway,
And wrath to see his kingdom fail,
Swinges the scaly horror of his folded tail.

The oracles are dumb,
No voice or hideous hum
   Runs through the archèd roof in words deceiving.
Apollo from his shrine
Can no more divine,
   With hollow shriek the steep of Delphos leaving.
No nightly trance, or breathèd spell,
Inspires the pale-eyed priest from the prophetic
    cell.

The lonely mountains o'er,
And the resounding shore,
   A voice of weeping heard, and loud lament;
From haunted spring, and dale
Edged with poplar pale,
   The parting genius is with sighing sent,

With flower-inwoven tresses torn
The nymphs in twilight shade of tangled thickets
    mourn.

In consecrated earth,
And on the holy hearth,
    The lars and lemures moan with midnight
      plaint,
In urns, and altars round,
A drear and dying sound
    Affrights the flamens at their service quaint;
And the chill marble seems to sweat,
While each peculiar power forgoes his wonted seat.

Peor, and Baalim,
Forsake their temples dim,
    With that twice-battered god of Palestine,
And moonèd Ashtaroth,
Heaven's Queen and Mother both,
    Now sits not girt with tapers' holy shine,
The Libyc Hammon shrinks his horn,
In vain the Tyrian maids their wounded Thamus
    mourn.

And sullen Moloch fled,
Hath left in shadows dread,
    His burning idol all of blackest hue,
In vain with cymbals' ring,
They call the grisly king,
    In dismal dance about the furnace blue;
The brutish gods of Nile as fast,
Isis and Orus, and the dog Anubis haste.

Nor is Osiris seen
In Memphian grove, or green,
    Trampling the unshow'red grass with lowings
      loud:

Nor can he be at rest
Within his sacred chest,
  Naught but profoundest hell can be his shroud,
In vain with timbrelled anthems dark
The sable-stolèd sorcerers bear his worshipped ark.

He feels from Juda's land
The dreaded Infant's hand,
  The rays of Bethlehem blind his dusky eyn;
Nor all the gods beside,
Longer dare abide,
  Not Typhon huge ending in snaky twine:
Our Babe to show his Godhead true,
Can in his swaddling bands control the damnèd
  crew.

So when the sun in bed,
Curtained with cloudy red,
  Pillows his chin upon an orient wave,
The flocking shadows pale,
Troop to the infernal jail,
  Each fettered ghost slips to his several grave,
And the yellow-skirted fays,
Fly after the night-steeds, leaving their moon-
  loved maze.

But see the Virgin blest,
Hath laid her Babe to rest.
  Time is our tedious song should here have ending,
Heavens youngest-teemèd star,
Hath fixed her polished car,
  Her sleeping Lord with handmaid lamp attend-
    ing:
And all about the courtly stable,
Bright-harnessed angels sit in order serviceable.

      youngest-teemed] youngest-born.

AT A SOLEMN MUSIC

BLEST pair of sirens, pledges of Heaven's joy,
Sphere-born harmonious sisters, voice and verse,
Wed your divine sounds, and mixed power employ
Dead things with inbreathed sense able to pierce,
And to our high-raised phantasy present,
That undisturbèd song of pure concent,
Aye sung before the sapphire-coloured throne
To him that sits thereon
With saintly shout, and solemn jubilee,
Where the bright Seraphim in burning row
Their loud uplifted angel trumpets blow,
And the cherubic host in thousand choirs
Touch their immortal harps of golden wires,
With those just spirits that wear victorious palms,
Hymns devout and holy psalms
Singing everlastingly:
That we on earth with undiscording voice
May rightly answer that melodious noise;
As once we did, till disproportioned sin
Jarred against nature's chime, and with harsh din
Broke the fair music that all creatures made
To their great Lord, whose love their motion
      swayed
In perfect diapason, whilst they stood
In first obedience, and their state of good.
O may we soon again renew that song
And keep in tune with heaven, till God ere long
To his celestial consort us unite,
To live with him, and sing in endless morn of
      light.

concent] harmony.   consort] company.

L'ALLEGRO

Hence, loathèd Melancholy
  Of Cerberus, and blackest midnight born,
In Stygian cave forlorn
  'Mongst horrid shapes, and shrieks, and sights
    unholy,
Find out some uncouth cell,
  Where brooding darkness spreads his jealous wings,
  And the night-raven sings;
    There under ebon shades, and low-browed rocks,
As ragged as thy locks,
  In dark Cimmerian desert ever dwell.
But come, thou goddess fair and free,
In heaven yclep'd Euphrosyne,
And by men, heart-easing mirth,
Whom lovely Venus at a birth
With two sister Graces more
To ivy-crownèd Bacchus bore;
Or whether (as some sager sing)
The frolic wind that breathes the spring,
Zephyr with Aurora playing,
As he met her once a-maying,
There on beds of violets blue,
And fresh-blown roses washed in dew,
Filled her with thee a daughter fair,
So buxom, blithe, and debonair.
Haste thee, nymph, and bring with thee
Jest and youthful jollity,
Quips and cranks, and wanton wiles,
Nods, and becks, and wreathèd smiles,
Such as hang on Hebe's cheek,
And love to live in dimple sleek;

           ebon] black.

Sport that wrinkled Care derides,
And Laughter holding both his sides.
Come, and trip it as ye go
On the light fantastic toe,
And in thy right hand lead with thee,
The mountain nymph, sweet Liberty;
And if I give thee honour due,
Mirth, admit me of thy crew
To live with her, and live with thee,
In unreprovèd pleasures free;
To hear the lark begin his flight,
And singing startle the dull night,
From his watch-tower in the skies,
Till the dappled dawn doth rise;
Then to come in spite of sorrow,
And at my window bid good morrow,
Through the sweet-briar, or the vine,
Or the twisted eglantine.
While the cock with lively din
Scatters the rear of darkness thin,
And to the stack, or the barn-door,
Stoutly struts his dames before,
Oft listening how the hounds and horn
Cheerly rouse the slumbering morn,
From the side of some hoar hill,
Through the high wood echoing shrill:
Some time walking not unseen
By hedge-row elms, on hillocks green,
Right against the eastern gate,
Where the great sun begins his state,
Robed in flames, and amber light,
The clouds in thousand liveries dight.
While the ploughman near at hand

dight] arrayed.

Whistles o'er the furrowed land,
And the milkmaid singeth blithe,
And the mower whets his scythe,
And every shepherd tells his tale
Under the hawthorn in the dale.
Straight mine eye hath caught new pleasures
Whilst the landscape round it measures,
Russet lawns, and fallows grey,
Where the nibbling flocks do stray,
Mountains on whose barren breast
The labouring clouds do often rest:
Meadows trim with daisies pied,
Shallow brooks, and rivers wide.
Towers and battlements it sees
Bosomed high in tufted trees,
Where perhaps some beauty lies,
The cynosure of neighbouring eyes.
Hard by, a cottage chimney smokes,
From betwixt two agèd oaks,
Where Corydon and Thyrsis met,
Are at their savoury dinner set
Of herbs, and other country messes,
Which the neat-handed Phillis dresses;
And then in haste her bower she leaves,
With Thestylis to bind the sheaves;
Or if the earlier season lead
To the tanned haycock in the mead.
Sometimes with secure delight
The upland hamlets will invite,
When the merry bells ring round,
And the jocund rebecks sound
To many a youth, and many a maid,
Dancing in the chequered shade;
And young and old come forth to play

On a sunshine holiday,
Till the livelong daylight fail,
Then to the spicy nut-brown ale,
With stories told of many a feat,
How Faery Mab the junkets ate,
She was pinched and pulled, she said,
And he by Friar's lanthorn led;
Tells how the drudging goblin sweat,
To earn his cream-bowl duly set,
When in one night, ere glimpse of morn,
His shadowy flail hath threshed the corn
That ten day-labourers could not end,
Then lies him down the lubber fiend,
And, stretched out all the chimney's length,
Basks at the fire his hairy strength;
And cropful out of doors he flings,
Ere the first cock his matin rings.
Thus done the tales, to bed they creep,
By whispering winds soon lulled asleep.
Towered cities please us then,
And the busy hum of men,
Where throngs of knights and barons bold
In weeds of peace high triumphs hold,
With store of ladies, whose bright eyes
Rain influence, and judge the prize
Of wit, or arms, while both contend
To win her grace, whom all commend.
There let Hymen oft appear
In saffron robe, with taper clear,
And pomp, and feast, and revelry,
With mask, and antique pageantry,
Such sights as youthful poets dream
On summer eves by haunted stream.
Then to the well-trod stage anon,

If Jonson's learnèd sock be on,
Or sweetest Shakespeare, fancy's child,
Warble his native wood-notes wild,
And ever against eating cares,
Lap me in soft Lydian airs,
Married to immortal verse
Such as the meeting soul may pierce
In notes, with many a winding bout
Of linkèd sweetness long drawn out,
With wanton heed, and giddy cunning,
The melting voice through mazes running;
Untwisting all the chains that tie
The hidden soul of harmony.
That Orpheus self may heave his head
From golden slumber on a bed
Of heaped Elysian flowers, and hear
Such strains as would have won the ear
Of Pluto, to have quite set free
His half-regained Eurydice.
These delights, if thou canst give,
Mirth with thee, I mean to live.

IL PENSEROSO

HENCE, vain deluding joys,
    The brood of Folly without father bred,
How little you bestead,
    Or fill the fixèd mind with all your toys;
Dwell in some idle brain,
    And fancies fond with gaudy shapes possess,
As thick and numberless
    As the gay motes that people the sunbeams,
Or likest hovering dreams
    The fickle pensioners of Morpheus' train.

But hail, thou Goddess, sage and holy,
Hail, divinest Melancholy,
Whose saintly visage is too bright
To hit the sense of human sight;
And therefore to our weaker view,
O'erlaid with black, staid Wisdom's hue.
Black, but such as in esteem,
Prince Memnon's sister might beseem,
Or that starred Ethiope queen that strove
To set her beauty's praise above
The sea nymphs, and their powers offended.
Yet thou art higher far descended,
Thee bright-haired Vesta long of yore,
To solitary Saturn bore;
His daughter she (in Saturn's reign,
Such mixture was not held a stain)
Oft in glimmering bowers and glades
He met her, and in secret shades
Of woody Ida's inmost grove,
Whilst yet there was no fear of Jove.
Come, pensive nun, devout and pure,
Sober, steadfast, and demure,
All in a robe of darkest grain,
Flowing with majestic train,
And sable stole of cypres lawn,
Over thy decent shoulders drawn.
Come, but keep thy wonted state,
With even step, and musing gait,
And looks commercing with the skies,
Thy rapt soul sitting in thine eyes:
There held in holy passion still,
Forget thy self to marble, till
With a sad leaden downward cast,
Thou fix them on the earth as fast.

And join with thee calm peace, and quiet,
Spare fast, that oft with gods doth diet,
And hears the Muses in a ring,
Aye round about Jove's altar sing.
And add to these retirèd leisure,
That in trim gardens takes his pleasure;
But first, and chiefest, with thee bring,
Him that yon soars on golden wing,
Guiding the fiery-wheelèd throne,
The cherub Contemplation,
And the mute Silence hist along,
'Less Philomel will deign a song,
In her sweetest, saddest plight,
Smoothing the rugged brow of night,
While Cynthia checks her dragon yoke,
Gently o'er th' accustomed oak;
Sweet bird that shunn'st the noise of folly,
Most musical, most melancholy!
Thee, chantress, oft the woods among,
I woo to hear thy evensong;
And missing thee, I walk unseen
On the dry smooth-shaven green,
To behold the wandering moon,
Riding near her highest noon,
Like one that had been led astray
Through the Heavens' wide pathless way;
And oft, as if her head she bowed,
Stooping through a fleecy cloud.
Oft on a plat of rising ground,
I hear the far-off curfew sound,
Over some wide-watered shore,
Swinging slow with sullen roar;
Or if the air will not permit,
   hist] summon silently.

Some still removèd place will fit,
Where glowing embers through the room
Teach light to counterfeit a gloom,
Far from all resort of mirth,
Save the cricket on the hearth,
Or the bellman's drowsy charm,
To bless the doors from nightly harm:
Or let my lamp at midnight hour
Be seen in some high lonely tower,
Where I may oft out-watch the Bear,
With thrice-great Hermes, or unsphere
The spirit of Plato to unfold
What worlds, or what vast regions hold
The immortal mind that hath forsook
Her mansion in this fleshly nook:
And of those demons that are found
In fire, air, flood, or under ground,
Whose power hath a true consent
With planet, or with element.
Some time let gorgeous tragedy
In sceptered pall come sweeping by,
Presenting Thebes, or Pelops' line,
Or the tale of Troy divine.
Or what (though rare) of later age,
Ennoblèd hath the buskin'd stage.
But, O sad virgin, that thy power
Might raise Musæus from his bower,
Or bid the soul of Orpheus sing
Such notes as warbled to the string,
Drew iron tears down Pluto's cheek,
And made hell grant what love did seek.
Or call up him that left half told
The story of Cambuscan bold,
Of Camball, and of Algarsife,

And who had Canacè to wife,
That owned the virtuous ring and glass,
And of the wondrous horse of brass,
On which the Tartar king did ride;
And if aught else, great bards beside
In sage and solemn tunes have sung,
Of tourneys and of trophies hung;
Of forests, and enchantments drear,
Where more is meant than meets the ear.
Thus, Night, oft see me in thy pale career,
Till civil-suited Morn appear,
Not tricked and frounced as she was wont,
With the Attic boy to hunt,
But kercheft in a comely cloud,
While rocking winds are piping loud,
Or ushered with a shower still,
When the gust hath blown his fill,
Ending on the rustling leaves,
With minute drops from off the eaves.
And when the sun begins to fling
His flaring beams, me, goddess, bring
To archèd walks of twilight groves,
And shadows brown that Sylvan loves,
Of pine, or monumental oak,
Where the rude axe with heavèd stroke,
Was never heard the nymphs to daunt,
Or fright them from their hallowed haunt.
There in close covert by some brook,
Where no profaner eye may look,
Hide me from day's garish eye,
While the bee with honey'd thigh
That at her flowery work doth sing,
And the waters murmuring

kercheft) kerchief-covered.

With such consort as they keep,
Entice the dewy-feathered Sleep;
And let some strange mysterious dream
Wave at his wings in airy stream
Of lively portraiture displayed,
Softly on my eyelids laid.
And as I wake, sweet music breathe
Above, about, or underneath,
Sent by some spirit to mortals good,
Or the unseen genius of the wood.
But let my due feet never fail,
To walk the studious cloister's pale,
And love the high embowèd roof,
With antique pillars massy-proof,
And storied windows richly dight,
Casting a dim religious light.
There let the pealing organ blow,
To the full voiced choir below,
In service high, and anthems clear,
As may with sweetness, through mine ear,
Dissolve me into ecstasies,
And bring all Heaven before mine eyes.
And may at last my weary age
Find out the peaceful hermitage,
The hairy gown and mossy cell,
Where I may sit and rightly spell
Of every star that heaven doth show,
And every herb that sips the dew;
Till old experience do attain
To something like prophetic strain.
These pleasures, Melancholy, give,
And I with thee will choose to live.

high embowèd] high-arched.

COMUS

*A Masque presented at Ludlow Castle, 1634, before
John, Earl of Bridgewater, then President
of Wales*

THE PERSONS

THE ATTENDANT SPIRIT, *afterwards in the habit of* Thyrsis.
COMUS, *with his Crew.*
THE LADY.
FIRST BROTHER.
SECOND BROTHER.
SABRINA, *the Nymph.*
    THE CHIEF PERSONS WHICH PRESENTED WERE
The Lord BRACKLEY.
Mr. THOMAS EGERTON, *his brother.*
The Lady ALICE EGERTON.

The first Scene discovers a wild wood

THE ATTENDANT SPIRIT *descends or enters.*

BEFORE the starry threshold of Jove's court
My mansion is, where those immortal shapes
Of bright aerial spirits live insphered
In regions mild of calm and serene air,
Above the smoke and stir of this dim spot,
Which men call Earth, and with low-thoughted
    care
Confined, and pestered in this pinfold here,
Strive to keep up a frail and feverish being
Unmindful of the crown that Virtue gives
After this mortal change, to her true servants
Amongst the enthronèd gods on sainted seats.
Yet some there be that by due steps aspire
To lay their just hands on that golden key
That opes the palace of eternity:
To such my errand is, and but for such,

I would not soil these pure ambrosial weeds,
With the rank vapours of this sin-worn mould.
  But to my task. Neptune, besides the sway
Of every salt flood, and each ebbing stream,
Took in by lot 'twixt high and nether Jove,
Imperial rule of all the sea-girt isles
That like to rich and various gems inlay
The unadornèd bosom of the deep,
Which he to grace his tributary gods
By course commits to several government,
And gives them leave to wear their sapphire
    crowns,
And wield their little tridents. But this isle,
The greatest and the best of all the main,
He quarters to his blue-haired deities,
And all this tract that fronts the falling sun
A noble peer of mickle trust and power
Has in his charge, with tempered awe to guide
An old and haughty nation proud in arms:
Where his fair offspring nursed in princely lore,
Are coming to attend their father's state,
And new-entrusted sceptre. But their way
Lies through the perplexed paths of this drear wood,
The nodding horror of whose shady brows
Threats the forlorn and wandering passenger.
And here their tender age might suffer peril,
But that by quick command from sovereign Jove
I was dispatched for their defence, and guard;
And listen why, for I will tell ye now
What never yet was heard in tale or song
From old or modern bard in hall or bower.
  Bacchus that first from out the purple grape
Crushed the sweet poison of misusèd wine,
After the Tuscan mariners transformed

Coasting the Tyrrhene shore, as the winds listed,
On Circe's island fell. (Who knows not Circe
The daughter of the Sun? whose charmèd cup
Whoever tasted, lost his upright shape,
And downward fell into a grovelling swine.)
This Nymph that gazed upon his clustering locks,
With ivy berries wreathed, and his blithe youth,
Had by him, ere he parted thence, a son
Much like his father, but his mother more,
Whom therefore she brought up and Comus named,
Who ripe, and frolic of his full-grown age,
Roving the Celtic and Iberian fields,
At last betakes him to this ominous wood,
And in thick shelter of black shades embowered,
Excels his mother at her mighty art,
Offering to every weary traveller
His orient liquor in a crystal glass,
To quench the drouth of Phœbus, which as they
          taste
(For most do taste through fond intemperate
          thirst)
Soon as the potion works, their human count'nance,
Th' express resemblance of the gods, is changed
Into some brutish form of wolf, or bear,
Or ounce, or tiger, hog, or bearded goat,
All other parts remaining as they were,
And they, so perfect is their misery,
Not once perceive their foul disfigurement,
But boast themselves more comely than before;
And all their friends, and native home forget
To roll with pleasure in a sensual sty.
Therefore when any favoured of high Jove
Chances to pass through this adventurous glade,
Swift as the sparkle of a glancing star,

I shoot from Heaven to give him safe convoy,
As now I do: but first I must put off
These my sky-robes spun out of Iris' woof,
And take the weeds and likeness of a swain,
That to the service of this house belongs,
Who with his soft pipe, and smooth-dittied song,
Well knows to still the wild winds when they roar,
And hush the waving woods, nor of less faith,
And in this office of his mountain watch
Likeliest, and nearest to the present aid
Of this occasion. But I hear the tread
Of hateful steps, I must be viewless now.

COMUS *enters with a charming-rod in one hand, his
    glass in the other; with him a rout of monsters,
    headed like sundry sorts of wild beasts, but
    otherwise like men and women, their apparel
    glistering, they come in making a riotous and
    unruly noise, with torches in their hands.*

COMUS

The star that bids the shepherd fold
Now the top of heaven doth hold,
And the gilded car of day
His glowing axle doth allay
In the steep Atlantic stream,
And the slope sun his upward beam
Shoots against the dusky pole,
Pacing toward the other goal
Of his chamber in the East.
Meanwhile welcome joy, and feast,
Midnight shout, and revelry,
Tipsy dance, and jollity.
Braid your locks with rosy twine,

Dropping odours, dropping wine.
Rigour now is gone to bed,
And advice with scrupulous head,
Strict age, and sour severity,
With their grave saws in slumber lie.
We that are of purer fire
Imitate the starry choir,
Who in their nightly watchful spheres
Lead in swift round the months and years.
The sounds, and seas with all their finny drove
Now to the moon in wavering morrice move,
And on the tawny sands and shelves,
Trip the pert fairies and the dapper elves.
By dimpled brook, and fountain brim,
The wood-nymphs decked with daisies trim,
Their merry wakes and pastimes keep:
What hath night to do with sleep?
Night hath better sweets to prove,
Venus now wakes, and wakens love.
Come, let us our rites begin,
'Tis only daylight that makes sin,
Which these dun shades will ne'er report.
Hail, Goddess of nocturnal sport
Dark veil'd Cotytto, t' whom the secret flame
Of midnight torches burns; mysterious dame
That ne'er art called, but when the dragon womb
Of Stygian darkness spits her thickest gloom,
And makes one blot of all the air,
Stay thy cloudy ebon chair,
Wherein thou ridest with Hecat', and befriend
Us thy vow'd priests, till utmost end
Of all thy dues be done, and none left out,
Ere the blabbing eastern scout,
The nice morn on the Indian steep,

From her cabined loophole peep,
And to the tell-tale sun descry
Our concealed solemnity.
Come, knit hands, and beat the ground,
In a light fantastic round.

THE MEASURE

Break off, break off, I feel the different pace
Of some chaste footing near about this ground.
Run to your shrouds, within these brakes and trees,
Our number may affright: some virgin sure
(For so I can distinguish by mine art)
Benighted in these woods. Now to my charms,
And to my wily trains; I shall ere long
Be well stocked with as fair a herd as grazed
About my mother Circe. Thus I hurl
My dazzling spells into the spongy air,
Of power to cheat the eye with blear illusion,
And give it false presentments, lest the place
And my quaint habits breed astonishment,
And put the damsel to suspicious flight,
Which must not be, for that's against my course;
I under fair pretence of friendly ends,
And well-placed words of glozing courtesy
Baited with reasons not unplausible,
Wind me into the easy-hearted man,
And hug him into snares. When once her eye
Hath met the virtue of this magic dust,
I shall appear some harmless villager
Whom thrift keeps up about his country gear.
But here she comes, I fairly step aside,
And hearken, if I may, her business here.

The LADY *enters*

Lady. This way the noise was, if mine ear be true,

My best guide now, methought it was the sound
Of riot, and ill-managed merriment,
Such as the jocund flute, or gamesome pipe
Stirs up among the loose unlettered hinds,
When for their teeming flocks, and granges full
In wanton dance they praise the bounteous Pan,
And thank the gods amiss. I should be loth
To meet the rudeness, and swilled insolence
Of such late wassailers; yet O where else
Shall I inform my unacquainted feet
In the blind mazes of this tangled wood?
My brothers when they saw me wearied out
With this long way, resolving here to lodge
Under the spreading favour of these pines,
Stept, as they said, to the next thicket side
To bring me berries, or such cooling fruit
As the kind hospitable woods provide.
They left me then, when the gray-hooded ev'n,
Like a sad votarist in palmer's weed
Rose from the hindmost wheels of Phœbus' wain.
But where they are, and why they came not back,
Is now the labour of my thoughts, 'tis likeliest
They had engaged their wandering steps too far,
And envious darkness, ere they could return,
Had stole them from me; else, O thievish night,
Why shouldst thou, but for some felonious end,
In thy dark lantern thus close up the stars,
That nature hung in heaven, and filled their lamps
With everlasting oil, to give due light
To the misled and lonely traveller?
This is the place, as well as I may guess,
Whence even now the tumult of loud mirth
Was rife, and perfect in my listening ear,
Yet nought but single darkness do I find.

What might this be? A thousand fantasies
Begin to throng into my memory
Of calling shapes, and beckoning shadows dire,
And airy tongues, that syllable men's names
On sands, and shores, and desert wildernesses.
These thoughts may startle well, but not astound,
The virtuous mind, that ever walks attended
By a strong siding champion, Conscience.—
O welcome, pure-eyed Faith, white-handed Hope,
Thou hovering angel girt with golden wings,
And thou unblemished form of Chastity!
I see ye visibly, and now believe
That he, the Supreme Good, to whom all things ill
Are but as slavish officers of vengeance,
Would send a glistering guardian, if need were,
To keep my life and honour unassailed.
Was I deceived, or did a sable cloud
Turn forth her silver lining on the night?
I did not err, there does a sable cloud
Turn forth her silver lining on the night,
And casts a gleam over this tufted grove.
I cannot halloo to my brothers, but
Such noise as I can make to be heard farthest
I'll venture, for my new-enlivened spirits
Prompt me; and they perhaps are not far off.

SONG

Sweet Echo, sweetest nymph, that liv'st unseen
        Within thy airy shell
     By slow Meander's margent green;
And in the violet-embroidered vale,
     Where the love-lorn nightingale
Nightly to thee her sad song mourneth well:
Canst thou not tell me of a gentle pair

That likest thy Narcissus are?
   O if thou have
Hid them in some flowery cave,
   Tell me but where,
Sweet queen of parley, daughter of the sphere,
So may'st thou be translated to the skies,
And give resounding grace to all heaven's har-
   monies.

   Comus. Can any mortal mixture of earth's
   mould
Breathe such divine enchanting ravishment?
Sure something holy lodges in that breast,
And with these raptures moves the vocal air
To testify his hidden residence;
How sweetly did they float upon the wings
Of silence, through the empty-vaulted night
At every fall smoothing the raven down
Of Darkness till it smiled: I have oft heard
My mother Circe with the Sirens three,
Amidst the flowery-kirtled Naiades
Culling their potent herbs and baleful drugs,
Who, as they sung, would take the prisoned soul
And lap it in Elysium, Scylla wept,
And chid her barking waves into attention,
And fell Charybdis murmured soft applause:
Yet they in pleasing slumber lulled the sense,
And in sweet madness robbed it of itself,
But such a sacred and home-felt delight,
Such sober certainty of waking bliss,
I never heard till now. I'll speak to her
And she shall be my queen. Hail, foreign wonder
Whom certain these rough shades did never breed
Unless the goddess that in rural shrine

Dwell'st here with Pan, or Sylvan, by blest song
Forbidding every bleak unkindly fog
To touch the prosperous growth of this tall wood.

    Lady. Nay, gentle shepherd, ill is lost that
        praise
That is addressed to unattending ears,
Not any boast of skill, but extreme shift
How to regain my severed company
Compelled me to awake the courteous Echo
To give me answer from her mossy couch.

    Com. What chance, good lady, hath bereft you
        thus?

    Lady. Dim darkness, and this leafy labyrinth.

    Com. Could that divide you from near-ushering
        guides?

    Lady. They left me weary on a grassy turf.

    Com. By falsehood, or discourtesy, or why?

    Lady. To seek i' the valley some cool friendly
        spring.

    Com. And left your fair side all unguarded, lady?

    Lady. They were but twain, and purposed quick
        return.

    Com. Perhaps forestalling night prevented
        them.

    Lady. How easy my misfortune is to hit!

    Com. Imports their loss, beside the present
        need?

    Lady. No less than if I should my brothers lose.

    Com. Were they of manly prime, or youthful
        bloom?

    Lady. As smooth as Hebe's their unrazored lips.

    Com. Two such I saw, what time the laboured
        ox
In his loose traces from the furrow came,

And the swinked hedger at his supper sate;
I saw them under a green mantling vine
That crawls along the side of yon small hill,
Plucking ripe clusters from the tender shoots,
Their port was more than human, as they stood;
I took it for a faëry vision
Of some gay creatures of the element
That in the colours of the rainbow live
And play i' the plighted clouds. I was awestruck,
And as I passed, I worshipped: if those you seek
It were a journey like the path to Heav'n,
To help you find them.

    Lady.   Gentle villager,
What readiest way would bring me to that place?
    Comus. Due west it rises from this shrubby
      point.
    Lady. To find out that, good shepherd, I sup-
      pose,
In such a scant allowance of star-light,
Would overtask the best land-pilot's art,
Without the sure guess of well-practised feet.
    Comus. I know each lane, and every alley green,
Dingle, or bushy dell of this wild wood,
And every bosky bourn from side to side,
My daily walks and ancient neighbourhood,
And if your stray attendance be yet lodged,
Or shroud within these limits, I shall know
Ere morrow wake, or the low-roosted lark
From her thatched pallet rouse, if otherwise
I can conduct you, lady, to a low
But loyal cottage, where you may be safe
Till further quest.
    Lady.   Shepherd, I take thy word,

      swinked] tired.   attendance] attendants.

And trust thy honest-offered courtesy,
Which oft is sooner found in lowly sheds
With smoky rafters, than in tapestry halls
In courts of princes, where it first was named,
And yet is most pretended: in a place
Less warranted than this, or less secure,
I cannot be, that I should fear to change it.
Eye me, blest Providence, and square my trial
To my proportioned strength. Shepherd, lead on.
                                             [*Exeunt.*

Enter the TWO BROTHERS

Elder Brother. Unmuffle, ye faint stars, and
    thou, fair Moon,
That wont'st to love the traveller's benison,
Stoop thy pale visage through an amber cloud,
And disinherit Chaos, that reigns here
In double night of darkness, and of shades;
Or if your influence be quite dammed up
With black usurping mists, some gentle taper,
Though a rush-candle from the wicker hole
Of some clay habitation, visit us
With thy long levelled rule of streaming light,
And thou shalt be our star of Arcady,
Or Tyrian cynosure.
    Second Brother.   Or if our eyes
Be barred that happiness, might we but hear
The folded flocks penned in their wattled cotes,
Or sound of pastoral reed with oaten stops,
Or whistle from the lodge, or village cock
Count the night watches to his feathery dames,
'Twould be some solace yet, some little cheering
In this close dungeon of innumerous boughs.
But O that hapless virgin our lost sister!
Where may she wander now, whither betake her

From the chill dew, among rude burs and thistles?
Perhaps some cold bank is her bolster now,
Or 'gainst the rugged bark of some broad elm
Leans her unpillowed head, fraught with sad fears.
What if in wild amazement, and affright,
Or, while we speak within the direful grasp
Of savage hunger, or of savage heat?

    Elder Brother. Peace, brother, be not over-
exquisite
To cast the fashion of uncertain evils;
For grant they be so, while they rest unknown,
What need a man forestall his date of grief,
And run to meet what he would most avoid?
Or if they be but false alarms of fear,
How bitter is such self-delusion!
I do not think my sister so to seek,
Or so unprincipled in virtue's book,
And the sweet peace that goodness bosoms ever,
As that the single want of light and noise
(Not being in danger, as I trust she is not),
Could stir the constant mood of her calm thoughts,
And put them into misbecoming plight.
Virtue could see to do what virtue would
By her own radiant light, though sun and moon
Were in the flat sea sunk. And Wisdom's self
Oft seeks to sweet retirèd solitude,
Where with her best nurse Contemplation
She plumes her feathers, and lets grow her wings,
That in the various bustle of resort
Were all to-ruffled and sometimes impaired.
He that has light within his own clear breast
May sit i' the centre, and enjoy bright day,
But he that hides a dark soul and foul thoughts
Benighted walks under the mid-day sun;

Himself is his own dungeon.

   Second Brother.   'Tis most true
That musing meditation most affects
The pensive secrecy of desert cell,
Far from the cheerful haunt of men, and herds,
And sits as safe as in a senate-house,
For who would rob a hermit of his weeds,
His few books, or his beads, or maple dish,
Or do his gray hairs any violence?
But beauty, like the fair Hesperian tree
Laden with blooming gold, had need the guard
Of dragon watch with unenchanted eye,
To save her blossoms, and defend her fruit
From the rash hand of bold incontinence.
You may as well spread out the unsunned heaps
Of misers' treasure by an outlaw's den,
And tell me it is safe, as bid me hope
Danger will wink on opportunity,
And let a single helpless maiden pass
Uninjured in this wild surrounding waste.
Of night or loneliness it recks me not,
I fear the dread events that dog them both,
Lest some ill-greeting touch attempt the person
Of our unownèd sister.

   Elder Brother.   I do not, brother,
Infer, as if I thought my sister's state
Secure without all doubt, or controversy:
Yet where an equal poise of hope and fear
Does arbitrate th' event, my nature is
That I incline to hope, rather than fear,
And gladly banish squint suspicion.
My sister is not so defenceless left
As you imagine, she has a hidden strength
Which you remember not.

Second Brother.   What hidden strength,
Unless the strength of heaven, if you mean that?
    Elder Brother. I mean that too, but yet a hidden
        strength
Which if Heaven gave it, may be termed her own:
'Tis chastity, my brother, chastity:
She that has that, is clad in complete steel,
And like a quivered nymph with arrows keen
May trace huge forests, and unharboured heaths,
Infamous hills, and sandy perilous wilds,
Where, through the sacred rays of chastity,
No savage fierce, bandit, or mountaineer
Will dare to soil her virgin purity,
Yea there, where very desolation dwells
By grots, and caverns shagged with horrid shades,
She may pass on with unblenched majesty,
Be it not done in pride, or in presumption.
Some say, no evil thing that walks by night
In fog, or fire, by lake, or moorish fen,
Blue meagre hag, or stubborn unlaid ghost,
That breaks his magic chains at curfew-time,
No goblin, or swart faëry of the mine,
Hath hurtful power o'er true virginity.
Do ye believe me yet, or shall I call
Antiquity from the old schools of Greece
To testify the arms of chastity?
Hence had the huntress Dian her dread bow,
Fair silver-shafted queen for ever chaste,
Wherewith she tamed the brinded lioness
And spotted mountain pard, but set at naught
The frivolous bolt of Cupid; gods and men
Feared her stern frown, and she was queen o' the
    woods.

unblenched] fearless.

What was that snaky-headed Gorgon shield
That wise Minerva wore, unconquered virgin,
Wherewith she freezed her foes to congealed stone,
But rigid looks of chaste austerity,
And noble grace that dashed brute violence
With sudden adoration, and blank awe?
So dear to heaven is saintly chastity,
That when a soul is found sincerely so,
A thousand liveried angels lackey her,
Driving far off each thing of sin and guilt,
And in clear dream, and solemn vision,
Tell her of things that no gross ear can hear,
Till oft converse with heavenly habitants
Begin to cast a beam on th' outward shape,
The unpolluted temple of the mind,
And turns it by degrees to the soul's essence,
Till all be made immortal: but when lust
By unchaste looks, loose gestures, and foul talk,
But most by lewd and lavish act of sin,
Lets in defilement to the inward parts,
The soul grows clotted by contagion,
Imbodies, and imbrutes, till she quite lose
The divine property of her first being.
Such are those thick and gloomy shadows damp
Oft seen in charnel-vaults and sepulchres
Lingering, and sitting by a new-made grave,
As loth to leave the body that it loved,
And linked itself by carnal sensualty
To a degenerate and degraded state.
    Second Brother. How charming is divine philo-
      sophy!
Not harsh and crabbèd as dull fools suppose,
But musical as is Apollo's lute,
And a perpetual feast of nectared sweets,

Where no crude surfeit reigns.

    Elder Brother.   List, list, I hear
Some far off halloo break the silent air.

    Second Brother. Methought so too; what should
      it be?

    Elder Brother.   For certain
Either some one like us night-foundered here,
Or else some neighbour woodman, or at worst,
Some roving robber calling to his fellows.

    Second Brother. Heaven keep my sister! Again,
      again, and near,
Best draw, and stand upon our guard.

    Elder Brother.   I'll halloo,
If he be friendly he comes well; if not,
Defence is a good cause, and Heaven be for us.

    Enter the ATTENDANT SPIRIT, *habited like a*
            shepherd.

That halloo I should know, what are you? speak;
Come not too near, you fall on iron stakes else.

    Spirit. What voice is that? my young lord?
      speak again.

    Sec. Br. O brother, 'tis my father's shepherd,
      sure.

    El. Br. Thyrsis? Whose artful strains have oft
      delayed
The huddling brook to hear his madrigal,
And sweetened every muskrose of the dale,
How cam'st thou here, good swain? hath any ram
Slipped from the fold, or young kid lost his dam,
Or straggling wether the pent flock forsook?
How could'st thou find this dark sequestered nook?

    Spirit. O my loved master's heir, and his next
      joy,

I came not here on such a trivial toy
As a strayed ewe, or to pursue the stealth
Of pilfering wolf; not all the fleecy wealth
That doth enrich these downs, is worth a thought
To this my errand, and the care it brought.
But O my virgin lady, where is she?
How chance she is not in your company?
   Elder Brother. To tell thee sadly, shepherd,
     without blame,
Or our neglect, we lost her as we came.
   Spirit. Ay me unhappy! then my fears are true.
   Elder Brother. What fears, good Thyrsis?
     Prithee briefly show.
   Spirit. I'll tell ye, 'tis not vain, or fabulous,
(Though so esteemed by shallow ignorance)
What the sage poets, taught by th' heavenly Muse,
Storied of old in high immortal verse
Of dire chimeras and enchanted isles,
And rifted rocks whose entrance leads to hell,
For such there be, but unbelief is blind.
   Within the navel of this hideous wood,
Immured in cypress shades a sorcerer dwells
Of Bacchus and of Circe born, great Comus,
Deep skilled in all his mother's witcheries,
And here to every thirsty wanderer
By sly enticement gives his baneful cup,
With many murmurs mixed; whose pleasing poison
The visage quite transforms of him that drinks,
And the inglorious likeness of a beast
Fixes instead, unmoulding reason's mintage,
Charactered in the face; this have I learnt
Tending my flocks hard by i' the hilly crofts,
That brow this bottom glade, whence night by
     night

He and his monstrous rout are heard to howl
Like stabled wolves, or tigers at their prey,
Doing abhorrèd rites to Hecate
In their obscurèd haunts of inmost bowers.
Yet have they many baits, and guileful spells
To inveigle and invite th' unwary sense
Of them that pass unweeting by the way.
This evening late, by then the chewing flocks
Had ta'en their supper on the savoury herb
Of knot-grass dew-besprent, and were in fold,
I sat me down to watch upon a bank
With ivy canopied, and interwove
With flaunting honeysuckle, and began
Wrapt in a pleasing fit of melancholy
To meditate my rural minstrelsy,
Till fancy had her fill, but ere a close
The wonted roar was up amidst the woods,
And filled the air with barbarous dissonance,
At which I ceased, and listened them awhile,
Till an unusual stop of sudden silence
Gave respite to the drowsy frighted steeds
That draw the litter of close-curtained sleep.
At last a soft and solemn-breathing sound
Rose like a steam of rich distilled perfumes,
And stole upon the air, that even Silence
Was took ere she was ware, and wished she might
Deny her nature, and be never more
Still to be so displaced. I was all ear,
And took in strains that might create a soul
Under the ribs of Death; but O ere long
Too well I did perceive it was the voice
Of my most honoured Lady, your dear sister.
Amazed I stood, harrowed with grief and fear,

unweeting] unwitting.

And 'O poor hapless nightingale,' thought I,
'How sweet thou sing'st, how near the deadly
   snare!'
Then down the lawns I ran with headlong haste
Through paths, and turnings often trod by day,
Till guided by mine ear I found the place
Where that damned wizard hid in sly disguise
(For so by certain signs I knew) had met
Already, ere my best speed could prevent,
The aidless innocent lady, his wished prey,
Who gently asked if he had seen such two,
Supposing him some neighbour villager;
Longer I durst not stay, but soon I guessed
Ye were the two she meant, with that I sprung
Into swift flight, till I had found you here,
But further know I not.

   Second Brother.   O night and shades,
How are ye join'd with hell in triple knot
Against the unarmed weakness of one virgin
Alone, and helpless! Is this the confidence
You gave me, brother?

   Elder Brother.   Yes, and keep it still;
Lean on it safely, not a period
Shall be unsaid for me: against the threats
Of malice or of sorcery, or that power
Which erring men call chance, this I hold firm,
Virtue may be assailed, but never hurt,
Surprised by unjust force, but not enthralled;
Yea even that which mischief meant most harm,
Shall in the happy trial prove most glory.
But evil on itself shall back recoil,
And mix no more with goodness, when at last
Gathered like scum, and settled to itself
It shall be in eternal restless change

Self-fed, and self-consumèd; if this fail,
The pillared firmament is rottenness,
And earth's base built on stubble. But come, let's
    on.
Against the opposing will and arm of heaven
May never this just sword be lifted up;
But for that damned magician, let him be girt
With all the grisly legions that troop
Under the sooty flag of Acheron,
Harpies and hydras, or all the monstrous forms
'Twixt Africa and Ind, I'll find him out,
And force him to return his purchase back,
Or drag him by the curls to a foul death,
Cursed as his life.

   Spirit.   Alas! good vent'rous youth,
I love thy courage yet, and bold emprise,
But here thy sword can do thee little stead,
Far other arms, and other weapons must
Be those that quell the might of hellish charms,
He with his bare wand can unthread thy joints,
And crumble all thy sinews.

   Elder Brother.   Why prithee shepherd
How durst thou then thyself approach so near
As to make this relation?

   Spirit.   Care and utmost shifts
How to secure the lady from surprisal,
Brought to my mind a certain shepherd lad
Of small regard to see to, yet well skilled
In every virtuous plant and healing herb
That spreads her verdant leaf to the morning ray,
He loved me well, and oft would beg me sing,
Which when I did, he on the tender grass
Would sit, and hearken even to ecstasy,
And in requital ope his leathern scrip,

And show me simples of a thousand names,
Telling their strange and vigorous faculties;
Amongst the rest a small unsightly root,
But of divine effect, he culled me out;
The leaf was darkish, and had prickles on it,
But in another country, as he said,
Bore a bright golden flower, but not in this soil:
Unknown, and like esteemed, and the dull swain
Treads on it daily with his clouted shoon,
And yet more med'cinal is it than that moly
That Hermes once to wise Ulysses gave;
He called it hæmony, and gave it me,
And bade me keep it as of sovereign use
'Gainst all enchantments, mildew blast, or damp,
Or ghastly furies' apparition;
I pursed it up, but little reckoning made,
Till now that this extremity compelled,
But now I find it true; for by this means
I knew the foul enchanter though disguised,
Entered the very lime-twigs of his spells,
And yet came off: if you have this about you
(As I will give you when we go) you may
Boldly assault the necromancer's hall;
Where if he be, with dauntless hardihood,
And brandished blade rush on him, break his glass,
And shed the luscious liquor on the ground,
But seize his wand, though he and his cursed
        crew
Fierce sign of battle make, and menace high,
Or like the sons of Vulcan vomit smoke,
Yet will they soon retire, if he but shrink.

    El. Br. Thyrsis, lead on apace, I'll follow thee,
And some good angel bear a shield before us.

moly] fabulous herb.

*The Scene changes to a stately palace, set out with all
manner of deliciousness; soft music, tables spread
with all dainties.* COMUS *appears with his rabble,
and the* LADY *set in an enchanted chair, to whom
he offers his glass, which she puts by, and goes
about to rise.*

COMUS

Nay, lady, sit; if I but wave this wand,
Your nerves are all chained up in alabaster,
And you a statue; or as Daphne was
Rootbound, that fled Apollo.

  Lady.   Fool, do not boast,
Thou canst not touch the freedom of my mind
With all thy charms, although this corporal rind
Thou hast immanacled, while heaven sees good.

  Comus. Why are you vexed, lady? why do you
   frown?
Here dwell no frowns, nor anger, from these gates
Sorrow flies far. See, here be all the pleasures
That fancy can beget on youthful thoughts,
When the fresh blood grows lively, and returns
Brisk as the April buds in primrose-season.
And first behold this cordial julep here,
That flames and dances in his crystal bounds
With spirits of balm, and fragrant syrups mixed.
Not that Nepenthes which the wife of Thone
In Egypt gave to Jove-born Helena,
Is of such power to stir up joy as this,
To life so friendly, or so cool to thirst.
Why should you be so cruel to yourself,
And to those dainty limbs which Nature lent
For gentle usage, and soft delicacy?
But you invert the covenants of her trust,

And harshly deal like an ill borrower
With that which you received on other terms,
Scorning the unexempt condition
By which all mortal frailty must subsist,
Refreshment after toil, ease after pain,
That have been tired all day without repast,
And timely rest have wanted, but, fair virgin,
This will restore all soon.

    Lady.   'Twill not, false traitor,
'Twill not restore the truth and honesty
That thou hast banished from thy tongue with lies,
Was this the cottage, and the safe abode
Thou told'st me of? What grim aspects are these,
These ugly-headed monsters? Mercy guard me!
Hence with thy brewed enchantments, foul de-
    ceiver,
Hast thou betrayed my credulous innocence
With visored falsehood, and base forgery,
And wouldst thou seek again to trap me here
With lickerish baits fit to ensnare a brute?
Were it a draught for Juno when she banquets,
I would not taste thy treasonous offer; none
But such as are good men can give good things;
And that which is not good, is not delicious
To a well-governed and wise appetite.

    Comus. O foolishness of men! that lend their
    ears
To those budge doctors of the Stoic fur,
And fetch their precepts from the Cynic tub,
Praising the lean and sallow abstinence.
Wherefore did Nature pour her bounties forth,
With such a full and unwithdrawing hand,
Covering the earth with odours, fruits, and flocks,

             budge] pompous, formal.

Thronging the seas with spawn innumerable,
But all to please and sate the curious taste?
And set to work millions of spinning worms,
That in their green shops weave the smooth-haired
    silk
To deck her sons, and that no corner might
Be vacant of her plenty, in her own loins
She hutched the all-worshipped ore and precious
    gems
To store her children with; if all the world
Should in a pet of temperance feed on pulse,
Drink the clear stream, and nothing wear but
    frieze,
The All-giver would be unthanked, would be un-
    praised,
Not half his riches known, and yet despised,
And we should serve him as a grudging master,
As a penurious niggard of his wealth,
And live like Nature's bastards, not her sons,
Who would be quite surcharged with her own
    weight,
And strangled with her waste fertility,
The earth cumbered, and the winged air darked
    with plumes,
The nerds would over-multitude their lords,
The sea o'erfraught would swell, and the unsought
    diamonds
Would so emblaze the forehead of the deep,
And so bestud with stars, that they below
Would grow inured to light, and come at last
To gaze upon the sun with shameless brows.
List, lady, be not coy, and be not cozened
With that same vaunted name virginity,

                    hutched] stored.

Beauty is nature's coin, must not be hoarded,
But must be current, and the good thereof
Consists in mutual and partaken bliss,
Unsavoury in th' enjoyment of itself;
If you let slip time, like a neglected rose
It withers on the stalk with languished head.
Beauty is Nature's brag, and must be shown
In courts, at feasts, and high solemnities
Where most may wonder at the workmanship;
It is for homely features to keep home,
They had their name thence; coarse complexions
And cheeks of sorry grain will serve to ply
The sampler, and to tease the huswife's wool.
What need a vermeil-tinctured lip for that
Love-darting eyes, or tresses like the morn?
There was another meaning in these gifts,
Think what, and be advised, you are but young yet.

    Lady. I had not thought to have unlocked my
        lips
In this unhallowed air, but that this juggler
Would think to charm my judgement, as mine eyes,
Obtruding false rules pranked in reason's garb.
I hate when vice can bolt her arguments,
And virtue has no tongue to check her pride:
Imposter, do not charge most innocent nature,
As if she would her children should be riotous
With her abundance, she, good cateress,
Means her provision only to the good
That live according to her sober laws,
And holy dictate of spare temperance:
If every just man that now pines with want
Had but a moderate and beseeming share
Of that which lewdly-pampered luxury

           vermeil] vermilion.

Now heaps upon some few with vast excess,
Nature's full blessings would be well dispensed
In unsuperfluous even proportion,
And she no whit encumbered with her store,
And then the Giver would be better thanked,
His praise due paid, for swinish gluttony
Ne'er looks to heaven amidst his gorgeous feast,
But with besotted base ingratitude
Crams, and blasphemes his feeder. Shall I go on?
Or have I said enough? To him that dares
Arm his profane tongue with contemptuous words
Against the sun-clad power of chastity,
Fain would I something say, yet to what end?
Thou hast nor ear nor soul to apprehend
The sublime notion and high mystery
That must be uttered to unfold the sage
And serious doctrine of virginity;
And thou art worthy that thou shouldst not know
More happiness than this thy present lot.
Enjoy your dear wit, and gay rhetoric
That hath so well been taught her dazzling fence,
Thou art not fit to hear thyself convinced;
Yet should I try, the uncontrollèd worth
Of this pure cause would kindle my rapt spirits
To such a flame of sacred vehemence,
That dumb things would be moved to sympathize,
And the brute earth would lend her nerves, and shake,
Till all thy magic structures reared so high,
Were shattered into heaps o'er thy false head.
   Comus. She fables not, I feel that I do fear
Her words set off by some superior power;
And though not mortal, yet a cold shuddering dew
Dips me all o'er, as when the wrath of Jove
Speaks thunder and the chains of Erebus

To some of Saturn's crew. I must dissemble,
And try her yet more strongly. Come, no more,
This is mere moral babble, and direct
Against the canon laws of our foundation;
I must not suffer this, yet 'tis but the lees
And settlings of a melancholy blood;
But this will cure all straight, one sip of this
Will bathe the drooping spirits in delight
Beyond the bliss of dreams. Be wise, and taste.

The BROTHERS *rush in with swords drawn, wrest his glass out of his hand, and break it against the ground; his rout make sign of resistance, but are all driven in; the* ATTENDANT SPIRIT *comes in.*

SPIRIT

What, have you let the false enchanter scape?
O ye mistook, ye should have snatched his wand
And bound him fast; without his rod reversed
And backward mutters of dissevering power,
We cannot free the lady that sits here
In stony fetters fixed and motionless;
Yet stay, be not disturbed, now I bethink me,
Some other means I have which may be used,
Which once of Melibœus old I learnt,
The soothest shepherd that e'er piped on plains.
   There is a gentle nymph not far from hence,
That with moist curb sways the smooth Severn
      stream,
Sabrina is her name, a virgin pure,
Whilom she was the daughter of Locrine,
That had the sceptre from his father Brute.
The guiltless damsel, flying the mad pursuit
Of her enragèd stepdame Guendolen,

Commended her fair innocence to the flood
That stayed her flight with his cross-flowing course.
The water-nymphs that in the bottom played,
Held up their pearlèd wrists and took her in,
Bearing her straight to aged Nereus' hall,
Who, piteous of her woes, reared her lank head,
And gave her to his daughters to imbathe
In nectared lavers strewed with asphodel,
And through the porch and inlet of each sense
Dropt in ambrosial oils till she reviv'd,
And underwent a quick immortal change
Made goddess of the river; still she retains
Her maiden gentleness, and oft at eve
Visits the herds along the twilight meadows,
Helping all urchin blasts, and ill-luck signs
That the shrewd meddling elf delights to make,
Which she with precious vialed liquors heals.
For which the shepherds at their festivals
Carol her goodness loud in rustic lays,
And throw sweet garland wreaths into her stream
Of pansies, pinks, and gaudy daffodils.
And, as the old swain said, she can unlock
The clasping charm, and thaw the numbing spell,
If she be right invoked in warbled song,
Fair maidenhood she loves, and will be swift
To aid a virgin, such as was herself
In hard-besetting need, this will I try
And add the power of some adjuring verse.

SONG

Sabrina fair
    Listen where thou art sitting
Under the glassy, cool, translucent wave,
    In twisted braids of lilies knitting

The loose train of thy amber-dropping hair,
    Listen for dear honour's sake,
    Goddess of the silver lake,
            Listen and save.
Listen and appear to us
In name of great Oceanus,
By the earth-shaking Neptune's mace,
And Tethys' grave majestic pace,
By hoary Nereus' wrinkled look,
And the Carpathian wizard's hook,
By scaly Triton's winding shell,
And old soothsaying Glaucus' spell,
By Leucothea's lovely hands,
And her son that rules the strands,
By Thetis' tinsel-slippered feet,
And the songs of Sirens sweet,
By dead Parthenope's dear tomb,
And fair Ligea's golden comb,
Wherewith she sits on diamond rocks
Sleeking her soft alluring locks,
By all the nymphs that nightly dance
Upon thy streams with wily glance,
Rise, rise, and heave thy rosy head
From thy coral-paven bed,
And bridle in thy headlong wave,
Till thou our summons answered have.
            Listen and save.

SABRINA *rises, attended by Water-Nymphs, and sings.*

By the rushy-fringèd bank,
Where grows the willow and the osier dank,
    My sliding chariot stays,
Thick-set with agate, and the azurn sheen
Of turkis blue, and em'rald green

That in the channel strays,
Whilst from off the waters fleet
Thus I set my printless feet
O'er the cowslip's velvet head,
    That bends not as I tread,
Gentle swain, at thy request
    I am here.
    Spirit. Goddess dear
We implore thy powerful hand
To undo the charmèd band
Of true virgin here distressed,
Through the force and through the wile
Of unblessed enchanter vile.
    Sabrina. Shepherd, 'tis my office best
To help ensnarèd chastity;
Brightest lady, look on me,
Thus I sprinkle on thy breast
Drops that from my fountain pure,
I have kept of precious cure,
Thrice upon thy finger's tip,
Thrice upon thy rubied lip,
Next this marble venomed seat
Smeared with gums of glutinous heat
I touch with chaste palms moist and cold,
Now the spell hath lost his hold;
And I must haste ere morning hour
To wait in Amphitrite's bower.

Sabrina *descends, and the* Lady *rises out of her seat.*

    Spirit. Virgin, daughter of Locrine,
Sprung of old Anchises' line,
May thy brimmèd waves for this
Their full tribute never miss
From a thousand petty rills,

That tumble down the snowy hills;
Summer drouth, or singèd air
Never scorch thy tresses fair,
Nor wet October's torrent flood
Thy molten crystal fill with mud,
May thy billows roll ashore
The beryl and the golden ore,
May thy lofty head be crowned
With many a tower and terrace round,
And here and there thy banks upon
With groves of myrrh, and cinnamon.

Come, lady, while heaven lends us grace,
Let us fly this cursed place,
Lest the sorcerer us entice
With some other new device.
Not a waste or needless sound
Till we come to holier ground,
I shall be your faithful guide
Through this gloomy covert wide,
And not many furlongs thence
Is your father's residence,
Where this night are met in state
Many a friend to gratulate
His wished presence; and beside
All the swains that there abide,
With jigs and rural dance resort,
We shall catch them at their sport,
And our sudden coming there
Will double all their mirth and cheer;
Come let us haste, the stars grow high,
But night sits monarch yet in the mid sky.

*The Scene changes, presenting Ludlow town, and
the President's castle; then come in country*

Dancers, after them the ATTENDANT SPIRIT, *with
the Two* BROTHERS, *and the* LADY.

SONG

Spirit. Back, Shepherds, back, enough your play,
Till next sunshine holiday;
Here be without duck or nod
Other trippings to be trod
Of lighter toes, and such court guise
As Mercury did first devise
With the mincing Dryades
On the lawns, and on the leas.

This second Song presents them to their Father and Mother.

Noble lord, and lady bright,
I have brought ye new delight,
Here behold so goodly grown
Three fair branches of your own,
Heaven hath timely tried their youth,
Their faith, their patience, and their truth.
And sent them here through hard assays
With a crown of deathless praise,
To triumph in victorious dance
O'er sensual Folly, and Intemperance.

The dances ended, the SPIRIT *epiloguizes.*

Spirit. To the ocean now I fly,
And those happy climes that lie
Where day never shuts his eye,
Up in the broad fields of the sky:
There I suck the liquid air
All amidst the gardens fair
Of Hesperus, and his daughters three
That sing about the golden tree:
Along the crispèd shades and bowers
Revels the spruce and jocund Spring,

The Graces, and the rosy-bosomed hours,
Thither all their bounties bring,
There eternal summer dwells,
And west winds with musky wing
About the cedarn alleys fling
Nard, and cassia's balmy smells.
Iris there with humid bow,
Waters the odorous banks that blow
Flowers of more mingled hue
Than her purfled scarf can show,
And drenches with Elysian dew
(List, mortals, if your ears be true)
Beds of hyacinth, and roses,
Where young Adonis oft reposes,
Waxing well of his deep wound
In slumber soft; and on the ground
Sadly sits the Assyrian queen;
But far above in spangled sheen
Celestial Cupid, her famed son, advanced,
Holds his dear Psyche sweet entranced
After her wandering labours long,
Till free consent the gods among
Make her his eternal bride,
And from her fair unspotted side
Two blissful twins are to be born,
Youth and Joy; so Jove hath sworn.
    But now my task is smoothly done,
I can fly, or I can run
Quickly to the green earth's end,
Where the bowed welkin slow doth bend,
And from thence can soar as soon
To the corners of the moon.
    Mortals that would follow me,
Love virtue, she alone is free,

She can teach ye how to climb
Higher than the sphery chime;
Or if virtue feeble were,
Heaven itself would stoop to her.

LYCIDAS

A LAMENT FOR A FRIEND DROWNED IN HIS PASSAGE FROM CHESTER ON THE IRISH SEAS, 1637

YET once more, O ye laurels, and once more,
Ye myrtles brown, with ivy never-sere,
I come to pluck your berries harsh and crude,
And with forced fingers rude,
Shatter your leaves before the mellowing year.
Bitter constraint, and sad occasion dear,
Compels me to disturb your season due:
For Lycidas is dead, dead ere his prime,
Young Lycidas, and hath not left his peer:
Who would not sing for Lycidas? he knew
Himself to sing, and build the lofty rhyme.
He must not float upon his watery bier
Unwept, and welter to the parching wind,
Without the meed of some melodious tear.

Begin then, sisters of the sacred well,
That from beneath the seat of Jove doth spring,
Begin, and somewhat loudly sweep the string.
Hence with denial vain, and coy excuse,
So may some gentle Muse
With lucky words favour my destined urn,
And as he passes turn,
And bid fair peace be to my sable shroud.
For we were nursed upon the self-same hill,
Fed the same flock, by fountain, shade, and rill.

Together both, ere the high lawns appeared
Under the opening eye-lids of the morn,

We drove afield, and both together heard
What time the grey-fly winds her sultry horn,
Battening our flocks with the fresh dews of night,
Oft till the star, that rose at evening bright,
Toward heaven's descent had sloped his westering
    wheel.
Meanwhile the rural ditties were not mute,
Tempered to the oaten flute;
Rough Satyrs danced, and Fauns with cloven heel
From the glad sound would not be absent long,
And old Damætas loved to hear our song.

    But O the heavy change, now thou art gone,
Now thou art gone and never must return!
Thee, shepherd, thee the woods, and desert caves,
With wild thyme and the gadding vine o'ergrown,
And all their echoes mourn.
The willows, and the hazel copses green,
Shall now no more be seen,
Fanning their joyous leaves to thy soft lays.
As killing as the canker to the rose,
Or taint-worm to the weanling herds that graze,
Or frost to flowers, that their gay wardrobe wear
When first the white thorn blows;
Such, Lycidas, thy loss to shepherds' ear.

    Where were ye, nymphs, when the remorseless deep
Closed o'er the head of your loved Lycidas?
For neither were ye playing on the steep,
Where your old bards, the famous Druids, lie,
Nor on the shaggy top of Mona high,
Nor yet where Deva spreads her wizard stream:
Ay me, I fondly dream!
Had ye been there—for what could that have done?
What could the Muse herself that Orpheus bore,
The Muse herself, for her enchanting son

Whom universal nature did lament,
When by the rout that made the hideous roar,
His gory visage down the stream was sent,
Down the swift Hebrus to the Lesbian shore?
    Alas! what boots it with incessant care
To tend the homely slighted shepherd's trade,
And strictly meditate the thankless Muse?
Were it not better done, as others use,
To sport with Amaryllis in the shade,
Or with the tangles of Neæra's hair?
Fame is the spur that the clear spirit doth raise
(That last infirmity of noble mind)
To scorn delights, and live laborious days;
But the fair guerdon when we hope to find,
And think to burst out into sudden blaze,
Comes the blind Fury with the abhorrèd shears,
And slits the thin-spun life. 'But not the praise,'
Phœbus replied, and touched my trembling ears;
'Fame is no plant that grows on mortal soil,
Nor in the glistering foil
Set off to the world, nor in broad rumour lies,
But lives and spreads aloft by those pure eyes,
And perfect witness of all-judging Jove;
As he pronounces lastly on each deed,
Of so much fame in heaven expect thy meed.'
    O fountain Arethuse, and thou honoured flood,
Smooth-sliding Mincius, crowned with vocal reeds,
That strain I heard was of a higher mood:
But now my oat proceeds,
And listens to the herald of the sea
That came in Neptune's plea,
He asked the waves, and asked the felon winds,
What hard mishap hath doomed this gentle swain?
And questioned every gust of rugged wings

That blows from off each beakèd promontory,
They knew not of his story,
And sage Hippotades their answer brings,
That not a blast was from his dungeon strayed;
The air was calm, and on the level brine
Sleek Panope with all her sisters played.
It was that fatal and perfidious bark
Built in the eclipse, and rigged with curses dark,
That sunk so low that sacred head of thine.

   Next Camus, reverend sire, went footing slow,
His mantle hairy, and his bonnet sedge,
Inwrought with figures dim, and on the edge
Like to that sanguine flower inscribed with woe.
'Ah! who hath reft', quoth he, 'my dearest pledge?'
Last came, and last did go,
The pilot of the Galilean lake,
Two massy keys he bore of metals twain
(The golden opes, the iron shuts amain);
He shook his mitred locks, and stern bespake:
'How well could I have spared for thee, young swain,
Enow of such as for their bellies' sake,
Creep and intrude, and climb into the fold!
Of other care they little reckoning make,
Than how to scramble at the shearers' feast,
And shove away the worthy bidden guest.
Blind mouths! that scarce themselves know how
    to hold
A sheep-hook, or have learned aught else the least
That to the faithful herdman's art belongs!
What recks it them? What need they? They are sped;
And when they list, their lean and flashy songs
Grate on their scrannel pipes of wretched straw;
The hungry sheep look up, and are not fed,
But swoln with wind, and the rank mist they draw,

Rot inwardly, and foul contagion spread:
Besides what the grim wolf with privy paw
Daily devours apace, and nothing said,
But that two-handed engine at the door,
Stands ready to smite once, and smite no more.'
    Return, Alpheus, the dread voice is past,
That shrunk thy streams; return, Sicilian Muse,
And call the vales, and bid them hither cast
Their bells, and flowerets of a thousand hues.
Ye valleys low where the mild whispers use,
Of shades and wanton winds, and gushing brooks
On whose fresh lap the swart-star sparely looks,
Throw hither all your quaint enamelled eyes,
That on the green turf suck the honied showers,
And purple all the ground with vernal flowers.
Bring the rathe primrose that forsaken dies,
The tufted crow-toe, and pale jessamine,
The white pink, and the pansy freaked with jet,
The glowing violet.
The musk-rose, and the well attired woodbine.
With cowslips wan that hang the pensive head,
And every flower that sad embroidery wears:
Bid amaranthus all his beauty shed,
And daffadillies fill their cups with tears,
To strew the laureat hearse where Lycid lies.
For so to interpose a little ease,
Let our frail thoughts dally with false surmise.
Ay me! Whilst thee the shores, and sounding seas
Wash far away, where'er thy bones are hurled,
Whether beyond the stormy Hebrides,
Where thou perhaps under the whelming tide
Visit'st the bottom of the monstrous world;
Or whether thou to our moist vows denied,

        rathe] early.

Sleep'st by the fable of Bellerus old,
Where the great vision of the guarded mount
Looks toward Namancos and Bayona's hold;
Look homeward, angel, now, and melt with ruth.
And, O ye dolphins, waft the hapless youth!

Weep no more, woeful shepherds, weep no more,
For Lycidas, your sorrow, is not dead,
Sunk though he be beneath the watery floor;
So sinks the day-star in the ocean bed,
And yet anon repairs his drooping head,
And tricks his beams, and with new-spangled ore,
Flames in the forehead of the morning sky:
So Lycidas sunk low, but mounted high,
Through the dear might of him that walked the waves
Where, other groves and other streams along,
With nectar pure his oozy locks he laves,
And hears the unexpressive nuptial song,
In the blest Kingdoms meek of joy and love.
There entertain him all the saints above,
In solemn troops, and sweet societies
That sing, and singing in their glory move,
And wipe the tears for ever from his eyes.
Now, Lycidas, the shepherds weep no more;
Henceforth thou art the genius of the shore,
In thy large recompense, and shalt be good
To all that wander in that perilous flood.

Thus sang the uncouth swain to the oaks and rills,
While the still morn went out with sandals grey;
He touched the tender stops of various quills,
With eager thought warbling his Doric lay:
And now the sun had stretched out all the hills,
And now was dropt into the western bay;
At last he rose, and twitched his mantle blue:
To-morrow to fresh woods, and pastures new.

SONNETS

O NIGHTINGALE THAT ON YON BLOOMY SPRAY

O NIGHTINGALE, that on yon bloomy spray
    Warblest at eve, when all the woods are still,
    Thou with fresh hope the lover's heart dost fill,
    While the jolly hours lead on propitious May,
Thy liquid notes that close the eye of day,
    First heard before the shallow cuckoo's bill
    Portend success in love, O if Jove's will
    Have linked that amorous power to thy soft lay,
Now timely sing, ere the rude bird of hate
    Foretell my hopeless doom in some grove nigh:
    As thou from year to year hast sung too late
For my relief, yet hadst no reason why,
    Whether the Muse or Love call thee his mate,
    Both them I serve, and of their train am I.

WHEN THE ASSAULT WAS INTENDED TO THE CITY

CAPTAIN, or Colonel, or Knight in arms,
    Whose chance on these defenceless doors may seize,
    If ever deed of honour did thee please,
Guard them, and him within protect from harms.
He can requite thee; for he knows the charms
    That call fame on such gentle acts as these,
    And he can spread thy name o'er lands and seas,
Whatever clime the sun's bright circle warms.
Lift not thy spear against the Muses' bower:
    The great Emathian conqueror bid spare
The house of Pindarus, when temple and tower
    Went to the ground: and the repeated air
Of sad Electra's poet had the power
    To save the Athenian walls from ruin bare.

TO THE LADY MARGARET LEY

DAUGHTER to that good Earl, once President
 Of England's Council and her Treasury,
 Who lived in both unstained with gold or fee,
And left them both more in himself content,
Till the sad breaking of that Parliament
 Broke him, as that dishonest victory
 At Chaeronea, fatal to liberty
Killed with report that old man eloquent,
Though later born than to have known the days
 Wherein your father flourished, yet by you,
 Madam, methinks I see him living yet;
So well your words his noble virtues praise,
 That all both judge you to relate them true,
 And to possess them, honoured Margaret.

ON THE LATE MASSACRE IN PIEDMONT

AVENGE, O Lord, Thy slaughtered Saints, whose
 bones
 Lie scattered on the Alpine mountains cold,
 Even them who kept Thy truth so pure of old
When all our fathers worshipped stocks and stones,
Forget not: in Thy book record their groans
 Who were Thy sheep and in their ancient fold
 Slain by the bloody Piemontese that rolled
Mother with infant down the rocks. Their moans
The vales redoubled to the hills, and they
 To Heaven. Their martyred blood and ashes sow
O'er all the Italian fields where still doth sway
 The triple tyrant: that from these may grow
A hundred-fold, who having learnt Thy way
 Early may fly the Babylonian woe.

ON HIS BLINDNESS

WHEN I consider how my light is spent,
  Ere half my days, in this dark world and wide,
  And that one talent which is death to hide,
Lodged with me useless, though my soul more bent
To serve therewith my Maker, and present
  My true account, lest He returning chide,
  Doth God exact day-labour, light denied,
I fondly ask;—But Patience to prevent
That murmur, soon replies, God doth not need
  Either man's work, or His own gifts; who best
    Bear His mild yoke, they serve Him best: His
    state
Is kingly. Thousands at His bidding speed
  And post o'er land and ocean without rest:
    They also serve who only stand and wait.

TO MR. LAWRENCE

LAWRENCE, of virtuous father virtuous son,
  Now that the fields are dank, and ways are mire,
  Where shall we sometimes meet, and by the fire
Help waste a sullen day; what may be won
From the hard season gaining: time will run
  On smoother, till Favonius re-inspire
  The frozen earth; and clothe in fresh attire
The lily and rose, that neither sowed nor spun.
What neat repast shall feast us, light and choice,
  Of Attic taste, with wine, whence we may rise
To hear the lute well touched, or artful voice
  Warble immortal notes and Tuscan air?
  He who of those delights can judge, and spare
To interpose them oft, is not unwise.

TO CYRIACK SKINNER

CYRIACK, whose grandsire on the royal bench
   Of British Themis, with no mean applause
   Pronounced and in his volumes taught our laws,
Which others at their bar so often wrench:
To-day deep thoughts resolve with me to drench
   In mirth, that after no repenting draws;
   Let Euclid rest, and Archimedes pause,
And what the Swede intend, and what the French.
To measure life, learn thou betimes, and know
   Toward solid good what leads the nearest way;
   For other things mild heaven a time ordains,
And disapproves that care, though wise in show,
   That with superfluous burden loads the day,
      And when God sends a cheerful hour, refrains.

ON HIS DECEASED WIFE

METHOUGHT I saw my late espousèd Saint
   Brought to me, like Alcestis, from the grave,
   Whom Jove's great Son to her glad husband gave,
   Rescued from death by force, though pale and
      faint.
Mine, as whom washed from spot of childbed taint,
   Purification in the old law did save,
   And such, as yet once more I trust to have
Full sight of her in heaven without restraint,
Came vested all in white, pure as her mind:
   Her face was veiled, yet to my fancied sight,
   Love, sweetness, goodness, in her person shined
So clear, as in no face with more delight.
   But O! as to embrace me she inclined
   I waked, she fled, and day brought back my
      night.

PARADISE LOST

BOOK I

THE ARGUMENT

This First Book proposes, first in brief, the whole subject—
Man's disobedience, and the loss thereupon of Paradise,
wherein he was placed: then touches the prime cause of his
fall—the Serpent, or rather Satan in the Serpent; who, re-
volting from God, and drawing to his side many legions of
Angels, was, by the command of God, driven out of Heaven,
with all his crew, into the great Deep. Which action passed
over, the Poem hastens into the midst of things; presenting
Satan, with his Angels, now fallen into Hell—described here
not in the Centre (for heaven and earth may be supposed as yet
not made, certainly not yet accursed), but in a place of utter
darkness, fitliest called Chaos. Here Satan, with his Angels
lying on the burning lake, thunderstruck and astonished, after
a certain space recovers, as from confusion; calls up him who,
next in order and dignity, lay by him: they confer of their
miserable fall. Satan awakens all his legions, who lay till
then in the same manner confounded. They rise: their num-
bers; array of battle; their chief leaders named, according to
the idols known afterwards in Canaan and the countries ad-
joining. To these Satan directs his speech; comforts them
with hope yet of regaining Heaven; but tells them, lastly, of a
new world and new kind of creature to be created, according
to an ancient prophecy, or report, in Heaven—for that Angels
were long before this visible creation was the opinion of many
ancient Fathers. To find out the truth of this prophecy, and
what to determine thereon, he refers to a full council. What
his associates thence attempt. Pandemonium, the palace of
Satan, rises, suddenly built out of the Deep; the infernal Peers
there sit in council.

OF Man's first disobedience, and the fruit
Of that forbidden tree whose mortal taste
Brought death into the world, and all our woe,
With loss of Eden, till one greater Man
Restore us, and regain the blissful seat,
Sing, Heavenly Muse, that, on the secret top

Of Oreb, or of Sinai, didst inspire
That shepherd who first taught the chosen seed
In the beginning how the heavens and earth
Rose out of Chaos: or, if Sion hill
Delight thee more, and Siloa's brook that flowed
Fast by the oracle of God, I thence
Invoke thy aid to my advent'rous song,
That with no middle flight intends to soar
Above the Aonian mount, while it pursues
Things unattempted yet in prose or rime.
And chiefly Thou, O Spirit, that dost prefer
Before all temples the upright heart and pure,
Instruct me, for Thou know'st; Thou from the
    first
Wast present, and, with mighty wings outspread,
Dove-like sat'st brooding on the vast Abyss,
And mad'st it pregnant: what in me is dark
Illumine, what is low raise and support;
That, to the height of this great argument,
I may assert Eternal Providence,
And justify the ways of God to men.
    Say first—for Heaven hides nothing from thy
        view,
Nor the deep tract of Hell—say first what cause
Moved our grand Parents, in that happy state,
Favoured of Heaven so highly, to fall off
From their Creator, and transgress his will
For one restraint, lords of the world besides?
Who first seduced them to that foul revolt?
The infernal Serpent; he it was whose guile,
Stirred up with envy and revenge, deceived
The mother of mankind, what time his pride
Had cast him out from Heaven, with all his host
Of rebel Angels, by whose aid, aspiring

To set himself in glory above his peers,
He trusted to have equalled the Most High,
If he opposed; and, with ambitious aim
Against the throne and monarchy of God,
Raised impious war in Heaven and battle proud,
With vain attempt. Him the Almighty Power
Hurled headlong flaming from the ethereal sky,
With hideous ruin and combustion, down
To bottomless perdition, there to dwell
In adamantine chains and penal fire,
Who durst defy the Omnipotent to arms.
Nine times the space that measures day and night
To mortal men, he, with his horrid crew,
Lay vanquished, rolling in the fiery gulf,
Confounded, though immortal; but his doom
Reserved him to more wrath; for now the thought
Both of lost happiness and lasting pain
Torments him: round he throws his baleful eyes,
That witnessed huge affliction and dismay,
Mixed with obdurate pride and steadfast hate.
At once, as far as angel's ken, he views
The dismal situation waste and wild.
A dungeon horrible, on all sides round,
As one great furnace flamed; yet from those flames
No light; but rather darkness visible
Served only to discover sights of woe,
Regions of sorrow, doleful shades, where peace
And rest can never dwell, hope never comes
That comes to all, but torture without end
Still urges, and a fiery deluge, fed
With ever-burning sulphur unconsumed.
Such place Eternal Justice had prepared
For those rebellious; here their prison ordained
In utter darkness, and their portion set,

As far removed from God and light of Heaven
As from the centre thrice to the utmost pole.
Oh, how unlike the place from whence they fell!
There the companions of his fall, o'er-whelmed
With floods and whirlwinds of tempestuous fire,
He soon discerns; and, weltering by his side,
One next himself in power, and next in crime,
Long after known in Palestine, and named
Beëlzebub. To whom the Arch-Enemy,
And thence in Heaven called Satan, with bold
    words
Breaking the horrid silence, thus began:—
  'If thou beest he—but Oh, how fallen! how
    changed
From him who, in the happy realms of light,
Clothed with transcendent brightness, didst out-
    shine
Myriads, though bright!—if he whom mutual
    league,
United thoughts and counsels, equal hope
And hazard in the glorious enterprise,
Joined with me once, now misery hath joined
In equal ruin; into what pit thou seest
From what height fallen: so much the stronger
    proved
He with his thunder: and till then who knew
The force of those dire arms? Yet not for those,
Nor what the potent Victor in his rage
Can else inflict, do I repent, or change,
Though changed in outward lustre, that fixed mind,
And high disdain from sense of injured merit,
That with the Mightiest raised me to contend,
And to the fierce contention brought along
Innumerable force of Spirits armed,

That durst dislike his reign, and, me preferring,
His utmost power with adverse power opposed
In dubious battle on the plains of Heaven,
And shook his throne. What though the field be
    lost?
All is not lost—the unconquerable will,
And study of revenge, immortal hate,
And courage never to submit or yield:
And what is else not to be overcome.
That glory never shall his wrath or might
Extort from me. To bow and sue for grace
With suppliant knee, and deify his power
Who, from the terror of this arm, so late
Doubted his empire—that were low indeed;
That were an ignominy and shame beneath
This downfall; since, by fate, the strength of Gods,
And this empyreal substance, cannot fail;
Since, through experience of this great event,
In arms not worse, in foresight much advanced,
We may with more successful hope resolve
To wage by force or guile eternal war,
Irreconcilable to our grand Foe,
Who now triumphs, and in the excess of joy
Sole reigning holds the tyranny of Heaven.'
  So spake the apostate Angel, though in pain,
Vaunting aloud, but racked with deep despair;
And him thus answered soon his bold compeer:—
  'O Prince, O Chief of many throned Powers
That led the embattled Seraphim to war
Under thy conduct, and, in dreadful deeds
Fearless, endangered Heaven's perpetual King,
And put to proof his high supremacy,
Whether upheld by strength, or chance, or fate!
Too well I see and rue the dire event

That, with sad overthrow and foul defeat,
Hath lost us Heaven, and all this mighty host
In horrible destruction laid thus low,
As far as Gods and Heavenly Essences
Can perish: for the mind and spirit remains
Invincible, and vigour soon returns,
Though all our glory extinct, and happy state
Here swallowed up in endless misery.
But what if he our Conqueror (whom I now
Of force believe almighty, since no less
Than such could have o'erpowered such force as
    ours)
Have left us this our spirit and strength entire,
Strongly to suffer and support our pains,
That we may so suffice his vengeful ire,
Or do him mightier service as his thralls
By right of war, whate'er his business be,
Here in the heart of Hell to work in fire,
Or do his errands in the gloomy Deep?
What can it then avail though yet we feel
Strength undiminished, or eternal being
To undergo eternal punishment?'
  Whereto with speedy words the Arch-Fiend
    replied:—
'Fallen Cherub, to be weak is miserable,
Doing or suffering: but of this be sure—
To do aught good never will be our task,
But ever to do ill our sole delight,
As being the contrary to his high will
Whom we resist. If then his providence
Out of our evil seek to bring forth good,
Our labour must be to pervert that end,
And out of good still to find means of evil;
Which ofttimes may succeed so as perhaps

Shall grieve him, if I fail not, and disturb
His inmost counsels from their destined aim.
But see! the angry Victor hath recalled
His ministers of vengeance and pursuit
Back to the gates of Heaven: the sulphurous hail,
Shot after us in storm, o'erblown hath laid
The fiery surge that from the precipice
Of Heaven received us falling; and the thunder,
Winged with red lightning and impetuous rage,
Perhaps hath spent his shafts, and ceases now
To bellow through the vast and boundless Deep.
Let us not slip the occasion, whether scorn
Or satiate fury yield it from our Foe.
Seest thou yon dreary plain, forlorn and wild,
The seat of desolation, void of light,
Save what the glimmering of these livid flames
Casts pale and dreadful? Thither let us tend
From off the tossing of these fiery waves;
There rest, if any rest can harbour there;
And, reassembling our afflicted powers,
Consult how we may henceforth most offend
Our Enemy, our own loss how repair,
How overcome this dire calamity,
What reinforcement we may gain from hope,
If not, what resolution from despair.'

    Thus Satan, talking to his nearest mate,
With head uplift above the wave, and eyes
That sparkling blazed; his other parts besides
Prone on the flood, extended long and large,
Lay floating many a rood, in bulk as huge
As whom the fables name of monstrous size,
Titanian or Earth-born, that warred on Jove,
Briareos or Typhon, whom the den
By ancient Tarsus held, or that sea-beast

Leviathan, which God of all his works
Created hugest that swim the ocean-stream.
Him, haply slumbering on the Norway foam,
The pilot of some small night-foundered skiff,
Deeming some island, oft, as seamen tell,
With fixèd anchor in his scaly rind,
Moors by his side under the lee, while night
Invests the sea, and wishèd morn delays.
So stretched out huge in length the Arch-Fiend
    lay,
Chained on the burning lake; nor ever thence
Had risen, or heaved his head, but that the will
And high permission of all-ruling Heaven
Left him at large to his own dark designs,
That with reiterated crimes he might
Heap on himself damnation, while he sought
Evil to others, and enraged might see
How all his malice served but to bring forth
Infinite goodness, grace, and mercy, shown
On Man by him seduced; but on himself
Treble confusion, wrath, and vengeance poured.
Forthwith upright he rears from off the pool
His mighty stature; on each hand the flames,
Driven backward, slope their pointing spires, and,
    rolled
In billows, leave i' the midst a horrid vale.
Then with expanded wings he steers his flight
Aloft, incumbent on the dusky air,
That felt unusual weight; till on dry land
He lights—if it were land that ever burned
With solid, as the lake with liquid fire,
And such appeared in hue as when the force
Of subterranean wind transports a hill
Torn from Pelorus, or the shattered side

Of thundering Aetna, whose combustible
And fuelled entrails, thence conceiving fire,
Sublimed with mineral fury, aid the winds,
And leave a singèd bottom all involved
With stench and smoke; such resting found the sole
Of unblest feet.   Him followed his next mate;
Both glorying to have 'scaped the Stygian flood
As gods, and by their own recovered strength,
Not by the sufferance of Supernal Power.

   'Is this the region, this the soil, the clime,'
Said then the lost Archangel, 'this the seat
That we must change for Heaven?—this mournful
    gloom
For that celestial light? Be it so, since he
Who now is sovereign can dispose and bid
What shall be right: farthest from him is best,
Whom reason hath equalled, force hath made
    supreme
Above his equals.   Farewell, happy fields,
Where joy for ever dwells! Hail, horrors! hail,
Infernal World! and thou, profoundest Hell,
Receive thy new possessor—one who brings
A mind not to be changed by place or time.
The mind is its own place, and in itself
Can make a Heaven of Hell, a Hell of Heaven.
What matter where, if I be still the same,
And what I should be, all but less than he
Whom thunder hath made greater? Here at least
We shall be free; the Almighty hath not built
Here for his envy, will not drive us hence:
Here we may reign secure; and, in my choice,
To reign is worth ambition, though in Hell:
Better to reign in Hell than serve in Heaven.
But wherefore let we then our faithful friends,

The associates and co-partners of our loss,
Lie thus astonished on the oblivious pool,
And call them not to share with us their part
In this unhappy mansion, or once more
With rallied arms to try what may be yet
Regained in Heaven, or what more lost in Hell? '
   So Satan spake; and him Beëlzebub
Thus answered:—'Leader of those armies bright
Which, but the Omnipotent, none could have
   foiled!
If once they hear that voice, their liveliest pledge
Of hope in fears and dangers—heard so oft
In worst extremes, and on the perilous edge
Of battle, when it raged, in all assaults
Their surest signal—they will soon resume
New courage and revive, though now they lie
Grovelling and prostrate on yon lake of fire,
As we erewhile, astounded and amazed;
No wonder, fallen such a pernicious height!'
   He scarce had ceased when the superior Fiend
Was moving toward the shore; his ponderous
   shield,
Ethereal temper, massy, large, and round,
Behind him cast. The broad circumference
Hung on his shoulders like the moon, whose orb
Through optic glass the Tuscan artist views
At evening, from the top of Fesolè,
Or in Valdarno, to descry new lands,
Rivers, or mountains, in her spotty globe.
His spear—to equal which the tallest pine
Hewn on Norwegian hills, to be the mast
Of some great ammiral, were but a wand—
He walked with, to support uneasy steps
Over the burning marle, not like those steps

On Heaven's azure; and the torrid clime
Smote on him so sore besides, vaulted with fire.
Nathless he so endured, till on the beach
Of that inflamèd sea he stood, and called
His legions—angel forms, who lay entranced
Thick as autumnal leaves that strow the brooks
In Vallombrosa, where the Etrurian shades
High over-arched embower; or scattered sedge
Afloat, when with fierce winds Orion armed
Hath vexed the Red Sea coast, whose waves o'er-
  threw
Busiris and his Memphian chivalry,
While with perfidious hatred they pursued
The sojourners of Goshen, who beheld
From the safe shore their floating carcases
And broken chariot-wheels. So thick bestrown,
Abject and lost, lay these, covering the flood,
Under amazement of their hideous change.
He called so loud that all the hollow deep
Of Hell resounded:—'Princes, Potentates,
Warriors, the Flower of Heaven—once yours, now
  lost,
If such astonishment as this can seize
Eternal Spirits! Or have ye chosen this place
After the toil of battle to repose
Your wearied virtue, for the ease you find
To slumber here, as in the vales of Heaven?
Or in this abject posture have ye sworn
To adore the Conqueror, who now beholds
Cherub and Seraph rolling in the flood
With scattered arms and ensigns, till anon
His swift pursuers from Heaven-gates discern
The advantage, and, descending, tread us down
Thus drooping, or with linkèd thunderbolts

Transfix us to the bottom of this gulf?—
Awake, arise, or be for ever fallen!'
    They heard, and were abashed, and up they
      sprung
Upon the wing; as when men wont to watch,
On duty sleeping, found by whom they dread,
Rouse and bestir themselves ere well awake.
Nor did they not perceive the evil plight
In which they were, or the fierce pains not feel;
Yet to their General's voice they soon obeyed
Innumerable. As when the potent rod
Of Amram's son, in Egypt's evil day,
Waved round the coast, up-called a pitchy cloud
Of locusts, warping on the eastern wind,
That o'er the realm of impious Pharaoh hung
Like night, and darkened all the land of Nile;
So numberless were those bad angels seen
Hovering on wing under the cope of Hell,
'Twixt upper, nether, and surrounding fires;
Till, as a signal given, the uplifted spear
Of their great Sultan waving to direct
Their course, in even balance down they light
On the firm brimstone, and fill all the plain:
A multitude like which the populous North
Poured never from her frozen loins to pass
Rhine or the Danaw, when her barbarous sons
Came like a deluge on the South, and spread
Beneath Gibraltar to the Libyan sands.
Forthwith, from every squadron and each band,
The heads and leaders thither haste where stood
Their great Commander—godlike Shapes, and
      Forms
Excelling human; princely Dignities;
And Powers that erst in Heaven sat on thrones,

Though of their names in heavenly records now
Be no memorial, blotted out and rased
By their rebellion from the Books of Life.
Nor had they yet among the sons of Eve
Got them new names, till, wandering o'er the
    earth,
Through God's high sufferance for the trial of man,
By falsities and lies the greatest part
Of mankind they corrupted to forsake
God their Creator, and the invisible
Glory of him that made them, to transform
Oft to the image of a brute, adorned
With gay religions full of pomp and gold,
And devils to adore for deities:
Then were they known to men by various names,
And various idols through the heathen world.
    Say, Muse, their names then known, who first,
      who last,
Roused from the slumber on that fiery couch,
At their great Emperor's call, as next in worth
Came singly where he stood on the bare strand,
While the promiscuous crowd stood yet aloof.
    The chief were those who, from the pit of Hell
Roaming to seek their prey on Earth, durst fix
Their seats, long after, next the seat of God,
Their altars by his altar, gods adored
Among the nations round, and durst abide
Jehovah thundering out of Sion, throned
Between the Cherubim; yea, often placed
Within his sanctuary itself their shrines,
Abominations; and with cursèd things
His holy rites and solemn feasts profaned,
And with their darkness durst affront his light.
First, Moloch, horrid king, besmeared with blood

Of human sacrifice, and parents' tears;
Though, for the noise of drums and timbrels loud,
Their children's cries unheard that passed through fire
To his grim idol. Him the Ammonite
Worshipped in Rabba and her watery plain,
In Argob and in Basan, to the stream
Of utmost Arnon. Nor content with such
Audacious neighbourhood, the wisest heart
Of Solomon he led by fraud to build
His temple right against the temple of God
On that opprobrious hill, and made his grove
The pleasant valley of Hinnom, Tophet thence
And black Gehenna called, the type of Hell.
Next Chemos, the obscene dread of Moab's sons,
From Aroer to Nebo and the wild
Of southmost Abarim; in Hesebon
And Horonaim, Seon's realm, beyond
The flowery dale of Sibma, clad with vines,
And Elealè to the Asphaltic Pool:
Peor his other name, when he enticed
Israel in Sittim, on their march from Nile,
To do him wanton rites, which cost them woe.
Yet thence his lustful orgies he enlarged
Even to that hill of scandal, by the grove
Of Moloch homicide, lust hard by hate,
Till good Josiah drove them thence to Hell.
With these came they who, from the bordering flood
Of old Euphrates to the brook that parts
Egypt from Syrian ground, had general names
Of Baalim and Ashtaroth—those male,
These feminine. For Spirits, when they please,

Can either sex assume, or both; so soft
And uncompounded is their essence pure,
Not tied or manacled with joint or limb,
Nor founded on the brittle strength of bones,
Like cumbrous flesh; but, in what shape they
    choose,
Dilated or condensed, bright or obscure,
Can execute their aery purposes,
And works of love or enmity fulfil.
For those the race of Israel oft forsook
Their Living Strength, and unfrequented left
His righteous altar, bowing lowly down
To bestial gods; for which their heads, as low
Bowed down in battle, sunk before the spear
Of despicable foes. With these in troop
Came Astoreth, whom the Phœnicians called
Astarte, queen of heaven, with crescent horns;
To whose bright image nightly by the moon
Sidonian virgins paid their vows and songs;
In Sion also not unsung, where stood
Her temple on the offensive mountain, built
By that uxorious king whose heart, though large,
Beguiled by fair idolatresses, fell
To idols foul. *Thammuz* came next behind,
Whose annual wound in Lebanon allured
The Syrian damsels to lament his fate
In amorous ditties all a summer's day,
While smooth Adonis from his native rock
Ran purple to the sea, supposed with blood
Of Thammuz yearly wounded: the love-tale
Infected Sion's daughters with like heat,
Whose wanton passions in the sacred porch
Ezekiel saw, when by the vision led,
His eye surveyed the dark idolatries

Of alienated Judah. Next came one
Who mourned in earnest, when the captive ark
Maimed his brute image, head and hands lopped
    off,
In his own temple, on the grunsel-edge,
Where he fell flat and shamed his worshippers:
Dagon his name, sea-monster, upward man
And downward fish; yet had his temple high
Reared in Azotus, dreaded through the coast
Of Palestine, in Gath and Ascalon,
And Accaron and Gaza's frontier bounds.
Him followed Rimmon, whose delightful seat
Was fair Damascus, on the fertile banks
Of Abbana and Pharphar, lucid streams.
He also against the house of God was bold:
A leper once he lost, and gained a king—
Ahaz, his sottish conqueror, whom he drew
God's altar to disparage and displace
For one of Syrian mode, whereon to burn
His odious offerings, and adore the gods
Whom he had vanquished. After these appeared
A crew who, under names of old renown—
Osiris, Isis, Orus, and their train—
With monstrous shapes and sorceries abused
Fanatic Egypt and her priests, to seek
Their wandering gods disguised in brutish forms
Rather than human. Nor did Israel 'scape
The infection, when their borrowed gold com-
    posed
The calf in Oreb; and the rebel king
Doubled that sin in Bethel and in Dan,
Likening his Maker to the grazèd ox—
Jehovah, who, in one night, when he passed
From Egypt marching, equalled with one stroke

Both her first-born and all her bleating gods.
Belial came last; than whom a Spirit more lewd
Fell not from Heaven, or more gross to love
Vice for itself. To him no temple stood
Or altar smoked; yet who more oft than he
In temples and at altars, when the priest
Turns atheist, as did Eli's sons, who filled
With lust and violence the house of God?
In courts and palaces he also reigns,
And in luxurious cities, where the noise
Of riot ascends above their loftiest towers,
And injury and outrage; and, when night
Darkens the streets, then wander forth the sons
Of Belial, flown with insolence and wine.
Witness the streets of Sodom, and that night
In Gibeah, when the hospitable door
Exposed a matron, to prevent worse rape.
　These were the prime in order and in might:
The rest were long to tell; though far renowned
The Ionian gods—of Javan's issue held
Gods, yet confessed later than Heaven and Earth,
Their boasted parents;—Titan, Heaven's first-
　　born,
With his enormous brood, and birthright seized
By younger Saturn: he from mightier Jove,
His own and Rhea's son, like measure found:
So Jove usurping reigned. These, first in Crete
And Ida known, thence on the snowy top
Of cold Olympus ruled the middle air,
Their highest heaven; or on the Delphian cliff,
Or in Dodona, and through all the bounds
Of Doric land; or who with Saturn old
Fled over Adria to the Hesperian fields,
And o'er the Celtic roamed the utmost Isles.

All these and more came flocking; but with looks
Downcast and damp; yet such wherein appeared
Obscure some glimpse of joy to have found their
    Chief
Not in despair, to have found themselves not
    lost
In loss itself; which on his countenance cast
Like doubtful hue. But he, his wonted pride
Soon recollecting, with high words, that bore
Semblance of worth, not substance, gently raised
Their fainted courage, and dispelled their fears:
Then straight commands that, at the warlike
    sound
Of trumpets loud and clarions, be upreared
His mighty standard. That proud honour claimed
Azazel as his right, a Cherub tall:
Who forthwith from the glittering staff unfurled
The imperial ensign; which, full high advanced,
Shone like a meteor streaming to the wind
With gems and golden lustre rich emblazed,
Seraphic arms and trophies; all the while
Sonorous metal blowing martial sounds:
At which the universal host up-sent
A shout that tore Hell's concave, and beyond
Frighted the reign of Chaos and old Night.
All in a moment through the gloom were seen
Ten thousand banners rise into the air,
With orient colours waving: with them rose
A forest huge of spears; and thronging helms
Appeared, and serried shields in thick array
Of depth immeasurable. Anon they move
In perfect phalanx to the Dorian mood
Of flutes and soft recorders—such as raised
To height of noblest temper heroes old

Arming to battle, and instead of rage
Deliberate valour breathed, firm, and unmoved
With dread of death to flight or foul retreat;
Nor wanting power to mitigate and swage
With solemn touches troubled thoughts, and chase
Anguish and doubt and fear and sorrow and pain
From mortal or immortal minds. Thus they,
Breathing united force with fixèd thought,
Moved on in silence to soft pipes that charmed
Their painful steps o'er the burnt soil. And now
Advanced in view they stand—a horrid front
Of dreadful length and dazzling arms, in guise
Of warriors old, with ordered spear and shield,
Awaiting what command their mighty Chief
Had to impose. He through the armèd files
Darts his experienced eye, and soon traverse
The whole battalion views—their order due,
Their visages and stature as of gods;
Their number last he sums. And now his heart
Distends with pride, and, hardening in his strength,
Glories: for never, since created Man,
Met such embodied force as, named with these,
Could merit more than that small infantry
Warred on by cranes—though all the giant brood
Of Phlegra with the heroic race were joined
That fought at Thebes and Ilium, on each side
Mixed with auxiliar gods; and what resounds
In fable or romance of Uther's son,
Begirt with British and Armoric knights;
And all who since, baptized or infidel,
Jousted in Aspramont, or Montalban,
Damasco, or Marocco, or Trebisond,
Or whom Biserta sent from Afric shore
When Charlemain with all his peerage fell

By Fontarabbia. Thus far these beyond
Compare of mortal prowess, yet observed
Their dread Commander. He, above the rest
In shape and gesture proudly eminent,
Stood like a tower. His form had yet not lost
All her original brightness, nor appeared
Less than Archangel ruined, and the excess
Of glory obscured: as when the sun new-risen
Looks through the horizontal misty air
Shorn of his beams, or, from behind the moon,
In dim eclipse, disastrous twilight sheds
On half the nations, and with fear of change
Perplexes monarchs. Darkened so, yet shone
Above them all the Archangel: but his face
Deep scars of thunder had intrenched, and care
Sat on his faded cheek, but under brows
Of dauntless courage, and considerate pride
Waiting revenge. Cruel his eye, but cast
Signs of remorse and passion, to behold
The fellows of his crime, the followers rather
(Far other once beheld in bliss), condemned
For ever now to have their lot in pain—
Millions of Spirits for his fault amerced
Of Heaven, and from eternal splendours flung
For his revolt—yet faithful how they stood,
Their glory withered; as, when Heaven's fire
Hath scathed the forest oaks or mountain pines,
With singèd top their stately growth, though bare,
Stands on the blasted heath. He now prepared
To speak; whereat their doubled ranks they bend
From wing to wing, and half enclose him round
With all his peers: attention held them mute.
Thrice he assayed, and thrice, in spite of scorn,
Tears, such as angels weep, burst forth: at last

Words interwove with sighs found out their way:—
'O myriads of immortal Spirits! O Powers
Matchless, but with the Almighty!—and that
    strife
Was not inglorious, though the event was dire,
As this place testifies, and this dire change,
Hateful to utter. But what power of mind,
Foreseeing or presaging, from the depth
Of knowledge past or present, could have feared
How such united force of gods, how such
As stood like these, could ever know repulse?
For who can yet believe, though after loss,
That all these puissant legions, whose exile
Hath emptied Heaven, shall fail to re-ascend
Self-raised, and repossess their native seat?
For me, be witness all the host of Heaven,
If counsels different, or danger shunned
By me, have lost our hopes. But he who reigns
Monarch in Heaven till then as one secure
Sat on his throne, upheld by old repute,
Consent or custom, and his regal state
Put forth at full, but still his strength concealed—
Which tempted our attempt, and wrought our fall.
Henceforth his might we know, and know our own,
So as not either to provoke, or dread
New war provoked: our better part remains
To work in close design, by fraud or guile,
What force effected not; that he no less
At length from us may find, Who overcomes
By force hath overcome but half his foe.
Space may produce new Worlds; whereof so rife
There went a fame in Heaven that he ere long
Intended to create, and therein plant
A generation whom his choice regard

Should favour equal to the Sons of Heaven.
Thither, if but to pry, shall be perhaps
Our first eruption—thither, or elsewhere;
For this infernal pit shall never hold
Celestial Spirits in bondage, nor the Abyss
Long under darkness cover. But these thoughts
Full counsel must mature. Peace is despaired;
For who can think submission? War then, war
Open or understood, must be resolved.'

He spake; and to confirm his words, out-flew
Millions of flaming swords, drawn from the thighs
Of mighty Cherubim; the sudden blaze
Far round illumined Hell. Highly they raged
Against the Highest, and fierce with graspèd arms
Clashed on their sounding shields the din of war,
Hurling defiance toward the vault of Heaven.

There stood a hill not far, whose grisly top
Belched fire and rolling smoke; the rest entire
Shone with a glossy scurf—undoubted sign
That in his womb was hid metallic ore,
The work of sulphur. Thither, winged with speed,
A numerous brigade hastened: as when bands
Of pioneers, with spade and pickaxe armed,
Forerun the royal camp, to trench a field,
Or cast a rampart. Mammon led them on—
Mammon, the least erected Spirit that fell
From Heaven; for even in Heaven his looks and
    thoughts
Were always downward bent, admiring more
The riches of Heaven's pavement, trodden gold,
Than aught divine or holy else enjoyed
In vision beatific. By him first
Men also, and by his suggestion taught,
Ransacked the centre, and with impious hands

Rifled the bowels of their mother Earth
For treasures better hid. Soon had his crew
Opened into the hill a spacious wound,
And digged out ribs of gold. Let none admire
That riches grow in Hell; that soil may best
Deserve the precious bane. And here let those
Who boast in mortal things, and wondering tell
Of Babel, and the works of Memphian kings,
Learn how their greatest monuments of fame,
And strength, and art, are easily outdone
By Spirits reprobate, and in an hour
What in an age they, with incessant toil
And hands innumerable, scarce perform.
Nigh on the plain, in many cells prepared,
That underneath had veins of liquid fire
Sluiced from the lake, a second multitude
With wondrous art founded the massy ore,
Severing each kind, and scummed the bullion-
        dross.
A third as soon had formed within the ground
A various mould, and from the boiling cells
By strange conveyance filled each hollow nook;
As in an organ, from one blast of wind,
To many a row of pipes the sound-board breathes.
Anon out of the earth a fabric huge
Rose like an exhalation, with the sound
Of dulcet symphonies and voices sweet—
Built like a temple, where pilasters round
Were set, and Doric pillars overlaid
With golden architrave; nor did there want
Cornice or frieze, with bossy sculptures graven:
The roof was fretted gold. Not Babylon
Nor great Alcairo such magnificence
Equalled in all their glories, to enshrine

Belus or Serapis their gods, or seat
Their kings, when Egypt with Assyria strove
In wealth and luxury. The ascending pile
Stood fixed her stately height; and straight the
    doors,
Opening their brazen folds, discover, wide
Within, her ample spaces o'er the smooth
And level pavement: from the archèd roof,
Pendent by subtle magic, many a row
Of starry lamps and blazing cressets, fed
With naphtha and asphaltus, yielded light
As from a sky. The hasty multitude
Admiring entered; and the work some praise
And some the architect. His hand was known
In Heaven by many a towered structure high,
Where sceptred angels held their residence,
And sat as princes, whom the supreme King
Exalted to such power, and gave to rule,
Each in his hierarchy, the Orders bright.
Nor was his name unheard or unadored
In ancient Greece; and in Ausonian land
Men called him Mulciber; and how he fell
From Heaven they fabled, thrown by angry Jove
Sheer o'er the crystal battlements: from morn
To noon he fell, from noon to dewy eve,
A summer's day, and with the setting sun
Dropped from the zenith, like a falling star,
On Lemnos, the Aegaean isle. Thus they relate,
Erring; for he with this rebellious rout
Fell long before; nor aught availed him now
To have built in Heaven high towers; nor did he
    scape
By all his engines, but was headlong sent,
With his industrious crew, to build in Hell.

Meanwhile the wingèd heralds, by command
Of sovereign power, with awful ceremony
And trumpet's sound, throughout the host proclaim
A solemn council forthwith to be held
At Pandemonium, the high capital
Of Satan and his peers. Their summons called
From every band and squarèd regiment
By place or choice the worthiest: they anon
With hundreds and with thousands trooping came
Attended. All access was thronged; the gates
And porches wide, but chief the spacious hall
(Though like a covered field, where champions bold
Wont ride in armed, and at the Soldan's chair
Defied the best of Paynim chivalry
To mortal combat, or career with lance),
Thick swarmed, both on the ground and in the air,
Brushed with the hiss of rustling wings. As bees
In spring-time, when the sun with Taurus rides,
Pour forth their populous youth about the hive
In clusters; they among fresh dews and flowers
Fly to and fro, or on the smoothèd plank,
The suburb of their straw-built citadel,
New rubbed with balm, expatiate, and confer
Their state-affairs: so thick the aery crowd
Swarmed and were straitened; till, the signal given,
Behold a wonder! They but now who seemed
In bigness to surpass Earth's giant sons,
Now less than smallest dwarfs, in narrow room
Throng numberless—like that pygmean race
Beyond the Indian mount; or faëry elves,
Whose midnight revels, by a forest-side
Or fountain, some belated peasant sees,
Or dreams he sees, while overhead the Moon
Sits arbitress, and nearer to the Earth

Wheels her pale course: they, on their mirth and
    dance
Intent, with jocund music charm his ear;
At once with joy and fear his heart rebounds.
Thus incorporeal Spirits to smallest forms
Reduced their shapes immense, and were at large,
Though without number still, amidst the hall
Of that infernal court. But far within,
And in their own dimensions like themselves,
The great Seraphic Lords and Cherubim
In close recess and secret conclave sat,
A thousand demi-gods on golden seats,
Frequent and full. After short silence then,
And summons read, the great consult began.

The End of the First Book.

PARADISE LOST, BOOK III (LINES 1-55)

THE INVOCATION TO LIGHT

HAIL, holy Light, offspring of Heaven first-
    born!
Or of the Eternal coeternal beam,
May I express thee unblamed? since God is light,
And never but in unapproachèd light
Dwelt from eternity—dwelt then in thee,
Bright effluence of bright essence increate!
Or hear'st thou rather pure ethereal stream,
Whose fountain who shall tell? Before the sun,
Before the heavens, thou wert, and at the voice
Of God, as with a mantle, didst invest
The rising world of waters dark and deep,
Won from the void and formless Infinite!
Thee I revisit now with bolder wing,
Escaped the Stygian Pool, though long detained

In that obscure sojourn, while in my flight,
Through utter and through middle darkness borne
With other notes than to the Orphean lyre
I sung of Chaos and eternal Night,
Taught by the Heavenly Muse to venture down
The dark descent, and up to reascend,
Though hard and rare. Thee I revisit safe,
And feel thy sovereign vital lamp; but thou
Revisit'st not these eyes, that roll in vain
To find thy piercing ray, and find no dawn;
So thick a drop serene hath quenched their orbs,
Or dim suffusion veiled. Yet not the more
Cease I to wander where the Muses haunt
Clear spring, or shady grove, or sunny hill,
Smit with the love of sacred song; but chief
Thee, Sion, and the flowery brooks beneath,
That wash thy hallowed feet, and warbling flow,
Nightly I visit: nor sometimes forget
Those other two equalled with me in fate,
So were I equalled with them in renown,
Blind Thamyris and blind Maeonides,
And Tiresias and Phineus, prophets old:
Then feed on thoughts that voluntary move
Harmonious numbers; as the wakeful bird
Sings darkling, and, in shadiest covert hid,
Tunes her nocturnal note. Thus with the year
Seasons return; but not to me returns
Day, or the sweet approach of even or morn,
Or sight of vernal bloom, or summer's rose,
Or flocks, or herds, or human face divine;
But cloud instead and ever-during dark
Surrounds me, from the cheerful ways of men
Cut off, and, for the book of knowledge fair,
Presented with a universal blank

Of Nature's works, to me expunged and rased,
And wisdom at one entrance quite shut out.
So much the rather thou, Celestial Light,
Shine inward, and the mind through all her powers
Irradiate; there plant eyes; all mist from thence
Purge and disperse, that I may see and tell
Of things invisible to mortal sight.

PARADISE LOST, BOOK IV (LINES 32–113)

SATAN'S ADDRESS TO THE SUN

'O THOU that, with surpassing glory crowned,
Look'st from thy sole dominion like the god
Of this new World—at whose sight all the stars
Hide their diminished heads—to thee I call,
But with no friendly voice, and add thy name,
O Sun, to tell thee how I hate thy beams,
That bring to my remembrance from what state
I fell, how glorious once above thy sphere,
Till pride and worse ambition threw me down,
Warring in Heaven against Heaven's matchless
    King!
Ah, wherefore? He deserved no such return
From me, whom he created what I was
In that bright eminence, and with his good
Upbraided none; nor was his service hard.
What could be less than to afford him praise,
The easiest recompense, and pay him thanks,
How due? Yet all his good proved ill in me,
And wrought but malice. Lifted up so high,
I 'sdained subjection, and thought one step higher
Would set me highest, and in a moment quit
The debt immense of endless gratitude,
So burdensome, still paying, still to owe;

Forgetful what from him I still received;
And understood not that a grateful mind
By owing owes not, but still pays, at once
Indebted and discharged—what burden then?
Oh, had his powerful destiny ordained
Me some inferior Angel, I had stood
Then happy; no unbounded hope had raised
Ambition. Yet why not? Some other Power
As great might have aspired, and me, though
    mean,
Drawn to his part. But other Powers as great
Fell not, but stand unshaken, from within
Or from without to all temptations armed!
Hadst thou the same free will and power to
    stand?
Thou hadst. Whom hast thou then, or what, to
    accuse,
But Heaven's free love dealt equally to all?
Be then his love accursed, since, love or hate,
To me alike it deals eternal woe.
Nay, cursed be thou; since against his thy will
Chose freely what it now so justly rues.
Me miserable! which way shall I fly
Infinite wrath and infinite despair?
Which way I fly is Hell; myself am Hell;
And, in the lowest deep, a lower deep
Still threatening to devour me opens wide,
To which the Hell I suffer seems a Heaven.
O, then, at last relent! Is there no place
Left for repentance, none for pardon left?
None left but by submission; and that word
Disdain forbids me, and my dread of shame
Among the Spirits beneath, whom I seduced
With other promises and other vaunts

Than to submit, boasting I could subdue
The Omnipotent. Ay me! they little know
How dearly I abide that boast so vain,
Under what torments inwardly I groan.
While they adore me on the throne of Hell,
With diadem and sceptre high advanced,
The lower still I fall, only supreme
In misery: such joy ambition finds!
But say I could repent, and could obtain,
By act of grace, my former state; how soon
Would height recall high thoughts, how soon unsay
What feigned submission swore! Ease would recant
Vows made in pain, as violent and void;
For never can true reconcilement grow
Where wounds of deadly hate have pierced so
    deep.
Which would but lead me to a worse relapse
And heavier fall; so should I purchase dear
Short intermission, bought with double smart.
This knows my Punisher; therefore as far
From granting he, as I from begging, peace.
All hope excluded thus, behold, instead
Of us, outcast, exiled, his new delight,
Mankind, created, and for him this World!
So farewell hope, and, with hope, farewell fear,
Farewell remorse! All good to me is lost;
Evil, be thou my Good: by thee at least
Divided empire with Heaven's King I hold,
By thee, and more than half perhaps will reign;
As Man ere long, and this new World, shall
    know.'

PARADISE LOST, BOOK IV (LINES 131–165)

THE GARDEN OF EDEN

So on he fares, and to the border comes
Of Eden, where delicious Paradise,
Now nearer, crowns with her enclosure green,
As with a rural mound, the champaign head
Of a steep wilderness, whose hairy sides
With thicket overgrown, grotesque and wild,
Access denied; and overhead up-grew
Insuperable height of loftiest shade,
Cedar, and pine, and fir, and branching palm,
A sylvan scene, and, as the ranks ascend
Shade above shade, a woody theatre
Of stateliest view. Yet higher than their tops
The verdurous wall of Paradise up-sprung;
Which to our general sire gave prospect large
Into his nether empire neighbouring round.
And higher than that wall a circling row
Of goodliest trees, loaden with fairest fruit,
Blossoms and fruits at once of golden hue,
Appeared, with gay enamelled colours mixed;
On which the sun more glad impressed his beams
Than in fair evening cloud, or humid bow,
When God hath showered the earth: so lovely
    seemed
That landscape; and of pure, now purer air
Meets his approach, and to the heart inspires
Vernal delight and joy, able to drive
All sadness but despair. Now gentle gales,
Fanning their odoriferous wings, dispense
Native perfumes, and whisper whence they stole
Those balmy spoils.

BOOK IV (LINES 288–351 and 598–688)

ADAM AND EVE IN THE GARDEN

Two of far nobler shape, erect and tall,
God-like erect, with native honour clad
In naked majesty, seemed lords of all,
And worthy seemed; for in their looks divine
The image of their glorious Maker shone,
Truth, wisdom, sanctitude severe and pure—
Severe, but in true filial freedom placed;
Whence true authority in men: though both
Not equal, as their sex not equal seemed;
For contemplation he and valour formed,
For softness she and sweet attractive grace;
He for God only, she for God in him.
His fair large front and eye sublime declared
Absolute rule; and hyacinthine locks
Round from his parted forelock manly hung
Clustering, but not beneath his shoulders broad:
She, as a veil down to the slender waist,
Her unadornèd golden tresses wore
Dishevelled, but in wanton ringlets waved
As the vine curls her tendrils—which implied
Subjection, but required with gentle sway,
And by her yielded, by him best received,
Yielded, with coy submission, modest pride,
And sweet, reluctant, amorous delay.
Nor those mysterious parts were then concealed;
Then was not guilty shame: dishonest shame
Of Nature's works, honour dishonourable.
Sin-bred, how have ye troubled all mankind
With shows instead, mere shows of seeming pure,
And banished from man's life his happiest life,
Simplicity and spotless innocence!

So passed they naked on, nor shunned the sight
Of God or Angel; for they thought no ill;
So hand in hand they passed, the loveliest pair
That ever since in love's embraces met—
Adam, the goodliest man of men since born
His sons; the fairest of her daughters Eve.
Under a tuft of shade that on a green
Stood whispering soft, by a fresh fountain-side
They sat them down; and, after no more toil
Of their sweet gardening labour than sufficed
To recommend cool Zephyr, and made ease
More easy, wholesome thirst and appetite
More grateful, to their supper-fruits they fell—
Nectarine fruits, which the compliant boughs
Yielded them, sidelong as they sat recline
On the soft downy bank damasked with flowers.
The savoury pulp they chew, and in the rind,
Still as they thirsted, scoop the brimming stream;
Nor gentle purpose, nor endearing smiles
Wanted, nor youthful dalliance, as beseems
Fair couple linked in happy nuptial league,
Alone as they. About them frisking played
All beasts of the earth, since wild, and of all chase
In wood or wilderness, forest or den.
Sporting the lion ramped, and in his paw
Dandled the kid; bears, tigers, ounces, pards,
Gambolled before them; the unwieldy elephant,
To make them mirth, used all his might, and wreathed
His lithe proboscis; close the serpent sly,
Insinuating, wove with Gordian twine
His braided train, and of his fatal guile
Gave proof unheeded. Others on the grass
Couched, and now filled with pasture, gazing
    sat. . . .

Now came still Evening on, and Twilight grey
Had in her sober livery all things clad;
Silence accompanied; for beast and bird,
They to their grassy couch, these to their nests
Were slunk, all but the wakeful nightingale;
She all night long her amorous descant sung:
Silence was pleased. Now glowed the firmament
With living sapphires; Hesperus, that led
The starry host, rode brightest, till the Moon,
Rising in clouded majesty, at length
Apparent queen, unveiled her peerless light,
And o'er the dark her silver mantle threw;
When Adam thus to Eve:—'Fair consort, the hour
Of night, and all things now retired to rest,
Mind us of like repose; since God hath set
Labour and rest, as day and night, to men
Successive, and the timely dew of sleep,
Now falling with soft slumberous weight inclines
Our eyelids. Other creatures all day long
Rove idle, unemployed, and less need rest;
Man hath his daily work of body or mind
Appointed, which declares his dignity,
And the regard of Heaven on all his ways;
While other animals unactive range,
And of their doings God takes no account.
To-morrow, ere fresh morning streak the east
With first approach of light, we must be risen,
And at our pleasant labour, to reform
Yon flowery arbours, yonder alleys green,
Our walks at noon, with branches overgrown,
That mock our scant manuring, and require
More hands than ours to lop their wanton growth.
Those blossoms also, and those dropping gums,

That lie bestrewn, unsightly and unsmooth,
Ask riddance, if we mean to tread with ease.
Meanwhile, as Nature wills, Night bids us rest.'
    To whom thus Eve, with perfect beauty ad-
      orned:—
'My author and disposer, what thou bidd'st
Unargued I obey. So God ordains:
God is thy law, thou mine: to know no more
Is woman's happiest knowledge, and her praise.
With thee conversing, I forget all time,
All seasons, and their change; all please alike.
Sweet is the breath of Morn, her rising sweet,
With charm of earliest birds; pleasant the Sun,
When first on this delightful land he spreads
His orient beams, on herb, tree, fruit, and flower,
Glistering with dew; fragrant the fertile Earth
After soft showers; and sweet the coming-on
Of grateful Evening mild: then silent Night,
With this her solemn bird, and this fair Moon,
And these the gems of Heaven, her starry train:
But neither breath of Morn, when she ascends
With charm of earliest birds; nor rising Sun
On this delightful land; nor herb, fruit, flower,
Glistering with dew; nor fragrance after showers;
Nor grateful Evening mild; nor silent Night,
With this her solemn bird; nor walk by moon,
Or glittering starlight, without thee is sweet.
But wherefore all night long shine these? for whom
This glorious sight, when sleep hath shut all eyes?'
    To whom our general ancestor replied:—
'Daughter of God and Man, accomplished Eve,
Those have their course to finish round the Earth
By morrow evening, and from land to land
In order, though to nations yet unborn,

Ministering light prepared, they set and rise;
Lest total darkness should by night regain
Her old possession, and extinguish life
In nature and all things; which these soft fires
Not only enlighten, but with kindly heat
Of various influence foment and warm,
Temper or nourish, or in part shed down
Their stellar virtue on all kinds that grow
On Earth, made hereby apter to receive
Perfection from the Sun's more potent ray.
These, then, though unbeheld in deep of night,
Shine not in vain. Nor think, though men were none,
That Heaven would want spectators, God want praise.
Millions of spiritual creatures walk the Earth
Unseen, both when we wake, and when we sleep:
All these with ceaseless praise his works behold
Both day and night. How often, from the steep
Of echoing hill or thicket, have we heard
Celestial voices to the midnight air,
Sole, or responsive each to other's note,
Singing their great Creator! Oft in bands
While they keep watch, or nightly rounding walk,
With heavenly touch of instrumental sounds
In full harmonic number joined, their songs
Divide the night, and lift our thoughts to Heaven.'

PARADISE REGAINED

BOOK II (LINES 260–284)

THE SON OF GOD IN THE WILDERNESS. HIS DREAM

It was the hour of night, when thus the Son
Communed in silent walk, then laid him down
Under the hospitable covert nigh
Of trees thick interwoven. There he slept,

And dreamed, as appetite is wont to dream,
Of meats and drinks, nature's refreshment sweet.
Him thought he by the brook of Cherith stood,
And saw the ravens with their horny beaks
Food to Elijah bringing even and morn—
Though ravenous, taught to abstain from what
        they brought;
He saw the Prophet also, how he fled
Into the desert, and how there he slept
Under a juniper—then how, awaked,
He found his supper on the coals prepared,
And by the Angel was bid rise and eat,
And eat the second time after repose,
The strength whereof sufficed him forty days:
Sometimes that with Elijah he partook,
Or as a guest with Daniel at his pulse.
Thus wore out night; and now the herald lark
Left his ground-nest, high towering to descry
The Morn's approach, and greet her with his song.
As lightly from his grassy couch uprose
Our Saviour, and found all was but a dream;
Fasting he went to sleep, and fasting waked.

PARADISE REGAINED, BOOK IV (LINES 237–284)

SATAN'S SURVEY OF GREECE

WESTWARD, much nearer by south-west, behold
Where on the Ægean shore a city stands,
Built nobly, pure the air and light the soil—
Athens, the eye of Greece, mother of arts
And eloquence, native to famous wits
Or hospitable, in her sweet recess,
City or suburban, studious walks and shades.
See there the olive-grove of Academe,

Plato's retirement, where the Attic bird
Trills her thick-warbled notes the summer long;
There, flowery hill, Hymettus, with the sound
Of bees' industrious murmur, oft invites
To studious musing; there Ilissus rolls
His whispering stream.   Within the walls then view
The schools of ancient sages—his who bred
Great Alexander to subdue the world,
Lyceum there; and painted Stoa next.
There thou shalt hear and learn the secret power
Of harmony, in tones and numbers hit
By voice or hand, and various-measured verse,
Æolian charms and Dorian lyric odes,
And his who gave them breath, but higher sung,
Blind Melesigenes, thence Homer called,
Whose poem Phœbus challenged for his own.
Thence what the lofty grave Tragedians taught
In chorus or iambic, teachers best
Of moral prudence, with delight received
In brief sententious precepts, while they treat
Of fate, and chance, and change in human life,
High actions and high passions best describing.
Thence to the famous Orators repair,
Those ancient, whose resistless eloquence
Wielded at will that fierce democraty,
Shook the Arsenal, and fulmined over Greece
To Macedon and Artaxerxes' throne.
To sage Philosophy next lend thine ear,
From Heaven descended to the low-roofed house
Of Socrates—see there his tenement—
Whom, well inspired, the oracle pronounced
Wisest of men; from whose mouth issued forth
Mellifluous streams, that watered all the schools
Of Academics old and new, with those

Surnamed Peripatetics, and the sect
Epicurean, and the Stoic severe.
These here revolve, or, as thou lik'st, at home,
Till time mature thee to a kingdom's weight;
These rules will render thee a king complete
Within thyself, much more with empire joined.

SAMSON AGONISTES (LINES 1596–1659)

SAMSON AT GAZA. HIS LAST TRIAL OF STRENGTH

Messenger

OCCASIONS drew me early to this city;
And, as the gates I entered with sun-rise,
The morning trumpets festival proclaimed
Through each high street. Little I had dispatched,
When all abroad was rumoured that this day
Samson should be brought forth, to show the
people
Proof of his mighty strength in feats and games.
I sorrowed at his captive state, but minded
Not to be absent at that spectacle.
The building was a spacious theatre,
Half round on two main pillars vaulted high,
With seats where all the lords, and each degree
Of sort, might sit in order to behold;
The other side was open, where the throng
On banks and scaffolds under sky might stand:
I among these aloof obscurely stood.
The feast and noon grew high, and sacrifice
Had filled their hearts with mirth, high cheer, and
wine,
When to their sports they turned. Immediately
Was Samson as a public servant brought,
In their state livery clad: before him pipes

And timbrels; on each side went armèd guards;
Both horse and foot before him and behind,
Archers and slingers, cataphracts, and spears.
At sight of him the people with a shout
Rifted the air, clamouring their god with praise,
Who had made their dreadful enemy their thrall.
He patient, but undaunted, where they led him,
Came to the place; and what was set before him,
Which without help of eye might be assayed,
To heave, pull, draw, or break, he still performed
All with incredible, stupendious force,
None daring to appear antagonist.
At length, for intermission sake, they led him
Between the pillars; he his guide requested
(For so from such as nearer stood we heard),
As over-tired, to let him lean a while
With both his arms on those two massy pillars,
That to the archèd roof gave main support.
He unsuspicious led him; which when Samson
Felt in his arms, with head a while inclined,
And eyes fast fixed, he stood, as one who prayed,
Or some great matter in his mind revolved:
At last, with head erect, thus cried aloud:—
'Hitherto, Lords, what your commands imposed
I have performed, as reason was, obeying,
Not without wonder or delight beheld;
Now, of my own accord, such other trial
I mean to show you of my strength, yet greater,
As with amaze shall strike all who behold.'
This uttered, straining all his nerves, he bowed;
As with the force of winds and waters pent,
When mountains tremble, those two massy pillars
With horrible convulsion to and fro
He tugged, he shook, till down they came, and drew

The whole roof after them with burst of thunder
Upon the heads of all who sat beneath,
Lords, ladies, captains, counsellors, or priests,
Their choice nobility and flower, not only
Of this, but each Philistian city round,
Met from all parts to solemnize this feast.
Samson, with these immixed, inevitably
Pulled down the same destruction on himself;
The vulgar only scaped, who stood without.

SIR JOHN SUCKLING

1609–1642

SONG

WHY so pale and wan, fond lover?
    Prythee, why so pale?
Will, when looking well can't move her,
    Looking ill prevail?
    Prythee, why so pale?

Why so dull and mute, young sinner?
    Prythee, why so mute?
Will, when speaking well can't win her,
    Saying nothing do't?
    Prythee, why so mute?

Quit, quit, for shame! this will not move,
    This cannot take her;
If of herself she will not love,
    Nothing can make her:
    The devil take her!

A CONSTANT LOVER

Out upon it, I have loved
  Three whole days together!
And am like to love three more,
  If it prove fair weather.

Time shall moult away his wings
  Ere he shall discover
In the whole wide world again
  Such a constant lover.

But the spite on 't is, no praise
  Is due at all to me:
Love with me had made no stays,
  Had it any been but she.

Had it any been but she,
  And that very face,
There had been at least ere this
  A dozen dozen in her place.

Last Remains, 1659.

FROM 'A BALLAD UPON A WEDDING'

I tell thee, Dick, where I have been,
Where I the rarest things have seen,
  Oh, things beyond compare!
Such sights again cannot be found
In any place on English ground,
  Be it at wake or fair.

At Charing Cross, hard by the way
Where we (thou know'st) do sell our hay,
  There is a house with stairs;
And there did I see coming down
Such folk as are not in our town,
  Forty at least, in pairs.

Amongst the rest, one pestilent fine
('His beard no bigger, though, than thine!)
    Walked on before the rest.
Our landlord looks like nothing to him;
The king (God bless him!), 'twould undo him,
    Should he go still so dressed. . . .

But wot you what? The youth was going
To make an end of all his wooing;
    The Parson for him stayed.
Yet, by his leave, for all his haste,
He did not so much wish all passed,
    Perchance, as did the maid.

The maid (and thereby hangs a tale)
For such a maid no Whitsun ale
    Could ever yet produce;
No grape that's kindly ripe could be
So round, so plump, so soft, as she;
    Nor half so full of juice!

Her finger was so small, the ring
Would not stay on; which they did bring.
    It was too wide a peck!
And to say truth, for out it must,
It looked like the great collar (just)
    About our young colt's neck.

Her feet, beneath her petticoat,
Like little mice stole in and out,
    As if they feared the light:
But oh! she dances such a way,
No sun, upon an Easter Day,
    Is half so fine a sight! . . .

Her cheeks so rare a white was on;
No daisy makes comparison,
    Who sees them is undone.

For streaks of red were mingled there,
Such as are on a Katherine pear
   (The side that 's next the sun).

Her lips were red, and one was thin
Compared to that was next her chin
   (Some bee had stung it newly).
But, Dick, her eyes so guard her face,
I durst no more upon them gaze,
   Than on the sun in July.

Her mouth so small, when she does speak
Thou'dst swear her teeth her words did break,
   That they might passage get:
But she so handled still the matter,
They came as good as ours or better,
   And are not spent a whit! . . .

Just in the nick, the cook knocked thrice,
And all the waiters, in a trice,
   His summons did obey.
Each serving-man, with dish in hand,
Marched boldly up like our trained band,
   Presented, and away!

The business of the kitchen 's great,
For it is fit that men should eat;
   Nor was it there denied.
Passion o' me! how I run on;
There 's that that would be thought upon,
   I trow, besides the bride:

When all the meat was on the table
What man of knife or teeth was able
   To stay to be entreated
And this the very reason was,
Before the parson could say grace
   The company was seated.

Now hats fly off; and youths carouse:
Healths first go round, and then the house.
    The bride's came thick and thick.
And when 'twas named another's health,
Perhaps he made it hers by stealth.
    (And who could help it, Dick?)

O' th' sudden, up they rise and dance:
Then sit again and sigh and glance,
    Then dance again and kiss.
Thus several ways the time did pass;
Whilst every woman wished her place,
    And every man wished his!

I PRITHEE SEND ME BACK MY HEART

I PRITHEE send me back my heart,
    Since I can not have thine;
For if from yours you will not part,
    Why, then, shouldst thou have mine?

Yet now I think on't, let it lie,
    To find it were in vain;
For th' hast a thief in either eye
    Would steal it back again.

Why should two hearts in one breast lie,
    And yet not lodge together?
O Love! where is thy sympathy,
    If thus our breasts thou sever?

But love is such a mystery,
    I cannot find it out:
For when I think I'm best resolved,
    I then am in most doubt.

Then farewell care, and farewell woe;
   I will no longer pine:
For I'll believe I have her heart,
   As much as she hath mine.

Last Remains, 1659.

WILLIAM CARTWRIGHT

1611–1643

A NEW YEAR'S GIFT

**TO BRIAN LORD BISHOP OF SARUM UPON THE AUTHOR'S
ENTERING INTO HOLY ORDERS, 1638**

Now that the village reverence doth lie hid,
   As Egypt's Wisdom did,
In birds and beasts, and that the tenant's soul
   Goes with his New Year's fowl;
   So that the cock and hen speak more
   Now than in fables heretofore;
   And that the feathered things
   Truly make love have wings:
Though we no flying present have to pay,
A quill yet snatch'd from thence may sign the day.

But, being the Canon bars me wit and wine,
   Enjoining the true Vine,
Being the bays must yield unto the Cross,
   And all be now one loss;
   So that my raptures are to steal
   And knit themselves in one pure zeal,
   And that my each day's breath
   Must be a daily death:

Without all strain of fury must I than
Tell you this New Year brings you a new man.

New, not as th' year, to run the same course o'er
  Which it hath run before,
Lest in the man himself there be a round,
  As in his humour's found,
  And that return seem to make good
  Circling of actions, as of blood.
   Motion as in a mill,
   Is busy standing still;
And by such wheeling we but thus prevail,
To make the serpent swallow his own tail.

Nor new by solemnizing looser toys,
  And erring with less noise,
Taking the flag and trumpet from the sin,
  So to offend within;
  As some men silence loud perfumes
  And draw them into shorter rooms:
   This will be understood
   More wary, not more good.
Sins too may be severe, and so, no doubt,
The vice but only sour'd, not rooted out.

But new, by th' using of each part aright,
  Changing both step and sight;
That false direction comes not from the eye,
  Nor the foot tread awry;
  That neither *that* the way aver
  Which doth toward fame, or profit, err,
   Nor *this* tread that path which
   Is not the right, but rich;
That thus the foot being fix'd, thus led the eye,
I pitch my walk low, but my prospect high.

    than] then.

New too, to teach my opinions not t' submit
  To favour, or to wit;
Nor yet to walk on edges, where they may
  Run safe in broader way;
  Nor to search out for new paths, where
  Nor tracks nor footsteps doth appear,
   Knowing that deeps are ways
   Where no impression stays;
Nor servile thus, nor curious, may I then
Approve my faith to heaven, my life to men.

But I who thus present myself as new,
  Am thus made new by you.
Had not your rays dwelt on me, one long night
  Had shut me up from sight.
  Your beams exhale me from among
  Things tumbling in the common throng.
   Who thus with your fire burns,
   Now gives not, but returns.
To others then be this a day of thrift:
They do receive; but you, sir, make the gift.

TO CHLOE, WHO WISHED HERSELF YOUNG
ENOUGH FOR ME

 Chloe, why wish you that your years
  Would backward run, till they meet mine,
That perfect likeness which endears
  Things unto things, might us combine?
Our ages so in date agree
That twins do differ more than we.

There are two births; the one when light
  First strikes the new awaken'd sense;

The other when two souls unite,
  And we must count our life from thence:
When you loved me and I loved you
Then both of us were born anew.

Love then to us did new souls give
  And in those souls did plant new powers;
Since when another life we live,
  The breath we breathe is his, not ours:
Love makes those young whom age doth chill,
And whom he finds young keeps young still.

Love, like that angel that shall call
  Our bodies from the silent grave,
Unto one age doth raise us all,
  None too much, none too little have.
Nay, that the difference may be none,
He makes two, not alike, but one.

And now since you and I are such,
  Tell me what's yours, and what is mine?
Our eyes, our ears, our taste, smell, touch,
  Do (like our souls) in one combine—
So by this, I as well may be
Too old for you, as you for me.

JAMES GRAHAM, MARQUIS OF MONTROSE

1612–1650

HEROIC LOVE

My dear and only love, I pray
  This noble world of thee
Be governed by no other sway
  But purest monarchy;

For if confusion have a part,
  (Which virtuous souls abhor),
And hold a synod in thy heart,
  I'll never love thee more.

Like Alexander I will reign,
  And I will reign alone;
My thoughts did evermore disdain
  A rival on my throne.
He either fears his fate too much,
  On his deserts are small,
That puts it not unto the touch
  To win or lose it all.

But I must rule and govern still
  And always give the law,
And have each subject at my will
  And all to stand in awe.
But 'gainst my battery, if I find
  Thou shunn'st the prize so sore
As that thou sett'st me up a blind,
  I'll never love thee more!

Or in the empire of thy heart,
  Where I should solely be,
Another do pretend a part
  And dares to vie with me,
Or if *committees* thou erect,
  And go on such a score,
I'll sing and laugh at thy neglect,
  And never love thee more.

But if thou wilt be constant then,
  And faithful of thy word;
I'll make thee glorious by my pen
  And famous by my sword,

    I'll serve thee in such noble ways
        Was never heard before!
    I'll crown and deck thee all with bays,
        And love thee evermore.

UPON THE DEATH OF KING CHARLES I

GREAT, good, and just, could I but rate
My grief to thy too rigid fate,
I'd weep the world in such a strain,
As it would deluge once again:
But since thy loud-tongued blood demands supplies
More from Briareus' hands than Argus' eyes,
I'll tune thy elegies to trumpet sounds,
And write thy epitaph in blood and wounds.

SAMUEL BUTLER

1612–1680

HUDIBRAS

WHEN civil fury first grew high,
And men fell out, they knew not why;
When hard words, jealousies, and fears,
Set folks together by the ears,
And made them fight, like mad or drunk,
For Dame Religion as for punk,
Whose honesty they all durst swear for,
Though not a man of them knew wherefore:
When gospel-trumpeter surrounded,
With long-eared rout to battle sounded,
And pulpit, drum ecclesiastic,
Was beat with fist, instead of a stick;
Then did Sir Knight abandon dwelling,
And out he rode a-colonelling.

A wight he was, whose very sight would
Entitle him Mirror of Knighthood;
That never bent his stubborn knee
To any thing but chivalry,
Nor put up blow, but that which laid
Right worshipful on shoulder-blade:
Chief of domestic knights and errant,
Either for cartel or for warrant;
Great on the bench, great in the saddle,
That could as well bind o'er, as swaddle,
Mighty he was at both of these,
And styled of war as well as peace
(So some rats, of amphibious nature,
Are either for the land or water).
But here our authors make a doubt
Whether he were more wise, or stout.
Some hold the one, and some the other;
But howsoe'er they make a pother,
The difference was so small, his brain
Outweighed his rage but half a grain;
Which made some take him for a tool
That knaves do work with, called a fool.
For 't has been held by many, that
As Montaigne, playing with his cat,
Complains she thought him but an ass,
Much more she would Sir Hudibras.
(For that 's the name our valiant knight
To all his challenges did write.)
But they're mistaken very much,
'Tis plain enough he was no such;
We grant, although he had much wit,
H' was very shy of using it;
As being loth to wear it out,

       swaddle] cudgel.

And therefore bore it not about,
Unless on holy-days, or so,
As men their best apparel do.
Beside, 'tis known he could speak Greek
As naturally as pigs squeak;
That Latin was no more difficile,
Than to a blackbird 'tis to whistle:
Being rich in both, he never scanted
His bounty unto such as wanted;
But much of either would afford
To many, that had not one word.
For Hebrew roots, although th' are found
To flourish most in barren ground,
He had such plenty, as sufficed
To make some think him circumcised;
And truly so, perhaps, he was,
'Tis many a pious Christian's case.

He was in logic a great critic,
Profoundly skilled in analytic;
He could distinguish, and divide
A hair 'twixt south and south-west side;
On either which he would dispute,
Confute, change hands, and still confute.
He'd undertake to prove by force
Of argument, a man 's no horse.
He'd prove a buzzard is no fowl,
And that a lord may be an owl,
A calf an alderman, a goose a justice,
And rooks committee-men and trustees.
He'd run in debt by disputation,
And pay with ratiocination.
All this by syllogism, true
In mood and figure, he would do.

For rhetoric, he could not ope

His mouth, but out there flew a trope;
And when he happened to break off
I' th' middle of his speech, or cough,
H' had hard words, ready to show why,
And tell what rules he did it by;
Else when with greatest art he spoke,
You'd think he talked like other folk.
For all a rhetorician's rules
Teach nothing but to name his tools.
But, when he pleased to show't, his speech
In loftiness of sound was rich;
A Babylonish dialect,
Which learnèd pedants much affect.
It was a parti-coloured dress
Of patched and piebald languages;
'Twas English cut on Greek and Latin,
Like fustian heretofore on satin;
It had an old promiscuous tone,
As if h' had talked three parts in one;
Which made some think, when he did gabble,
Th' had heard three labourers of Babel;
Or Cerberus himself pronounce
A leash of languages at once.
This he as volubly would vent
As if his stock would ne'er be spent:
And truly, to support that charge,
He had supplies as vast and large;
For he could coin, or counterfeit
New words, with little or no wit;
Words so debased and hard, no stone
Was hard enough to touch them on;
And when with hasty noise he spoke 'em;
The ignorant for current took 'em;
That had the orator, who once

Did fill his mouth with pebble stones
When he harangued, but known his phrase,
He would have used no other ways.

In mathematics he was greater
Than Tycho Brahe, or Erra Pater:
For he, by geometric scale,
Could take the size of pots of ale;
Resolve, by sines and tangents straight,
If bread or butter wanted weight;
And wisely tell what hour o' th' day
The clock doth strike, by Algebra.

Beside, he was a shrewd philosopher,
And had read ev'ry text and gloss over;
Whate'er the crabbed'st author hath,
He understood b' implicit faith:
Whatever sceptic could inquire for,
For ev'ry why he had a wherefore;
Knew more than forty of them do,
As far as words and terms could go.
All which he understood by rote,
And, as occasion served, would quote;
No matter whether right or wrong:
They might be either said or sung.
His notions fitted things so well,
That which was which he could not tell;
But oftentimes mistook th' one
For th' other, as great clerks have done.
He could reduce all things to acts,
And knew their natures by abstracts;
Where entity and quiddity,
The ghosts of defunct bodies, fly;
Where truth in person does appear
Like words congealed in Northern air.
He knew what 's what, and that 's as high

As metaphysic wit can fly,
In school divinity as able
As he that hight Irrefragable;
Profound in all the nominal
And real ways beyond them all;
And with as delicate a hand,
Could twist as tough a rope of sand.
And weave fine cobwebs, fit for skull
That's empty when the moon is full;
Such as take lodgings in a head
That's to be let unfurnishèd.
He could raise scruples dark and nice,
And after solve 'em in a trice:
As if divinity had catched
The itch, of purpose to be scratched;
Or, like a mountebank, did wound
And stab herself with doubts profound,
Only to show with how small pain
The sores of faith are cured again;
Although by woful proof we find
They always leave a scar behind.
He knew the seat of paradise,
Could tell in what degree it lies:
And, as he was disposed, could prove it,
Below the moon, or else above it.
What Adam dreamt of when his bride
Came from her closet in his side:
Whether the Devil tempted her
By a High Dutch interpreter:
If either of them had a navel;
Who first made music malleable:
Whether the Serpent at the Fall
Had cloven feet or none at all.
All this without a gloss or comment,

He would unriddle in a moment:
In proper terms, such as men smatter
When they throw out and miss the matter.
  For his Religion, it was fit
To match his learning and his wit;
'Twas Presbyterian true blue;
For he was of that stubborn crew
Of errant saints, whom all men grant
To be the true church militant;
Such as do build their faith upon
The holy text of pike and gun;
Decide all controversies by
Infallible artillery;
And prove their doctrine orthodox
By apostolic blows and knocks;
Call fire and sword and desolation,
A godly-thorough-reformation,
Which always must be carried on,
And still be doing, never done;
As if religion were intended
For nothing else but to be mended.
A sect, whose chief devotion lies
In odd perverse antipathies;
In falling out with that or this,
And finding somewhat still amiss;
More peevish, cross, and splenetic,
Than dog distract or monkey sick;
That with more care keep holy-day
The wrong, than others the right way;
Compound for sins they are inclined to,
By damning those they have no mind to:
Still so perverse and opposite,
As if they worshipped God for spite.

distract] distraught.

The self-same thing they will abhor
One way, and long another for.
Free will they one way disavow,
Another, nothing else allow.
All piety consists therein
In them, in other men all sin.
Rather than fail, they will defy
That which they love most tenderly,
Quarrel with minced-pies, and disparage
Their best and dearest friend, plum-porridge;
Fat pig and goose itself oppose,
And blaspheme custard through the nose.
Th' apostles of this fierce religion,
Like Mahomet's, were ass and widgeon,
To whom our knight, by fast instinct
Of wit and temper, was so linked,
As if hypocrisy and nonsense
Had got th'advowson of his conscience.

RICHARD CRASHAW

1613–1649

THE SHEPHERD'S HYMN

Chorus. COME, we shepherds, whose blest sight
     Hath met Love's noon in Nature's night;
Come lift we up our loftier song
     And wake the sun that lies too long.

     To all our world of well-stol'n joy
He slept; and dreamt of no such thing.
     While we found out heaven's fairer eye
And kissed the cradle of our king.
     Tell him he rises now, too late
To show us ought worth looking at.

Tell him we now can show him more
Than he e'er showed to mortal sight;
   Than he himself e'er saw before;
Which to be seen needs not his light.
   Tell him, Tityrus, where th' hast been,
Tell him, Thyrsis, what th' hast seen.

Tityrus. Gloomy night embraced the place
   Where the noble Infant lay.
   The Babe looked up and showed His face;
In spite of darkness, it was day.
   It was Thy day, Sweet! and did rise
Not from the East, but from Thine eyes.

   Chorus. It was Thy day, Sweet, etc.

Thyrsis. Winter chid aloud; and sent
   The angry North to wage his wars.
   The North forgot his fierce intent;
And left perfumes instead of scars.
   By those sweet eyes' persuasive powers
Where he meant frost, he scattered flowers.

   Chorus. By those sweet eyes, etc.

Both. We saw Thee in Thy balmy nest,
   Young dawn of our eternal day!
   We saw Thine eyes break from their East
And chase the trembling shades away.
   We saw Thee; and we blest the sight,
We saw Thee by Thine own sweet light.

Tity. Poor world (said I) what wilt thou do
   To entertain this starry stranger?
   Is this the best thou canst bestow?
A cold, and not too cleanly, manger?

Contend, ye powers of heaven and earth,
To fit a bed for this huge birth.

  Chorus. Contend, ye powers, etc.

Thyr. Proud world, said I; cease your contest,
  And let the mighty Babe alone.
The phœnix builds the phœnix' nest,
  Love's architecture is His own.
The Babe whose birth embraves this morn,
Made His own bed ere He was born.

  Chorus. The Babe, etc.

Tit. I saw the curled drops, soft and slow,
  Come hovering o'er the place's head;
Off'ring their whitest sheets of snow
  To furnish the fair Infant's bed.
Forbear, said I; be not too bold.
Your fleece is white, but 'tis too cold.

  Chorus. Forbear, said I, etc.

Thyr. I saw the obsequious Seraphims
  Their rosy fleece of fire bestow.
For well they now can spare their wings
  Since heaven itself lies here below.
Well done, said I: but are you sure
Your down so warm, will pass for pure?

  Chorus. Well done, said I, etc.

No, no, your King's not yet to seek
  Where to repose His royal head;
See, see how soon His new-bloomed cheek
  'Twixt mother's breasts is gone to bed.
Sweet choice, said we! no way but so,
Not to lie cold, yet sleep in snow.

  Chorus. Sweet choice, said we, etc.

Both.   We saw Thee in Thy balmy nest,
     Bright dawn of our eternal day!
     We saw Thine eyes break from their East
     And chase the trembling shades away.
     We saw Thee: and we blest the sight.
     We saw Thee, by Thine own sweet light.

       Chorus.   We saw Thee, etc.

Full Chorus.

     Welcome, all wonders in one sight!
     Eternity shut in a span,
       Summer in winter—day in night,
     Heaven in earth, and God in man.
       Great little one! whose all-embracing birth
     Lifts earth to heaven, stoops heaven to earth.

     Welcome, though nor to gold nor silk,
     To more than Cæsar's birthright is;
       Two sister-seas of Virgin-milk,
     With many a rarely-tempered kiss
       That breathes at once both Maid and Mother,
     Warms in the one, cools in the other.

     Welcome, though not to those gay flies
     Gilded 'i th' beams of earthly kings;
       Slippery souls in smiling eyes;
     But to poor shepherds, home-spun things:
       Whose wealth's their flock: whose wit, to be
     Well read in their simplicity.

     Yet when young April's husband showers
     Shall bless the fruitful Maia's bed
       We'll bring the firstborn of her flowers
     To kiss Thy feet and crown Thy head.
       To Thee, dread Lamb! whose love must keep
     The shepherds, more than they the sheep;

To Thee, meek Majesty! soft King
Of simple graces and sweet loves.
   Each of us his lamb will bring,
Each his pair of silver doves;
   Till burnt at last in fire of Thy fair eyes,
Ourselves become our own best sacrifice.

WISHES TO HIS SUPPOSED MISTRESS

WHOE'ER she be,
That not impossible she
That shall command my heart and me:

Where'er she lie,
Locked up from mortal eye,
In shady leaves of destiny:

Till that ripe birth
Of studied fate stand forth,
And teach her fair steps to our earth:

Till that divine
Idea take a shrine
Of crystal flesh, through which to shine:

Meet you her, my wishes,
Bespeak her to my blisses,
And be ye called my absent kisses.

I wish her beauty,
That owes not all its duty
To gaudy tire, or glist'ring shoe-tie.

Something more than
Taffata or tissue can,
Or rampant feather, or rich fan.

A face that's best
By its own beauty drest,
And can alone commend the rest.

A face made up
Out of no other shop,
Than what nature's white hand sets ope.

A cheek where youth,
And blood, with pen of truth,
Write, what the reader sweetly ru'th.

A cheek, where grows
More than a morning rose:
Which to no box his being owes.

Lips, where all day
A lover's kiss may play,
Yet carry nothing thence away.

Looks that oppress
Their richest tires, but dress
And clothe their simplest nakedness.

Eyes, that displaces
The neighbour diamond, and outfaces
That sunshine by their own sweet graces.

Tresses that wear
Jewels, but to declare
How much themselves more precious are:

Whose native ray,
Can tame the wanton day
Of gems, that in their bright shades play.

Each ruby there,
Or pearl that dare appear,
Be its own blush, be its own tear.

A well-tamed heart,
For whose more noble smart,
Love may be long choosing a dart.

Eyes, that bestow
Full quivers on love's bow;
Yet pay less arrows than they owe.

Smiles, that can warm
The blood, yet teach a charm,
That chastity shall take no harm.

Blushes, that bin
The burnish of no sin,
Nor flames of aught too hot within.

Joys, that confess
Virtue their mistress,
And have no other head to dress.

Fears, fond and slight,
As the coy bride's, when night
First does the longing lover right.

Days, that need borrow
No part of their good-morrow
From a fore-spent night of sorrow.

Days, that in spite
Of darkness, by the light
Of a clear mind are day all night.

Nights, sweet as they,
Made short by lovers' play,
Yet long by th' absence of the day.

Life, that dares send
A challenge to his end,
And when it comes say 'Welcome, friend!'

Sydneian showers
Of sweet discourse, whose powers
Can crown old winter's head with flowers.

Soft silken hours,
Open suns; shady bowers,
'Bove all; nothing within that lowers.

Whate'er delight
Can make day's forehead bright;
Or give down to the wings of night.

I wish her store
Of worth may leave her poor
Of wishes; and I wish—no more.

Now if time knows
That Her whose radiant brows
Weave them a garland of my vows;

Her whose just bays
My future hopes can raise
A trophy to her present praise;

Her that dares be
What these lines wish to see:
I seek no further, it is she.

'Tis she, and here
Lo I unclothe and clear
My wishes' cloudy character.

May she enjoy it,
Whose merit dare apply it,
But modesty dares still deny it.

Such worth as this is
Shall fix my flying wishes,
And determine them to kisses.

Let her full glory,
My fancies, fly before ye,
Be ye my fictions; but her story.

AN EPITAPH UPON HUSBAND AND WIFE WHO DIED AND WERE BURIED TOGETHER

To these, whom death again did wed,
This grave's the second marriage-bed.
For though the hand of Fate could force,
'Twixt soul and body a divorce.
It could not sever man and wife,
Because they both lived but one life.
Peace, good reader, do not weep;
Peace, the lovers are asleep:
They, sweet turtles, folded lie,
In the last knot that love could tie.
Let them sleep, let them sleep on,
Till this stormy night be gone.
And the eternal morrow dawn,
Then the curtains will be drawn,
And they waken with that light,
Whose day shall never sleep in night.

FROM 'THE FLAMING HEART'

LIVE in these conquering leaves; live all the same;
And walk through all tongues one triumphant
flame.
Live here, great Heart: and love and die and kill;
And bleed and wound; and yield and conquer still.
Let this immortal life where'er it comes
Walk in a crowd of loves and martyrdoms.
Let mystic deaths wait on 't; and wise souls be
The love-slain witnesses of this life of thee.

O sweet incendiary! show here thy art,
Upon this carcass of a hard, cold, heart,
Let all thy scattered shafts of light, that play
Among the leaves of thy large books of day,
Combined against this breast at once break in
And take away from me myself and sin,
This gracious robbery shall thy bounty be;
And my best fortunes such fair spoils of me.
O thou undaunted daughter of desires!
By all thy dower of lights and fires;
By all the eagle in thee, all the dove;
By all thy lives and deaths of love;
By thy large draughts of intellectual day,
And by thy thirsts of love more large than they;
By all thy brim-filled bowls of fierce desire,
By thy last morning's draught of liquid fire;
By the full kingdom of that final kiss
That seized thy parting soul, and sealed thee
    His;
By all the heavens thou hast in Him
Fair sister of the seraphim!
By all of Him we have in thee;
Leave nothing of myself in me.
Let me so read my life, that I
Unto all life of mine may die.

FROM 'THE WEEPER.'

The dew no more will weep,
  The primrose's pale cheek to deck,
The dew no more will sleep,
  Nuzzled in the lily's neck.
     Much rather would it tremble here,
     And leave them both to be thy tear.

When sorrow would be seen
In her brightest majesty,
—For she is a Queen—
Then is she dressed by none but thee.
  Then, and only then she wears
  Her richest pearls, I mean thy tears.

Not in the evening's eyes,
When they red with weeping are
  For the sun that dies,
Sits sorrow with a face so fair.
  Nowhere but here did ever meet
  Sweetness so sad, sadness so sweet.

Does the night arise?
Still thy tears do fall, and fall.
  Does night lose her eyes?
Still the fountain weeps for all.
  Let night or day do what they will,
  Thou hast thy task, thou weepest still.

Not, *so long she lived*
Will thy tomb report of this
  But *so long she grieved*;
Thus must we date thy memory.
  Others by days, by months, by years
  Measure their ages, thou by tears.

ON GEORGE HERBERT'S 'THE TEMPLE' SENT
TO A GENTLEWOMAN

Know you, fair, on what you look;
Divinest love lies in this book:
Expecting fire from your eyes,
To kindle this his sacrifice.
When your hands untie these strings,
Think you have an angel by th' wings.

One that gladly will be nigh,
To wait upon each morning sigh.
To flutter in the balmy air
Of your well-perfumèd prayer.

These white plumes of his he'll lend you,
Which every day to heaven will send you:
To take acquaintance of the sphere,
And all the smooth-faced kindred there.
And though Herbert's name do owe
These devotions, fairest, know
That while I lay them on the shrine
Of your white hand, they are mine.

A HYMN TO THE NAME AND HONOUR OF THE ADMIRABLE SAINT TERESA

LOVE, thou art absolute sole Lord
Of life and death. To prove the word,
We'll now appeal to none of all
Those thy old soldiers, great and tall,
Ripe men of martyrdom, that could reach down
With strong arms, their triumphant crown;
Such as could with lusty breath
Speak loud into the face of death
Their great Lord's glorious name, to none
Of those whose spacious bosoms spread a throne
For love at large to fill: spare blood and sweat;
And see Him take a private seat,
Making His mansion in the mild
And milky soul of a soft child.

Scarce has she learnt to lisp the name
Of martyr; yet she thinks it shame
Life should so long play with that breath
Which spent can buy so brave a death.

She never undertook to know
What death with love should have to do;
Nor has she e'er yet understood
Why to show love, she should shed blood;
Yet though she cannot tell you why,
She can love, and she can die.

    Scarce has she blood enough to make
A guilty sword blush for her sake;
Yet has she a heart dares hope to prove
How much less strong is death than love. . . .

Since 'tis not to be had at home
She'll travel to a martyrdom.
No home for hers confesses she
But where she may a martyr be.
    She'll to the Moors; and trade with them,
For this unvalued diadem.
She'll offer them her dearest breath,
With Christ's name in 't, in change for death.
She'll bargain with them, and will give
Them God; teach them how to live
In Him: or, if they this deny,
For Him she'll teach them how to die.
So shall she leave amongst them sown
Her Lord's blood; or at least her own.

Farewell then, all the world! Adieu.
Teresa is no more for you.
Farewell, all pleasures, sports, and joys,
Never till now esteemèd toys;
Farewell whatever dear may be,
Mother's arms or father's knee.
Farewell house, and farewell home!
She's for the Moors, and Martyrdom.

Sweet, not so fast! lo thy fair Spouse
Whom thou seek'st with so swift vows,
Calls thee back, and bids thee come
T' embrace a milder martyrdom. . . .

O how oft shalt thou complain
Of a sweet and subtle pain,
Of intolerable joys;
Of a death, in which who dies
Loves his death, and dies again,
And would for ever so be slain.
And lives, and dies; and knows not why
To live, but that he thus may never leave to die.
  How kindly will thy gentle heart
Kiss the sweetly-killing dart!
And close in His embraces keep
Those delicious wounds, that weep
Balsam to heal themselves with. Thus
When these thy deaths, so numerous,
Shall all at last die into one,
And melt thy soul's sweet mansion;
Like a soft lump of incense, hasted
By too hot a fire, and wasted
Into perfuming clouds, so fast
Shalt thou exhale to heaven at last
In a resolving sigh, and then
O what? Ask not the tongues of men.
Angels cannot tell, suffice
Thyself shalt feel thine own full joys
And hold them fast for ever. There
So soon as thou shalt first appear,
The moon of maiden stars, thy white
Mistress, attended by such bright
Souls as thy shining self, shall come

And in her first ranks make thee room;
Where 'mongst her snowy family
Immortal welcomes wait for thee.
   O what delight, when revealed Life shall stand
And teach thy lips heaven with His hand,
On which thou now may'st to thy wishes
Heap up thy consecrated kisses.
What joys shall seize thy soul, when she
Bending her blessèd eyes on thee,
Those second smiles of heaven, shall dart
Her mild rays through thy melting heart!
   Angels, thy old friends, there shall greet thee
Glad at their own home now to meet thee.
   All thy good works which went before
And waited for thee, at the door,
Shall own thee there; and all in one
Weave a constellation
Of crowns, with which the King thy spouse
Shall build up thy triumphant brows.
   All thy old woes shall now smile on thee,
And thy pains sit bright upon thee;
All thy sorrows here shall shine,
And thy sufferings be divine.
Tears shall take comfort, and turn gems
And wrongs repent to diadems.
Even thy deaths shall live; and new
Dress the soul that erst they slew.
Thy wounds shall blush to such bright scars
As keep account of the Lamb's wars.
   Those rare works where thou shalt leave writ
Love's noble history, with wit
Taught thee by none but Him, while here
They feed our souls, shall clothe thine there.
Each heavenly word by whose hid flame

Our hard hearts shall strike fire, the same
Shall flourish on thy brows, and be
Both fire to us and flame to thee;
Whose light shall live bright in thy face
By glory, in our hearts by grace.

   Thou shalt look round about, and see
Thousands of crowned souls throng to be
Themselves thy crown, sons of thy vows,
The virgin-births with which thy sovereign spouse
Made fruitful thy fair soul, go now
And with them all about thee bow
To Him, Put on, He'll say, put on,
My rosy love, that thy rich zone
Sparkling with the sacred flames
Of thousand souls, whose happy names
Heaven keeps upon thy score. Thy bright
Life brought them first to kiss the light
That kindled them to stars. And so
Thou with the Lamb, thy Lord, shalt go;
And wheresoe'er He sets His white
Steps, walk with Him those ways of light
Which who in death would live to see,
Must learn in life to die like thee.

AN ECSTACY

LORD, when the sense of Thy sweet grace
   Sends up my soul to seek Thy face.
Thy blessed eyes breed such desire,
I die in love's delicious fire.
   O love, I am Thy sacrifice.
Be still triumphant, blessed eyes.
Still shine on me, fair suns! that I
Still may behold, though still I die.

Though still I die, I live again;
Still longing so to be still slain,
So gainful is such loss of breath.
I die even in desire of death.
        Still live in me this loving strife
Of living Death and dying Life.
For while Thou sweetly slayest me,
Dead to myself, I live in Thee.

RICHARD LOVELACE

1618–1658

TO LUCASTA, GOING BEYOND THE SEAS

If to be absent were to be
        Away from thee;
    Or that when I am gone,
        You or I were alone;
    Then, my Lucasta, might I crave
Pity from blustering wind, or swallowing wave.

    But I'll not sigh one blast or gale
        To swell my sail,
    Or pay a tear to 'suage
        The foaming blue god's rage;
    For whether he will let me pass
Or no, I'm still as happy as I was.

    Though seas and land betwixt us both,
        Our faith and troth,
    Like separated souls,
        All time and space controls:
    Above the highest sphere we meet
Unseen, unknown, and greet as angels greet.

So then we do anticipate
    Our after-fate,
      And are alive i' the skies,
      If thus our lips and eyes
Can speak like spirits unconfined
In Heaven, their earthy bodies left behind.

TO ALTHEA FROM PRISON

When Love with unconfinèd wings
    Hovers within my gates;
And my divine Althea brings
    To whisper at the grates:
When I lie tangled in her hair,
    And fettered to her eye;
The birds that wanton in the air,
    Know no such liberty.

When flowing cups run swiftly round
    With no allaying Thames,
Our careless heads with roses bound,
    Our hearts with loyal flames;
When thirsty grief in wine we steep,
    When healths and draughts go free,
Fishes that tipple in the deep,
    Know no such liberty.

When, like committed linnets, I
    With shriller throat shall sing
The sweetness, mercy, majesty,
    And glories of my King;
When I shall voice aloud, how good
    He is, how great should be;
Enlargèd winds that curl the flood,
    Know no such liberty.

Stone walls do not a prison make,
    Nor iron bars a cage;
Minds innocent and quiet take
    That for an hermitage;
If I have freedom in my love,
    And in my soul am free;
Angels alone that soar above,
    Enjoy such liberty.

TO LUCASTA, GOING TO THE WARS

TELL me not, Sweet, I am unkind,
    That from the nunnery
Of thy chaste breast, and quiet mind,
    To war and arms I fly.

True; a new mistress now I chase,
    The first foe in the field;
And with a stronger faith embrace
    A sword, a horse, a shield.

Yet this inconstancy is such,
    As you too shall adore;
I could not love thee, dear, so much,
    Loved I not honour more.

TO THE GRASSHOPPER

OH thou that swingest upon the waving hair
  Of some well-fillèd oaten beard,
Drunk ev'ry night with a delicious tear
  Dropt thee from heaven, where now th' art
    reared.

The joys of earth and air are thine entire,
  That with thy feet and wings doth hop and fly,
And when thy poppy works thou dost retire
  To thy carved acron-bed to lie.

      acron] acorn

Up with the day, the sun thou welcomest then,
  Sportest in the gilt plaits of his beams,
And all these merry days makest merry men,
  Thyself, and melancholy streams.

But ah the sickle! golden ears are cropped;
  Ceres and Bacchus bid good night;
Sharp frosty fingers all your flowers have topped
  And what scythes spared, winds shave off quite.

Poor verdant fool! and now green ice! thy joys,
  Large and as lasting as thy perch of grass,
Bid us lay in 'gainst winter, rain, and poise
  Their floods, with an o'erflowing glass.

Thou best of men and friends! we will create
  A genuine summer in each other's breast;
And spite of this cold time and frozen fate
  Thaw us a warm seat to our rest.

Our sacred hearths shall burn eternally
  As vestal flames, the north-wind, he
Shall strike his frost-stretched wings, dissolve and fly
  This Œtna in epitome.

Dropping December shall come weeping in,
  Bewail the usurping of his reign;
But when in showers of old Greek we begin,
  Shall cry, he hath his crown again!

Night as clear Hesper shall our tapers whip
  From the light casements where we play,
And the dark hag from her black mantle strip,
  And stick there everlasting day.

Thus richer than untempted Kings are we,
  That asking nothing, nothing need:
Though Lord of all what seas embrace; yet he
  That wants himself, is poor indeed.

GRATIANA DANCING, AND SINGING

SEE! with what constant motion
Even, and glorious, as the sun,
　Gratiana steers that noble frame,
　　Soft as her breast, sweet as her voice
　　　That gave each winding law and poise,
　And swifter than the wings of fame.

She beat the happy pavèment
By such a star made firmament,
　Which now no more the roof envies;
　　But swells up high, with Atlas even,
　　　Bearing the brighter, nobler heaven,
　And in her, all the deities.

Each step trod out a lover's thought,
And the ambitious hopes he brought,
　Chained to her brave feet with such arts,
　　Such sweet command, and gentle awe,
　　　As when she ceased, we sighing saw
　The floor lay paved with broken hearts.

So did she move; so did she sing
Like the harmonious spheres that bring
　Unto their rounds their music's aid;
　　Which she performèd such a way,
　　　As all the enamoured world will say
　'The Graces dancèd, and Apollo played.'

ON THE DEATH OF MRS. ELIZABETH FILMER

　　CHASTE as the air whither she 's fled,
　　She making her celestial bed
　　　In her warm alabaster lay
　　As cold as in this house of clay;

Nor were the rooms unfit to feast
Or circumscribe this angel-guest;
The radiant gem was brightly set
In as divine a carcanet;
For which the clearer was not known,
Her mind, or her complexion;
Such an everlasting grace,
Such a beatific face
Incloisters here this narrow floor
That possessed all hearts before.

. . . . . .

Thus, although this marble must,
As all things, crumble into dust,
And though you find this fair-built tomb
Ashes, as what lies in its womb;
Yet her saint-like name shall shine
A living glory to this shrine,
And her eternal fame be read,
When all but very virtue's dead.

THE ROSE

SWEET serene sky-like flower,
Haste to adorn her bower:
    From thy long cloudy bed,
    Shoot forth thy damask head.

New-startled blush of Flora!
The grief of pale Aurora,
    Who will contest no more;
    Haste, haste, to strow her floor.

Vermilion ball that's given
From lip to lip in Heaven;
    Love's couch's coverlet:
    Haste, haste, to make her bed.

Dear offspring of pleased Venus,
And jolly, plump Silenus;
    Haste, haste to deck the hair
    Of the only, sweetly fair.

See! Rosy is her bower,
Her floor is all this flower;
    Her bed a rosy nest
    By a bed of roses pressed.

But early as she dresses,
Why fly you her bright tresses?
    Ah! I have found, I fear;
    Because her cheeks are near.

SIR JOHN DENHAM

1615–1669

PRAISE OF THE THAMES

My eye descending from the hill, surveys
Where Thames amongst the wanton valleys strays.
Thames, the most loved of all the Ocean's sons,
By his old sire, to his embraces runs,
Hasting to pay his tribute to the sea,
Like mortal life to meet eternity;
Though with those streams he no resemblance hold,
Whose foam is amber, and their gravel gold,
His genuine and less guilty wealth t' explore,
Search not his bottom, but survey his shore,
O'er which he kindly spreads his spacious wing,
And hatches plenty for th' ensuing spring;
Nor then destroys it with too fond a stay,
Like mothers which their infants overlay,
Nor, with a sudden and impetuous wave,
Like profuse kings, resumes the wealth he gave.

No unexpected inundations spoil
The mower's hopes, nor mock the ploughman's toil:
But godlike his unwearied bounty flows,
First loves to do, then loves the good he does;
Nor are his blessings to his banks confined,
But free and common, as the sea or wind;
When he to boast, or to disperse his stores,
Full of the tributes of his grateful shores,
Visits the world, and in his flying towers,
Brings home to us, and makes both Indies ours;
Finds wealth where 'tis, bestows it where it wants,
Cities in deserts, woods in cities plants.
So that to us no thing, no place is strange,
While his fair bosom is the world's exchange.
O could I flow like thee, and make thy stream
My great example, as it is my theme!
Though deep, yet clear, though gentle, yet not dull,
Strong without rage, without o'erflowing full.

From Cooper's Hill.

ABRAHAM COWLEY

1618–1667

IN PRAISE OF HOPE

HOPE, of all ills that men endure,
    The only cheap and universal cure!
Thou captives' freedom, and thou sick man's
    health,
Thou loser's victory, and thou beggar's wealth!
    Thou manna, which from Heaven we eat,
    To every taste a several meat!
Thou strong retreat! Thou sure entailed estate,
    Which naught has power to alienate!

Thou pleasant, honest flatterer! for none
Flatter unhappy men, but thou alone!

Hope, thou first-fruits of happiness!
Thou gentle dawning of a bright success!
Thou good preparative, without which our joy
Does work too strong, and whilst it cures, destroy;
    Who out of Fortune's reach dost stand,
    And art a blessing still in hand!
Whilst thee, her earnest-money, we retain,
    We certain are to gain,
Whether she her bargain break, or else fulfil;
Thou only good, not worse, for ending ill!

    Brother of Faith, twixt whom and thee
The joys of heaven and earth divided be!
Though faith be heir, and have the fixed estate,
Thy portion yet in moveables is great.
    Happiness itself's all one
    In thee, or in possession!
Only the future's thine, the present his!
    Thine's the more hard and noble bliss;
Best apprehender of our joys, which hast
So long a reach, and yet canst hold so fast.

    Hope, thou sad lovers' only friend!
Thou way that mayest dispute it with the end!
For love I fear 's a fruit that does delight
The taste itself less than the smell and sight.
    Fruition more deceitful is
    Than thou canst be, when thou dost miss;
Men leave thee by obtaining, and straight flee
    Some other way again to thee;
And that 's a pleasant country, without doubt,
To which all soon return that travel out.

THE CHRONICLE

A BALLAD

MARGARITA first possessed,
If I remember well, my breast;
　　Margarita first of all!
　　　　But when awhile the wanton maid
　　　　With my restless heart had played,
　　Martha took the flying ball.

Martha soon did it resign
To the beauteous Catharine,
　　Beauteous Catharine gave place
　　　　(Though loth and angry she to part
　　　　With the possession of my heart)
　　To Eliza's conquering face.

Eliza to this hour might reign,
Had not she evil counsels ta'en.
　　Fundamental laws she broke;
　　　　And still new favourites she chose,
　　　　Till up in arms my passions rose,
　　And cast away her yoke.

Mary then and gentle Anne
Both to reign at once began.
　　Alternately they swayed;
　　　　And sometimes Mary was the fair,
　　　　And sometimes Anne the crown did wear;
　　And sometimes both I obeyed.

Another Mary then arose
And did rigorous laws impose;
　　A mighty tyrant she!
　　　　Long, alas, should I have been
　　　　Under that iron-sceptred Queen,
　　Had not Rebecca set me free.

When fair Rebecca set me free,
'Twas then a golden time with me.
  But soon these pleasures fled,
    For the gracious Princess died
    In her youth and beauty's pride,
  And Judith reigned in her stead.

One month, three days, and half an hour
Judith held the sovereign power.
  Wondrous beautiful her face;
    But so weak and small her wit
    That she to govern was unfit,
  And so Susanna took her place.

But when Isabella came,
Armed with a resistless flame
  And the artillery of her eye,
    Whilst she proudly marched about
    Greater conquests to find out,
  She beat out Susan by the by.

But in her place I then obeyed
Black-eyed Bess, her viceroy maid,
  To whom ensued a vacancy.
    Thousand worse passions then possessed
    The interregnum of my breast;
  Bless me from such an anarchy!

Gentle Henrietta then,
And a third Mary next began;
  Then Joan and Jane and Audria,
    And then a pretty Thomasine,
    And then another Katharine,
  And then a long et cetera.

But should I now to you relate
The strength and riches of their state,

The powder, patches, and the pins,
  The ribands, jewels, and the rings,
  The lace, the paint and warlike things
That make up all their magazines;

If I should tell the politic arts
To take and keep men's hearts,
  The letters, embassies and spies,
    The frowns, and smiles and flatteries,
    The quarrels, tears, and perjuries
Numberless, nameless, mysteries;

And all the little lime-twigs laid
By Machiavel, the waiting-maid,
  I more voluminous should grow
    (Chiefly if I, like them, should tell
    All change of weathers that befell)
Than Holinshed or Stow.

But I will briefer with them be,
Since few of them were long with me.
  A higher and a nobler strain
    My present Emperess does claim:
    Heleonora first o' th' name,
Whom God grant long to reign.

THE SPRING

THOUGH you be absent here, I needs must say
The trees as beauteous are, the flowers as gay,
  As ever they were wont to be;
  Nay, the birds' rural music too
  Is as melodious and free,
  As if they sung to pleasure you:
I saw a rose-bud ope this morn; I'll swear
The blushing morning opened not more fair.

How could it be so fair, and you away?
How could the trees be beauteous, flowers so gay?
    Could they remember, but last year,
      How you did them, they you delight,
    The sprouting leaves which saw you here,
      And called their fellows to the sight,
Would, looking round for the same sight in vain,
Creep back into their silent barks again.

Where'er you walked trees were as reverend
    made,
As when of old gods dwelt in every shade.
    Is 't possible they should not know,
      What loss of honour they sustain,
    That thus they smile and flourish now,
      And still their former pride retain?
Dull creatures! 'tis not without cause that she,
Who fled the god of wit, was made a tree.

In ancient times sure they much wiser were,
When they rejoiced the Thracian verse to hear;
    In vain did Nature bid them stay,
      When Orpheus had his song begun,
    They called their wondering roots away,
      And bade them silent to him run.
How would those learned trees have followed you?
You would have drawn them, and their poet too.

But who can blame them now? for, since you're
    gone,
They're here the only fair, and shine alone.
    You did their natural rights invade;
      Wherever you did walk or sit,
    The thickest boughs could make no shade,
      Although the Sun had granted it:

The fairest flowers could please no more, near
    you,
Than painted flowers, set next to them, could do.

Whene'er then you come hither, that shall be
The time, which this to others is, to me.
    The little joys which here are now,
      The name of punishments do bear;
    When by their sight they let us know
      How we deprived of greater are.
'Tis you the best of seasons with you bring;
This is for beasts, and that for men, the spring.

CHEER UP, MY MATES

CHEER up, my mates, the wind does fairly blow;
    Clap on more sail, and never spare;
    Farewell, all lands, for now we are
    In the wide sea of drink, and merrily we go.
Bless me, 'tis hot! another bowl of wine,
    And we shall cut the burning Line:
Hey, boys! she scuds away, and by my head I
    know
    We round the world are sailing now.
What dull men are those who tarry at home,
When abroad they might wantonly roam,
    And gain such experience, and spy, too,
    Such countries and wonders, as I do!
But pr'ythee, good pilot, take heed what you do,
    And fail not to touch at Peru!
    With gold there the vessel we'll store,
    And never, and never be poor,
    No, never be poor any more.

ANACREONTICS

(1) *Drinking*

THE thirsty earth soaks up the rain,
And drinks and gapes for drink again;
The plants suck in the earth, and are
With constant drinking fresh and fair;
The sea itself (which one would think
Should have but little need of drink)
Drinks ten thousand rivers up,
So fill'd that they o'erflow the cup.
The busy Sun (and one would guess
By 's drunken fiery face no less)
Drinks up the sea, and when he 's done,
The Moon and Stars drink up the Sun.
They drink and dance by their own light,
They drink and revel all the night.
Nothing in Nature 's sober found,
But an eternal health goes round.
Fill up the bowl, then, fill it high,
Fill all the glasses there, for why
Should every creature drink but I?
Why, man of morals, tell me why?

(2) *The Epicure*

UNDERNEATH this myrtle shade,
On flowery beds supinely laid,
With odorous oils my head o'erflowing,
And around it roses growing,
What should I do but drink away
The heat and troubles of the day?
In this more than kingly state
Love himself shall on me wait.

Fill to me, Love! nay, fill it up!
And mingled cast into the cup
Wit and mirth and noble fires,
Vigorous health and gay desires.
The wheel of life no less will stay
In a smooth than rugged way:
Since it equally does flee,
Let the motion pleasant be.
Why do we precious ointments shower?—
Nobler wines why do we pour?—
Beauteous flowers why do we spread
Upon the monuments of the dead?
Nothing they but dust can show,
Or bones that hasten to be so.
Crown me with roses whilst I live,
Now your wines and ointments give.
After death I nothing crave,
Let me alive my pleasures have:
All are Stoics in the grave.

(3) *The Swallow*

FOOLISH prater, what dost thou
So early at my window do
With thy tuneless serenade?
Well 't had been had Tereus made
Thee as dumb as Philomel;
There his knife had done but well.
In thy undiscovered nest
Thou dost all the winter rest,
And dreamest o'er thy summer joys
Free from the stormy season's noise:
Free from th' ill thou'st done to me;
Who disturbs or seeks out thee?
Hadst thou all the charming notes

Of the woods' poetic throats,
All thy art could never pay
What thou'st ta'en from me away;
Cruel bird, thou'st ta'en away
A dream out of my arms to-day;
A dream that ne'er must equall'd be
By all that waking eyes may see.
Thou this damage to repair
Nothing half so sweet or fair,
Nothing half so good canst bring,
Tho' men say thou bring'st the Spring.

THE GRASSHOPPER

HAPPY insect, what can be
In happiness compared to thee?
Fed with nourishment divine,
The dewy morning's gentle wine!
Nature waits upon thee still,
And thy verdant cup does fill;
'Tis fill'd wherever thou dost tread,
Nature self's thy Ganymede.
Thou dost drink, and dance, and sing;
Happier than the happiest king!
All the fields, which thou dost see,
All the plants belong to thee,
All that summer hours produce,
Fertile made with early juice—
Man for thee doth sow and plough;
Farmer he, and landlord thou!—
Thou dost innocently enjoy;
Nor does thy luxury destroy;
The shepherd gladly heareth thee,
More harmonious than he.

Thee country minds with gladness hear,
Prophet of the ripened year!
Thee Phoebus loves, and does inspire;
Phoebus is himself thy sire.
To thee of all things upon earth,
Life is no longer than thy mirth.
Happy insect, happy thou,
Dost neither age nor winter know.
But when thou 'st drunk, and danc'd, and sung
Thy fill, thy flow'ry leaves among,
(Voluptuous and wise withal,
Epicurean animal!)
Sated with thy summer feast,
Thou retir'st to endless rest.

TO HIS MISTRESS

TYRIAN dye why do you wear,
You whose cheeks best scarlet are?
  Why do you fondly pin
  Pure linens o'er your skin,
  Your skin that 's whiter far—
Casting a dusky cloud before a star?

Why bears your neck a golden chain?
Did Nature make your hair in vain,
  Of gold most pure and fine?
  With gems why do you shine?
  They, neighbours to your eyes,
Show but like Phosphor when the Sun doth rise.

I would have all my mistress' parts
Owe more to Nature than to arts;
  I would not woo the dress,
  Or one whose nights give less

Contentment than the day;
She's fair whose beauty only makes her gay.

For 'tis not buildings make a court
Or pomp, but 'tis the King's resort:
   If Jupiter down pour
   Himself, and in a shower
   Hide such bright majesty
Less than a golden one it cannot be.

MUSIC

   AWAKE, awake, my Lyre!
And tell thy silent master's humble tale
   In sounds that may prevail;
   Sounds that gentle thoughts inspire:
   Though so exalted she
   And I so lowly be,
Tell her, such different notes make all thy harmony.

   Hark! how the strings awake:
And, though the moving hand approach not near,
   Themselves with awful fear
   A kind of numerous trembling make.
   Now all thy forces try;
   Now all thy charms apply;
Revenge upon her ear the conquests of her eye.

   Weak Lyre! thy virtue sure
Is useless here, since thou art only found
   To cure, but not to wound,
   And she to wound, but not to cure.
   Too weak too wilt thou prove
   My passion to remove;
Physic to other ills, thou'rt nourishment to love.

Sleep, sleep again, my Lyre!
For thou canst never tell my humble tale
 In sounds that will prevail,
 Nor gentle thoughts in her inspire;
  All thy vain mirth lay by,
  Bid thy strings silent lie,
Sleep, sleep again, my Lyre, and let thy master die.

HYMN TO LIGHT

FIRST born of chaos, who so fair didst come
  From the old negro's darksome womb!
  Which when it saw the lovely child,
The melancholy mass put on kind looks and smiled.

Thou tide of glory which no rest dost know,
  But ever ebb, and ever flow!
  Thou golden shower of a true Jove!
Who dost in thee descend, and heaven to earth
 make love!

Hail, active nature's watchful life and health!
  Her joy, her ornament, and wealth!
  Hail to thy husband Heat, and thee!
Thou the world's beauteous bride, the lusty bride-
 groom he!

Say from what golden quivers of the sky
  Do all thy wingèd arrows fly?
  Swiftness and power by birth are thine.
From thy great sire they came, thy sire the word
 divine.

'Tis, I believe, this archery to show,
  That so much cost in colours thou,
  And skill in painting dost bestow,
Upon thy ancient arms, the gaudy heavenly bow.

Swift as light thoughts their empty carriere run,
  Thy race is finished, when begun,
   Let a post-angel start with thee,
And thou the goal of earth shalt reach as soon as
  he:

Thou in the moon's bright chariot proud and gay,
  Dost thy bright wood of stars survey;
   And all the year dost with thee bring
Of thousand flowery lights thine own nocturnal
  spring.

Thou Scythian-like dost round thy lands above
  The sun's gilt tent for ever move,
   And still as thou in pomp dost go
The shining pageants of the world attend thy show.

Nor amidst all these triumphs dost thou scorn
  The humble glow-worms to adorn,
   And with those living spangles gild,
O greatness without pride! the bushes of the field.

Night, and her ugly subjects thou dost fright,
  And sleep, the lazy owl of light;
   Ashamed and fearful to appear
They screen their horrid shapes with the black
  hemisphere.

With them there hastes, and wildly takes the alarm
  Of painted dreams, a busy swarm,
   At the first opening of thine eye,
The various clusters break, the antic atoms fly.

The guilty serpents, and obscener beasts,
  Creep conscious to their secret rests:
   Nature to thee does reverence pay,
Ill omens, and ill sights removes out of thy way.

    carriere] career, course.

At thy appearance, grief itself is said
   To shake his wings and rouse his head.
   And cloudy care has often took
A gentle beamy smile reflected from thy look.

At thy appearance, fear itself grows bold;
   Thy sunshine melts away his cold.
   Encouraged at the sight of thee,
To the cheek colour comes, and firmness to the
   knee.

Even lust, the master of a hardened face,
   Blushes if thou beest in the place,
   To darkness' curtain he retires,
In sympathizing night he rolls his smoky fires.

When goddess, thou liftst up thy wakened head,
   Out of the morning's purple bed,
   Thy choir of birds about thee play,
And all the joyful world salutes the rising day.

The ghosts, and monster spirits, that did presume
   A body's privilege to assume,
   Vanish again invisibly,
And bodies gain again their visibility.

All the world's bravery that delights our eyes
   Is but thy several liveries,
   Thou the rich day on them bestowest,
Thy nimble pencil paints this landscape as thou
   goest.

A crimson garment in the rose thou wear'st;
   A crown of studded gold thou bear'st,
   The virgin lillies in their white,
Are clad but with the lawns of almost naked light.

The violet, spring's little infant, stands,
   Girt in thy purple swaddling-bands:

On the fair tulip thou dost dote;
Thou cloth'st it in a gay and parti-coloured coat.

With flame condensed thou dost the jewels fix,
    And solid colours in it mix:
    Flora herself envies to see
Flowers fairer than her own, and durable as she.

Ah, goddess! would thou could'st thy hand with-
    hold,
    And be less liberal to gold;
    Didst thou less value to it give,
Of how much care, alas, might'st thou poor man
    relieve!

To me the sun is more delightful far,
    And all fair days much fairer are.
    But few, ah wondrous few there be,
Who do not gold prefer, O goddess, even to thee.

Through the soft way of heaven, and air, and sea,
    Which open all their pores to thee;
    Like a clear river thou dost glide,
And with thy living stream through the close
    channels slide.

But where firm bodies thy free course oppose,
    Gently thy source the land o'erflows;
    Takes there possession, and does make
Of colours mingled Light, a thick and standing lake.

But the vast ocean of unbounded day
    In the empyræan heaven does stay.
    Thy rivers, lakes, and springs below
From thence took first their rise, thither at last
    must flow.

THE WISH

WELL then; I now do plainly see
This busy world and I shall ne'er agree.
The very honey of all earthly joy
Does of all meats the soonest cloy;
    And they, methinks, deserve my pity
Who for it can endure the stings,
The crowd and buzz and murmurings,
    Of this great hive, the city.

Ah yet, ere I descend to th' grave
May I a small house and large garden have;
And a few friends, and many books, both true,
Both wise, and both delightful too!
    And since love ne'er will from me flee,
A mistress moderately fair,
And good as guardian-angels are,
    Only beloved, and loving me.

O fountains! when in you shall I
Myself, eased of unpeaceful thoughts, espy?
O fields! O woods! when, when shall I be made
The happy tenant of your shade?
    Here's the spring-head of pleasure's flood:
Here's wealthy Nature's treasury,
Where all the riches lie that she
    Has coin'd and stamped for good.

Pride and ambition here
Only in far-fetched metaphors appear;
Here nought but winds can hurtful murmurs scatter,
And nought but Echo flatter.
    The gods, when they descended, hither
From heaven did always choose their way:
And therefore we may boldly say
    That 'tis the way too thither.

How happy here should I
And one dear She live, and embracing die!
She who is all the world, and can exclude
In deserts solitude.

 I should have then this only fear:
Lest men, when they my pleasures see,
Should hither throng to live like me,
 And so make a city here.

TO THE ROYAL SOCIETY

PHILOSOPHY! the great and only heir
Of all that human knowledge which has been
Unforfeited by man's rebellious sin,
Though full of years he do appear,
(Philosophy! I say, and call it he,
For whatsoe'er the painter's fancy be,
It a male virtue seems to me)
Has still been kept in nonage till of late,
Nor managed or enjoyed his vast estate.
Three or four thousand years one would have
  thought,
To ripeness and perfection might have brought
A science so well bred and nursed,
And of such hopeful parts, too, at the first;
But oh! the guardians and the tutors then,
(Some negligent, and some ambitious men)
Would ne'er consent to set him free.
Or his own natural powers to let him see,
Lest that should put an end to their authority.

That his own business he might quite forget,
They amused him with the sports of wanton wit;
With the desserts of poetry they fed him,
Instead of solid meats t' increase his force;
Instead of vigorous exercise they led him

Into the pleasant labyrinths of ever-fresh discourse:
Instead of carrying him to see
The riches which do hoarded for him lie
In Nature's endless treasury,
They chose his eye to entertain
(His curious, but not covetous, eye)
With painted scenes and pageants of the brain.
Some few exalted spirits this latter age has shown,
That laboured to assert the liberty
(From guardians who were now usurpers grown)
Of this old minor still, captured Philosophy;
But 'twas rebellion called, to fight
For such a long-oppressèd right.
Bacon, at last, a mighty man, arose,
Whom a wise king and nature chose
Lord Chancellor of both their laws,
And boldly undertook the injured pupil's cause.

Authority, which did a body boast
Though 'twas but air condensed, and stalked about
Like some old giant's more gigantic ghost,
To terrify the learnèd rout,
With the plain magic of true reason's light
He chased out of our sight,
Nor suffered living men to be misled
By the vain shadows of the dead:
To graves, from whence it rose, the conquered
    phantom fled.
He broke that monstrous god which stood,
In midst of the orchard, and the whole did claim,
Which with a useless scythe of wood,
And something else not worth a name,
(Both vast for show, yet neither fit
Or to defend, or to beget;

Ridiculous and senseless terrors!) made
Children and superstitious men afraid.
The orchard's open now, and free:
Bacon has broke that scarecrow Deity;
Come, enter, all that will,
Behold the ripened Fruit, come gather now your
    fill.
Yet still, methinks, we fain would be
Catching at the forbidden tree;
We would be like the Deity
When truth and falsehood, good and evil, we
Without the senses and within ourselves would see;
For 'tis God only who can find
All nature in his mind.

From words, which are but pictures of the thought
(Though we our thoughts from them perversely
    drew),
To things, the mind's right object, he it brought;
Like foolish birds to painted grapes we flew.
He sought and gathered for our use the true;
And when on heaps the chosen bunches lay,
He pressed them wisely the mechanic way,
Till all their juice did in one vessel join,
Ferment into a nourishment divine
The thirsty soul's refreshing wine.
Who to the life an exact piece would make,
Must not from others' work a copy take;
No, not from Rubens or Vandyck;
Much less content himself to make it like
The ideas and the images which lie
In his own fancy or his memory:
No, he before his sight must place
The natural and living face;

The real object must command
Each judgement of his eye, and motion of his hand.

From these, and all long errors of the way,
In which our wandering predecessors went,
And, like the old Hebrews, many years did stray,
In deserts, but of small extent,
Bacon, like Moses, led us forth at last;
The barren wilderness he passed,
Did on the very border stand
Of the blessed Promised Land,
And from the mountain's top of his exalted wit,
Saw it himself, and showed us it.
But life did never to one man allow
Time to discover worlds and conquer too;
Nor can so short a line sufficient be
To fathom the vast depths of Nature's sea:
The work he did we ought t' admire,
And were unjust if we should more require
From his few years, divided 'twixt excess
Of low affliction and high happiness:
For who on things remote can fix his sight,
That 's always in a triumph or a fight?

From you, great champions, we expect to get
These spacious countries but discovered yet;
Countries where yet, instead of Nature, we
Her images and idols worshipped see:
These large and wealthy regions to subdue,
Though Learning has whole armies at command,
Quartered about in every land,
A better troop she ne'er together drew.
Methinks, like Gideon's little band,
God with design has picked out you,
To do these noble wonders by a few.

When the whole host He saw, they are, said He,
Too many to o'ercome for Me:
And now he chooses out his men,
Much in the way that He did then:
Not those many, whom He found
Idly extended on the ground,
To drink with their dejected head
The stream just so as by their mouths it fled:
No; but those few who took the waters up,
And made of their laborious hands the cup.

Thus you prepared, and in the glorious fight
Their wondrous pattern too you take:
Their old and empty pitchers first they brake,
And with their hands then lifted up the light.
Iö! sound too the trumpets here!
Already your victorious lights appear;
New scenes of heaven already we espy,
And crowds of golden worlds on high,
Which from the spacious plains of earth and sea
Could never yet discovered be
By sailor's or Chaldean's watchful eye.
Nature's great works no distance can obscure,
No smallness her near objects can secure.
You have taught the curious sight to press
Into the privatest recess
Of her imperceptible littleness:
She with much stranger art than his who put
All the Iliads in a nut,
The numerous work of life does into atoms shut;
You have learned to read her smallest hand,
And well begun her deepest sense to understand.

Mischief and true dishonour fall on those
Who would to laughter or to scorn expose

So virtuous and so noble a design,
So human for its use, for knowledge so divine.
The things which these proud men despise, and
     call
Impertinent, and vain, and small,
Those smallest things of nature let me know,
Rather than all their greatest actions do.
Whoever would desposèd truth advance
Into the throne usurped from it,
Must feel at first the blows of ignorance,
And the sharp points of envious wit.
So when, by various turns of the celestial dance,
In many thousand years
A star, so long unknown, appears,
Though heaven itself more beauteous by it grow,
It troubles and alarms the world below,
Does to the wise a star, to fools a meteor, show.

With courage and success you the bold work begin;
Your cradle has not idle been;
None e'er but Hercules and you could be
At five years' age worthy a history:
And ne'er did fortune better yet
The historian to the story fit.
As you from all old errors free
And purge the body of Philosophy,
So from all modern follies he
Has vindicated eloquence and wit:
His candid style like a clean stream does slide,
And his bright fancy all the way
Does, like the sunshine, in it play;
It does like Thames, the best of rivers, glide,
Where the god does not rudely overturn,
But gently pour, the crystal urn,

And with judicious hand does the whole current
    guide.
'T has all the beauties Nature can impart,
And all the comely dress, without the paint, of
    Art.

ON THE DEATH OF MR. WILLIAM HARVEY

IT was a dismal and a fearful night:
    Scarce could the Morn drive on th' unwilling
        light,
When sleep, death's image, left my troubled
        breast
            By something liker death possessed.
My eyes with tears did uncommanded flow,
            And on my soul hung the dull weight
            Of some intolerable fate.
What bell was that? Ah me! too much I know!

My sweet companion and my gentle peer,
Why hast thou left me thus unkindly here,
Thy end for ever and my life to moan?
        O, thou hast left me all alone!
Thy soul and body, when death's agony
        Besieged around thy noble heart,
        Did not with more reluctance part
Than I, my dearest friend, do part from thee.

My dearest friend, would I had died for thee!
Life and this world henceforth will tedious be:
Nor shall I know hereafter what to do
        If once my griefs prove tedious too.
Silent and sad I walk about all day,
        As sullen ghosts stalk speechless by
        Where their hid treasures lie;
Alas! my treasure 's gone, why do I stay?

He was my friend, the truest friend on earth;
A strong and mighty influence joined our birth.
Nor did we envy the most sounding name
    By friendship given of old to fame.
None but his brethren he, and sisters knew
    Whom the kind youth preferred to me;
    And even in that we did agree,
For much above myself I loved them too.

Say, for you saw us, ye immortal lights,
How oft unwearied have we spent the nights,
Till the Ledæan stars, so famed for love,
    Wonder'd at us from above!
We spent them not in toys, in lusts, or wine;
    But search of deep philosophy,
    Wit, eloquence, and poetry—
Arts which I loved, for they, my friend, were
    thine.

Ye fields of Cambridge, our dear Cambridge, say,
Have ye not seen us walking every day?
Was there a tree about which did not know
    The love betwixt us two?
Henceforth, ye gentle trees, for ever fade;
    Or your sad branches thicker join
    And into darksome shades combine,
Dark as the grave wherein my friend is laid! . . .

Large was his soul: as large a soul as e'er
Submitted to inform a body here;
High as the place 'twas shortly in heaven to have,
    But low and humble as his grave.
So high that all the virtues there did come,
    As to their chiefest seat
    Conspicuous and great;
So low, that for me too it made a room. . . .

Knowledge he only sought, and so soon caught
As if for him knowledge had rather sought;
Nor did more learning ever crowded lie
    In such a short mortality.
Whene'er the skilful youth discoursed or writ,
      Still did the notions throng
      About his eloquent tongue;
Nor could his ink flow faster than his wit.

So strong a wit did nature to him frame
As all things but his judgment overcame;
His judgment like the heavenly moon did show,
    Tempering that mighty sea below.
Oh had he lived in learning's world, what bound
      Would have been able to control
      His over-powering soul?
We have lost in him arts that not yet are found.

His mirth was the pure spirits of various wit,
Yet never did his God or friends forget;
And when deep talk and wisdom came in view,
    Retired, and gave to them their due.
For the rich help of books he always took,
      Though his own searching mind before
      Was so with notions written o'er,
As if wise Nature had made that her book. . . .

With as much zeal, devotion, piety,
He always lived, as other saints do die.
Still with his soul severe account he kept,
    Weeping all debts out ere he slept.
Then down in peace and innocence he lay,
      Like the sun's laborious light,
      Which still in water sets at night,
Unsullied with his journey of the day. . . .

But happy thou, ta'en from this frantic age,
Where ignorance and hypocrisy does rage!
A fitter time for heaven no soul e'er chose—
    The place now only free from those.
There 'mong the blest thou dost forever shine;
       And wheresoe'er thou cast'st thy view
       Upon that white and radiant crew,
See'st not a soul clothed with more light than
    thine.

ON SOLITUDE

HAIL, old patrician trees, so great and good!
      Hail, ye plebeian underwood!
      Where the poetic birds rejoice,
And for their quiet nests and plenteous food,
      Pay with their grateful voice.

Hail, the poor muse's richest manor seat!
      Ye country houses and retreat,
      Which all the happy gods so love,
That for you oft they quit their bright and great
      Metropolis above.

Here nature does a house for me erect,
      Nature the wisest architect,
      Who those fond artists does despise
That can the fair and living trees neglect,
      Yet the dead timber prize.

Here let me careless and unthoughtful lying,
      Hear the soft winds above me flying
      With all their wanton boughs dispute,
And the more tuneful birds to both replying,
      Nor be myself too mute.

A silver stream shall roll his waters near,
    Gilt with the sunbeams here and there,
    On whose enamelled bank I'll walk,
And see how prettily they smile, and hear
    How prettily they talk.

Ah wretched, and too solitary he
    Who loves not his own company!
    He'll feel the weight of 't many a day
Unless he call in sin or vanity
    To help to bear 't away.

O Solitude, first state of human-kind!
    Which blest remain'd till man did find
    Even his own helper's company.
As soon as two (alas!) together joined,
    The serpent made up three.

The god himself, through countless ages thee
    His sole companion chose to be,
    Thee, sacred Solitude alone,
Before the branchy head of number's tree
    Sprang from the trunk of one.

Thou (though men think thine an unactive part)
    Dost break and tame th' unruly heart,
    Which else would know no settled pace,
Making it more well manag'd by thy art
    With swiftness and with grace.

Thou the faint beams of reason's scattered light,
    Dost like a burning-glass unite,
    Dost multiply the feeble heat,
And fortify the strength, till thou dost bright
    And noble fires beget.

Whilst this hard truth I teach, methinks, I see
  The monster London laugh at me,
    I should at thee too, foolish city,
If it were fit to laugh at misery,
    But thy estate I pity.

Let but thy wicked men from out thee go,
    And all the fools that crowd thee so,
      Even thou who dost thy millions boast,
A village less than Islington wilt grow,
    A solitude almost.

ANDREW MARVELL

1621–1678

THOUGHTS IN A GARDEN

How vainly men themselves amaze
To win the palm, the oak, or bays;
And their uncessant labours see
Crowned from some single herb or tree.
Whose short and narrow-vergèd shade
Does prudently their toils upbraid;
While all flowers and all trees do close
To weave the garlands of repose.

Fair quiet, have I found thee here,
And innocence thy sister dear!
Mistaken long, I sought you then
In busy companies of men.
Your sacred plants, if here below,
Only among the plants will grow.
Society is all but rude,
To this delicious solitude.

No white nor red was ever seen
So amorous as this lovely green.

Fond lovers, cruel as their flame,
Cut in these trees their mistress' name.
Little, alas, they know, or heed,
How far these beauties hers exceed!
Fair trees! wheres'e'er your barks I wound,
No name shall but your own be found.

When we have run our passions' heat,
Love hither makes his best retreat.
The gods, that mortal beauty chase,
Still in a tree did end their race.
Apollo hunted Daphne so,
Only that she might laurel grow.
And Pan did after Syrinx speed,
Not as a nymph, but for a reed.

What wondrous life in this I lead!
Ripe apples drop about my head;
The luscious clusters of the vine
Upon my mouth do crush their wine;
The nectarine, and curious peach,
Into my hands themselves do reach;
Stumbling on melons, as I pass,
Ensnared with flowers, I fall on grass.

Meanwhile the mind, from pleasure less,
Withdraws into its happiness.
The mind, that ocean where each kind
Does straight its own resemblance find;
Yet it creates, transcending these,
Far other worlds, and other seas;
Annihilating all that's made
To a green thought in a green shade.

Here at the fountain's sliding foot,
Or at some fruit-tree's mossy root,

Casting the body's vest aside,
My soul into the boughs does glide;
There like a bird it sits and sings,
Then whets, and combs its silver wings;
And, till prepared for longer flight,
Waves in its plumes the various light.

Such was that happy garden state
While man there walked without a mate:
After a place so pure and sweet,
What other help could yet be meet!
But 'twas beyond a mortal's share
To wander solitary there:
Two paradises 'twere in one
To live in Paradise alone.

How well the skilful gardener drew
Of flowers and herbs this dial new;
Where from above the milder sun
Does through a fragrant zodiac run;
And, as it works, th' industrious bee
Computes its time as well as we.
How could such sweet and wholesome hours
Be reckoned but with herbs and flowers!

HORATIAN ODE UPON CROMWELL'S RETURN
FROM IRELAND

THE forward youth that would appear
Must now forsake his Muses dear,
        Nor in the shadows sing
        His numbers languishing.
'Tis time to leave the books in dust,
And oil the unuséd armour's rust:
        Removing from the wall
        The corslet of the hall.

So restless Cromwell could not cease
In the inglorious arts of peace,
 But through adventurous war
 Urgéd his active star.
And, like the three-forked lightning, first
Breaking the clouds where it was nurst,
 Did thorough his own side
 His fiery way divide.
For 'tis all one to courage high
The emulous or enemy;
 And with such to enclose
 Is more than to oppose.
Then burning through the air he went
And palaces and temples rent:
 And Caesar's head at last
 Did through his laurels blast.
'Tis madness to resist or blame
The face of angry heaven's flame:
 And, if we would speak true,
 Much to the man is due,
Who, from his private gardens where
He lived reservèd and austere,
 As if his highest plot
 To plant the bergamot,
Could by industrious valour climb
To ruin the great work of Time,
 And cast the kingdom old
 Into another mould.
Though Justice against Fate complain,
And plead the ancient rights in vain:
 But those do hold or break
 As men are strong or weak.

thorough] through.

Nature that hateth emptiness,
Allows of penetration less:
    And therefore must make room
    Where greater spirits come.
What field of all the Civil Wars
Where his were not the deepest scars?
    And Hampton shows what part
    He had of wiser art,
Where, twining subtle fears with hope,
He wove a net of such a scope,
    That Charles himself might chase
    To Carisbrook's narrow case:
That thence the Royal actor borne
The tragic scaffold might adorn:
    While round the armèd bands
    Did clap their bloody hands.
He nothing common did or mean
Upon that memorable scene:
    But with his keener eye
    The axe's edge did try.
Nor called the gods with vulgar spite
To vindicate his helpless right,
    But bowed his comely head,
    Down as upon a bed.
This was that memorable hour
Which first assured the forcèd power.
    So when they did design
    The Capitol's first line,
A Bleeding Head where they begun,
Did fright the architects to run;
    And yet in that the State
    Foresaw its happy fate.
And now the Irish are ashamed
To see themselves in one year tamed:

So much one man can do,
That does both act and know.
They can affirm his praises best,
And have, though overcome, confest
How good he is, how just,
And fit for highest trust:
Not yet grown stiffer with command,
But still in the Republic's hand:
How fit he is to sway
That can so well obey.
He to the Commons' feet presents
A Kingdom for his first year's rents;
And, what he may, forbears
His fame to make it theirs:
And has his sword and spoils ungirt,
To lay them at the public's skirt.
So when the falcon high
Falls heavy from the sky,
She, having killed, no more does search,
But on the next green bough to perch;
Where, when he first does lure,
The falconer has her sure.
What may not then our Isle presume
While victory his crest does plume!
What may not others fear
If thus he crowns each year!
A Caesar he ere long to Gaul,
To Italy an Hannibal,
And to all states not free
Shall climacteric be.
The Pict no shelter now shall find
Within his parti-coloured mind;
But from this valour sad
Shrink underneath the plaid:

Happy if in the tufted brake
The English hunter him mistake;
    Nor lay his hounds in near
    The Caledonian deer.
But thou, the war's and fortune's son,
March indefatigably on;
    And for the last effect
    Still keep the sword erect:
Besides the force it has to fright
The spirits of the shady night,
    The same arts that did gain
    A power must it maintain.

TO HIS COY MISTRESS

HAD we but world enough, and time,
This coyness, Lady, were no crime.
We would sit down, and think which way
To walk, and pass our long love's day.
Thou by the Indian Ganges' side
Shouldst rubies find: I by the tide
Of Humber would complain. I would
Love you ten years before the Flood:
And you should, if you please, refuse
Till the conversion of the Jews.
My vegetable love should grow
Vaster than empires, and more slow.
An hundred years should go to praise
Thine eyes, and on thy forehead gaze.
Two hundred to adore each breast:
But thirty thousand to the rest.
An age at least to every part,
And the last age should show your heart.
For, Lady, you deserve this state;
Nor would I love at lower rate.

But at my back I always hear
Time's wingèd chariot hurrying near:
And yonder all before us lie
Deserts of vast eternity.
Thy beauty shall no more be found;
Nor, in thy marble vault, shall sound
My echoing song: then worms shall try
That long preserved virginity:
And your quaint honour turn to dust;
And into ashes all my lust.
The grave's a fine and private place,
But none I think do there embrace.
 Now therefore, while the youthful hue
Sits on thy skin like morning dew,
And while thy willing soul transpires
At every pore with instant fires,
Now let us sport us while we may;
And now, like amorous birds of prey,
Rather at once our time devour,
Than languish in his slow-chapt power.
Let us roll all our strength, and all
Our sweetness, up into one ball:
And tear our pleasures with rough strife,
Thorough the iron gates of life.
Thus, though we cannot make our sun
Stand still, yet we will make him run.

SONG OF THE EMIGRANTS IN BERMUDA

WHERE the remote Bermudas ride
In the ocean's bosom unespied,
From a small boat, that rowed along,
The listening winds received this song.

     slow-chapt power] slow-consuming power.

'What should we do but sing His praise
That led us through the watery maze,
Unto an isle so long unknown,
And yet far kinder than our own?
Where He the huge sea-monsters wracks,
That lift the deep upon their backs.
He lands us on a grassy stage;
Safe from the storms, and prelate's rage.
He gave us this eternal spring,
Which here enamels everything;
And sends the fowls to us in care,
On daily visits through the air.
He hangs in shades the orange bright,
Like golden lamps in a green night.
And does in the pomegranates close
Jewels more rich than Ormus shows.
He makes the figs our mouths to meet;
And throws the melons at our feet.
But apples plants of such a price,
No tree could ever bear them twice.
With cedars, chosen by His hand,
From Lebanon, He stores the land :
And makes the hollow seas that roar
Proclaim the ambergris on shore.
He cast (of which we rather boast)
The Gospel's pearl upon our coast.
And in these rocks for us did frame
A temple, where to sound His name.
Oh! let our voice His praise exalt,
Till it arrive at heaven's vault:
Which thence (perhaps) rebounding, may
Echo beyond the Mexique bay.'
Thus sung they, in the English boat,

wracks] wrecks.

An holy and a cheerful note,
And all the way, to guide their chime,
With falling oars they kept the time.

THE PICTURE OF LITTLE T. C. IN A PROSPECT OF FLOWERS

SEE with what simplicity
This nymph begins her golden days!
In the green grass she loves to lie,
And there with her fair aspect tames
The wilder flowers, and gives them names:
But only with the roses plays;
And them does tell
What colour best becomes them, and what smell.

Who can foretell for what high cause
This darling of the gods was born?
Yet this is she whose chaster laws
The wanton Love shall one day fear,
And, under her command severe,
See his bow broke and ensigns torn.
Happy who can
Appease this virtuous enemy of man!

O then let me in time compound,
And parley with those conquering eyes;
Ere they have tried their force to wound,
Ere, with their glancing wheels, they drive
In triumph over hearts that strive,
And them that yield but more despise.
Let me be laid,
Where I may see thy glories from some shade.

Meantime, whilst every verdant thing
Itself does at thy beauty charm,
Reform the errors of the Spring;

Make that the tulips may have share
Of sweetness, seeing they are fair;
    And roses of their thorns disarm:
                    But most procure
That violets may a longer age endure.

But O young beauty of the woods,
  Whom Nature courts with fruits and flowers,
    Gather the flowers, but spare the buds;
Lest Flora angry at thy crime,
To kill her infants in their prime,
  Do quickly make the example yours;
              And, ere we see,
Nip in the blossom all our hopes and thee.

IN A FOREST

From Upon Appleton House.

DARK all without it knits; within
It opens passable and thin;
And in as loose an order grows,
As the Corinthian porticoes.
The arching boughs unite between
The columns of the temple green;
And underneath the wingèd choirs
Echo about their tunèd fires.

The Nightingale does here make choice
To sing the trials of her voice.
Low shrubs she sits in, and adorns
With music high the squatted thorns.
But highest oaks stoop down to hear,
And list'ning elders prick the ear.
The thorn, lest it should hurt her, draws
Within the skin its shrunken claws.

But I have for my music found
A sadder, yet more pleasing sound:
The stock-doves, whose fair necks are graced
With nuptial rings, their ensigns chaste;
Yet always, for some cause unknown,
Sad pair, into the elms they moan.
O why should such a couple mourn,
That in so equal flames do burn?

Then as I careless on the bed
Of gelid strawberries do tread,
And through the hazels thick espy
The hatching throstle's shining eye.
The heron from the ash's top,
The eldest of its young lets drop,
As if it stork-like did pretend
That tribute to its lord to send.

But most the hewel's wonders are,
Who here has the holt-felster's care.
He walks still upright from the root,
Measuring the timber with his foot;
And all the way, to keep it clean,
Doth from the bark the wood-moths glean.
He, with his beak, examines well
Which fit to stand and which to fell.

The good he numbers up, and hacks;
As if he marked them with his axe.
But where he, tinkling with his beak,
Does find the hollow oak to speak,
That for his building he designs,
And through the tainted side he mines.
Who could have thought the tallest oak
Should fall by such a feeble stroke!

hewel's wonders] woodpecker's wonders.

Nor would it, had the tree not fed
A traitor-worm, within it bred
(As first our flesh corrupt within
Tempts impotent and bashful sin).
And yet that worm triumphs not long,
But serves to feed the hewel's young.
While the oak seems to fall content,
Viewing the treason's punishment.

Thus I, easy philosopher,
Among the birds and trees confer:
And little now to make me, wants
Or of the fowls, or of the plants.
Give me but wings as they, and I
Straight floating on the air shall fly:
Or turn me but, and you shall see
I was but an inverted tree.

Already I begin to call
In their most learned original,
And where I language want, my signs
The bird upon the bough divines;
And more attentive there doth sit
Than if she were with lime-twigs knit.
No leaf does tremble in the wind
Which I returning cannot find.

Out of these scattered Sibyl's leaves
Strange prophecies my fancy weaves:
And in one history consumes,
Like Mexique paintings, all the plumes.
What Rome, Greece, Palestine, e'er said
I in this light mosaic read.
Thrice happy he who, not mistook,
Hath read in nature's mystic book.

And see how chance's better wit
Could with a mask my studies hit!
The oak-leaves me embroider all
Between which caterpillars crawl:
And ivy, with familiar trails,
Me licks, and clasps, and curls, and hales.
Under this antic cope I move
Like some great prelate of the grove.

Then, languishing with ease, I toss
On pallets swoln of velvet moss;
While the wind, cooling through the boughs,
Flatters with air my panting brows.
Thanks for my rest, ye mossy banks,
And unto you cool zephyrs thanks,
Who, as my hair, my thoughts too shed,
And winnow from the chaff my head.

ON A DROP OF DEW

SEE how the orient dew,
Shed from the bosom of the morn
  Into the blowing roses,
Yet careless of its mansion new;
For the clear region where 'twas born
  Round in itself encloses:
  And in its little globe's extent,
Frames as it can its native element.
  How it the purple flower does slight,
    Scarce touching where it lies,
    But gazing back upon the skies,
    Shines with a mournful light;
      Like its own tear,
Because so long divided from the sphere.
  Restless it rolls and unsecure,

Trembling lest it grow impure:
Till the warm sun pity its pain,
And to the skies exhale it back again.
So the soul, that drop, that ray
Of the clear fountain of eternal day,
Could it within the human flower be seen,
Remembering still its former height,
Shuns the sweet leaves and blossoms green;
And, recollecting its own light,
Does, in its pure and circling thoughts, express
The greater heaven in an heaven less.
In how coy a figure wound,
Every way it turns away:
So the world excluding round,
Yet receiving in the day.
Dark beneath, but bright above:
Here disdaining, there in love.
How loose and easy hence to go:
How girt and ready to ascend.
Moving but on a point below,
It all about does upwards bend.
Such did the manna's sacred dew distil;
White, and entire, though congealed and chill.
Congealed on earth; but does, dissolving, run
Into the glories of the Almighty Sun.

THE NYMPH COMPLAINING FOR THE DEATH OF HER FAWN

THE wanton troopers riding by
Have shot my fawn and it will die.
Ungentle men! they cannot thrive
To kill thee. Thou ne'er didst, alive,
Them any harm: alas! nor could
Thy death yet do them any good.

I'm sure I never wished them ill;
Nor do I for all this; nor will:
But, if my simple prayers may yet
Prevail with heaven to forget
Thy murder, I will join my tears,
Rather than fail. But, O my fears!
It cannot die so. Heaven's king
Keeps register of everything:
And nothing may we use in vain.
Even beasts must be with justice slain;
Else men are made their deodands.
Though they should wash their guilty hands
In this warm life-blood, which doth part
From thine, and wound me to the heart,
Yet could they not be clean: their stain
Is dyed in such a purple grain.
There is not such another in
The world, to offer for their sin.

Unconstant Sylvio, when yet
I had not found him counterfeit,
One morning (I remember well)
Tied in this silver chain and bell,
Gave it to me: nay and I know
What he said then; I'm sure I do.
Said he, 'Look how your huntsman here
Hath taught a fawn to hunt his dear.'
But Sylvio soon had me beguiled.
This waxèd tame, while he grew wild,
And quite regardless of my smart,
Left me his fawn, but took his heart.

Thenceforth I set myself to play
My solitary time away,

deodands] forfeits for crimes.

With this: and very well content,
Could so mine idle life have spent.
For it was full of sport; and light
Of foot, and heart; and did invite
Me to its game: it seemed to bless
Itself in me. How could I less
Than love it? O I cannot be
Unkind to a beast that loveth me.

Had it lived long, I do not know
Whether it too might have done so
As Sylvio did: his gifts might be
Perhaps as false or more than he.
But I am sure, for aught that I
Could in so short a time espy,
Thy love was far more better than
The love of false and cruel man.

With sweetest milk, and sugar, first
I it at my own fingers nursed.
And as it grew, so every day
It waxed more white and sweet than they.
It had so sweet a breath! And oft
I blushed to see its foot more soft,
And white, shall I say than my hand?
Nay, any lady's of the land.

It is a wond'rous thing, how fleet
'Twas on those little silver feet.
With what a pretty skipping grace,
It oft would challenge me the race:
And when 't had left me far away,
'Twould stay, and run again, and stay:
For it was nimbler much than hinds;
And trod, as on the four winds.

I have a garden of my own,
But so with roses overgrown,
And lilies, that you would it guess
To be a little wilderness.
And all the springtime of the year
It only lovèd to be there.
Among the beds of lilies, I
Have sought it oft, where it should lie,
Yet could not, till itself would rise,
Find it, although before mine eyes.
For, in the flaxen lilies' shade,
It like a bank of lilies laid.
Upon the roses it would feed,
Until its lips ev'n seemed to bleed;
And then to me 'twould boldly trip,
And print those roses on my lip.
But all its chief delight was still
On roses thus itself to fill.
And its pure virgin limbs to fold
In whitest sheets of lilies cold.
Had it lived long, it would have been
Lilies without, roses within.

O help! O help! I see it faint
And die as calmly as a saint.
See how it weeps! the tears do come
Sad, slowly dropping like a gum.
So weeps the wounded balsam: so
The holy frankincense doth flow.
The brotherless Heliades
Melt in such amber tears as these.

I in a golden vial will
Keep these two crystal tears; and fill

It till it doth o'erflow with mine;
Then place it in Diana's shrine.

Now my sweet fawn is vanished to
Whither the swans and turtles go:
In fair Elysium to endure,
With milk-white lambs, and ermines pure.
O do not run too fast: for I
Will but bespeak thy grave, and die.

First, my unhappy statue shall
Be cut in marble; and withal,
Let it be weeping too: but there
Th' engraver sure his art may spare;
For I so truly thee bemoan,
That I shall weep though I be stone,
Until my tears, still dropping, wear
My breast, themselves engraving there.
There at my feet shalt thou be laid,
Of purest alabaster made:
For I would have thine image be
White as I can, though not as thee.

YOUNG LOVE

Come, little infant, love me now,
  While thine unsuspected years
Clear thine aged father's brow
  From cold jealousy and fears.

Pretty surely 'twere to see
  By young love old time beguiled:
While our sportings are as free
  As the nurses with the child.

Common beauties stay fifteen;
  Such as yours should swifter move:

Whose fair blossoms are too green
  Yet for lust, but not for love.

Love as much the snowy lamb
  Or the wanton kid does prize,
As the lusty bull or ram,
  For his morning sacrifice.

Now then love me: time may take
  Thee before thy time away:
Of this need we'll virtue make,
  And learn love before we may.

So we win of doubtful fate;
  And, if good she to us meant,
We that good shall antedate,
  Or, if ill, that ill prevent.

Thus as kingdoms frustrating
  Other titles to their crown,
In their cradle crown their king,
  So all foreign claims to drown;

So, to make all rivals vain,
  Now I crown thee with my love:
Crown me with thy love again,
  And we both shall monarchs prove.

EYES AND TEARS

How wisely nature did decree,
With the same eyes to weep and see!
That, having viewed the object vain,
They might be ready to complain.

And, since the self-deluding sight
In a false angle takes each height;
These tears which better measure all,
Like watery lines and plummets fall.

Two tears, which sorrow long did weigh
Within the scales of either eye,
And then paid out in equal poise,
Are the true price of all my joys.

What in the world most fair appears,
Yea even laughter, turns to tears:
And all the jewels which we prize,
Melt in these pendants of the eyes.

I have through every garden been,
Amongst the red, the white, the green;
And yet, from all the flowers I saw,
No honey but these tears could draw.

So the all-seeing sun each day
Distils the world with chemic ray;
But finds the essence only showers,
Which straight in pity back he pours.

Yet happy they whom grief doth bless,
That weep the more, and see the less:
And, to preserve their sight more true,
Bathe still their eyes in their own dew.

So Magdalen in tears more wise
Dissolved those captivating eyes,
Whose liquid chains could flowing meet
To fetter her Redeemer's feet.

Not full sails hasting laden home,
Nor the chaste lady's pregnant womb,
Nor Cynthia teeming shows so fair,
As two eyes swol'n with weeping are.

The sparkling glance that shoots desire,
Drenched in these waves, does lose its fire.
Yea oft the thunderer pity takes
And here the hissing lightning slakes.

The incense was to heaven dear,
Not as a perfume, but a tear.
And stars show lovely in the night,
But as they seem the tears of light.

Ope then, mine eyes, your double sluice,
And practise so your noblest use.
For others too can see, or sleep;
But only human eyes can weep.

Now like two clouds dissolving, drop,
And at each tear in distance stop;
Now like two fountains trickle down:
Now like two floods o'erturn and drown.

Then let your stream o'erflow your springs,
Till eyes and tears be the same things:
And each the other's difference bears;
These weeping eyes, those seeing tears.

HENRY VAUGHAN

1622-1695

THE RETREAT

HAPPY those early days! when I
Shined in my angel-infancy.
Before I understood this place
Appointed for my second race,
Or taught my soul to fancy aught
But a white, celestial thought,
When yet I had not walk'd above
A mile, or two, from my first Love,
And looking back (at that short space,)
Could see a glimpse of His bright face;
When on some gilded cloud or flower
My gazing soul would dwell an hour,

And in those weaker glories spy
Some shadows of eternity;
Before I taught my tongue to wound
My conscience with a sinful sound,
Or had the black art to dispense
A several sin to every sense,
But felt through all this fleshly dress
Bright shoots of everlastingness.
O how I long to travel back,
And tread again that ancient track!
That I might once more reach that plain,
Where first I left my glorious train,
From whence th' enlighten'd spirit sees
That shady City of palm trees;
But ah! my soul with too much stay
Is drunk, and staggers in the way.
Some men a forward motion love,
But I by backward steps would move;
And when this dust falls to the urn
In that state I came return.

PEACE

My soul, there is a country
    Far beyond the stars,
Where stands a wingèd sentry
    All skilful in the wars,
There above noise and danger
    Sweet Peace sits crown'd with smiles,
And One born in a manger
    Commands the beauteous files.
He is thy gracious Friend,
    And (O my soul, awake!)

    several] separate.   files] hosts.

Did in pure love descend
  To die here for thy sake,
If thou canst get but thither,
  There grows the flower of Peace,
The Rose that cannot wither,
  Thy fortress, and thy ease;
Leave then thy foolish ranges;
  For none can thee secure,
But One, who never changes,
  Thy God, thy life, thy cure.

FROM 'CHILDHOOD'

I CANNOT reach it; and my striving eye
Dazzles at it, as at eternity.
Were now that chronicle alive,
Those white designs which children drive,
And the thoughts of each harmless hour
With their content too in my power,
Quickly would I make my path even,
And by mere playing go to heaven.

   *   *   *   *   *   *

Dear, harmless age! the short, swift span,
Where weeping virtue parts with man;
Where love without lust dwells, and bends
What way we please without self-ends.
An age of mysteries! which he
Must live twice, that would God's face see;
Which angels guard, and with it play,
Angels! which foul men drive away.
How do I study now, and scan
Thee more than e'er I studied man,

white] pure, innocent.   drive] follow after.

And only see through a long night
Thy edges and thy bordering light!
O for thy centre and mid-day!
For sure that is the narrow way.

BEYOND THE VEIL

THEY are all gone into the world of light!
　　And I alone sit lingering here;
Their very memory is fair and bright,
　　　　And my sad thoughts doth clear.

It glows and glitters in my cloudy breast
　　Like stars upon some gloomy grove,
Or those faint beams in which this hill is dressed
　　　　After the sun's remove.

I see them walking in an air of glory,
　　Whose light doth trample on my days:
My days, which are at best but dull and hoary,
　　　　Mere glimmerings and decays.

O holy hope! and high humility,
　　High as the heavens above!
These are your walks, and you have showed them me
　　　　To kindle my cold love,

Dear, beauteous Death! the jewel of the just,
　　Shining nowhere, but in the dark;
What mysteries do lie beyond thy dust;
　　　　Could man outlook that mark!

He that hath found some fledged bird's nest, may
　　know
　　At first sight, if the bird be flown;
But what fair well or grove he sings in now,
　　　　That is to him unknown.

And yet, as angels in some brighter dreams
　　Call to the soul, when man doth sleep:

So some strange thoughts transcend our wonted
    themes,
        And into glory peep.

If a star were confined into a tomb,
  Her captive flames must needs burn there;
But when the hand that locked her up, gives room,
      She'll shine through all the sphere.

O Father of eternal life, and all
  Created glories under Thee!
Resume Thy spirit from this world of thrall
      Into true liberty.

Either disperse these mists, which blot and fill
  My perspective, still as they pass;
Or else remove me hence unto that hill
      Where I shall need no glass.

THE TIMBER

Sure thou didst flourish once! and many springs,
Many bright mornings, much dew, many showers
Passed o'er thy head: many light hearts and wings
Which now are dead, lodged in thy living bowers.

And still a new succession sings and flies;
Fresh groves grow up, and their green branches
    shoot
Towards the old and still enduring skies,
While the low violet thrives at their root.

But thou beneath the sad and heavy line
Of death, doth waste all senseless, cold, and dark;
Where not so much as dreams of light may shine,
Nor any thought of greenness, leaf or bark.

And yet (as if some deep hate and dissent,
Bred in thy growth betwixt high winds and thee,

Were still alive) thou dost great storms resent
Before they come, and know'st how near they be.

Else all at rest thou liest, and the fierce breath
Of tempests can no more disturb thy ease;
But this thy strange resentment after death
Means only those, who broke (in life) thy peace.

So murdered man, when lovely life is done,
And his blood freezed, keeps in the centre still
Some secret sense, which makes the dead blood run
At his approach that did the body kill.

And is there any murderer worse than sin?
Or any storms more foul than a lewd life?
Or what resentient can work more within,
Than true remorse, when with past sins at strife?

THE DAWNING

Ah! what time wilt Thou come? when shall that
    cry
      The Bridegroom's coming! fill the sky?
Shall it in the evening run
When our words and works are done?
Or will Thy all-surprising light
      Break at midnight?
When either sleep, or some dark pleasure
Possesseth mad man without measure;
Or shall these early, fragrant hours
      Unlock Thy bowers?
And with their blush of light descry
Thy locks crowned with eternity;
Indeed, it is the only time
That with Thy glory doth best chime,
All now are stirring, every field
      Full hymns doth yield,

The whole creation shakes off night,
And for Thy shadow looks the light,
Stars now vanish without number,
Sleepy planets set, and slumber,
The pursy clouds disband, and scatter,
All expect some sudden matter,
Not one beam triumphs, but from far
    That morning-star.

O at what time soever Thou,
(Unknown to us) the heavens wilt bow,
And, with Thy angels in the van,
Descend to judge poor careless man,
Grant, I may not like puddle lie
In a corrupt security,
Where, if a traveller water crave,
He finds it dead, and in a grave;
But as this restless, vocal spring
All day and night doth run, and sing,
And though here born, yet is acquainted
Elsewhere, and flowing keeps untainted;
So let me all my busy age
In Thy free services engage,
And though (while here) of force I must
Have commerce sometimes with poor dust,
And in my flesh, though vile and low,
As this doth in her channel, flow,
Yet let my course, my aim, my love,
And chief acquaintance be above;
So when that day, and hour shall come
In which Thyself will be the Sun,
Thou'lt find me drest and on my way,
Watching the break of Thy great day.

  acquainted elsewhere] has knowledge of other places;

MAN

WEIGHING the steadfastness and state
Of some mean things which here below reside,
Where birds, like watchful clocks the noiseless date
   And intercourse of times divide,
Where bees at night get home and hive, and
      flowers,
         Early, as well as late,
Rise with the sun, and set in the same bowers;

   I would (said I) my God would give
The staidness of these things to man! for these
To His divine appointments ever cleave,
   And no new business breaks their peace;
The birds nor sow, nor reap, yet sup and dine,
      The flowers without clothes live,
Yet Solomon was never dressed so fine.

   Man hath still either toys, or care,
He hath no root, nor to one place is tied,
But ever restless and irregular
   About this earth doth run and ride,
He knows he hath a home, but scarce knows
      where,
         He says it is so far
That he hath quite forgot how to go there.

   He knocks at all doors, strays and roams,
Nay, hath not so much wit as some stones have
Which in the darkest nights point to their homes,
   By some hid sense their Maker gave;
Man is the shuttle, to whose winding quest
      And passage through these looms
God ordered motion, but ordained no rest.

THE FAVOUR

O THY bright looks! thy glance of love
Shown, and but shown me from above!
Rare looks! that can dispense such joy
As without wooing wins the coy,
And makes him mourn, and pine and die
Like a starved eaglet, for Thine eye.
Some kind herbs here, though low and far,
Watch for, and know their loving star.
O let no star compare with Thee!
Nor any herb outduty me!
So shall my nights and mornings be
Thy time to shine, and mine to see.

THE BOOK

ETERNAL God! Maker of all
That have lived here, since the Man's fall;
The Rock of Ages! in whose shade
They live unseen, when here they fade.

Thou knew'st this paper, when it was
Mere seed, and after that but grass;
Before 'twas drest or spun, and when
Made linen, who did wear it then:
What were their lives, their thoughts and deeds
Whether good corn, or fruitless weeds.

Thou knew'st this tree, when a green shade
Cover'd it, since a cover made,
And where it flourish'd, grew, and spread,
As if it never should be dead.

Thou knew'st this harmless beast, when he
Did live and feed by Thy decree
On each green thing; then slept (well-fed)
Clothed with this skin, which now lies spread

A covering o'er this aged book,
Which makes me wisely weep and look
On my own dust; mere dust it is,
But not so dry and clean as this.
Thou knew'st and saw'st them all and though
Now scatter'd thus, dost know them so.

   O knowing, glorious Spirit! when
Thou shalt restore trees, beasts and men,
When Thou shalt make all new again,
Destroying only death and pain,
Give him amongst Thy works a place,
Who in them loved and sought Thy face!

THE WORLD

I saw Eternity the other night
Like a great ring of pure and endless light,
      All calm, as it was bright,
And round beneath it, Time, in hours, days, years
      Driven by the spheres
Like a vast shadow moved, in which the world
      And all her train were hurl'd;

The doting Lover in his quaintest strain
      Did there complain,
Near him, his lute, his fancy, and his flights,
      Wit's sour delights,
With gloves, and knots the silly snares of pleasure;
      Yet his dear treasure
All scatter'd lay, while he his eyes did pour
      Upon a flower.

The darksome Statesman hung with weights and
    woe
Like a thick midnight-fog moved there so slow
      He did not stay, nor go;
Condemning thoughts (like sad eclipses) scowl
        Upon his soul,
And clouds of crying witnesses without
      Pursued him with one shout.
Yet digg'd the mole, and lest his ways be found,
      Work'd under ground,
Where he did clutch his prey, but One did see
      That policy,
Churches and altars fed him, perjuries
      Were gnats and flies,
It rain'd about him blood and tears, but he
      Drank them as free.

The fearful Miser on a heap of rust
Sat pining all his life there, did scarce trust
      His own hands with the dust,
Yet would not place one piece above, but lives
      In fear of thieves.
Thousands there were as frantic as himself,
      And hugg'd each one his pelf,
The downright Epicure placed heaven in sense,
      And scorn'd pretence,
While others, slipped into a wide excess
      Said little less;
The weaker sort, slight, trivial wares enslave
      Who think them brave,
And poor, despisèd Truth sat counting by
      Their victory.

Yet some, who all this while did weep and sing,
And sing, and weep, soar'd up into the ring,

But most would use no wing.
O fools (said I) thus to prefer dark night
      Before true light,
To live in grots, and caves, and hate the day
      Because it shows the way,
The way which from this dead and dark abode
      Leads up to GOD,
A way where you might tread the sun, and be
      More bright than he.
But as I did their madness so discuss,
      One whisper'd thus,
This ring the Bridegroom did for none provide
      But for His Bride.

THE FLOWER

I WALK'D the other day (to spend my hour,)
      Into a field
Where I sometimes had seen the soil to yield
      A gallant flower,
But Winter now had ruffled all the bower
      And curious store,
    I knew there heretofore.

Yet I, whose search loved not to peep and peer
      I' th' face of things,
Thought with myself, there might be other springs
      Besides this here
Which, like cold friends, sees us but once a year,
      And so the flower
    Might have some other bower.

Then taking up what I could nearest spy
      I digg'd about
That place where I had seen him to grow out,
      And by and by

I saw the warm Recluse alone to lie
          Where fresh and green
     He lived of us unseen.

Many a question intricate and rare
          Did I there strow;
But all I could extort was, that he now
          Did there repair
Such losses as befell him in this air,
          And would ere long
     Come forth most fair and young.

This past, I threw the clothes quite o'er his head,
          And stung with fear
Of my own frailty, dropp'd down many a tear
          Upon his bed,
Then sighing whisper'd, 'Happy are the dead!
          What peace doth now
     Rock him asleep below!'

And yet, how few believe such doctrine springs
          From a poor root
Which all the Winter sleeps here underfoot
          And hath no wings
To raise it to the truth and light of things,
          But is still trod
     By every wandering clod.

O Thou! Whose Spirit did at first inflame
          And warm the dead,
And by a sacred incubation fed
          With life this frame
Which once had neither being, form, nor name,
          Grant I may so
     Thy steps track here below,

          clod] clod-hopper

That in these masques and shadows I may see
        Thy sacred way,
And by those hid ascents climb to that day
        Which breaks from Thee
Who art in all things, though invisibly;
        Show me Thy peace,
      Thy mercy, love, and ease.

And from this care, where dreams and sorrows
    reign,
        Lead me above
Where light, joy, leisure, and true comforts move
        Without all pain,
There, hid in thee, show me his life again
        At whose dumb urn
    Thus all the year I mourn.

EARLY RISING AND PRAYER

WHEN first thy eyes unveil, give thy soul leave
To do the like; our bodies but forerun
The spirit's duty; true hearts spread, and heave
Unto their GOD, as flowers do to the sun.
    Give Him thy first thoughts then; so shalt thou
      keep
    Him company all day, and in Him sleep.

Yet never sleep the sun up; prayer should
Dawn with the day; there are set, awful hours
'Twixt Heaven, and us; the manna was not good
After sun-rising, far-day sullies flowers.
    Rise to prevent the sun; sleep doth sins glut,
    And Heaven's gate opens, when this world's is
    shut.

prevent] anticipate or meet.

Walk with thy fellow-creatures: note the hush
And whispers amongst them. There's not a spring
Or leaf but hath his morning-hymn; each bush
And oak doth know I AM. Canst thou not sing?
    O leave thy cares, and follies! go this way,
    And thou art sure to prosper all the day.

To heighten thy devotions, and keep low
All mutinous thoughts, what business e'er thou hast,
Observe GOD in His works; here fountains flow,
Birds sing, beasts feed, fish leap, and th' earth
        stands fast;
    Above are restless motions, running lights,
    Vast circling azure, giddy clouds, days, nights.

When Seasons change, then lay before thine eyes
His wondrous method; mark the various scenes
In heaven; hail, thunder, rainbows, snow, and ice,
Calms, tempests, light, and darkness, by His
        means;
    Thou canst not miss His praise; each tree, herb,
        flower
    Are shadows of His wisdom, and His power.

THE NIGHT

THROUGH that pure virgin shrine,
    That sacred veil drawn o'er Thy glorious noon,
That men might look and live, as glow-worms
        shine,
            And face the moon:
    Wise Nicodemus saw such light
As made him know his GOD by night.

Most blest believer he!
Who in that land of darkness and blind eyes

Thy long expected healing wings could see,
  When Thou didst rise,
 And what can never more be done,
 Did at midnight speak with the sun.

 O who will tell me, where
He found Thee at that dead and silent hour!
What hallowed solitary ground did bear
  So rare a flower,
 Within those sacred leaves did lie
 The fullness of the Deity.

 No mercy-seat of gold,
No dead and dusty cherub, nor carved stone,
But His own living works did my LORD hold
  And lodge alone;
 Where trees and herbs did watch and peep
 And wonder, while the Jews did sleep.

 Dear night! this world's defeat;
The stop to busy fools; care's check and curb;
The day of spirits; my soul's calm retreat
  Which none disturb!
 CHRIST'S progress, and His prayer time;
 The hours to which high heaven doth chime.

 God's silent searching flight:
When my Lord's head is filled with dew, and all
His locks are wet with the clear drops of night;
  His still, soft call;
 His knocking time; the soul's dumb watch,
 When spirits their fair kindred catch.

 Were all my loud, evil days
Calm and unhaunted as in thy dark tent,
Whose peace but by some angel's wing or voice
  Is seldom rent;

Then I in Heaven all the long year
Would keep, and never wander here.

But living where the sun
Doth all things wake, and where all mix and tire
Themselves and others, I consent and run
To every mire,
And by this world's ill-guiding light,
Err more than I can do by night.

There is in GOD (some say)
A deep, but dazzling darkness; as men here
Say it is late and dusky, because they
See not all clear;
O for that Night! where I in Him
Might live invisible and dim!

THOMAS STANLEY

1625–1678

A DEPOSITION FROM BEAUTY

THOUGH when I loved thee thou wert fair,
Thou art no longer so;
Those glories all the pride they wear
Unto opinion owe;
Beauties, like stars, in borrowed lustre shine;
And 'twas my love that gave thee thine.

The flames that dwelt within thine eye
Do now, with mine, expire;
Thy brightest graces fade and die
At once with my desire;
Love's fires thus mutual influence return;
Thine cease to shine, when mine to burn.

Then, proud Celinda, hope no more
To be implored or wooed,

Since by thy scorn thou dost restore
    The wealth my love bestowed;
And thy despised disdain too late shall find
That none are fair but who are kind.

THE RELAPSE

O, TURN away those cruel eyes,
    The stars of my undoing!
Or death, in such a bright disguise,
    May tempt a second wooing.

Punish their blindly impious pride,
    Who dare contemn thy glory;
It was my fall that deified
    Thy name, and sealed thy story.

Yet no new sufferings can prepare
    A higher praise to crown thee;
Though my first death proclaim thee fair,
    My second will unthrone thee.

Lovers will doubt thou canst entice
    No other for thy fuel,
And if thou burn one victim twice,
    Both think thee poor and cruel.

CHARLES COTTON

1630–1687

CONTENTATION

DIRECTED TO MY DEAR FATHER, AND MOST WORTHY FRIEND
MR. IZAAK WALTON

HEAV'N, what an age is this! what race
    Of giants are sprung up, that dare
Thus fly in the Almighty's face,
    And with his Providence make war!

I can go nowhere but I meet
  With malcontents and mutineers,
As if in life was nothing sweet,
  And we must blessings reap in tears.

O senseless Man, that murmurs still
  For happiness, and does not know
Even though he might enjoy his will,
  What he would have to make him so.

Is it true happiness to be
  By undiscerning Fortune placed
In the most eminent degree,
  Where few arrive, and none stand fast?

Titles and wealth are Fortune's toils
  Wherewith the vain themselves ensnare;
The great are proud of borrowed spoils,
  The miser's plenty breeds his care.

The one supinely yawns at rest,
  Th' other eternally doth toil;
Each of them equally a beast,
  A pampered horse, or labouring moil.

The titulado's oft disgraced
  By public hate, or private frown,
And he whose hand the creature raised,
  Has yet a foot to kick him down.

The drudge who would all get, all save,
  Like a brute beast both feeds and lies;
Prone to the earth, he digs his grave,
  And in the very labour dies.

Excess of ill-got, ill-kept, pelf
  Does only death and danger breed;

moil] drudge.

Whilst one rich worldling starves himself
　　With what would thousand others feed.

By which we see that wealth and power,
　　Although they make men rich and great,
The sweets of life do often sour,
　　And gull ambition with a cheat.

Nor is he happier than these,
　　Who in a moderate estate,
Where he might safely live at ease,
　　Has lusts that are immoderate.

For he, by those desires misled,
　　Quits his own vine's securing shade,
T' expose his naked empty head
　　To all the storms man's peace invade.

Nor is he happy who is trim,
　　Tricked up in favours of the fair,
Mirrors, with every breath made dim,
　　Birds, caught in every wanton snare.

Woman, man's greatest woe, or bliss,
　　Does often far, than serve, enslave,
And with the magic of a kiss
　　Destroy whom she was made to save.

Oh! fruitful grief, the world's disease!
　　And vainer man, to make it so,
Who gives his miseries increase
　　By cultivating his own woe.

There are no ills but what we make
　　By giving shapes and names to things;
Which is the dangerous mistake
　　That causes all our sufferings.

We call that sickness, which is health;
    That persecution, which is grace;
That poverty, which is true wealth,
    And that dishonour, which is praise. . . .

Alas! our time is here so short,
    That in what state soe'er 'tis spent,
Of joy or woe does not import,
    Provided it be innocent.

But we may make it pleasant too
    If we will take our measures right,
And not what heaven has done, undo
    By an unruly appetite. . . .

The world is full of beaten roads,
    But yet so slippery withal,
That where one walks secure, 'tis odds
    A hundred and a hundred fall.

Untrodden paths are then the best,
    Where the frequented are unsure,
And he comes soonest to his rest,
    Whose journey has been most secure.

It is content alone that makes
    Our pilgrimage a pleasure here;
And who buys sorrow cheapest, takes
    An ill commodity too dear.

TO CELIA

WHEN, Celia, must my old day set,
    And my young morning rise
In beams of joy so bright as yet
    Ne'er bless'd a lover's eyes?

My state is more advanced than when
   I first attempted thee:
I sued to be a servant then,
   But now to be made free.

I've served my time faithful and true,
   Expecting to be placed
In happy freedom, as my due,
   To all the joys thou hast:
Ill husbandry in love is such
   A scandal to love's power,
We ought not to misspend so much
   As one poor short-lived hour.

Yet think not, Sweet, I'm weary grown,
   That I pretend such haste;
Since none to surfeit e'er was known
   Before he had a taste:
My infant love could humbly wait
   When, young, it scarce knew how
To plead; but grown to man's estate,
   He is impatient now.

TO CHLORIS

FAREWELL, my sweet, until I come,
   Improved in merit, for thy sake,
With characters of honour, home,
   Such as thou canst not then but take.

To loyalty my love must bow,
   My honour, too, calls to the field,
Where for a lady's busk I now
   Must keen and sturdy iron wield.

Yet, when I rush into those arms,
   When death and danger do combine,

I shall less subject be to harms
  Than to those killing eyes of thine.

Since I could live in thy disdain,
  Thou art so far become my fate,
That I by nothing can be slain
  Until thy sentence speaks my date.

But if I seem to fall in war,
  T' excuse the murder you commit,
Be to my memory just so far
  As in thy heart to acknowledge it;

That's all I ask; which thou must give
  To him that dying takes a pride
It is for thee; and would not live
  Sole Prince of all the world beside.

JOHN BUNYAN

1628–1688

THE SHEPHERD BOY SINGS IN THE VALLEY OF HUMILIATION

HE that is down, needs fear no fall,
  He that is low, no pride;
He that is humble ever shall
  Have God to be his guide.

I am content with what I have,
  Little be it or much:
And, Lord, contentment still I crave
  Because Thou savest such.

Fullness to such a burden is
  That go on pilgrimage:
Here little, and hereafter bliss,
  Is best from age to age.

THE PILGRIM

  WHO would true valour see,
Let him come hither;
One here will constant be,
Come wind, come weather.
There's no discouragement,
Shall make him once relent
His first avowed intent
To be a pilgrim.

  Who so beset him round
With dismal stories,
Do but themselves confound,
His strength the more is.
No lion can him fright,
He'll with a giant fight,
But he will have a right
To be a pilgrim.

  Hobgoblin, nor foul fiend,
Can daunt his spirit;
He knows he at the end
Shall life inherit.
Then fancies fly away,
He'll fear not what men say,
He'll labour night and day
To be a pilgrim.

KATHERINE PHILLIPS ('ORINDA')

1631–1664

TO A FRIEND BEFORE TAKING A JOURNEY

I

WELL, we will do that rigid thing
  Which makes spectators think we part;
Though absence hath for none a sting
  But those who keep each other's heart.

II

And when our sense is dispossest,
  Our labouring souls will heave and pant,
And gasp for one another's breast,
  Since their conveyances they want.

III

Nay, we have felt the tedious smart
  Of absent friendship, and do know
That when we die we can but part;
  And who know what we shall do now?

IV

Yet I must go: we will submit,
  And so our own disposers be;
For while we nobly suffer it,
  We triumph o'er necessity.

V

By this we shall be truly great,
  If having other things o'ercome,
To make our victory complete
  We can be conquerors at home.

VI

Nay then to meet we may conclude,
   And all our obstructions overthrow,
Since we our passions have subdued,
   Which is the strongest thing I know.

TO ONE PERSUADING A LADY TO MARRIAGE

FORBEAR, bold youth; all's heaven here,
   And what you do aver
To others courtship may appear,
   'Tis sacrilege to her.
She is a public deity,
   And were't not very odd
She should dispose herself to be
   A petty household god?

First make the sun in private shine,
   And bid the world adieu,
That so he may his beams confine
   In compliment to you.
But if of that you do despair,
   Think how you did amiss,
To strive to fix her beams which are
   More bright and large than his.

ANONYMOUS

BALLADS, SONGS, CAROLS, ETC.

SIR PATRICK SPENS

THE king sits in Dunfermline toun,
   Drinking the blude-red wine;
'Oh whare will I get gude sailor,
   To sail this ship o' mine?'

Up and spake an eldern knight
  Sat at the king's right knee;
'Sir Patrick Spens is the best sailor,
  That ever sail'd the sea.'

The king has written a braid letter,
  And sign'd it wi' his hand,
And sent it to Sir Patrick Spens,
  Was walking on the strand.

'To Noroway, to Noroway,
  To Noroway o'er the faem;
The king's daughter of Noroway,
  'Tis thou maun bring her hame.'

The first line that Sir Patrick read,
  A loud laugh laughèd he;
The neist line that Sir Patrick read,
  The tear blinded his ee.

'O wha is this has done this deed,
  And tauld the king o' me,
To send us out at this time o' the year,
  To sail upon the sea?'

'Be't wind, be it weet, be't hail, be it sleet,
  Our ship must sail the faem,
The king's daughter of Noroway,
  'Tis we must fetch her hame.'

They hoysed their sails on Monenday morn,
  Wi' a' the speed they may;
And they hae landed in Noroway,
  Upon a Wodensday.

They hadna been a week, a week,
  In Noroway, but twae,
When that the lords o' Noroway
  Began aloud to say,

'Ye Scottishmen spend a' our king's goud,
  And a' our queenis fee!'
'Ye lee, ye lee, ye liars loud!
  Fu' loud I hear ye lie!

'For I brought as much white monie,
  As gane my men and me,
And I brought a half-fou o' gude red goud,
  Out o'er the sea wi' me.

'Make ready, make ready, my merrymen a'!
  Our gude ship sails the morn.'
'Now, ever alake, my master dear,
  I fear a deadly storm!

'I saw the new moon, late yestreen,
  Wi' the auld moon in her arm;
And if we gang to sea, master,
  I fear we'll come to harm!'

They hadna sail'd a league, a league,
  A league but barely three,
When the lift grew dark, and the wind blew loud,
  And gurly grew the sea.

The ankers brak, and the topmasts lap,
  It was sic a deadly storm;
And the waves came o'er the broken ship,
  Till a' her sides were torn.

'O where will I get a gude sailor,
  To take my helm in hand,
Till I get up to the tall topmast,
  To see if I can spy land?'

'O here am I, a sailor gude,
  To take the helm in hand,

gane] would suffice.   alake] alack.
lift] sky.   gurly] rough.   lap] sprang.

Till you go up to the tall topmast,
    But I fear you'll ne'er spy land.'

He hadna gane a step, a step,
    A step but barely ane,
When a bout flew out of our goodly ship,
    And the salt sea it came in.

'Gae, fetch a web o' the silken claith,
    Another o' the twine,
And wap them into our ships' side,
    And let na the sea come in.'

They fetch'd a web o' the silken claith,
    Another o' the twine,
And they wapp'd them round the gude ship's side,
    But still the sea came in.

O laith, laith were our gude Scots lords
    To weet their cork-heeled shoon!
But lang or a' the play was play'd,
    They wat their hats aboon.

And mony was the feather-bed
    That flattered on the faem;
And mony was the gude lord's son
    That never mair cam hame.

The ladyes wrang their fingers white,
    The maidens tore their hair,
A' for the sake of their true loves;
    For them they'll see na mair.

O lang, lang may the ladyes sit,
    Wi' their fans into their hand,
Before they see Sir Patrick Spens
    Come sailing to the strand!

      bout] bolt.   wap] warp.   flattered] floated.

And lang, lang may the maidens sit,
　Wi' the goud kaims in their hair,
A' waiting for their ain dear loves!
　For them they'll see nae mair.

O forty miles off Aberdeen,
　'Tis fifty fathom deep,
And there lies gude Sir Patrick Spens
　Wi' the Scots lords at his feet.

CHEVY CHACE

I

GOD prosper long our noble king,
　Our lives and safeties all;
A woeful hunting once there did
　In Chevy-Chace befall;

To drive the deer with hound and horn
　Erle Percy took his way;
The child may rue that is unborn
　The hunting of that day.

The stout Erle of Northumberland
　A vow to God did make,
His pleasure in the Scottish woods
　Three summer's days to take,

The chiefest harts in Chevy-Chace
　To kill and bear away.
These tydings to Erle Douglas came,
　In Scotland where he lay:

Who sent Erle Percy present word,
　He wold prevent his sport.
The English Erle, not fearing that,
　Did to the woods resort

　　　　　　kaims] combs.

With fifteen hundred bow-men bold,
  All chosen men of might,
Who knew full well in time of neede
  To ayme their shafts aright.

The gallant greyhounds swiftly ran,
  To chase the fallow deere:
On Monday they began to hunt,
  Ere daylight did appeare;

And long before high noone they had
  An hundred fat buckes slaine;
Then having dined, the drovyers went
  To rouse the deere againe.

The bow-men mustered on the hills,
  Well able to endure;
Their backsides all with special care
  That day were guarded sure.

The hounds ran swiftly through the woods,
  The nimble deere to take,
And with their cryes the hills and dales
  An echo shrill did make.

Lord Percy to the quarry went,
  To view the slaughtered deere:
Quoth he, 'Erle Douglas promisèd
  This day to meet me here,

'But if I thought he wold not come
  No longer wold I stay.'
With that, a brave younge gentleman
  Thus to the Erle did say:

'Lo, yonder doth Erle Douglas come,
  His men in armour bright;
Full twenty hundred Scottish speares
  All marching in our sight;

'All men of pleasant Tivydale,
  Fast by the river Tweede':
'O, cease your sports,' Erle Percy said,
  'And take your bowes with speede;

'And now with me, my countrymen,
  Your courage forth advance,
For there was never champion yet,
  In Scotland or in France,

'That ever did on horsebacke come,
  But if my hap it were,
I durst encounter man for man,
  And with him break a speare.'

II

Erle Douglas on his milke-white steede,
  Most like a baron bold,
Rode foremost of his company,
  Whose armour shone like gold.

'Show me,' said he, 'whose men ye be,
  That hunt so boldly here,
That, without my consent, do chase
  And kill my fallow-deere.'

The first man that did answer make,
  Was noble Percy he;
Who sayd, 'We list not to declare,
  Nor shew whose men we be,

'Yet we will spend our dearest blood,
  Thy chiefest harts to slay.'
Then Douglas swore a solemn oath,
  And thus in rage did say:

'Ere thus I will out-bravèd be,
  One of us two shall dye:

I know thee well, an erle thou art;
  Lord Percy, so am I.

'But trust me, Percy, pittye it were,
  And great offence to kill
Any of these our guiltlesse men,
  For they have done no ill.

'Let thou and I the battle trye,
  And set our men aside.'
'Accurst be he,' Erle Percy said,
  'By whom this is denied.'

Then stept a gallant squier forth,
  Witherington was his name,
Who said, 'I would not have it told
  To Henry our king for shame,

'That ere my captaine fought on foote,
  And I stood looking on.
Ye be two erles,' said Witherington,
  'And I a squier alone:

'Ile do the best that do I may,
  While I have power to stand:
While I have power to wield my sword,
  Ile fight with heart and hand.'

III

Our English archers bent their bowes,
  Their hearts were good and trew,
At the first flight of arrowes sent,
  Full fourscore Scots they slew.

Yet bides Erle Douglas on the bent,
  As chieftain stout and good.
As valiant captain, all unmoved
  The shock he firmly stood.

His host he parted had in three,
  As leader ware and try'd,
And soon his spearmen on their foes
  Bare down on every side.

Throughout the English archery
  They dealt full many a wound;
But still our valiant Englishmen
  All firmly kept their ground,

And, throwing strait their bowes away,
  They grasped their swords so bright,
And now sharp blows, a heavy shower,
  On shields and helmets light.

They closed full fast on every side,
  No slackness there was found;
And many a gallant gentleman
  Lay gasping on the ground.

O Christ! it was a griefe to see,
  And likewise for to heare,
The cries of men lying in their gore,
  And scattered here and there!

At last these two stout erles did meet,
  Like captaines of great might:
Like lions wode, they laid on lode,
  And made a cruel fight:

They fought untill they both did sweat
  With swords of tempered steele,
Until the blood like drops of rain
  They trickling down did feele.

'Yield thee, Lord Percy,' Douglas said;
  'In faith I will thee bringe,

wode] mad.   laid on lode] dealt heavy blows.

Where thou shalt high advancèd be
  By James our Scottish king:

'Thy ransome I will freely give,
  And this report of thee,
Thou art the most courageous knight,
  That ever I did see.'

'No, Douglas,' quoth Erle Percy then,
  'Thy proffer I do scorne;
I will not yield to any Scot,
  That ever yet was borne.'

With that, there came an arrow keene
  Out of an English bow,
Which struck Erle Douglas to the heart,
  A deep and deadly blow:

Who never spake more words than these,
  'Fight on, my merry men all;
For why, my life is at an end;
  Lord Percy sees my fall.'

Then leaving life, Erle Percy tooke
  The dead man by the hand;
And said, 'Erle Douglas, for thy life
  Wold I had lost my land!

'O Christ! my very heart doth bleed
  With sorrow for thy sake,
For sure, a more redoubted knight
  Mischance could never take.'

A knight amongst the Scots there was,
  Which saw Erle Douglas dye,
Who straight in wrath did vow revenge
  Upon the Lord Percye.

Sir Hugh Mountgomery was he called
   Who, with a speare most bright,
Well-mounted on a gallant steed,
   Ran fiercely through the fight,

And past the English archers all,
   Without or dread or feare,
And through Erle Percy's body then
   He thrust his hateful speare.

With such a vehement force and might
   He did his body gore,
The staff ran through the other side
   A large cloth-yard, and more.

So thus did both these nobles dye,
   Whose courage none could staine!
An English archer then perceived
   The noble Erle was slaine:

He had a bow bent in his hand,
   Made of a trusty tree;
An arrow of a cloth-yard long
   Up to the head drew he;

Against Sir Hugh Mountgomerye
   So right the shaft he set,
The grey goose-winge that was thereon
   In his heart's bloode was wet.

This fight did last from breake of day
   Till setting of the sun;
For when they rung the evening-bell,
   The battle scarce was done.

IV

With stout Erle Percy, there was slaine
   Sir John of Egerton,

Sir Robert Ratcliff, and Sir John,
  Sir James, that bold barôn;

And with Sir George and stout Sir James,
  Both knights of good account,
Good Sir Ralph Raby there was slaine,
  Whose prowesse did surmount.

For Witherington needs must I wayle,
  As one in doleful dumpes;
For when his legs were smitten off,
  He fought upon his stumpes.

And with Erle Douglas, there was slaine
  Sir Hugh Mountgomerye,
Sir Charles Murray, that from the field
  One foote would never flee;

Sir Charles Murray, of Ratcliff, too,
  His sister's sonne was he;
Sir David Lamb, so well esteemed,
  Yet saved he could not be;

And the Lord Maxwell in like case
  Did with Erle Douglas dye:
Of twenty hundred Scottish speares,
  Scarce fifty-five did flye.

Of fifteen hundred Englishmen,
  Went home but fifty-three:
The rest were slaine in Chevy-Chace,
  Under the greenewoode tree.

Next day did many widdowes come,
  Their husbands to bewayle;
They washt their wounds in brinish teares,
  But all wold not prevayle;

Their bodyes, bathed in purple gore,
　　They bore with them away;
They kist them dead a thousand times,
　　Ere they were clad in clay.

V

The newes was brought to Eddenborrow,
　　Where Scotland's king did raigne,
That brave Erle Douglas suddenlye
　　Was with an arrow slaine:

'O heavy newes,' King James did say,
　　'Scotland may witnesse be,
I have not any captaine more
　　Of such account as he.'

Like tydings to King Henry came,
　　Within as short a space,
That Percy of Northumberland
　　Was slaine in Chevy-Chace:

'Now God be with him,' said our king,
　　'Sith it will no better be;
I trust I have, within my realme,
　　Five hundred as good as he:

'Yet shall not Scots nor Scotland say,
　　But I will vengeance take:
Ile be revengèd on them all,
　　For brave Erle Percy's sake.'

This vow full well the king performed
　　After, at Humbledowne;
In one day, fifty knights were slayne,
　　With lords of great renowne,

And of the rest, of small account,
　　Did many thousands dye.

Thus endeth the hunting of Chevy-Chace,
  Made by the Erle Percye.

God save our king, and bless this land
  With plentye, joy, and peace,
And grant henceforth that foule debate
  'Twixt noblemen may cease.

BRAVE LORD WILLOUGHBY

The fifteenth of July,
  With glistening spear and shield,
A famous fight in Flanders
  Was foughten in the field;
The most courageous officers
  Were English captains three,
But the bravest man in battle
  Was brave Lord Willoughby.

The next was Captain Morris,
  A valiant man was he;
The other, Captain Turner,
  From field would never flee.
With fifteen hundred fighting men——
  Alas, there were no more,—
They fought with fourteen thousand men
  Upon the bloody shore.

'Stand to it, noble pikemen,
  And look you round about!
And shoot you right, you bowmen,
  And we will keep them out!
You musquet and caliver men,
  Do you prove true to me;
I'll be the foremost in the fight!'
  Says brave Lord Willoughby.

And then the bloody enemy
   They fiercely did assail;
And fought it out most furiously,
   Not doubting to prevail.
The wounded men on both sides fell,
   Most piteous for to see,
Yet nothing could the courage quell
   Of brave Lord Willoughby.

For seven hours, to all men's view,
   The fight endurèd sore,
Until our men so feeble grew
   That they could fight no more.
And then upon their dead horses
   Full savoury they ate,
And drank the puddle-water—
   They could not better get.

When they had fed so freely,
   They kneelèd on the ground,
And praisèd God devoutly
   For the favour they had found;
And beating up their colours,
   The fight they did renew,
And turning tow'rds the Spaniard,
   A thousand more they slew.

The sharp steel-pointed arrows
   And bullets thick did fly;
Then did our valiant soldiers
   Charge on most furiously;
Which made the Spaniards waver,
   They thought it best to flee;
They feared the stout behaviour
   Of brave Lord Willoughby.

And then the fearful enemy
  Was quickly put to flight;
Our men pursued courageously
  And caught their forces quite.
But at the last they gave a shout
  Which echoed through the sky;
'God and Saint George for England!'
  The conquerors did cry.

The news was brought to England,
  With all the speed might be,
And soon our gracious Queen was told
  Of this same victory.
'O this is brave Lord Willoughby,
  My love that ever won;
Of all the lords of honour
  'Tis he great deeds hath done.'

To the soldiers that were maimèd
  And wounded in the fray,
The Queen allowed a pension
  Of fifteenpence a day:
And from all costs and charges
  She quit and set them free;
And this she did all for the sake
  Of brave Lord Willoughby.

Then, courage! noble Englishmen,
  And never be dismayed:
If that we be but one to ten
  We will not be afraid
To fight with foreign enemies,
  And set our nation free;
And thus I end the bloody bout
  Of brave Lord Willoughby.

ROBIN HOOD AND THE CURTAL FRIAR

But how many months be in the year?
There are thirteen, I say;
The midsummer moon is the merryest of all
Next to the merry month of May.

I

IN summer time, when leaves grow green,
    And flowers are fresh and gay,
Robin Hood and his merry men
    Were [all] disposed to play.

II

Then some would leap, and some would run,
    And some would use artillery;
'Which of you can a good bow draw,
    A good archer for to be?

III

'Which of you can kill a buck,
    Or who can kill a doe?
Or who can kill a hart of grease,
    Five hundred foot him fro?'

IV

Will Scadlocke he kill'd a buck,
    And Midge he kill'd a doe,
And Little John kill'd a hart of grease,
    Five hundred foot him fro.

V

'God's blessing on thy heart,' said Robin Hood,
    'That hath [shot] such a shot for me;
I would ride my horse a hundred miles,
    To find one could match with thee.'

Curtal] short-frocked.   hart of grease] fat hart.

VI

That caus'd Will Scadlocke to laugh,
  He laugh'd full heartily:
'There lives a curtal friar in Fountains Abbey
  Will beat both him and thee.

VII

'The curtal friar in Fountains Abbey
  Well can a strong bow draw;
He will beat you and your yeomen,
  Set them all on a row.'

VIII

Robin Hood he took a solemn oath,
  It was by Mary free,
That he would neither eat nor drink
  Till the friar he did see.

IX

Robin Hood put on his harness good,
  And on his head a cap of steel,
Broad sword and buckler by his side,
  And they became him weel.

X

He took his bow into his hand,
  It was made of a trusty tree,
With a sheaf of arrows at his belt,
  To the Fountains Dale went he.

XI

And coming unto Fountains Dale,
  No farther would he ride;
There he was aware of a curtal friar,
  Walking by the water-side.

XII

The friar had on a harness good,
    And on his head a cap of steel,
Broad sword and buckler by his side,
    And they became him weel.

XIII

Robin Hood lighted off his horse,
    And tied him to a thorn:
'Carry me over the water, thou curtal friar,
    Or else thy life's forlorn.'

XIV

The friar took Robin Hood on his back,
    Deep water he did bestride,
And spake neither good word nor bad,
    Till he came at the other side.

XV

Lightly leapt Robin Hood off the friar's back;
    The friar said to him again,
'Carry me over this water, fine fellow,
    Or it shall breed thy pain.'

XVI

Robin Hood took the friar on 's back,
    Deep water he did bestride,
And spake neither good word nor bad,
    Till he came at the other side.

XVII

Lightly leapt the friar off Robin Hood's back;
    Robin Hood said to him again,
'Carry me over this water, thou curtal friar,
    Or it shall breed thy pain.'

XVIII

The friar took Robin Hood on's back again,
  And stept up to the knee;
Till he came at the middle stream,
  Neither good nor bad spake he.

XIX

And coming to the middle stream,
  There he threw Robin in:
'And choose thee, choose thee, fine fellow,
  Whether thou wilt sink or swim.'

XX

Robin Hood swam to a bush of broom,
  The friar to a wicker wand;
Bold Robin Hood is gone to shore,
  And took his bow in his hand.

XXI

One of his best arrows under his belt
  To the friar he let flye;
The curtal friar with his steel buckler,
  He put that arrow by.

XXII

'Shoot on, shoot on, thou fine fellow,
  Shoot as thou hast begun;
If thou shoot here a summer's day,
  Thy mark I will not shun.'

XXIII

Robin Hood shot passing well,
  Till his arrows all were gone;
They took their swords and steel bucklers,
  And fought with might and main,

XXIV

From ten o' th' clock that day,
   Till four i' th' afternoon;
Then Robin Hood, came to his knees,
   Of the friar to beg a boon.

XXV

'A boon, a boon, thou curtal friar,
   I beg it on my knee;
Give me leave to set my horn to my mouth,
   And to blow blasts three.'

XXVI

'That will I do,' said the curtal friar,
   'Of thy blasts I have no doubt;
I hope thou 'lt blow so passing well,
   Till both thy eyes fall out.'

XXVII

Robin Hood set his horn to his mouth
   He blew but blasts three;
Half a hundred yeomen, with bows bent,
   Came raking over the lee.

XXVIII

'Whose men are these,' said the friar,
   'That come so hastily?'
'These men are mine,' said Robin Hood;
   'Friar, what is that to thee?'

XXIX

'A boon, a boon,' said the curtal friar,
   'The like I gave to thee!
Give me leave to set my fist to my mouth,
   And to whute whutès three.'

raking] advancing.   whute] whistle.

XXX

'That will I do,' said Robin Hood,
  'Or else I were to blame;
Three whutès in a friar's fist
  Would make me glad and fain.'

XXXI

The friar set his fist to his mouth,
  And whuted whutès three;
Half a hundred good ban-dogs
  Came running over the lee.

XXXII

'Here's for every man of thine a dog;
  And I myself for thee:'
'Nay, by my faith,' quoth Robin Hood,
  'Friar, that may not be.'

XXXIII

Two dogs at once to Robin Hood did go,
  The one behind, the other before;
Robin Hood's mantle of Lincoln green
  Off from his back they tore.

XXXIV

And whether his men shot east or west,
  Or they shot north or south,
The curtal dogs, so taught they were,
  They kept their arrows in their mouth.

XXXV

'Take up thy dogs,' said Little John,
  'Friar, at my bidding be;'
'Whose man art thou,' said the curtal friar,
  'Comes here to prate with me?'

XXXVI

'I am Little John, Robin Hood's man,
    Friar, I will not lie;
If thou take not up thy dogs soon,
    I'll take up them and thee.'

XXXVII

Little John had a bow in his hand,
    He shot with might and main;
Soon half a score of the friar's dogs
    Lay dead upon the plain.

XXXVIII

'Hold thy hand, good fellow,' said the curtal friar,
    'Thy master and I will agree;
And we will have new orders taken,
    With all the haste that may be.'

XXXIX

'If thou wilt forsake fair Fountains Dale,
    And Fountains Abbey free,
Every Sunday throughout the year
    A noble shall be thy fee;

XL

'And every holy day throughout the year
    Changed shall thy garment be,
If thou wilt go to fair Nottingham,
    And there remain with me.'

XLI

This curtal friar had kept Fountains Dale
    Seven long years or more;
There was neither knight, lord, nor earl,
    Could make him yield before.

ROBIN HOOD AND THE PINDER OF WAKEFIELD

In Wakefield there lives a jolly pinder,
    In Wakefield, all on a green;

'There is neither knight nor squire,' said the
      pinder,
    'Nor baron that is so bold,
Dare make a trespass to the town of Wakefield,
    But his pledge goes to the pinfold.'

All this beheard three witty young men,
    'Twas Robin Hood, Scarlet, and John;
With that they spied the jolly pinder,
    As he sat under a thorn.

'Now turn again, turn again,' said the pinder,
    'For a wrong way have you gone;
For you have forsaken the king his highway,
    And made a path over the corn.'

'O that were great shame,' said jolly Robin,
    'We being three, and thou but one':
The pinder leapt back then thirty good foot,
    'Twas thirty good foot and one.

He leaned his back fast unto a thorn,
    And his foot unto a stone,
And there he fought a long summer's day,
    A summer's day so long,
Till that their swords, on their broad bucklers,
    Were broken fast unto their hands.

'Hold thy hand, hold thy hand,' said Robin Hood,
    'And my merry men every one;
For this is one of the best pinders
    That ever I tried with sword.

'And wilt thou forsake thy pinder his craft,
　　And live in the green wood with me?'

'At Michaelmas next my covenant comes out,
　　When every man gathers his fee;
I'll take my blue blade all in my hand,
　　And plod to the green wood with thee.'

'Hast thou either meat or drink,' said **Robin
　　Hood,**
　　'For my merry men and me?'

'I have both bread and beef,' said the pinder,
　　'And good ale of the best';
'And that is meat good enough,' said **Robin
　　Hood,**
　　'For such unbidden guest.

'O wilt thou forsake the pinder his craft
　　And go to the green wood with me?
Thou shalt have a livery twice in the year,
　　The one green, the other brown shall be.

'If Michaelmas day were once come and gone,
　　And my master had paid me my fee,
Then would I set as little by him
　　As my master doth set by me.

ROBIN HOOD AND THE WIDOW'S THREE SONS

I

THERE are twelve months in all the year.
　　As I hear many say,
But the merriest month in all the year
　　Is the merry month of May.

II

Now Robin Hood is to Nottingham gone,
  With a link a down and a day,
And there he met a silly old woman,
  Was weeping on the way.

III

'What news? what news, thou silly old woman?
  What news hast thou for me?'
Said she, 'There's three squires in Nottingham
    town
  To-day is condemn'd to die.'

IV

'O have they parishes burnt?' he said,
  'Or have they ministers slain?
Or have they robb'd any virgin,
  Or with other men's wives have lain?'—

V

'They have no parishes burnt, good sir,
  Nor yet have ministers slain,
Nor have they robbed any virgin,
  Nor with other men's wives have lain.'

VI

'O what have they done?' said Robin Hood,
  'I pray thee tell to me.'—
'It's for slaying of the King's fallow deer,
  Bearing their long bows with thee.'—

VII

'Dost thou not mind, old woman,' he said,
  'Since thou made me sup and dine?
By the truth of my body,' quoth bold Robin Hood,
  'You could not tell it in better time.'

VIII

Now Robin Hood is to Nottingham gone,
  With a link a down and a day,
And there he met with a silly old palmer,
  Was walking along the highway.

IX

'What news? what news, thou silly old man?
  What news, I do thee pray?'—
Said he, 'Three squires in Nottingham town
  Are condemned to die this day.'—

X

'Come change thy apparel with me, old man,
  Come change thy apparel for mine;
Here is forty shillings in good silver,
  Go drink it in beer or wine.'—

XI

'O thine apparel is good,' he said,
  'And mine is ragged and torn;
Wherever you go, wherever you ride,
  Laugh ne'er an old man to scorn.'—

XII

'Come change thy apparel with me, old churl,
  Come change thy apparel with mine;
Here are twenty pieces of good broad gold,
  Go feast thy brethren with wine.'

XIII

Then he put on the old man's hat,
  It stood full high on the crown:
'The first bold bargain that I come at,
  It shall make thee come down.'

XIV

Then he put on the old man's cloak,
  Was patch'd black, blue, and red;
He thought it no shame, all the day long,
  To wear the bags of bread.

XV

Then he put on the old man's breeks,
  Was patch'd from ballup to side;
'By the truth of my body,' bold Robin can say,
  'This man lov'd little pride!'

XVI

Then he put on the old man's hose,
  Were patch'd from knee to wrist;
'By the truth of my body,' said bold Robin Hood,
  'I'd laugh if I had any list.'

XVII

Then he put on the old man's shoes,
  Were patch'd both beneath and aboon;
Then Robin Hood swore a solemn oath,
  'It's good habit that makes a man!'

XVIII

Now Robin Hood is to Nottingham gone,
  With a link a down and a down,
And there he met with the proud Sheriff,
  Was walking along the town.

XIX

'O save, O save, O Sheriff,' he said,
  'O save, and you may see!
And what will you give to a silly old man
  To-day will your hangman be?'

ballup] front, or flap.   list] inclination for it.

XX

'Some suits, some suits,' the Sheriff he said,
  'Some suits I'll give to thee;
Some suits, some suits, and pence thirteen
  To-day's a hangman's fee.'

XXI

Then Robin he turns him round about,
  And jumps from stock to stone;
'By the truth of my body,' the Sheriff he said,
  'That's well jumpt, thou nimble old man.'—

XXII

'I was ne'er a hangman in all my life,
  Nor yet intends to trade;
But curst be he,' said bold Robin,
  'That first a hangman was made!

XXIII

'I've a bag for meal, and a bag for malt,
  And a bag for barley and corn;
A bag for bread, and a bag for beef,
  And a bag for my little small horn.

XXIV

'I have a horn in my pockèt,
  I got it from Robin Hood,
And still when I set it to my mouth,
  For thee it blows little good.'—

XXV

'O wind thy horn, thou proud fellòw,
  Of thee I have no doubt;
I wish that thou give such a blast
  Till both thy eyes fall out.'

XXVI

The first loud blast that he did blow,
   He blew both loud and shrill;
A hundred and fifty of Robin Hood's men
   Came riding over the hill.

XXVII

The next loud blast that he did give,
   He blew both loud and amain;
And quickly sixty of Robin Hood's men
   Came shining over the plain.

XXVIII

'O who are yon,' the Sheriff he said,
   'Come tripping over the lee?'
'They're my attendants,' brave Robin did say,
   'They'll pay a visit to thee.'

XXIX

They took the gallows from the slack,
   They set it in the glen,
They hang'd the proud Sheriff on that,
   And releas'd their own three men.

ROBIN HOOD AND ALAN A DALE

I

Come listen to me, you gallants so free,
   All you that love mirth for to hear,
And I will you tell of a bold outlàw,
   That lived in Nottinghamshire.

II

As Robin Hood in the forest stood,
   All under the green-wood tree,

       slack] hollow, dell.

There he was ware of a brave young man,
    As fine as fine might be.

III

The youngster was clothed in scarlet red,
    In scarlet fine and gay,
And he did frisk it over the plain,
    And chanted a roundelay.

IV

As Robin Hood next morning stood,
    Amongst the leaves so gay,
There did he espy the same young man
    Come drooping along the way.

V

The scarlet he wore the day before,
    It was clean cast away;
And every step he fetcht a sigh,
    'Alack and a well a day!'

VI

Then steppèd forth brave Little John,
    And Much the miller's son,
Which made the young man bend his bow,
    When as he saw them come.

VII

'Stand off, stand off!' the young man said,
    'What is your will with me?'—
'You must come before our master straight,
    Under yon green-wood tree.'

VIII

And when he came bold Robin before,
    Robin asked him courteously,

'O hast thou any money to spare,
  For my merry men and me?'

IX

'I have no money,' the young man said,
  'But five shillings and a ring;
And that I have kept this seven long years,
  To have it at my wedding.

X

'Yesterday I should have married a maid,
  But she from me is tane,
And chosen to be an old knight's delight,
  Whereby my poor heart is slain.'

XI

'What is thy name?' then said Robin Hood,
  'Come tell me, without any fail.'—
'By the faith of my body,' then said the young
    man,
  'My name it is Alan a Dale.'

XII

'What wilt thou give me,' said Robin Hood,
  'In ready gold or fee,
To help thee to thy true-love again,
  And deliver her unto thee?'

XIII

'I have no money,' then quoth the young man,
  'No ready gold nor fee,
But I will swear upon a book
  Thy true servant for to be.'—

XIV

'How many miles is it to thy true-love?
  Come tell me without guile.'—

'By the faith of my body,' then said the young
    man,
  'It is but five little mile.'

XV

Then Robin he hasted over the plain,
  He did neither stint nor lin,
Until he came unto the church
  Where Alan should keep his wedding.

XVI

'What hast thou here?' the Bishop then said,
  'I prithee now tell unto me:'
'I am a bold harper,' quoth Robin Hood,
  'And the best in the north countrey.'

XVII

O welcome, O welcome!' the Bishop he said,
  'That musick best pleaseth me.'—
'You shall have no musick,' quoth Robin Hood,
  'Till the bride and the bridegroom I see.'

XVIII

With that came in a wealthy knight,
  Which was both grave and old,
And after him a finikin lass,
  Did shine like the glistering gold.

XIX

'This is no fit match,' quoth bold Robin Hood,
  'That you do seem to make here;
For since we are come into the church,
  The bride she shall choose her own dear.'

lin] stop.

XX

Then Robin Hood put his horn to his mouth,
  And blew blasts two or three;
When four and twenty bowmen bold
  Come leaping over the lee.

XXI

And when they came into the churchyard,
  Marching all on a row,
The first man was Alan a Dale,
  To give bold Robin his bow.

XXII

'This is thy true-love,' Robin he said,
  'Young Alan, as I hear say;
And you shall be married at this same time,
  Before we depart away.'

XXIII

'That shall not be,' the Bishop he said,
  'For thy word shall not stand;
They shall be three times asked in the church,
  As the law is of our land.'

XXIV

Robin Hood pull'd off the Bishop's coat,
  And put it upon Little John;
'By the faith of my body,' then Robin said,
  'This cloth doth make thee a man.'

XXV

When Little John went into the quire,
  The people began to laugh;
He asked them seven times in the church,
  Least three times should not be enough.

XXVI

'Who gives me this maid?' said Little John;
    Quoth Robin Hood, 'That do I!
And he that takes her from Alan a Dale
    Full dearly he shall her buy.'

XXVII

And thus having ended this merry weddìng,
    The bride looked like a queen,
And so they return'd to the merry green-wood,
    Amongst the leaves so green.

                    Ritson's *Robin Hood*, 1795.

KINMONT WILLIE

I

O HAVE ye na heard o' the fause Sakelde?
    O have ye na heard o' the keen Lord Scroope?
How they hae ta'en bauld Kinmont Willie,
    On Haribee to hang him up?

II

Had Willie had but twenty men,
    But twenty men as stout as he,
Fause Sakelde had never the Kinmont ta'en,
    Wi' eight score in his companie.

III

They band his legs beneath the steed,
    They tied his hands behind his back;
They guarded him, fivesome on each side,
    And they brought him ower the Liddel-rack.

        Liddel-rack] a ford on the Liddel.

IV

They led him thro' the Liddel-rack,
    And also thro' the Carlisle sands;
They brought him in to Carlisle castell,
    To be at my Lord Scroope's commands.

V

'My hands are tied, but my tongue is free.
    And whae will dare this deed avow?
Or answer by the Border law?
    Or answer to the bauld Buccleuch?'—

VI

'Now haud thy tongue, thou rank reiver!
    There's never a Scot shall set ye free:
Before ye cross my castle yate,
    I trow ye shall take farewell o' me.'

VII

'Fear na ye that, my lord,' quo' Willie:
    'By the faith o' my body, Lord Scroope,' he said,
'I never yet lodged in a hostelrie
    But I paid my lawing before I gaed.'

VIII

Now word is gane to the bauld Keeper,
    In Branksome Ha', where that he lay,
That Lord Scroope has ta'en the Kinmont Willie,
    Between the hours of night and day.

IX

He has ta'en the table wi' his hand,
    He garr'd the red wine spring on hie—
'Now Christ's curse on my head,' he said,
    'But avengèd of Lord Scroope I'll be!

rank reiver] common thief.   lawing] reckoning.

X

'O is my basnet a widow's curch?
    Or my lance a wand of the willow-tree?
Or my arm a ladye's lilye hand,
    That an English lord should lightly me?

XI

'And have they ta'en him, Kinmont Willie,
    Against the truce of Border tide?
And forgotten that the bauld Buccleuch
    Is Keeper here on the Scottish side?

XII

'And have they e'en ta'en him, Kinmont Willie,
    Withouten either dread or fear?
And forgotten that the bauld Buccleuch
    Can back a steed, or shake a spear?

XIII

'O were there war between the lands,
    As well I wot that there is none,
I would slight Carlisle castell high,
    Though it were builded of marble stone.

XIV

'I would set that castell in a low,
    And sloken it with English blood!
There 's never a man in Cumberland
    Should ken where Carlisle castell stood.

XV

But since nae war 's between the lands,
    And there is peace, and peace should be;
I'll neither harm English lad or lass,
    And yet the Kinmont freed shall be!'—

basnet] helmet.   curch] kerchief, coif.   lightly]
treat disrespectfully.   low] flame.   sloken] slake.

XVI

He has call'd him forty Marchmen bauld,
  I trow they were of his ain name,
Except Sir Gilbert Elliot call'd,
  The Laird of Stobs, I mean the same.

XVII

He has call'd him forty Marchmen bauld,
  Were kinsmen to the bauld Buccleuch;
With spur on heel, and splent on spauld,
  And gluves of green, and feathers blue.

XVIII

There were five and five before them a',
  Wi' hunting-horns and bugles bright:
And five and five came wi' Buccleuch,
  Like warden's men, array'd for fight.

XIX

And five and five, like a mason-gang,
  That carried the ladders lang and hie;
And five and five, like broken men;
  And so they reach'd the Woodhouselee.

XX

And as we cross'd the Bateable Land,
  When to the English side we held,
The first o' men that we met wi',
  Whae sould it be but fause Sakelde?

XXI

'Where be ye gaun, ye hunters keen?'
  Quo' fause Sakelde; 'come tell to me!'

splent] split, or overlapping armour.   spauld] shoulder.
Bateable Land] debateable land; a stretch of frontier
between the Solway Frith and Scots Dyke, claimed by
both nations.

'We go to hunt an English stag,
    Has trespass'd on the Scots countrie.'

XXII

'Where be ye gaun, ye marshal men?'
    Quo' fause Sakelde; 'come tell me true!'
'We go to catch a rank reiver,
    Has broken faith wi' the bauld Buccleuch.'

XXIII

'Where be ye gaun, ye mason lads,
    Wi' a' your ladders, lang and hie?'
'We gang to herry a corbie's nest,
    That wons not far frae Woodhouselee.'—

XXIV

'Where be ye gaun, ye broken men?'
    Quo' fause Sakelde; 'come tell to me!'
Now Dickie of Dryhope led that band,
    And the never a word o' lear had he.

XXV

'Why trespass ye on the English side?
    Row-footed outlaws, stand!' quo' he;
The never a word had Dickie to say,
    Sae he thrust the lance through his fause bodie.

XXVI

Then on we held for Carlisle toun,
    And at Staneshaw-bank the Eden we cross'd;
The water was great and meikle of spait,
    But the never a horse nor man we lost.

    marshal men] officers of law.   herry] harry.   corbie]
crow.   lear] lore.   row-footed] rough-footed.   spait]
flood.

XXVII

And when we reach'd the Staneshaw-bank,
    The wind was rising loud and hie;
And there the Laird garr'd leave our steeds,
    For fear that they should stamp and neigh.

XXVIII

And when we left the Staneshaw-bank,
    The wind began full loud to blaw;
But 'twas wind and weet, and fire and sleet,
    When we came beneath the castle wa'.

XXIX

We crept on knees, and held our breath,
    Till we placed the ladders against the wa';
And sae ready was Buccleuch himsell
    To mount the first, before us a'.

XXX

He has ta'en the watchman by the throat,
    He flung him down upon the lead—
'Had there not been peace between our land,
    Upon the other side thou hadst gaed!—

XXXI

'Now sound out, trumpets!' quo' Buccleuch;
    'Let's waken Lord Scroope right merrilie!'
Then loud the warden's trumpet blew—
    'O wha dare meddle wi' me?'

XXXII

Then speedilie to wark we gaed,
    And raised the slogan ane and a',
And cut a hole through a sheet of lead,
    And so we wan to the castle ha'.

slogan] battle-cry.

XXXIII

They thought King James and a' his men
  Had won the house wi' bow and spear;
It was but twenty Scots and ten
  That put a thousand in sic a stear!

XXXIV

Wi' coulters, and wi' fore-hammers,
  We garred the bars bang merrilie,
Until we came to the inner prison,
  Where Willie o' Kinmont he did lie.

XXXV

And when we cam to the lower prison,
  Where Willie o' Kinmont he did lie—
O sleep ye, wake ye, Kinmont Willie,
  Upon the morn that thou 's to die?'

XXXVI

'O I sleep saft, and I wake aft;
  It's lang since sleeping was fley'd frae me!
Gie my service back to my wife and bairns,
  And a' gude fellows that spier for me.'

XXXVII

The Red Rowan has hente him up,
  The starkest man in Teviotdale—
'Abide, abide now, Red Rowan,
  Till of my Lord Scroope I take farewell.

XXXVIII

'Farewell, farewell, my gude Lord Scroope!
  My gude Lord Scroope, farewell!' he cried—

stear] stir, commotion.   forehammers] sledge-ham-
mers.   garred] made.   fley'd] scared.   spier]
inquire.   hente] lifted.

'I'll pay you for my lodging mail
  When first we meet on the Border side.'—

XXXIX

Then shoulder high, with shout and cry,
  We bore him down the ladder lang;
At every stride Red Rowan made,
  I wot the Kinmont's airns play'd clang!

XL

'O mony a time,' quo' Kinmont Willie,
  'I have ridden horse baith wild and wood;
But a rougher beast than Red Rowan,
  I ween my legs have ne'er bestrode.

XLI

'And mony a time,' quo' Kinmont Willie,
  'I've prick'd a horse out owre the furs;
But since the day I backed a steed,
  I never wore sic cumbrous spurs!'

XLII

We scarce had won the Staneshaw-bank
  When a' the Carlisle bells were rung,
And a thousand men, in horse and foot,
  Cam wi' the keen Lord Scroope along.

XLIII

Buccleuch has turn'd to Eden Water,
  Even where it flow'd frae bank to brim,
And he has plunged in wi' a' his band,
  And safely swam them through the stream.

XLIV

He turn'd him on the other side,
  And at Lord Scroope his glove flung he—

mail] rent.   wood] mad.   furs] furrows.

'If ye like na my visit in merry England,
   In fair Scotland come visit me!'

XLV

All sore astonish'd stood Lord Scroope,
   He stood as still as rock of stane;
He scarcely dared to trew his eyes,
   When through the water they had gane.

XLVI

'He is either himsell a devil frae hell,
   Or else his mother a witch maun be;
I wadna have ridden that wan water
   For a' the gowd in Christentie.'

THE ABBOT OF CANTERBURY

An ancient story I'll tell you anon
Of a notable prince that was called King John;
And he ruled England with main and with might,
For he did great wrong and maintained little right.

And I'll tell you a story, a story so merry,
Concerning the Abbot of Canterbury;
How for his housekeeping, and high renown,
They rode post for him to fair London town.

An hundred men, the king did hear say,
The abbot kept in his house every day;
And fifty gold chains, without any doubt,
In velvet coats waited the abbot about.

'How now, father abbot? I hear it of thee,
Thou keepest a far better house than me;
And, for thy housekeeping and high renown,
I fear thou work'st treason against my crown.'

      trew] trust.   Christentie] Christendom.

'My liege,' quoth the abbot, 'I would it were
    known,
I never spend nothing but what is my own;
And I trust your grace will do me no dere
For spending of my own true-gotten gear.'

'Yes, yes, father abbot, thy fault it is high,
And now for the same thou needest must die;
For except thou canst answer me questions three,
Thy head shall be smitten from thy body.

'And first,' quoth the king, 'when I'm in this stead,
With my crown of gold so fair on my head,
Among all my liege-men so noble of birth,
Thou must tell me to one penny what I am worth.

'Secondly, tell me, without any doubt,
How soon I may ride the whole world about.
And at the third question thou must not shrink,
But tell me here truly what I do think.'

'O, these are hard questions for my shallow wit,
Nor I cannot answer your grace as yet;
But if you will give me but three weeks' space,
I'll do my endeavour to answer your grace.'

'Now three weeks' space to thee will I give,
And that is the longest time thou hast to live;
For if thou dost not answer my questions three,
Thy lands and thy living are forfeit to me.'

Away rode the abbot all sad at that word,
And he rode to Cambridge and Oxenford;
But never a doctor there was so wise
That could with his learning an answer devise.

Then home rode the abbot of comfort so cold,
And he met his shepherd a-going to fold:

            dere] harm.

'How now, my lord abbot, you are welcome home;
What news do you bring us from good King John?'

'Sad news, sad news, shepherd, I must give:
That I have but three days more to live;
For if I do not answer him questions three,
My head will be smitten from my body.

'The first is to tell him there in that stead,
With his crown of gold so fair on his head,
Among all his liege-men so noble of birth,
To within one penny of what he is worth.

'The second, to tell him, without any doubt,
How soon he may ride this whole world about:
And at the third question I must not shrink
To tell him there truly what he does think.'

'Now cheer up, sir abbot! Did you never hear yet
That a fool he may learn a wise man wit?
Lend me horse, and serving-men, and your apparel,
And I'll ride to London to answer your quarrel.

'Nay, frown not, if it hath been told unto me,
I am like your lordship as ever may be:
And if you will but lend me your gown,
There is none shall know us at fair London town.'

'Now horses and serving-men thou shalt have,
With sumptuous array most gallant and brave,
With crozier and mitre, and rochet and cope,
Fit to appear 'fore our father the Pope.'

'Now welcome, sir abbot,' the king he did say,
''Tis well thou'rt come back to keep thy day;
For and if thou canst answer my questions three,
Thy life and thy living both savèd shall be.

'And first, when thou seest me here in this stead,
With my crown of gold so fair on my head,
Among all my liege-men so noble of birth,
Tell me to one penny what I am worth.'

'*For thirty pence our Saviour was sold
Among the false Jews, as I have been told;
And twenty-nine is the worth of thee,
For I think thou'rt one penny worser than He.*'

The king he laughed, and swore by St. Bittel:
'I did not think I had been worth so little!
—Now secondly tell me, without any doubt,
How soon I may ride this whole world about.'

'*You must rise with the sun, and ride with the same,
Until the next morning he riseth again,
And then your grace need not make any doubt,
But in twenty-four hours you'll ride it about.*'

The king he laughed, and swore by St. John:
'I did not think it could be done so soon!
—Now from the third question thou must not
    shrink,
But tell me here truly what I do think.'

'*Yea, that shall I do, and make your grace merry:
You think I'm the abbot of Canterbury;
But I'm his poor shepherd, as plain you may see,
That am come to beg pardon for him and for me.*

The king he laughed, and swore by the mass,
'I'll make thee lord abbot this day in his place!'
'Now nay, my liege, be not in such speed,
For alack I can neither write nor read.'

'Four nobles a week, then, I will give thee,
For this merry jest thou hast shown unto me;
And tell the old abbot, when thou comest home,
Thou hast brought him a pardon from good King
    John.'

CLERK SAUNDERS

CLERK SAUNDERS and May Margaret
    Walked ower yon garden green;
And sad and heavy was the love
    That fell thir twa between.

'A bed, a bed,' Clerk Saunders said,
    'A bed for you and me!'—
'Fye na, fye na,' said May Margaret,
    'Till anes we married be;

'For in may come my seven bauld brothers,
    Wi' torches burning bright;
They'll say, we hae but ae sister,
    And behold, she's wi' a knight!'—

'Then take the sword frae my scabbard
    And slowly lift the pin;
And you may swear, and save your aith,
    Ye never let Clerk Saunders in.

'And take a napkin in your hand,
    And tie up baith your bonnie e'en,
And you may swear, and save your aith,
    Ye saw me na since late yestreen.'

It was about the midnight hour,
    When they asleep were laid,
When in and came her seven brothers,
    Wi' torches burning red:

    anes] once.   ae] one.

When in and came her seven brothers,
  Wi' torches burning bright:
They said, 'We hae but ae sister,
  And behold her lying with a knight!'

Then out and spake the first o' them,
  'I bear the sword shall gar him die.'
And out and spake the second o' them,
  'His father has nae mair than he.'

And out and spake the third o' them,
  'I wot that they are lovers dear.'
And out and spake the fourth o' them,
  'They hae been in love this mony a year.'

Then out and spake the fifth o' them,
  'It were great sin true love to twain.'
And out and spake the sixth o' them,
  'It were shame to slay a sleeping man.'

Then up and gat the seventh o' them,
  And never a word spake he;
But he has striped his bright brown brand
  Out through Clerk Saunders' fair bodye.

Clerk Saunders he started, and Margaret she turn'd
  Into his arms as asleep she lay;
And sad and silent was the night
  That was atween thir twae.

And they lay still and sleepit sound
  Until the day began to draw';
And kindly she to him did say,
  'It is time, true love, you were awa'.'

But he lay still, and sleepit sound,
  Albeit the sun began to sheen;

striped] thrust.

She look'd atween her and the wa',
　　And dull and drowsie were his e'en.

Then in and came her father dear;
　　Said, 'Let a' your mourning be;
I'll carry the dead corse to the clay,
　　And I'll come back and comfort thee.'

'Comfort weel your seven sons,
　　For comforted will I never be:
I ween 'twas neither knave nor loon
　　Was in the bower last night wi' me.'

The clinking bell gaed through the town,
　　To carry the dead corse to the clay;
And Clerk Saunders stood at May Margaret's
　　　window,
　　I wot, an hour before the day.

'Are ye sleeping, Margaret?' he says,
　　'Or are ye waking presentlie?
Give me my faith and troth again,
　　I wot, true love, I gied to thee.'

'Your faith and troth ye sall never get,
　　Nor our true love sall never twin,
Until ye come within my bower,
　　And kiss me cheik and chin.'

'My mouth it is full cold, Margaret;
　　It has the smell, now, of the ground;
And if I kiss thy comely mouth,
　　Thy days of life will not be lang.

'O cocks are crowing a merry midnight;
　　I wot the wild fowls are boding day;
Give me my faith and troth again,
　　And let me fare me on my way.'

　　　　　wot] know.　　　twin] part in two.

'Thy faith and troth thou sallna get,
　And our true love sall never twin,
Until ye tell what comes of women,
　I wot, who die in strong traivelling?'

'Their beds are made in the heavens high,
　Down at the foot of our good Lord's knee,
Weel set about wi' gillyflowers;
　I wot, sweet company for to see.

'O cocks are crowing a merry midnight;
　I wot the wild fowl are boding day;
The psalms of heaven will soon be sung,
　And I, ere now, will be miss'd away.'

Then she has taken a crystal wand,
　And she has stroken her troth thereon;
She has given it him out at the shot-window,
　Wi' mony a sad sigh and heavy groan.

'I thank ye, Marg'ret; I thank ye, Marg'ret;
　And ay I thank ye heartilie;
Gin ever the dead come for the quick,
　Be sure, Marg'ret, I'll come for thee.'

It's hosen and shoon, and gown alone,
　She climb'd the wall, and follow'd him,
Until she came to the green forest,
　And there she lost the sight o' him.

'Is there ony room at your head, Saunders?
　Is there ony room at your feet?
Or ony room at your side, Saunders,
　Where fain, fain, I wad sleep?'

'There's nae room at my head, Marg'ret,
　There's nae room at my feet;
My bed it is full lowly now,
　Amang the hungry worms I sleep.

'Cauld mould is my covering now,
    But and my winding-sheet;
The dew it falls nae sooner down
    Than my resting-place is weet.

'But plait a wand o' bonny birk,
    And lay it on my breast;
And shed a tear upon my grave,
    And wish my saul gude rest.'

Then up and crew the red, red cock,
    And up and crew the gray:
''Tis time, 'tis time, my dear Marg'ret,
    That you were going away.

'And fair Marg'ret, and rare Marg'ret,
    And Marg'ret o' veritie,
Gin e'er ye love another man,
    Ne'er love him as ye did me.'

THE BATTLE OF OTTERBOURNE

It fell about the Lammas tide,
    When the muir-men win their hay,
The doughty earl of Douglas rode
    Into England, to catch a prey.

He chose the Gordons and the Græmes,
    With them the Lindesays, light and gay;
But the Jardines wald not with him ride,
    And they rue it to this day.

And he has burn'd the dales of Tyne,
    And part of Bambrough shire;
And three good towers on Roxburgh fells,
    He left them all on fire.

saul] soul.

And he march'd up to Newcastle,
  And rode it round about;
'O wha's the lord of this castle,
  Or wha's the lady o't?'

But up spake proud Lord Percy, then,
  And O but he spake hie!
'I am the Lord of this castle,
  My wife's the lady gay.'

'If thou'rt the lord of this castle,
  Sae weel it pleases me!
For, ere I cross the border fells,
  The tane of us shall die.'

He took a long spear in his hand,
  Shod with the metal free,
And for to meet the Douglas there
  He rode right furiouslie.

But O how pale his lady look'd
  Frae aff the castle wa',
When down, before the Scottish spear,
  She saw proud Percy fa'.

'Had we twa been upon the green,
  And never an eye to see,
I wad hae had you, flesh and fell;
  But your sword sall gae wi' me.'

'But gae ye up to Otterbourne,
  And wait there dayis three;
And, if I come not ere three dayis end,
  A fause knight ca' ye me.'

'The Otterbourne's a bonnie burn;
  'Tis pleasant there to be;
But there is nought at Otterbourne
  To feed my men and me.

'The deer rins wild on hill and dale,
  The birds fly wild from tree to tree;
But there is neither bread nor kale
  To fend my men and me.

'Yet I will stay at Otterbourne,
  Where you shall welcome be;
And, if ye come not at three dayis end,
  A fause lord I'll ca' thee.'

'Thither will I come,' proud Percy said,
  'By the might of Our Ladye!'—
'There will I bide thee,' said the Douglas,
  'My trowth I plight to thee.'

They lighted high on Otterbourne,
  Upon the bent sae brown;
They lighted high on Otterbourne,
  And threw their pallions down.

And he that had a bonnie boy,
  Sent out his horse to grass;
And he that had not a bonnie boy,
  His ain servant he was.

But up then spake a little page,
  Before the peep of dawn—
'O waken ye, waken ye, my good lord,
  For Percy's hard at hand.'

'Ye lie, ye lie, ye liar loud!
  Sae loud I hear ye lie:
For Percy had not men yestreen,
  To dight my men and me.

'But I hae dream'd a dreary dream,
  Beyond the Isle of Sky;
I saw a dead man win a fight,
  And I think that man was I.'

He belted on his good braid sword,
   And to the field he ran;
But he forgot the helmet good,
   That should have kept his brain.

When Percy wi' the Douglas met,
   I wat he was fu' fain!
They swakked their swords, till sair they swat,
   And the blood ran down like rain.

But Percy with his good broad sword,
   That could so sharply wound,
Has wounded Douglas on the brow,
   Till he fell to the ground.

Then he call'd on his little foot-page,
   And said—'Run speedilie,
And fetch my ain dear sister's son,
   Sir Hugh Montgomery.'

'My nephew good,' the Douglas said,
   'What recks the death of ane!
Last night I dream'd a dreary dream,
   And I ken the day's thy ain.

'My wound is deep; I fain would sleep;
   Take thou the vanguard of the three,
And hide me by the braken bush,
   That grows on yonder lilye lee.

'O bury me by the braken bush,
   Beneath the blooming briar,
Let never living mortal ken
   That ere a kindly Scot lies here.'

He lifted up that noble lord,
   Wi' the saut tear in his e'e;
He hid him in the braken bush,
   That his merrie men might not see.

The moon was clear, the day drew near,
   The spears in flinders flew,
But many a gallant Englishman
   Ere day the Scotsmen slew.

The Gordons good, in English blood
   They steep'd their hose and shoon;
The Lindsays flew like fire about,
   Till all the fray was done.

The Percy and Montgomery met,
   That either of other were fain;
They swappèd swords, and they twa swat,
   And aye the blude ran down between.

'Yield thee, O yield thee, Percy!' he said,
   'Or else I vow I'll lay thee low!'
'Whom to shall I yield,' said Earl Percy,
   'Now that I see it must be so?'

'Thou shalt not yield to lord nor loun,
   Nor yet shalt thou yield to me;
But yield thee to the braken bush,
   That grows upon yon lilye lee!'

'I will not yield to a braken bush,
   Nor yet will I yield to a briar;
But I would yield to Earl Douglas,
   Or Sir Hugh the Montgomery, if he were here.'

As soon as he knew it was Montgomery,
   He struck his sword's point in the groand;
And the Montgomery was a courteous knight,
   And quickly took him by the hand.

This deed was done at Otterbourne,
   About the breaking of the day;
Earl Douglas was buried at the braken bush,
   And the Percy led captive away.

EDOM O' GORDON

IT fell about the Martinmas,
  When the wind blew shrill and cauld,
Said Edom o' Gordon to his men,
  'We maun draw to a hauld.

'And whatna hauld sall we draw to,
  My merry men and me?
We will gae to the house of the Rodes,
  To see that fair ladye.'

The lady stood on her castle wa',
  Beheld baith dale and down;
There she was ware of a host of men
  Came riding towards the town.

'O see ye not, my merry men a',
  O see ye not what I see?
Methinks I see a host of men;
  I marvel wha they be.'

She ween'd it had been her lovely lord,
  As he cam' riding hame;
It was the traitor, Edom o' Gordon,
  Wha reck'd nor sin nor shame.

She had nae sooner buskit hersell,
  And putten on her gown,
But Edom o' Gordon an' his men
  Were round about the town.

They had nae sooner supper set,
  Nae sooner said the grace,
But Edom o' Gordon an' his men
  Were lighted about the place.

town] house or farm buildings.   buskit] attired.

The lady ran up to her tower-head,
    Sae fast as she could hie,
To see if by her fair speeches
    She could wi' him agree.

But whan he see this lady saif,
    And her gates all lockèd fast,
He fell into a rage of wrath,
    And his heart was all aghast.

'Come doun to me, ye lady gay,
    Come doun, come doun to me;
This night sall ye lig within mine arms,
    To-morrow my bride sall be.'

'I winna come down, ye fals Gordon,
    I winna come down to thee;
I winna forsake my ain dear lord,
    That is sae far frae me.'

'Gie owre your house, ye lady fair,
    Gie owre your house to me;
Or I sall brenn yoursel therein,
    But and your babies three.'

'I winna gie owre, ye fals Gordon,
    To nae sic traitor as yee;
And if ye brenn my ain dear babes,
    My lord sall mak ye dree.

'Now reach my pistol, Glaud, my man,
    And charge ye weel my gun;
For, but an I pierce that bluidy butcher,
    My babes, we been undone!'

She stood upon her castle wa',
    And let twa bullets flee:

brenn] burn.

She miss'd that bluidy butcher's heart,
　　And only razed his knee.

'Set fire to the house!' quo' fals Gordon,
　　All wud wi' dule and ire:
'Fals lady, ye sall rue this deid
　　As ye brenn in the fire!'

'Wae worth, wae worth ye, Jock, my man!
　　I paid ye weel your fee;
Why pu' ye out the grund-wa' stane,
　　Lets in the reek to me?

'And e'en wae worth ye, Jock, my man!
　　I paid ye weel your hire;
Why pu' ye out the grund-wa' stane,
　　To me lets in the fire?'

'Ye paid me weel my hire, ladye,
　　Ye paid me weel my fee:
But now I'm Edom o' Gordon's man—
　　Maun either do or die.'

O then bespake her her little son,
　　Sat on the nurse's knee:
Says, 'Mither dear, gie owre this house,
　　For the reek it smithers me.'

'I wad gie a' my gowd, my bairn,
　　Sae wad I a' my fee,
For ae blast o' the western wind,
　　To blaw the reek frae thee.'

O then bespake her dochter dear—
　　She was baith jimp and sma':
'O row me in a pair o' sheets,
　　And tow me owre the wa'!'

wud] mad.　　grund-wa'] ground-wall.　　jimp]
slender.　　row] wrap.

They row'd her in a pair o' sheets,
    And tow'd her owre the wa';
But on the point o' Gordon's spear
    She gat a deadly fa'.

O bonnie, bonnie was her mouth,
    And cherry were her cheiks,
And clear, clear was her yellow hair,
    Whereon the red blood dreips.

Then wi' his spear he turn'd her owre;
    O gin her face was wan!
He said, 'Ye are the first that e'er
    I wish'd alive again.'

He turn'd her owre and owre again;
    O gin her skin was white!
'I might hae spared that bonnie face
    To hae been some man's delight.

'Busk and boun, my merry men a',
    For ill dooms I do guess;
I canna look in that bonnie face
    As it lies on the grass.'

'Wha looks to freits, my master dear,
    It's freits will follow them;
Let it ne'er be said that Edom o' Gordon
    Was daunted by a dame.'

But when the lady saw the fire
    Come flaming owre her head,
She wept, and kiss'd her children twain,
    Says, 'Bairns, we been but dead.'

The Gordon then his bugle blew,
    And said, 'Awa', awa'!

freits] omens.

This house o' the Rodes is a' in a flame;
    I hauld it time to ga'.'

And this way lookit her ain dear lord,
    As he cam owre the lea;
He saw his castle a' in a lowe,
    As far as he could see.

Then sair, O sair, his mind misgave,
    And all his heart was wae:
'Put on, put on, my wighty men,
    Sae fast as ye can gae.

'Put on, put on, my wighty men,
    Sae fast as ye can drie!
For he that's hindmost o' the thrang
    Sall ne'er get good o' me.'

Then some they rade, and some they ran,
    Out owre the grass and bent;
But ere the foremost could win up,
    Baith lady and babes were brent.

He wrang his hands, he rent his hair;
    And wept in teerfu' mood:
'O traitors, for this cruel deid
    Ye sall weep teirs o' bluid.'

And after the Gordon he is gane,
    Sae fast as he might drie;
And soon i' the Gordon's foul heart's blude
    He's wroken his dear ladye.

lowe] flame.   wighty] active, nimble.   wroken]
avenged.

THE WIFE OF USHER'S WELL

THERE lived a wife at Usher's well,
    And a wealthy wife was she;
She had three stout and stalwart sons,
    And sent them o'er the sea.

They hadna been a week from her,
    A week but barely ane,
When word came to the carline wife
    That her three sons were gane.

They hadna been a week from her,
    A week but barely three,
When word came to the carline wife
    That her sons she'd never see.

'I wish the wind may never cease,
    Nor fashes in the flood,
Till my three sons come hame to me,
    In earthly flesh and blood!'

It fell about the Martinmas,
    When nights are lang and mirk,
The carline wife's three sons cam hame,
    And their hats were o' the birk.

It neither grew in syke nor ditch,
    Nor yet in ony sheugh;
But at the gates o' Paradise,
    That birk grew fair eneuch.

'Blow up the fire, my maidens!
    Bring water from the well!
For a' my house shall feast this night,
    Since my three sons are well.'—

ane] one.   carline] aged.   fashes] troubles   mirk]
dark.   syke] marsh.   sheugh] trench, water-furrow.

And she has made to them a bed,
  She's made it large and wide;
And she's ta'en her mantle her about,
  Sat down at the bedside.

Up then crew the red red cock,
  And up and crew the gray;
The eldest to the youngest said,
  ''Tis time we were away.'

The cock he hadna craw'd but ance
  And clapp'd his wings at a',
When the youngest to the eldest said,
  'Brother, we must awa'.—

The cock doth craw, the day doth daw,
  The channerin' worm doth chide;
Gin we be miss'd out o' our place,
  A sair pain we maun bide.'

'Lie still, lie still but a little wee while,
  Lie still but if we may;
Gin my mother should miss us when she wakes,
  She'll go mad ere it be day.'

'Fare ye weel, my mother dear!
  Fareweel to barn and byre!
And fare ye weel, the bonny lass,
  That kindles my mother's fire!'

JAMIE TELFER IN THE FAIR DODHEAD

I

IT fell about the Martinmas tyde,
  When our Border steeds get corn and hay,
The Captain of Bewcastle hath bound him to ryde,
  And he's ower to Tividale to drive a prey.

channerin'] complaining, fretting.

II

The first ae guide that they met wi',
  It was high up in Hardhaughswire!
The second guide that they met wi',
  It was laigh down in Borthwick Water.

III

'What tidings, what tidings, my trusty guide?'—
  'Nae tidings, nae tidings, I hae to thee;
But gin ye'll gae to the fair Dodhead,
  Mony a cow's cauf I'll let thee see.'

IV

And when they cam to the fair Dodhead,
  Right hastily they clam the peel;
They loosed the kye out, ane and a',
  And ranshackled the house right weel.

V

Now Jamie Telfer's heart was sair,
  The tear aye rowing in his ee;
He pled wi' the Captain to hae his gear,
  Or else revengèd he wad be.

VI

The Captain turned him round and leugh;
  Said—'Man, there's naething in thy house,
But ae auld sword without a sheath,
  That hardly now would fell a mouse.'

VII

The sun wasna up, but the moon was down,
  It was the gryming of a new-fa'n snaw,

laigh] low.   clam] climbed.   peel] tower, keep.
ranshackled] ransacked.   rowing] rolling.   gryming]
sprinkling.

Jamie Telfer has run ten myles a-foot,
   Between the Dodhead and the Stobs's Ha .

VIII

And when he cam to the fair tower-yate,
   He shouted loud, and cried weel hie,
Till out bespak auld Gibby Elliot—
   'Whae's this that brings the fray to me?'—

IX

'It's I, Jamie Telfer, o' the fair Dodhead,
   And a harried man I think I be!
There's naething left at the fair Dodhead,
   But a waefu' wife and bairnies three.'

X

'Gae seek your succour at Branksome Ha',
   For succour ye'se get nane frae me!
Gae seek your succour where ye paid black-mail,
   For, man, ye ne'er paid money to me.'—

XI

Jamie has turned him round about,
   I wat the tear blinded his ee—
'I'll ne'er pay mail to Elliot again,
   And the fair Dodhead I'll never see!

XII

'My hounds may a' rin masterless,
   My hawks may fly frae tree to tree,
My lord may grip my vassal lands,
   For there again maun I never be!'—

XIII

He has turn'd him to the Tiviotside,
   E'en as fast as he could drie,

           fray] alarm.

Till he cam to the Coultart Cleugh,
　　And there he shouted baith loud and hie.

XIV

Then up bespak him auld Jock Grieve—
　　'Whae 's this that brings the fray to me?'—
'It 's I, Jamie Telfer o' the fair Dodhead;
　　A harried man I trow I be.

XV

'There 's naething left in the fair Dodhead,
　　But a greeting wife and bairnies three,
And sax poor ca's stand in the sta',
　　A' routing loud for their minnie.'—

XVI

'Alack a wae!' quo' auld Jock Grieve,
　　'Alack! my heart is sair for thee!
For I was married on the elder sister,
　　And you on the youngest of a' the three.'

XVII

Then he has ta'en out a bonny black,
　　Was right weel fed with corn and hay,
And he 's set Jamie Telfer on his back,
　　To the Catslockhill to tak the fray.

XVIII

And when he cam to the Catslockhill,
　　He shouted loud, and cried weel hie,
Till out and spak him William's Wat—
　　'O whae 's this brings the fray to me?'—

---

greeting] weeping.　　ca's] calves.　　sta'] stall.
routing] lowing.　　minnie] mother.

XIX

'It's I, Jamie Telfer of the fair Dodhead,
   A harried man I think I be!
The Captain of Bewcastle has driven my gear;
   For God's sake rise, and succour me!'—

XX

'Alas for wae!' quoth William's Wat,
   'Alack, for thee my heart is sair!
I never cam by the fair Dodhead,
   That ever I fand thy basket bare.'—

XXI

He's set his twa sons on coal-black steeds,
   Himsell upon a freckled gray,
And they are on wi' Jamie Telfer,
   To Branksome Ha' to tak the fray.

XXII

And when they cam to Branksome Ha',
   They shouted a' baith loud and hie,
Till up and spak him auld Buccleuch,
   Said 'Whae's this brings the fray to me?'—

XXIII

'It's I, Jamie Telfer of the fair Dodhead,
   And a harried man I think I be!
There's nought left in the fair Dodhead,
   But a greeting wife and bairnies three.'—

XXIV

'Alack for wae!' quoth the gude auld lord,
   'And ever my heart is wae for thee!
But fye gar cry on Willie, my son,
   And see that he come to me speedilie!

wae] woe.

XXV

'Gar warn the water, braid and wide,
  Gar warn it sune and hastilie!
They that winna ride for Telfer's kye,
  Let them never look in the face o' me

XXVI

'Warn Wat o' Harden and his sons,
  Wi' them will Borthwick Water ride;
Warn Gaudilands, and Allanhaugh,
  And Gilmanscleugh, and Commonside,

XXVII

'Ride by the gate at Priesthaughswire,
  And warn the Currors o' the Lee;
As ye cum down the Hermitage Slack,
  Warn doughty Willie o' Gorrinberry.'—

XXVIII

The Scotts they rade, the Scotts they ran,
  Sae starkly and sae steadilie!
And aye the ower-word o' the thrang
  Was—'Rise for Branksome readilie!'

XXIX

The gear was driven the Frostylee up,
  Frae the Frostylee unto the plain,
Whan Willie has look'd his men before,
  And saw the kye right fast drivand.

XXX

'Whae drives thir kye?' 'gan Willie say,
  'To make an outspeckle o' me?'
'It's I, the Captain o' Bewcastle, Willie;
  I winna layne my name for thee.'—

warn the water] give the alarm along its banks.   out-
speckle] laughing-stock.   layne] deny, hide.

XXXI

'O will ye let Telfer's kye gae back?
   Or will ye do aught for regard o' me?
Or by the faith of my body,' quo' Willie Scott,
   'I'se ware my dame's cauf skin on thee!'

XXXII

'I winna let the kye gae back,
   Neither for thy love, nor yet thy fear;
But I will drive Jamie Telfer's kye,
   In spite of every Scott that's here.'—

XXXIII

'Set on them, lads!' quo' Willie than;
   'Fye, lads, set on them cruellie!
For ere they win to the Ritterford,
   Mony a toom saddle there sall be!'

XXXIV

Then till't they gaed, wi' heart and hand,
   The blows fell fast as bickering hail;
And mony a horse ran masterless,
   And mony a comely cheek was pale.

XXXV

But Willie was stricken ower the head,
   And thro' the knapscap the sword has gane;
And Harden grat for very rage,
   Whan Willie on the grund lay slane.

XXXVI

But he's ta'en aff his gude steel cap,
   And thrice he's waved it in the air—

ware] spend.   cauf-skin] shoe-leather.   toom] empty.   till't] to it.   bickering] thrashing.   knapcap] headpiece.   grat] wept.

The Dinlay snaw was ne'er mair white
   Nor the lyart locks of Harden's hair.

XXXVII

'Revenge! revenge!' auld Wat 'gan cry;
   'Fye, lads, lay on them cruellie!
We'll ne'er see Teviotside again,
   Or Willie's death revenged sall be.'

XXXVIII

O mony a horse ran masterless,
   The splinter'd lances flew on hie;
But or they wan to the Kershope ford,
   The Scotts had gotten the victory.

XXXIX

John o' Brigham there was slane,
   And John o' Barlow, as I heard say;
And thirty mae o' the Captain's men
   Lay bleeding on the grund that day.

XL

The Captain was run through the thick of the thigh,
   And broken was his right leg-bane;
If he had lived this hundred years,
   He had never been loved by woman again.

XLI

'Hae back the kye!' the Captain said;
   'Dear kye, I trow, to some they be!
For gin I suld live a hundred years,
   There will ne'er fair lady smile on me.'

XLII

Then word is gane to the Captain's bride,
   Even in the bower where that she lay,

       lyart] grizzled.   mae] more.

That her lord was prisoner in enemy's land,
    Since into Tividale he had led the way.

XLIII

'I wad lourd have had a winding-sheet,
    And helped to put it ower his head,
Ere he had been disgraced by the Border Scot
    Whan he ower Liddel his men did lead!'—

XLIV

There was a wild gallant amang us a',
    His name was Watty wi' the Wudspurs,
Cried—'On for his house in Stanegirthside,
    If ony man will ride with us!'

XLV

When they cam to the Stanegirthside,
    They dang wi' trees, and burst the door;
They loosed out a' the Captain's kye,
    And set them forth our lads before.

XLVI

There was an auld wyfe ayont the fire,
    A wee bit o' the Captain's kin—
'Whae dar loose out the Captain's kye,
    Or answer to him and his men?'—

XLVII

'It's I, Watty Wudspurs, loose the kye,
    I winna layne my name frae thee!
And I will loose out the Captain's kye,
    In scorn of a' his men and he.'

lourd] rather.   Wudspurs] Madspurs.   dang]
banged.   trees] logs.

XLVIII

Whan they cam to the fair Dodhead,
   They were a wellcum sight to see!
For instead of his ain ten milk kye,
   Jamie Telfer has gotten thirty and three.

XLIX

And he has paid the rescue shot,
   Baith wi' gowd and white monie;
And at the burial o' Willie Scott,
   I wat was mony a weeping e'e.

FAIR HELEN

I WISH I were where Helen lies;
Night and day on me she cries;
O that I were where Helen lies
      On fair Kirconnell lea!

Curst be the heart that thought the thought,
And curst the hand that fired the shot,
When in my arms burd Helen dropt,
      And died to succour me!

O think na ye my heart was sair
When my Love dropt down and spak nae mair!
There did she swoon wi' meikle care
      On fair Kirconnell lea.

As I went down the water-side,
None but my foe to be my guide,
None but my foe to be my guide,
      On fair Kirconnell lea;

I lighted down my sword to draw,
I hackèd him in pieces sma'.

                              burd] lady.

I hackèd him in pieces sma',
   For her sake that died for me.

O Helen fair, beyond compare!
I'll make a garland of thy hair
Shall bind my heart for evermair
   Until the day I die.

O that I were where Helen lies!
Night and day on me she cries;
Out of my bed she bids me rise,
   Says, 'Haste and come to me!'

O Helen fair! O Helen chaste!
If I were with thee, I were blest,
Where thou lies low and takes thy rest
   On fair Kirconnell lea.

I wish my grave were growing green,
A winding-sheet drawn ower my een,
And I in Helen's arms lying,
   On fair Kirconnell lea.

I wish I were where Helen lies;
Night and day on me she cries;
And I am weary of the skies,
   For her sake that died for me.

WILLIE DROWNED IN YARROW

Down in yon garden sweet and gay
   Where bonnie grows the lily,
I heard a fair maid sighing say,
  'My wish be wi' sweet Willie!

'Willie's rare, and Willie's fair,
   And Willie's wondrous bonny;
And Willie hecht to marry me
   Gin e'er he married ony.

'O gentle wind, that bloweth south
 From where my Love repaireth,
Convey a kiss frae his dear mouth
 And tell me how he fareth!

'O tell sweet Willie to come down
 And hear the mavis singing,
And see the birds on ilka bush
 And leaves around them hinging.

'The lav'rock there, wi' her white breast
 And gentle throat sae narrow!
There's sport eneuch for gentlemen
 On Leader haughs and Yarrow.

'O Leader haughs are wide and braid,
 And Yarrow haughs are bonny;
There Willie hecht to marry me
 If e'er he married ony.

'But Willie's gone, whom I thought on,
 And does not hear me weeping;
Draws many a tear frae's true love's e'e,
 When other maids are sleeping.

'Yestreen I made my bed fu' braid,
 The night I'll mak' it narrow
For a' the live-lang winter night
 I lie twined o' my marrow.

'O came ye by yon water-side?
 Pou'd you the rose or lily?
Or came you by yon meadow green,
 Or saw you my sweet Willie?'

She sought him up, she sought him down,
 She sought him braid and narrow;
Syne, in the cleaving of a crag,
 She found him drowned in Yarrow.

THE GAY GOSHAWK

'O WELL is me, my gay goshawk,
    That you can speak and flee;
For you can carry a love-letter
    To my true Love from me.'

—'O how can I carry a letter to her?
    Or how should I her know?
I bear a tongue ne'er with her spake,
    And eyes that ne'er her saw.'

—'O well shall ye my true Love ken
    So soon as ye her see:
For of all the flowers of fair England,
    The fairest flower is she.

'And when she goes into the house,
    Sit ye upon the whin;
And sit you there and sing our loves
    As she goes out and in.'

Lord William has written a love-letter,
    Put it under his pinion gray:
And he's awa' to Southern land
    As fast as wings can gae.

And first he sang a low, low note,
    And then he sang a clear;
And aye the o'erword of the sang
    Was 'Your Love can no win here.'

'Feast on, feast on, my maidens all,
    The wine flows you amang;
While I gang to my shot-window
    And hear yon bonnie bird's sang.'

goshawk] a large short-winged hawk.

O first he sang a merry sang,
  And then he sang a grave:
And then he peck'd his feathers gray;
  To her the letter gave.

'Have there a letter from Lord William:
  He says, he sent ye three;
He cannot wait your love longer,
  But for your sake he'll die.'

—'I send him the rings from my white fingers,
  The garlands of my hair;
I send him the heart that's in my breast;
  What would my love have mair?
And at Mary's kirk in fair Scotland,
  Ye'll bid him wait for me there.'

She hied her to her father dear
  As fast as go could she:
'An asking, an asking, my father dear,
  An asking grant you me!
That if I die in fair England,
  In Scotland bury me.

'At the first kirk of fair Scotland,
  You cause the bells be rung;
At the second kirk of fair Scotland,
  You cause the mass be sung;

'And when ye come to Saint Mary's kirk,
  Ye'll tarry there till night.'
And so her father pledged his word,
  And so his promise plight.

The Lady's gone to her chamber
  As fast as she could fare;
And she has drunk a sleepy draught
  That she had mix'd with care.

And pale, pale, grew her rosy cheek,
   And pale and cold was she:—
She seem'd to be as surely dead
   As any corpse could be.

Then spake her cruel stepminnie,
   'Take ye the burning lead,
And drop a drop on her bosom,
   To try if she be dead.'

They dropp'd the hot lead on her cheek,
   They dropp'd it on her chin,
They dropp'd it on her bosom white;
   But she spake none again.

Then up arose her seven brethren,
   And hew'd to her a bier;
They hew'd it from the solid oak;
   Laid it o'er with silver clear.

The first Scots kirk that they came to
   They gart the bells be rung;
The next Scots kirk that they came to
   They gart the mass be sung.

But when they came to Saint Mary's kirk,
   There stood spearmen in a row;
And up and started Lord William,
   The chieftain among them a'.

He rent the sheet upon her face
   A little above her chin:
With rosy cheek, and ruby lip,
   She look'd and laugh'd to him.

—'A morsel of your bread, my lord!
   And one glass of your wine!
For I have fasted these three long days
   All for your sake and mine!'

               gart] made.

ANNAN WATER

'ANNAN Water's wading deep,
   And my love Annie's wondrous bonny;
And I am loath she shall wet her feet,
   Because I love her best of ony.'

He's loupen on his bonny gray,
   He rode the right gate and the ready;
For all the storm he wadna stay,
   For seeking of his bonny lady.

And he has ridden o'er field and fell,
   Through moor, and moss, and many a mire;
His spurs of steel were sair to bide,
   And from her four feet flew the fire.

'My bonny gray, now play your part!
   If ye be the steed that wins my dearie,
With corn and hay ye'll feed for aye,
   And never spur shall make you wearie!'

The gray was a mare, and a right gude mare;
   But when she wan the Annan Water,
She could not have ridden the ford that night
   Had a thousand merks been wadded at her.

'O boatman, boatman, put off your boat,
   Put off your boat for golden money!'
But for all the gold in fair Scotland,
   He dared not take him through to Annie.

'O I was sworn so late yestreen,
   Not by a single oath, but mony!
I'll cross the drumly stream to-night,
   Or never could I face my honey!'

      wadded] wagered.   drumly] turbid.

The side was stey, and the bottom deep,
  From bank to brae the water pouring;
The bonny gray mare she swat for fear,
  For she heard the water-kelpy roaring.

He spurr'd her forth into the flood,
  I wot she swam both strong and steady;
But the stream was broad, and her strength did fail,
  And he never saw his bonny lady!

THOMAS THE RHYMER

TRUE Thomas lay on Huntlie bank;
  A ferlie he spied wi' his e'e;
And there he saw a ladye bright
  Come riding down by the Eildon Tree.

Her skirt was o' the grass-green silk,
  Her mantle o' the velvet fyne;
At ilka tett o' her horse's mane,
  Hung fifty siller bells and nine.

True Thomas he pull'd aff his cap,
  And louted low down to his knee:
'Hail to thee, Mary, Queen of Heaven!
  For thy peer on earth could never be.'

'O no, O no, Thomas,' she said,
  'That name does not belang to me;
I'm but the Queen o' fair Elfland,
  That am hither come to visit thee.

'Harp and carp, Thomas,' she said;
  'Harp and carp along wi' me;
And if ye dare to kiss my lips,
  Sure of your bodie I will be.'

stey] steep.   swat] sweated.   water-kelpy] water-sprite.
ferlie] marvel.   tett] tuft, lock, tassel.   carp] sing,
recite.

'Betide me weal, betide me woe,
    That weird shall never daunten me.'
Syne he has kiss'd her rosy lips,
    All underneath the Eildon Tree.

'Now ye maun go wi' me,' she said,
    'True Thomas, ye maun go wi' me;
And ye maun serve me seven years,
    Thro' weal or woe as may chance to be.'

She's mounted on her milk-white steed,
    She's ta'en true Thomas up behind;
And aye, whene'er her bridle rang,
    The steed gaed swifter than the wind.

O they rade on, and farther on,
    The steed gaed swifter than the wind;
Until they reach'd a desert wide,
    And living land was left behind.

'Light down, light down now, true Thomas,
    And lean your head upon my knee;
Abide ye there a little space,
    And I will show you ferlies three.

'O see ye not yon narrow road,
    So thick beset wi' thorns and briers?
That is the Path of Righteousness,
    Though after it but few enquires.

'And see ye not yon braid, braid road,
    That lies across the lily leven?
That is the Path of Wickedness,
    Though some call it the Road to Heaven.

'And see ye not yon bonny road
    That winds about the fernie brae?
That is the road to fair Elfland,
    Where thou and I this night maun gae.

'But, Thomas, ye sall haud your tongue,
   Whatever ye may hear or see;
For speak ye word in Elfyn-land,
   Ye'll ne'er win back to your ain countrie.'

O they rade on, and farther on,
   And they waded rivers abune the knee;
And they saw neither sun nor moon,
   But they heard the roaring of the sea.

It was mirk, mirk night, there was nae starlight,
   They waded thro' red blude to the knee;
For a' the blude that's shed on the earth
   Rins through the springs o' that countrie.

Syne they came to a garden green,
   And she pu'd an apple frae a tree:
'Take this for thy wages, true Thomas;
   It will give thee the tongue that can never lee.'

'My tongue is my ain,' true Thomas he said;
   'A gudely gift ye wad gie to me!
I neither dought to buy or sell
   At fair or tryst where I might be.

'I dought neither speak to prince or peer,
   Nor ask of grace from fair ladye!'—
'Now haud thy peace, Thomas,' she said,
   'For as I say, so must it be.'

He has gotten a coat of the even cloth,
   And a pair o' shoon of the velvet green;
And till seven years were gane and past,
   True Thomas on earth was never seen.

mirk] dark.   dought to] could.

THE HEIR OF LINNE

PART I

LITHE and listen, gentlemen,
   To sing a song I will begin:
It is of a lord of fair Scotlànd,
   Which was the unthrifty heir of Linne.

His father was a right good lord,
   His mother a lady of high degree;
But they, alas! were dead, him froe,
   And he lov'd keeping companie.

To spend the day with merry cheer,
   To drink and revel every night,
To card and dice from eve to morn,
   It was, I ween, his heart's delight.

To ride, to run, to rant, to roar,
   To alway spend and never spare,
I wot, an' it were the king himself,
   Of gold and fee he mote be bare.

So fares the unthrifty lord of Linne
   Till all his gold is gone and spent;
And he maun sell his lands so broad,
   His house, and lands, and all his rent.

His father had a keen stewàrd,
   And John o' the Scales was callèd he:
But John is become a gentleman,
   And John has got both gold and fee.

Says, Welcome, welcome, lord of Linne,
   Let nought disturb thy merry cheer;
If thou wilt sell thy lands so broad,
   Good store of gold I'll give thee here.

My gold is gone, my money is spent;
   My land now take it unto thee:
Give me the gold, good John o' the Scales,
   And thine for aye my land shall be.

Then John he did him to record draw,
   And John he cast him a gods-pennie;
But for every pound that John agreed,
   The land, I wis, was well worth three.

He told him the gold upon the board,
   He was right glad his land to win:
The gold is thine, the land is mine,
   And now I'll be the lord of Linne.

Thus he hath sold his land so broad,
   Both hill and holt, and moor and fen,
All but a poor and lonesome lodge,
   That stood far off in a lonely glen.

For so he to his father hight.
   My son, when I am gone, said he,
Then thou wilt spend thy land so broad,
   And thou wilt spend thy gold so free:

But swear me now upon the rood,
   That lonesome lodge thou'lt never spend;
For when all the world doth frown on thee,
   Thou there shalt find a faithful friend.

The heir of Linne is full of gold:
   And come with me, my friends, said he,
Let's drink, and rant, and merry make,
   And he that spares, ne'er mote he thee.

They ranted, drank, and merry made,
   Till all his gold it waxèd thin;
And then his friends they slunk away;
   They left the unthrifty heir of Linne.

He had never a penny left in his purse,
   Never a penny left but three,
And one was brass, another was lead,
   And another it was white monèy.

Now welladay, said the heir of Linne,
   Now welladay, and woe is me,
For when I was the lord of Linne,
   I never wanted gold nor fee.

But many a trusty friend have I,
   And why should I feel dole or care?
I'll borrow of them all by turns,
   So need I not be never bare.

But one, I wis, was not at home;
   Another had paid his gold away;
Another call'd him thriftless loon,
   And bade him sharply wend his way.

Now welladay, said the heir of Linne,
   Now welladay, and woe is me!
For when I had my lands so broad,
   On me they liv'd right merrilee.

To beg my bread from door to door,
   I wis it were a burning shame:
To rob and steal it were a sin:
   To work my limbs I cannot frame.

Now I'll away to lonesome lodge,
   For there my father bade me wend;
When all the world should frown on me,
   I there should find a trusty friend.

PART II

Away then hied the heir of Linne
   O'er hill and holt and moor and fen,

Until he came to lonesome lodge,
    That stood so low in a lonely glen.

He lookèd up, he lookèd down,
    In hope some comfort for to win:
But bare and loathly were the walls.
    Here's sorry cheer, quo' the heir of Linne.

The little window dim and dark
    Was hung with ivy, brier, and yew;
No shimmering sun here ever shone;
    No halesome breeze here ever blew.

Nor chair, ne table he mote spy,
    No cheerful hearth, ne welcome bed,
Nought save a rope with renning noose,
    That dangling hung up o'er his head.

And over it in broad lettèrs,
    These words were written so plain to see:
'Ah! graceless wretch, hast spent thine all,
    And brought thyself to penurie?

'And this my boding mind misgave,
    I therefore left this trusty friend:
Let it now shield thy foule disgrace,
    And all thy shame and sorrows end.'

Sorely shent wi' this rebuke,
    Sorely shent was the heir of Linne;
His heart, I wis, was near to brast
    With guilt and sorrow, shame and sin.

Never a word spake the heir of Linne,
    Never a word he spake but three:
'This is a trusty friend indeed,
    And is right welcome unto me.'

shent] reproved.   brast] burst.

Then round his neck the cord he drew,
  And sprang aloft with his body:
When lo! the ceiling burst in twain,
  And to the ground came tumbling he.

Astonied lay the heir of Linne,
  Ne knew if he were live or dead:
At length he looked, and saw a bill,
  And in it a key of gold so red.

He took the bill, and looked it on,
  Straight good comfort found he there:
It told him of a hole in the wall,
  In which there stood three chests in-fere.

Two were full of the beaten gold,
  The third was full of white monèy;
And over them in broad lettèrs
  These words were written so plain to see:

'Once more, my son, I set thee clear;
  Amend thy life and follies past;
For but thou amend thee of thy life,
  That rope must be thy end at last.'

'And let it be,' said the heir of Linne;
  'And let it be, but if I amend:
For here I will make mine avow,
  This rede shall guide me to the end.'

Away then went with a merry cheer,
  Away then went the heir of Linne;
I wis, he neither ceas'd ne blanne
  Till John o' the Scales' house he did win.

bill] billet, letter.   in-fere] together.   white money]
silver.   blanne] lingered.

And when he came to John o' the Scales,
   Up at the speere then lookèd he:
There sat three lords upon a row,
   Were drinking of the wine so free.

And John himself sat at the board-head,
   Because now lord of Linne was he.
'I pray thee,' he said, 'good John o' the Scales,
   One forty pence for to lend me.'

'Away, away, thou thriftless loon;
   Away, away, this may not be:
For Christ's curse on my head,' he said,
   'If ever I trust thee one pennie.'

Then bespake the heir of Linne,
   To John o' the Scales' wife then spake he:
'Madame, some alms on me bestow,
   I pray for sweet saint Charitie.'

'Away, away, thou thriftless loon,
   I swear thou gettest no alms of me;
For if we should hang any losel here,
   The first we would begin with thee.'

Then bespake a good fellow,
   Which sat at John o' the Scales his board;
Said, 'Turn again, thou heir of Linne;
   Some time thou wast a well good lord:

'Some time a good fellow thou hast been,
   And sparedst not thy gold and fee:
Therefore I'll lend thee forty pence,
   And other forty if need be.

'And ever, I pray thee, John o' the Scales,
   To let him sit in thy company:

     losel] profligate, scoundrel.

For well I wot thou hadst his land,
   And a good bargain it was to thee.'

Up then spake him John o' the Scales,
   All wood he answered him again:
'Now Christ's curse on my head,' he said,
   'But I did lose by that bargàin.'

'And here I proffer thee, heir of Linne,
   Before these lords so fair and free,
Thou shalt have it back again better cheap,
   By a hundred marks, than I had it of thee.

'I draw you to record, lords,' he said.
   With that he cast him a god's pennie:
'Now by my fay,' said the heir of Linne,
   'And here, good John, is thy monèy.'

And he pull'd forth three bags of gold,
   And laid them down upon the board:
All woebegone was John o' the Scales,
   So shent he could say never a word.

He told him forth the good red gold,
   He tŏld it forth with mickle din,
'The gold is thine, the land is mine,
   And now I'm again the lord of Linne.'

Says, 'Have thou here, thou good fellow,
   Forty pence thou didst lend me:
Now I am again the lord of Linne,
   And forty pounds I will give thee.

'I'll make thee keeper of my forest,
   Both of the wild deer and the tame;
For but I reward thy bounteous heart,
   I wis, good fellow, I were to blame.'

wood] furious.   god's pennie] earnest or luck-penny.

'Now welladay!' saith Joan o' the Scales:
  'Now welladay! and woe is my life!
Yesterday I was lady of Linne,
  Now I'm but John o' the Scales his wife.'

'Now fare thee well,' said the heir of Linne;
  'Farewell now, John o' the Scales,' said he:
'Christ's curse light on me, if ever again
  I bring my lands in jeopardy.'

THE OLD AND YOUNG COURTIER

An old song made by an agèd old pate,
Of an old worshipful gentleman, who had a great
    estate,
That kept a brave old house at a bountiful rate,
And an old porter to relieve the poor at his gate;
        Like an old courtier of the queen's,
        And the queen's old courtier.

With an old lady, whose anger one word assuages;
They every quarter paid their old servants their
    wages,
And never knew what belong'd to coachman, foot-
    men, nor pages,
But kept twenty old fellows with blue coats and
    badges;
        Like an old courtier, &c.

With an old study fill'd full of learnèd old books,
With an old reverend chaplain, you might know
    him by his looks.
With an old buttery hatch worn quite off the hooks,
And an old kitchen, that maintain'd half a dozen
    old cooks:
        Like an old courtier, &c.

With an old hall, hung about with pikes, guns and
      bows,
With old swords, and bucklers, that had borne
      many shrewd blows,
And an old frieze coat to cover his worship's trunk
      hose,
And a cup of old sherry, to comfort his copper
      nose;
        Like an old courtier, &c.

With a good old fashion, when Christmas was
      come,
To call in all his old neighbours with bagpipe and
      drum,
With good cheer enough to furnish every old room,
And old liquor able to make a cat speak, and man
      dumb,
        Like an old courtier, &c.

With an old falconer, huntsman, and a kennel of
      hounds,
That never hawked, nor hunted, but in his own
      grounds,
Who, like a wise man, kept himself within his own
      bounds,
And when he died gave every child a thousand
      good pounds;
        Like an old courtier, &c.

But to his eldest son his house and land he assign'd,
Charging him in his will to keep the old bountiful
      mind,
To be good to his old tenants, and to his neighbours
      be kind:

But in the ensuing ditty you shall hear how he was
 inclin'd;
   Like a young courtier of the king's,
   And the king's young courtier.

Like a flourishing young gallant, newly come to his
 land,
Who keeps a brace of painted madams at his command,
And takes up a thousand pound upon his father's
 land,
And gets drunk in a tavern, till he can neither go
 nor stand;
   Like a young courtier, &c.

With a new-fangled lady, that is dainty, nice, and
 spare,
Who never knew what belong'd to good house-
 keeping, or care,
Who buys gaudy-colour'd fans to play with wanton
 air,
And seven or eight different dressings of other
 women's hair;
   Like a young courtier, &c.

With a new-fashion'd hall, built where the old one
 stood,
Hung round with new pictures, that do the poor no
 good,
With a fine marble chimney, wherein burns neither
 coal nor wood,
And a new smooth shovelboard, whereon no
 victuals ne'er stood;
   Like a young courtier, &c.

With a new study, stuffed full of pamphlets, and
    plays,
And a new chaplain, that swears faster than he
    prays,
With a new buttery hatch, that opens once in four
    or five days,
And a new French cook, to devise fine kickshaws,
    and toys;
       Like a young courtier, &c.

With a new fashion, when Christmas is drawing on,
On a new journey to London straight we all must
    begone,
And leave none to keep house, but our new porter
    John,
Who relieves the poor with a thump on the back
    with a stone;
       Like a young courtier, &c.

With a new gentleman-usher, whose carriage is
    complete,
With a new coachman, footmen, and pages to carry
    up the meat,
With a waiting-gentlewoman, whose dressing is
    very neat,
Who when her lady has din'd, lets the servants not
    eat;
       Like a young courtier, &c.

With new titles of honour bought with his father's
    old gold,
For which sundry of his ancestors' old manors are
    sold;
And this is the course most of our new gallants
    hold,

Which makes that good house-keeping **is now**
   grown so cold,
        Among the young courtiers of the k'ng,
        Or the king's young courtiers.

THE HONOUR OF BRISTOL

ATTEND you and give ear awhile,
   And you shall understand,
Of a battle fought upon the seas
   By a ship of brave command:
That fight it was so famous
   That all men's hearts did fill
And made them cry 'To sea,
   With the *Angel Gabriel*.'

The lusty ship of Bristol
   Sailed out adventurously
Against the foes of England,
   Her strength with them to try:
Well victualled, rigged, and manned
   And good provision still,
Which made them cry 'To sea
   With the *Angel Gabriel*.'

The Captain famous Netheway,
   So was he called by name,
The master's name John Mines
   A man of noted fame:
The gunner Thomas Watson,
   A man of perfect skill,
With other valiant hearts
   In the *Angel Gabriel*.

They waving up and down the seas
   Upon the ocean main;

'It is not long ago,' quoth they,
  'Since England fought with Spain,
Would we with them might meet,
  Our minds for to fulfil;
We would play a noble bout
  With our *Angel Gabriel*.'

They had no sooner spoken,
  But straight appeared in sight
Three lusty Spanish vessels
  Of warlike force and might;
With bloody resolution
  They thought our blood to spill,
And vowed to make a prize
  Of our *Angel Gabriel*.

Then first came up their Admiral
  Themselves for to advance;
In her she bore full forty-eight
  Pieces of ordinance.
The next that then came near us
  Was their Vice-Admiral,
Which shot most furiously
  At our *Angel Gabriel*.

Our gallant ship had in her
  Full forty fighting men;
With twenty pieces of ordnance
  We played about them then:
And with powder, shot, and bullets,
  We did employ them still,
And thus began the fight
  With our *Angel Gabriel*.

Our Captain to our Master said,
  'Take courage, Master bold.'

The Master to the seamen said,
  'Stand fast, my hearts of gold.'
The Gunner unto all the rest,
  'Brave hearts, be valiant still;
Let us fight in the defence
  Of our *Angel Gabriel.*'

Then we gave them a broadside
  Which shot their mast asunder,
And tore the bow-sprit of their ship,
  Which made the Spaniards wonder:
And caus̀d them to cry
  With voices loud and shrill
'Help! help! or else we sink
  By the *Angel Gabriel.*'

Yet desperately they boarded us
  For all our valiant shot.
Threescore of their best fighting men
  Upon our decks were got.
And then at their first entrance
  Full thirty we did kill,
And thus we cleared the decks
  Of the *Angel Gabriel.*

With that their three ships boarded us
  Again with might and main,
But still our noble Englishmen
  Cried out 'A fig for Spain!'
Though seven times they boarded us,
  At last we showed our skill,
And made them feel the force
  Of our *Angel Gabriel.*

Seven hours this fight continued,
  And many men lay dead,

With purple gore and Spanish blood
   The sea was coloured red.
Five hundred of their men
   We there outright did kill
And many more were maimed
   By the *Angel Gabriel*.

Then seeing of these bloody spoils,
   The rest made haste away:
For why?—they saw it was no boot
   Any longer for to stay.
Then they fled into Calès,
   And there they must lie still,
For they never more will dare to meet
   Our *Angel Gabriel*.

We had within our English ship
   But only three men slain,
And five men hurt, the which I hope
   Will soon be well again.
At Bristol we were landed,
   And let us praise God still
That thus hath blessed our men
   And our *Angel Gabriel*.

Now let me not forget to speak
   O' the gift given by the Owner
Of the *Angel Gabriel*
   That many years had known her;
Two hundred crowns in coin and plate
   He gave with free goodwill
Unto them that bravely fought
   In the *Angel Gabriel*.

Calès] Cadiz.

THE TWA CORBIES

As I was walking all alane
I heard twa corbies making a mane;
The tane unto the t'other say,
'Where sall we gang and dine to-day?'

'—In behint yon auld fail dyke,
I wot there lies a new-slain Knight;
And naebody kens that he lies there,
But his hawk, his hound, and lady fair.

'His hound is to the hunting gane,
His hawk to fetch the wild-fowl hame,
His lady's ta'en another mate,
So we may make our dinner sweet.

'Ye'll sit on his white hause-bane,
And I'll pick out his bonny blue een:
Wi' ae lock o' his gowden hair
We'll theek our nest when it grows bare.

'Mony a one for him makes mane,
But nane sall ken where he is gane;
O'er his white banes, when they are bare,
The wind sall blaw for evermair.'

LOVE'S DARING

Over the mountains
  And over the waves,
Under the fountains
  And under the graves;
Under floods that are deepest,
  Which Neptune obey,
Over rocks that are steepest,
  Love will find out the way.

corbies] carrion crows.   fail] turf.   hause-bane] neck-bone.   theek] thatch.

When there is no place
　For the glow-worm to lie,
Where there is no space
　For receipt of a fly;
Where the midge dares not venture
　Lest herself fast she lay,
If Love come, he will enter
　And will find out the way.

You may esteem him
　A child for his might;
Or you may deem him
　A coward from his flight;
But if she whom Love doth honour
　Be conceal'd from the day—
Set a thousand guards upon her,
　Love will find out the way.

Some think to lose him
　By having him confined;
And some do suppose him,
　Poor heart! to be blind;
But if ne'er so close ye wall him,
　Do the best that you may,
Blind Love, if so you call him,
　Will find out his way.

You may train the eagle
　To stoop to your fist;
Or you may inveigle
　The Phœnix of the east;
The lioness, ye may move her
　To give over her prey;
But you'll ne'er stop a lover—
　He will find out his way.

If the earth it should part him,
  He would gallop it o'er;
If the seas should o'erthwart him,
  He would swim to the shore;
Should his Love become a swallow,
  Through the air to stray,
Love will lend wings to follow,
  And will find out the way.

There is no striving
  To cross his intent;
There is no contriving
  His plots to prevent;
But if once the message greet him
  That his True Love doth stay,
If Death should come and meet him,
  Love will find out the way!

WALY, WALY

O WALY waly up the bank,
  And waly waly down the brae,
And waly waly yon burn-side
  Where I and my Love were wont to gae!
I leant my back unto an aik,
  I thought it was a trusty tree;
But first it bow'd, and syne it brak,
  Sae my true love did lichtly me.

O waly waly gin love be bonny
  A little time while it is new;
But when it's auld it waxeth cauld
  And fades awa' like morning dew.
O wherfore shuld I busk my heid?
  Or wherfore shuld I kame my hair?

waly] a cry of grief.   aik] oak.   busk] dress up.
kame] comb.

For my true Love has me forsook,
    And says he'll never loe me mair.

Now Arthur-Seat sall be my bed;
    The sheets shall ne'er be fyl'd by me:
Saint Anton's well sall be my drink,
    Since my true Love has forsaken me.
Marti'mas wind, when wilt thou blaw
    And shake the green leaves aff the tree?
O gentle Death, when wilt thou come?
    For of my life I am wearîe.

'Tis not the frost, that freezes fell,
    Nor blawing snaw's inclemencie,
'Tis not sic cauld that makes me cry,
    But my Love's heart grown cauld to me.
When we came in by Glasgow town,
    We were a comely sight to see;
My Love was clad in the black velvèt,
    And I myself in cramasie.

But had I wist, before I kist,
    That love had been sae ill to win;
I had lockt my heart in a case of gowd
    And pinn'd it with a siller pin.
And O! if my young babe were born,
    And set upon the nurse's knee.
And I myself were dead and gane,
    For a maid again I'se never be.

THE BAILIFF'S DAUGHTER OF ISLINGTON

There was a youth, and a well-beloved youth,
    And he was a squire's son;
He loved the bailiff's daughter dear,
    That lived in Islington.

        fell] fierce.   cramasie] crimson.

She was coy, and she would not believe
   That he did love her so,
No, nor at any time she would
   Any countenance to him show.

But when his friends did understand
   His fond and foolish mind,
They sent him up to fair London
   An apprentice for to bind.

And when he had been seven long years,
   And his love he had not seen,
'Many a tear have I shed for her sake,
   When she little thought of me'.

All the maids of Islington
   Went forth to sport and play;
All but the bailiff's daughter dear;
   She secretly stole away.

She put off her gown of gray,
   And put on her puggish attire;
She's up to fair London gone
   Her true-love to require.

As she went along the road,
   The weather being hot and dry,
There was she aware of her true-love,
   At length came riding by.

She stept to him, as red as any rose,
   And took him by the bridle-ring;
'I pray you, kind sir, give me one penny,
   To ease my weary limb.'

'I prithee, sweetheart, canst thou tell me
   Where that thou wast born?'

     puggish] tramp's, ragged.

'At Islington, kind sir,' said she,
  'Where I have had many a scorn.'

'I prithee, sweetheart, canst thou tell me,
  Whether thou dost know,
The bailiff's daughter of Islington?'
  'She's dead, sir, long ago.'

'Then will I sell my goodly steed,
  My saddle and my bow;
I will into some far country,
  Where no man doth me know.'

'O stay, O stay, thou goodly youth!
  Here she standeth by thy side,
She's alive, she is not dead;
  And is ready to be thy bride.'

'O farewell grief, and welcome joy,
  Ten thousand times and more!
For now I have seen mine own true-love,
  That I thought I should have seen no more.'

THE BLIND BEGGAR'S DAUGHTER OF BEDNALL-GREEN

PART I

IT was a blind beggar, had long lost his sight,
He had a fair daughter of beauty most bright;
And many a gallant brave suitor had she,
For none was so comely as pretty Bessee.

And though she was of favour most fair,
Yet seeing she was but a poor beggar's heir,
Of ancient housekeepers despisèd was she,
Whose sons came as suitors to pretty Bessee.

Wherefore in great sorrow fair Bessy did say,
Good father, and mother, let me go away
To seek out my fortune, whatever it be,
This suit then they granted to pretty Bessee.

Then Bessy, that was of beauty so bright,
All clad in grey russet, and late in the night
From father and mother alone parted she;
Who sighèd and sobbèd for pretty Bessee.

She went till she came to Stratford-le-Bow;
Then knew she not whither, nor which way to go:
With tears she lamented her hard destinîe,
So sad and so heavy was pretty Bessee.

She kept on her journey until it was day,
And went unto Rumford along the high way;
Where at the Queen's Arms entertainèd was she:
So fair and well-favoured was pretty Bessee.

She had not been there a month to an end,
But master and mistress and all was her friend:
And every brave gallant, that once did her see,
Was straightway enamour'd of pretty Bessee.

Great gifts they did send her of silver and gold,
And in their songs daily her love was extolled;
Her beauty was blazèd in every degree;
So fair and so comely was pretty Bessee.

The young men of Rumford in her had their joy;
She showed herself courteous, and modestly coy;
And at her commandment still would they be;
So fair and so comely was pretty Bessee.

Four suitors at once unto her did go;
They craved her favour, but still she said no;
I would not wish gentles to marry with me;
Yet ever they honoured pretty Bessee.

The first of them was a gallant young knight,
And he came unto her disguised in the night:
The second a gentleman of good degree,
Who wooèd and suèd for pretty Bessee.

A merchant of London, whose wealth was not small,
He was the third suitor, and proper withal:
Her master's own son the fourth man must be,
Who swore he would die for pretty Bessee.

And, if thou wilt marry with me, quoth the knight,
I'll make thee a lady with joy and delight;
My heart's so enthrallèd by thy beautie,
That soon I shall die for pretty Bessee.

The gentleman said, Come, marry with me,
As fine as a lady my Bessy shall be:
My life is distressed: O hear me, quoth he;
And grant me thy love, my pretty Bessee.

Let me be thy husband, the merchant could say,
Thou shalt live in London both gallant and gay;
My ships shall bring home rich jewels for thee,
And I will for ever love pretty Bessee.

Then Bessy she sighed, and thus she did say,
My father and mother I mean to obey;
First get their good will, and be faithful to me,
And then you shall marry your pretty Bessee.

To every one this answer she made,
Wherefore unto her they joyfully said,
This thing to fulfil we all do agree;
But where dwells thy father, my pretty Bessee?

My father, she said, is soon to be seen:
The silly blind beggar of Bednall-green,
That daily sits begging for charitie,
He is the good father of pretty Bessee.

His marks and his tokens are known very well;
He always is led with a dog and a bell:
A silly old man, God knoweth, is he,
Yet he is the father of pretty Bessee.

Nay then, quoth the merchant, thou art not for me.
Nor, quoth the inholder, my wife thou shalt be:
I loathe, said the gentle, a beggar's degree,
And therefore adieu, my pretty Bessee.

Why then, quoth the knight, hap better or worse,
I weigh not true love by the weight of the purse,
And beauty is beauty in every degree;
Then welcome unto me, my pretty Bessee.

With thee to thy father forthwith I will go.
Nay soft, quoth his kinsmen, it must not be so;
A poor beggar's daughter no lady shall be,
Then take thy adieu of pretty Bessee.

But soon after this, by break of the day
The knight had from Rumford stole Bessy away.
The young men of Rumford, as thick as might be,
Rode after to fetch again pretty Bessee.

As swift as the wind to ride they were seen,
Until they came near unto Bednall-green;
And as the knight lighted most courteouslìe,
They all fought against him for pretty Bessee.

But rescue came speedily over the plain,
Or else the young knight for his love had been slain.
This fray being ended, then straightway he see
His kinsmen come railing at pretty Bessee.

Then spake the blind beggar, Although I be poor,
Yet rail not against my child at my own door:
Though she be not deckèd in velvet and pearl,
Yet will I drop angels with you for my girl.

And then, if my gold may better her birth,
And equal the gold that you lay on the earth,
Then neither rail nor grudge you to see
The blind beggar's daughter a lady to be.

But first you shall promise, and have it well known,
The gold that you drop shall all be your own.
With that they replied, Contented be we.
Then here's, quoth the beggar, for pretty Bessee.

With that an angel he cast on the ground,
And droppèd in angels full three thousand pound;
And oftentimes it was proved most plain,
For the gentlemen's one the beggar dropt twain:

So that the place, wherein they did sit,
With gold it was coverèd every whit.
The gentlemen then having dropt all their store,
Said, Now, beggar, hold, for we have no more.

Thou hast fulfilled thy promise aright.
Then marry, quoth he, my girl to this knight;
And here, added he, I will now throw you down
A hundred pounds more to buy her a gown.

The gentlemen all, that this treasure had seen,
Admirèd the beggar of Bednall-green:
And all those, that were her suitors before,
Their flesh for very anger they tore.

Thus was fair Bessy matched to the knight,
And then made a lady in others' despite:
A fairer lady there never was seen,
Than the blind beggar's daughter of Bednall-green.

But of their sumptuous marriage and feast,
What brave lords and knights thither were prest,
The second fitt shall set forth to your sight
With marvellous pleasure and wishèd delight.

PART II

Of a blind beggar's daughter most bright,
That late was betrothed unto a young knight;
All the discourse thereof you did see:
But now comes the wedding of pretty Bessee.

Within a gorgeous palace most brave,
Adorned with all the cost they could have,
This wedding was kept most sumptuouslie,
And all for the credit of pretty Bessee.

All kind of dainties and delicates sweet
Were bought for the banquet, as it was most meet;
Partridge, and plover, and venison most free,
Against the brave wedding of pretty Bessee.

The marriage through England was spread by
    report,
So that a great number thereto did resort
Of nobles and gentles in every degree;
And all for the fame of pretty Bessee.

To church then went this gallant young knight;
His bride followed after, an angel most bright,
With troops of ladies, the like ne'er was seen,
As went with Bessy of Bednall-green.

This marriage being solemnizèd then,
With musick performed by the skilfullest men,
The nobles and gentles sat down at that tide,
Each one admiring the beautiful bride.

Now, after the sumptuous dinner was done,
To talk, and to reason a number begun:
They talked of the blind beggar's daughter most
    bright,
And what with his daughter he gave to the knight.

Then spake the nobles, Much marvel have we,
This jolly blind beggar we cannot here see.
My lords, quoth the bride, my father's so base,
He is loth with his presence these states to disgrace.

The praise of a woman in question to bring
Before her own face, were a flattering thing,
But we think thy father's baseness, quoth they,
Might by thy beauty be clean put away.

They had no sooner these pleasant words spoke,
But in comes the beggar clad in a silk cloak;
A fair velvet cap, and a feather had he,
And now a musician forsooth he would be.

He had a dainty lute under his arm,
He touched the strings, which made such a charm,
Says, Please you to hear any musick of me,
I'll sing you a song of pretty Bessee.

With that his lute he twangèd straightway,
And thereon began most sweetly to play;
And after that lessons were played two or three,
He strain'd out this song most delicatelie.

'A poor beggar's daughter did dwell on a green,
Who for her fairness might well be a queen:
A blithe bonny lass, and a dainty was she,
And many one called her pretty Bessee.

'Her father he had no goods, nor no land,
But begged for a penny all day with his hand;
And yet to her marriage he gave thousands three,
And still he hath somewhat for pretty Bessee.

'And if any one here her birth do disdain,
Her father is ready, with might and with main,
To prove she is come of noble degree:
Therefore never flout at pretty Bessee.'

With that the lords and the company round
With hearty laughter were ready to swound;
At last said the lords, Full well we may see,
The bride and the beggar's beholden to thee.

On this the bride all blushing did rise,
The pearly drops standing within her fair eyes,
O pardon my father, grave nobles, quoth she,
That through blind affection thus doteth on me.

If this be thy father, the nobles did say,
Well may he be proud of this happy day;
Yet by his countenance well may we see,
His birth and his fortune did never agree:

And therefore, blind man, we pray thee bewray
(And look that the truth thou to us do say)
Thy birth and thy parentage, what it may be;
For the love that thou bearest to pretty Bessee.

'Then give me leave, nobles and gentles, each one,
One song more to sing, and then I have done;
And if that it may not win good report,
Then do not give me a *groat* for my sport.

'Sir Simon de Montfort my subject shall be;
Once chief of all the great barons was he,
Yet fortune so cruel this lord did abase,
Now lost and forgotten are he and his race.

'When the barons in arms did king Henry oppose,
Sir Simon de Montfort their leader they chose;
A leader of courage undaunted was he,
And ofttimes he made their enemies flee.

'At length in the battle on Evesham plain,
The barons were routed, and Montfort was slain;
Most fatal that battle did prove unto thee,
Though thou wast not born then, my pretty Bessee!

'Along with the nobles, that fell at that tide,
His eldest son Henry, who fought by his side,
Was felled by a blow he received in the fight;
A blow that deprived him for ever of sight.

'Among the dead bodies all lifeless he lay,
Till evening drew on of the following day,
When by a young lady discovered was he;
And this was thy mother, my pretty Bessee!

'A baron's fair daughter stept forth in the night
To search for her father, who fell in the fight,
And seeing young Montfort, where gasping he lay,
Was movèd with pity, and brought him away.

'In secret she nurst him, and suagèd his pain,
While he through the realm was believed to be
        slain:
At length his fair bride she consented to be,
And made him glad father of pretty Bessee.

'And now, lest our foes our lives should betray,
We clothèd ourselves in beggars' array;
Her jewels she sold, and hither came we:
All our comfort and care was our pretty Bessee.

'And here have we lived in fortune's despite,
Though poor, yet contented with humble delight:
Full forty winters thus have I been
A silly blind beggar of Bednall-green.

'And here, noble lords, is ended the song
Of one, that once to your own rank did belong:
And thus have you learned a secret from me,
That ne'er had been known, but for pretty Bessee.'

Now when the fair company every one,
Had heard the strange tale in the song he had
        shown,

They all were amazed, as well they might be,
Both at the blind beggar, and pretty Bessee.

With that the fair bride they all did embrace,
Saying, Sure thou art come of an honourable race,
Thy father likewise is of noble degree,
And thou art well worthy a lady to be.

Thus was the feast ended with joy and delight,
A bridegroom most happy then was the young
    knight,
In joy and felicitie long livèd he,
All with his fair lady, the pretty Bessee.

THE TWA BROTHERS

I

THERE were twa brethren in the North,
    They went to school the gither;
The one unto the other said,
    Will you try a warsle, afore?

II

They warsled up, they warsled down,
    Till Sir John fell to the ground,
And there was a knife in Sir Willie's pouch
    Gied him a deadlie wound.

III

'Tak' aff, tak' aff my holland sark,
    Rive it frae gare to gare,
And stap it in my bleeding wound—
    'Twill aiblins bleed nae mair.'

sark] shirt.   rive] tear.   gare] gusset.   aiblins]
perhaps.

IV

He's pu'it aff his holland sark,
   Rave it frae gare to gare,
And stapt it in his bleeding wound—
   But aye it bled the mair.

V

'O tak' now aff my green sleiding
   And row me saftly in,
And carry me up to Chester kirk,
   Whar the grass grows fair and green.

VI

'But what will ye say to your father dear
   When ye gae home at e'en?'—
'I'll say ye're lying at Chester kirk,
   Whar the grass grows fair and green.'—

VII

'O no, O no, when he speers for me
   Saying, 'William, whar is John?'
Ye'll say ye left me at Chester school
   Leaving the school alone.'

VIII

He's ta'en him up upo' his back,
   And borne him hence away,
And carried him to Chester kirk,
   And laid him in the clay.

IX

But when he sat in his father's chair,
   He grew baith pale and wan:
'O what blude's that upon your brow?
   And whar is your brither John?'—

sleiding] clothing.   row] wrap.   speers] enquires.

X

'O John's awa' to Chester school,
    A scholar he'll return;
He bade me tell his father dear
    About him no' to mourn.

XI

'And it is the blude o' my gude grey steed;
    He wadna hunt for me.'—
'O thy steed's blude was ne'er so red,
    Nor ne'er so dear to me!

XII

'And whaten blude's that upon your dirk?
    Dear Willie, tell to me.'—
'It is the blude o' my ae brither
    And dule and wae is me!'—

XIII

'O what sall I say to your mither?
    Dear Willie, tell to me.'—
'I'll saddle my steed and awa' I'll ride,
    To dwell in some far countrie.'—

XIV

'O when will ye come hame again?
    Dear Willie, tell to me!'—
'When the sun and moon dance on yon green:
    And that will never be!'

THE TWA SISTERS

THERE were twa sisters sat in a bour;
    Binnorie, O Binnorie!
There cam a knight to be their wooer,
    By the bonnie milldams o' Binnorie.

He courted the eldest with glove and ring,
But he lo'ed the youngest abune a' thing.

The eldest she was vexèd sair,
And sair envìed her sister fair.

Upon a morning fair and clear,
She cried upon her sister dear:

'O sister, sister, tak' my hand,
And let's go down to the river-strand.'

She's ta'en her by the lily hand,
And led her down to the river-strand.

The youngest stood upon a stane,
The eldest cam' and push'd her in.

'O sister, sister, reach your hand!
And ye sall be heir o' half my land:

'O sister, reach me but your glove!
And sweet William sall be your love.'

Sometimes she sank, sometimes she swam,
Until she cam' to the miller's dam.

Out then cam' the miller's son,
And saw the fair maid soummin' in.

'O father, father, draw your dam!
There's either a mermaid or a milk-white swan.'

The miller hasted and drew his dam,
And there he found a drown'd womàn.

You couldna see her middle sma',
Her gowden girdle was sae braw.

You couldna see her lily feet,
Her gowden fringes were sae deep.

soummin'] swimming.

All amang her yellow hair
A string o' pearls was twisted rare.

You couldna see her fingers sma',
Wi' diamond rings they were cover'd a'.

And by there cam' a harper fine,
That harpit to the king at dine.

And when he look'd that lady on,
He sigh'd and made a heavy moan.

He's made a harp of her breast-bane,
Whose sound wad melt a heart of stane.

He's ta'en three locks o' her yellow hair,
And wi' them strung his harp sae rare.

He went into her father's hall,
And there was the court assembled all.

He laid his harp upon a stane,
And straight it began to play by lane.

'O yonder sits my father, the King,
And yonder sits my mother, the Queen;

'And yonder stands my brother Hugh,
And by him my William, sweet and true.'

But the last tune that the harp play'd then—
    Binnorie, O Binnorie !
Was, 'Woe to my sister, false Helèn!'
    By the bonnie milldams o' Binnorie.

THE THREE RAVENS

THERE were three ravens sat on a tree,
They were as black as they might be.

The one of them said to his make,
'Where shall we our breakfast take?'

      by lane] alone.   make] mate.

'Down in yonder greenë field
There lies a knight slain under his shield;

'His hounds they lie down at his feet,
So well they their master keep;

'His hawks they flie so eagerly,
There's no fowl dare him come nigh.'

Down there comes a fallow doe
As great with young as she might goe.

She lift up his bloudy head
And kist his wounds that were so red.

She got him up upon her back
And carried him to earthen lake.

She buried him before the prime,
She was dead herself ere evensong time.

God send every gentleman
Such hounds, such hawks, and such a leman.

GENTLE HERDSMAN TELL TO ME

DIALOGUE BETWEEN A PILGRIM AND A HERDSMAN

GENTLE herdsman tell to me,
　　Of curtesy I thee pray,
Unto the towne of Walsingham
　　Which is the right and ready way.

'Unto the towne of Walsingham
　　The way is hard for to be gone;
And very crooked are those pathes
　　For you to find out all alone.'

Were the miles doubled thrice,
　　And the way never soe ill,

leman] lover.

It were not enough for mine offence;
  It is soe grievous and so ill.

'Thy years are young, thy face is faire,
  Thy wits are weake, thy thoughts are green;
Time hath not given thee leave, as yet,
  For to commit so great a sin.'

Yes, herdsman, yes, soe woldst thou say,
  If thou knewest soe much as I;
My wits, and thoughts, and all the rest,
  Have well deservèd for to die.

I am not what I seem to be,
  My clothes and sex do differ far:
I am a woman, woe is me!
  Born to grief and irksome care.

For my beloved, and well-beloved
  My wayward cruelty could kill:
And though my tears will nought avail,
  Most dearely I bewail him still.

He was the flower of noble wights,
  None ever more sincere co'ld be;
Of comely mien and shape he was,
  And tenderlye he lovèd mee.

When thus I saw he loved me well,
  I grewe so proud his paine to see,
That I, who did not know mysell,
  Thought scorne of such a youth as he.

And grewe so coy and nice to please,
  As women's lookes are often soe,
He might not kisse nor hand forsooth,
  Unlesse I willed him so to do.

Thus being wearyed with delayes
  To see I pitied not his grief.

He got him to a secret place
    And there he died without relief.

And for his sake these weeds I weare,
    And sacrifice my tender age;
And every day I'le beg my bread,
    To undergoe this pilgrimage.

Thus every day I fast and pray,
    And ever will doe till I die;
And get me to some secret place,
    For soe did he, and soe will I.

Now, gentle herdsman, aske no more,
    But keepe my secrets I thee pray;
Unto the town of Walsingham
    Show me the right and readye way.

'Now goe thy wayes, and God before!
    For he must ever guide thee still:
Turne downe that dale, the right hand path,
    And soe, faire Pilgrim, fare thee well!'

THE BABES IN THE WOOD

I

Now ponder well, you parents dear,
    These words, which I shall write;
A doleful story you shall hear
    In time brought forth to light.
A gentleman of good account
    In Norfolk dwelt of late,
Who did in honour far surmount
    Most men of his estate.

II

Sore sick he was, and like to die,
    No help his life could save;

His wife by him as sick did lie,
 And both possessed one grave.
No love between these two was lost,
 Each was to other kind,
In love they lived, in love they died,
 And left two babes behind:

III

The one a fine and pretty boy,
 Not passing three years old;
The other a girl more young than he,
 And framed in beauty's mould.
The father left his little son,
 As plainly did appear,
When he to perfect age should come,
 Three hundred pounds a year.

IV

And to his little daughter Jane
 Five hundred pounds in gold,
To be paid down on marriage-day,
 Which might not be controlled.
But if the children chanced to die,
 Ere they to age should come,
Their uncle should possess their wealth;
 For so the will did run.

V

'Now, brother,' said the dying man,
 'Look to my children dear;
Be good unto my boy and girl,
 No friends else have they here:
To God and you I recommend
 My children dear this day;
But little while be sure we have
 Within this world to stay.

VI

'You must be father and mother both,
　　And uncle all in one;
God knows what will become of them,
　　When I am dead and gone.'
With that bespake their mother dear,
　　'O brother kind,' quoth she,
'You are the man must bring our babes
　　To wealth or misery:

VII

'And if you keep them carefully,
　　Then God will you reward;
But if you otherwise should deal,
　　God will your deeds regard.'
With lips as cold as any stone,
　　They kissed their children small:
'God bless you both, my children dear;'
　　With that the tears did fall.

VIII

These speeches then their brother spake
　　To this sick couple there,
'The keeping of your little ones,
　　Sweet sister, do not fear;
God never prosper me nor mine,
　　Nor aught else that I have,
If I do wrong your children dear,
　　When you are laid in grave.'

IX

The parents being dead and gone,
　　The children home he takes,
And brings them straight unto his house,
　　Where much of them he makes.

He had not kept these pretty babes
   A twelvemonth and a day,
But, for their wealth, he did devise
   To make them both away.

X

He bargained with two ruffians strong,
   Which were of furious mood,
That they should take these children young,
   And slay them in a wood.
He told his wife an artful tale,
   He would the children send
To be brought up in fair Londòn
   With one that was his friend.

XI

Away then went those pretty babes,
   Rejoicing at that tide,
Rejoicing with a merry mind,
   They should on cock-horse ride.
They prate and prattle pleasantly,
   As they rode on the way,
To those that should their butchers be,
   And work their lives' decay:

XII

So that the pretty speech they had,
   Made Murder's heart relent;
And they that undertook the deed,
   Full sore did now repent.
Yet one of them, more hard of heart,
   Did vow to do his charge,
Because the wretch, that hirèd him,
   Had paid him very large.

XIII

The other won't agree thereto,
    So here they fall to strife;
With one another they did fight,
    About the children's life:
And he that was of mildest mood,
    Did slay the other there,
Within an unfrequented wood;
    The babes did quake for fear!

XIV

He took the children by the hand,
    Tears standing in their eye,
And bade them straightway follow him,
    And look they did not cry;
And two long miles he led them on,
    While they for food complain:
'Stay here,' quoth he; 'I'll bring you bread
    When I come back again.'

XV

These pretty babes, with hand in hand,
    Went wandering up and down;
But never more could see the man
    Approaching from the town;
Their pretty lips with blackberries
    Were all besmeared and dyed,
And when they saw the darksome night,
    They sat them down and cried.

XVI

Thus wandered these poor innocents,
    Till death did end their grief,
In one another's arms they died,
    As wanting due relief:

No burial this pretty pair
   From any man receives,
Till Robin-redbreast piously
   Did cover them with leaves.

XVII

And now the heavy wrath of God
   Upon their uncle fell;
Yea, fearful fiends did haunt his house,
   His conscience felt an hell:
His barns were fired, his goods consumed,
   His lands were barren made;
His cattle died within the field,
   And nothing with him stayed.

XVIII

And in a voyage to Portugal
   Two of his sons did die;
And to conclude, himself was brought
   To want and misery:
He pawned and mortgaged all his land
   Ere seven years came about,
And now at length this wicked act
   Did by this means come out.

XIX

The fellow, that did take in hand
   These children for to kill,
Was for a robbery judged to die,
   Such was God's blessèd will:
Who did confess the very truth
   As here hath been displayed:
The uncle having died in gaol,
   Where he for debt was laid.

XX

You that executors be made,
  And overseërs eke,
Of children that be fatherless,
  And infants mild and meek;
Take you example by this thing,
  And yield to each his right,
Lest God with such like misery
  Your wicked minds requite.

FAIR ANNIE

THE reivers they stole Fair Annie,
  As she walked by the sea;
But a noble knight was her ransom soon,
  Wi' gowd and white monie.

She bided in strangers' land wi' him,
  And none knew whence she came;
She lived in the castle wi' her love,
  But never told her name.

'It's narrow, narrow, mak your bed,
  And learn to lie your lane;
For I'm gaun owre the sea, Fair Annie,
  A braw bride to bring hame.
Wi' her I will get gowd and gear,
  Wi' you I ne'er gat nane.

'But wha will bake my bridal bread,
  Or brew my bridal ale?
And wha will welcome my bright bride,
  That I bring owre the dale?'

'It's I will bake your bridal bread,
  And brew your bridal ale;

reivers] robbers.   white monie] silver.

And I will welcome your bright bride,
   That you bring owre the dale.'

'But she that welcomes my bright bride
   Maun gang like maiden fair;
She maun lace on her robe sae jimp,
   And comely braid her hair.

'Bind up, bind up your yellow hair,
   And tie it on your neck;
And see you look as maiden-like
   As the day that first we met.'

'O how can I gang maiden-like,
   When maiden I am nane?
Have I not borne six sons to thee,
   And am wi' child again?'

'I'll put cooks into my kitchen,
   And stewards in my hall,
And I'll have bakers for my bread,
   And brewers for my ale;
But you're to welcome my bright bride,
   That I bring owre the dale.'

Three months and a day were gane and past,
   Fair Annie she gat word
That her love's ship was come at last,
   Wi' his bright young bride aboard.

She's ta'en her young son in her arms,
   Anither in her hand;
And she's gane up to the highest tower,
   Looks over sea and land.

'Come up, come up, my eldest son,
   And look o'er yon sea strand,
And see your father's new come bride,
   Before she come to land.'

          jimp] trim.

'Come doun, come doun, my mother dear,
  Come aff the castle wa'!
I fear if langer ye stand there,
  Ye'll let yoursell doun fa'.'

She's ta'en a cake o' the best bread,
  A stoup o' the best wine,
And a' the keys upon her arm,
  And to the yett is gane.

'O ye're welcome hame, my ain gude lord,
  To your castles and your towers;
Ye're welcome hame, my ain gude lord,
  To your ha's, but and your bowers.

And welcome to your hame, fair lady!
  For a' that's here is yours.'
'O whatna lady's that, my lord,
  That welcomes you and me?

Gin I be lang about this place,
  Her friend I mean to be.'
Fair Annie served the lang tables
  Wi' the white bread and the wine;

But ay she drank the wan water
  To keep her colour fine.
And she gaed by the first table,
  And smiled upon them a';

But ere she reach'd the second table,
  The tears began to fa'.
She took a napkin lang and white,
  And hung it on a pin;

It was to wipe away the tears,
  As she gaed out and in.
When bells were rung and mass was sung,
  And a' men bound for bed,

        yett] gate.

The bridegroom and the bonny bride
  In ae chamber were laid.

Fair Annie's ta'en a harp in her hand,
  To harp thir twa asleep;
But ay, as she harpit and she sang,
  Fu' sairly did she weep.

'O gin my sons were seven rats,
  Rinnin' on the castle wa',
And I mysell a great grey cat,
  I soon wad worry them a'!

'O gin my sons were seven hares,
  Rinnin' owre yon lily lea,
And I mysell a good greyhound,
  Soon worried they a' should be!'

Then out and spak the bonny young bride,
  In bride-bed where she lay:
'That's like my sister Annie,' she says;
  'Wha is it doth sing and play?

'I'll put on my gown,' said the new-come bride,
  'And my shoes upon my feet;
I will see wha doth sae sadly sing,
  And what is it gars her greet.

'What ails you, what ails you, my housekeeper,
  That ye mak sic a mane?
Has ony wine-barrel cast its girds,
  Or is a' your white bread gane?'

'It isna because my wine is spilt,
  Or that my white bread's gane;
But because I've lost my true love's love,
  And he's wed to anither ane.'

'Noo tell me wha was your father?' she says,
  'Noo tell me wha was your mother?

      gars her greet] makes her weep.

And had ye ony sister?' she says,
  'And had ye ever a brother?'

'The Earl of Wemyss was my father,
  The Countess of Wemyss my mother,
Young Elinor she was my sister dear,
  And Lord John he was my brother.'

'If the Earl of Wemyss was your father,
  I wot sae was he mine;
And it's O my sister Annie!
  Your love ye sallna tyne.

'Tak your husband, my sister dear;
  You ne'er were wrang'd for me,
Beyond a kiss o' his merry mouth
  As we cam owre the sea.

'Seven ships, loaded weel,
  Cam owre the sea wi' me;
Ane o' them will tak me hame,
  And six I'll gie to thee.'

THE FROLICSOME DUKE, OR THE TINKER'S GOOD FORTUNE

Now as fame does report, a young duke keeps a
    court,
One that pleases his fancy with frolicksome sport:
But amongst all the rest, here is one I protest,
Which will make you to smile when you hear the
    true jest:
A poor tinker he found, lying drunk on the ground,
As secure in a sleep as if laid in a swound.

tyne] lose.

The duke said to his men, William, Richard, and
    Ben,
Take him home to my palace, we'll sport with him
    then.
O'er a horse he was laid, and with care soon con-
    vey'd
To the palace, altho' he was poorly array'd:
Then they stripped off his clothes, both his shirt,
    shoes and hose,
And they put him to bed for to take his repose.

Having pull'd off his shirt, which was all over dirt,
They did give him clean holland, this was no
    great hurt;
On a bed of soft down, like a lord of renown,
They did lay him to sleep the drink out of his
    crown:
In the morning when day, then admiring he lay,
For to see the rich chamber both gaudy and gay.

Now he lay something late, in his rich bed of state,
Till at last knights and squires they on him did
    wait;
And the chamberling bare, then did likewise
    declare,
He desir'd to know what apparel he'd wear:
The poor tinker amaz'd, on the gentleman gaz'd,
And admired how he to this honour was rais'd.

Tho' he seem'd something mute, yet he chose a
    rich suit,
Which he straitways put on without longer dispute;
With a star on his side, which the tinker oft ey'd,
And it seem'd for to swell him no little with pride;

For he said to himself, where is Joan my sweet
    wife?
Sure she never did see me so fine in her life.

From a convenient place, the right duke his good
    grace
Did observe his behaviour in every case.
To a garden of state, on the tinker they wait,
Trumpets sounding before him: thought he, this
    is great:
Where an hour or two, pleasant walks he would
    view,
With commanders and squires in scarlet and blue.

A fine dinner was dressed, both for him and his guests,
He was plac'd at the table above all the rest,
In a rich chair or bed, lin'd with fine crimson red,
With a rich golden canopy over his head:
As he sat at his meat, the music play'd sweet,
With the choicest of singing his joys to complete.

While the tinker did dine, he had plenty of wine,
Rich canary with sherry and tent superfine.
Like a right honest soul, faith, he took off his bowl,
Till at last he began for to tumble and roll
From his chair to the floor, where he sleeping did
    snore,
Being seven times drunker than ever before.

Then the duke did ordain, they should strip him
    amain,
And restore him his old leather garments again:
'Twas a point next the worst, yet perform it they
    must,
And they carried him straight where they found
    him at first;

Then he slept all the night, as indeed well he
  might;
But when he did waken, his joys took their flight.

For his glory to him so pleasant did seem,
That he thought it to be but a mere golden dream;
Till at length being brought to the duke, where he
  sought
For a pardon, as fearing he had set him at nought;
But his highness he said, Thou'rt a jolly bold
  blade,
Such a frolic before I think never was played.

Then his highness bespoke him a new suit and
  cloak,
Which he gave for the sake of this frolicsome
  joke;
Nay, and five hundred pound, with ten acres of
  ground,
Thou shalt never, said he, range the countries
  around,
Crying old brass to mend, for I'll be thy good
  friend,
Nay, and Joan thy sweet wife shall my duchess
  attend.

Then the tinker reply'd, What! must Joan my
  sweet bride
Be a lady in chariots of pleasure to ride?
Must we have gold and land ev'ry day at com-
  mand?
Then I shall be a squire I well understand.
Well, I thank your good grace, and your love I
  embrace,
I was never before in so happy a case.

SIR ANDREW BARTON

I

As it befel in midsummer-time,
  When birds singe sweetlye on every tree,
Our noble king, King Henry the Eighth,
  Over the river of Thames pass'd he.

II

He was no sooner over the river,
  Downe in a forrest to take the ayre,
But eighty merchants of London citye
  Came kneeling before King Henry there.

III

'O ye are welcome, rich merchànts,
  Good saylers, welcome unto me!'
They swore by the rood they were saylers good,
  But rich merchànts they co'ld not be.

IV

'To France nor Flanders dare we not passe,
  Nor Bourdeaux voyage we dare not fare,
All for a false robber that lyes on the seas,
  And robbs us of our merchants-ware.'

V

King Henry was stout, and he turned him about,
  And swore by the Lord that was mickle of might,
'I thought he'd not been in the world throughout
  That durst have wrought England such unright.'

VI

But ever they sighèd and said, alas!
  Unto King Harry this answer againe:
'He is a proud Scott that will robb us all
  Were we twenty shipps and he but one.'

VII

The King looket over his left shouldèr,
    Amongst his lords and barons so free:
'Have I never a lord in all my realme
    Will fetch yond traitor unto me?'

VIII

'Yes, that dare I!' says my lord Charles Howard,
    Neere to the King wheras he did stand;
'If that Your Grace will give me leave,
    My self will perform what you command.'

IX

'Thou shalt have six hundred men,' saith our King,
    'And chuse them out of my realme so free;
[Moreover] mariners and ship boyes,
    To guide the great ship on the sea.'

X

'I'le goe speake with Sir Andrew,' says my Lord
    Howard;
    'Upon the sea, if he be there;
I will bring him and his ship to shore,
    Or before my prince I will ne'er come neere.'

XI

The first of all my Lord did call,
    A noble gunner he was one;
This man was three score yeares and ten,
    And Peter Simon was his name.

XII

'Peter,' says he, 'I must sayle to the sea,
    To seek out an enemy; God be my speed!
Before all others I have chosen thee;
    Of a hundred gunners thou'st be my head.'

XIII

'My lord,' says he, 'if you've chosen me
  Of a hundred gunners to be the head,
You may hang me at your maine-mast tree
  If I miss my mark past three pence bread.'

XIV

The next of all my lord he did call,
  A noble bowman he was one;
In Yorkshire was this gentleman borne,
  And William Horsley was his name.

XV

'Horsley,' says he, 'I must sayle to the sea,
  To seek out an enemy; God be my speede!
Before all others I have chosen thee;
  Of a hundred bowemen thou'st be my head '

XVI

'My lord,' says he, 'if you've chosen me
  Of a hundred bowemen to be the head,
Hang me at your main-mast tree
  If I miss my mark past twelve pence bread.'

XVII

With pikes, and gunnes, and bowmen bold,
  This noble Howard is gone to the sea
On the day before Midsummer-even,
  And out at Thames' mouth saylèd they.

XVIII

They had not saylèd dayès three
  Upon their journey they took in hand,
But there they met with a noble ship,
  And stoutely made it both stay and stand.

three pence bread] the breadth of a threepenny piece.

XIX

'Thou must tell me thy name,' says Charles my
  lord Howard,
 'Or who thou art, or from whence thou came,
Yea, and where thy dwelling is,
  To whom and where thy ship does belong.'

XX

'My name,' says he, 'is Henery Hunt,
 With a pure hart and a penitent mind;
I and my ship they doe belong
  Unto the New-castle that stands upon Tyne.'—

XXI

'Now thou must tell me, Henery Hunt,
 As thou hast saylèd by day and by night
Hast thou not heard of a stout robbèr?
  Men calls him Sir Andrew Barton, Knight.'

XXII

But ever he sighèd, and said, 'Alas!
 Full well, my lord, I know that wight;
He has robb'd me of my merchants-ware,
  And I was his pris'ner but yesternight.

XXIII

'As I was sayling upon the sea,
 And a Bourdeaux voyage as I did fare,
He claspèd me to his archèborde,
  And robb'd me of all my merchants-ware.

XXIV

'And I am a man both poor and bare,
 Every man will have his own of me;
And I am bound towards London to fare,
  To complain unto my prince Henrye.

 archèborde] hatch-board, part of the side of a ship.

XXV

'That shall not need,' says my Lord Howard;
  'If thou canst let me this robber see,
For every penny he hath taken thee fro'
  Thou shalt be rewarded a shilling,' quoth he.

XXVI

'Now God forfend,' says Henery Hunt,
  'My lord, you sho'ld work so far amisse!
God keep you out of that traitor's hands!
  For you wot full little what man he is.

XXVII

'He is brasse within, and steele without,
  And beams he bears in his topcastle stronge;
His ship hath ordinance clean round about;
  Besides, my lord, he is very well mann'd.

XXVIII

'He hath a pinnace is dearlye dight,
  Saint Andrew's cross, that is his guide;
His pinnace bears nine-score men and more,
  With fifteen cannons on every side.

XXIX

'Were you twenty ships, and he but one,
  Either in archbord or in hall,
He wo'ld overcome you everye one,
  And if his beams they doe down fall.'

XXX

'This is cold comfort,' says my Lord Howard,
  'To welcome a stranger thus to the sea;
I'le bring him and his ship to shore,
  Or else into Scotland he shall carry me.'

dight] adorned.   hall] hull.

XXXI

'Then, my lord, you must get a noble ganner;
  One that can set well with his e'e,
And sink his pinnace into the sea,
  And soon then overcome will he be.

XXXII

'And when that you have done all this,
  If you chance Sir Andrew for to board,
Let no man to his topcastle go;
  And I will give you a glass, my lord,

XXXIII

'And then you need to fear no Scot,
  Whether you sayle by day or by night;
And to-morrow, by seven of the clocke,
  You shall meete with Sir Andrew Barton,
    Knight.'

XXXIV

The merchant set Lord Howard a glass
  So well apparent in his sight
That on the morrow by seven of the clock
  He spy'd Sir Andrew Barton, Knight.

XXXV

Lord Howard he swore a mighty oath
  When he saw his hache-bords dearly dight;
'Now by my faith and by my troth,
  Yonder proud Scott is a worthy wight.

XXXVI

'Take in your ancients and your standards,
  Yea, that no man shall them see,
And put me forth a white willow wand,
  As merchants use to sayle the sea.'

ancients] ensigns.

XXXVII

But they stirr'd neither top nor mast,
    But Sir Andrew they passèd by.—
'What English are yonder,' said Sir Andrew,
    'That can so little curtesye?

XXXVIII

'I have been admiral over the sea
    [Methinketh] more then these yeeres three;
There is never an English nor Portingall dog,
    Can pass this way without leave of me.

XXXIX

'But now yonder pedlars, they are pass'd,
    Which is no little grief to me:
Fetch them backe,' sayes Sir Andrew Barton,
    'They shall all hang at my maine-mast tree.'

XL

With that the pinnace it shot off,
    That my Lord Howard might it well ken;
It strokè down my lord's fore-màst,
    And kill'd fourteen of my lord his men.

XLI

'Come hither, Simon!' says my Lord Howard,
    'Look that thy words be true thou said;
I'le hang thee at my maine-mast tree
    If thou miss thy mark past three pence bread.'

XLII

Simon was old, but his hart it was bold;
    He tooke downe a piece, and laid it full low;
Chaine yeards nine he put therein,
    Besides other great shot less and moe.

can] know.

XLIII

With that he let his gun-shot go;
  So well he settled it with his e'e,
The first sight that Sir Andrew saw,
  He saw his pinnace sunk in the sea.

XLIV

When Sir Andrew saw his pinnace sunk,
  Lord! in his heart he was not well!
'Cut my ropes! it is time to be gone!
  I'le goe fetch yond pedlars back mysell!'

XLV

When my Lord Howard saw Sir Andrew loose,
  Lord! in his heart that he was faine!
'Strike on your drums! spread out your ancients!
  Sound out your trumpets! sound out amain!'

XLVI

'Fight on, my men!' says Sir Andrew Barton;
  'Weate, howsoever this geare will sway,
It is my Lord Admiral of England
  Is come to seek me on the sea.'

XLVII

Simon had a sone; with shot of a gun—
  Well Sir Andrew might it ken—
He shot it in at the middle deck,
  And killed sixty more of Sir Andrew's men.

XLVIII

[Bold] Hunt came in at the other side,
  And at Sir Andrew he shot then;
He drove down his fore-mast tree,
  And kill'd eighty more of Sir Andrew's men.

weate] know. geare] business, affair. sway]
turn out, result.

XLIX

'I have done a good turne,' sayes Henery Hunt;
  'Sir Andrew is not our King's friend;
He hoped t' have undone me yesternight,
  But I hope I have quit him well in the end.'

L

'Ever alas!' sayd Sir Andrew Barton,
  'What sho'ld a man either thinke or say?
Yonder false thief is my strongest enemy,
  Who was my prisoner but yesterday.

LI

'Come hither to me, thou Gourden good,
  And be thou ready at my call,
And I will give thee three hundred pound
  If thou wilt let my beames downe fall.'

LII

With that hee swarm'd the main-mast tree,
  Soe did he it with might and maine;
But Horsley, with a bearing arrow,
  Stroke the Gourden through the braine.

LIII

And he fell into the hatches againe,
  And sore of his wound that he did bleed;
Then word went through Sir Andrew's men,
  How that the Gourden he was dead.

LIV

'Come hither to me, James Hamilton,
  Thou'rt my sister's son, I have no more;
I will give thee six hundred pound
  If thou wilt let my beames downe fall.'

LV

With that he swarm'd the main-mast tree,
  Soe did he it with might and main:
Horsley, with another broad arrow,
  Strake the yeaman thoro' the brain.

LVI

That he fell downe to the hatches againe;
  Sore of his wound that hee did bleed;
Covetousness gets no gaine,
  It is very true, as the Welshman said.

LVII

But when he saw his nephew slaine,
  Lord! in his heart he was not well!
'Go fetch me downe my armour of proof,
  For I will to the topcastle mysell.

LVIII

'Go fetch me downe my armour of proof,
  For it is gilded with gold so cleere;
God be with my brother, John of Barton!
  Amongst the Portingalls he did it weare.'

LIX

But when he had his armour of proof,
  And on his body he had it on,
Every man that lookèd at him
  Said, Gun nor arrow he need fear none.

LX

'Come hither, Horsley!' says my Lord Howard,
  'And look your shaft that it goe right;
Shoot a good shoote in the time of need,
  And for thy shooting thou'st be made knight.'

LXI

'I'le do my best,' sayes Horsley then,
  'Your Honour shall see before I goe;
If I sno'ld be hang'd at your maine-mast tree,
  I have in my ship but arrows two.'

LXII

But at Sir Andrew he shot then;
  He made so sure to hit his mark;
Under the spole of his right arme
  He smote Sir Andrew quite thro' the heart.

LXIII

Yet from the tree he wo'ld not start,
  But he cling'd to it with might and main;
Under the collar then of his jacke,
  He stroke Sir Andrew thoro' the brain.

LXIV

'Fight on, my men!' says Sir Andrew Barton,
  'I am hurt, but I am not slain;
I'le lay me downe and bleed a-while,
  And then I'le rise and fight again.

LXV

'Fight on, my men!' says Sir Andrew Barton,
  'These English dogs they bite so lowe;
Fight on for Scotland and Saint Andrew
  While that you hear my whistle blowe!'

LXVI

But when they co'ld not hear his whistle,
  Says Henery Hunt, 'I'le lay my head
You may board yonder noble ship, my lord,
  For I know Sir Andrew he is dead.'

spole] shoulder.

LXVII

With that they boarded this noble ship,
 So did they it with might and main;
They found eighteen score Scots alive,
 Besides the rest were maim'd and slaine.

LXVIII

Lord Howard took a sword in his hand,
 And so smote off Sir Andrew's head;
The Scots stood by did weepe and mourne,
 But never a word they spoke or sayd.

LXIX

He caused his body to be taken downe,
 And over the hatch-bord cast into the sea,
And about his middle three hundred crownes:
 'Wheresoever thou lands, it will bury thee!'

LXX

With his head they sayl'd into England againe,
 With right good will and force and main,
And on the day before New-Year's Even
 Into Thames' mouth they came againe.

LXXI

Lord Howard wrote to King Henry's grace,
 With all the newes he co'ld him bring:
'Such a New Year's gift I have brought to your
 Grace
As never did subject to any King.

LXXII

'For merchandise, yea and manhood,
 The like is nowhere to be found;
The sight of these wo'ld do you good,
 For you have not the like in your English
 ground.'

LXXIII

When the King heard tell that they were come,
  Full royally he welcomed them home;
Sir Andrew's ship was his New-Year's gift;
  A braver ship you never saw none.

LXXIV

Now hath our King Sir Andrew's ship,
  Beset with pearles and precyous stones;
And now hath England two ships of war,
  Two ships of war, before but one.

LXXV

'Who holpe to this?' says King Henrye,
  'That I may reward him for his paine.'—
'Henery Hunt, and Peter Simon,
  William Horsley, and I the same.'—

LXXVI

'Harry Hunt shall have his whistle and chaine,
  And all his jewels whatsoe'er they be,
And other rich gifts that I will not name,
  For his good service he hath done me.

LXXVII

'Horsley, right thou'st be a knight,
  Lands, and livings thou shalt have store;
Howard shall be Earl of Nottingham,
  And so was never Howard before.

LXXVIII

'Now, Peter Simon, thou art old;
  I will maintaine thee and thy son;
Thou shalt have five hundred pound all in gold
  For the good service that thou hast done.'

LXXIX

With that King Henrye shifted his room;
  In came the Queen and Ladyes bright;
Other arrands they had none
  But to see Sir Andrew Barton, Knight.

LXXX

But when they saw his deadly face,
  His eyes were hollow in his head;
'I wo'ld give a hundred pound,' says his grace,
  'The man were alive as he is dead.

LXXXI

'Yet for the manful part he hath play'd,
  Both here at home and beyond the sea,
His men shall have half-a-crown a day
  Till they come to my brother, King Jamie.'

WINIFREDA

Away; let nought to love displeasing,
  My Winifreda, move your care;
Let nought delay the heavenly blessing,
  Nor squeamish pride, nor gloomy fear.

What tho' no grants of royal donors
  With pompous titles grace our blood!
We'll shine in more substantial honours,
  And to be noble we'll be good.

Our name, while virtue thus we tender,
  Will sweetly sound where-e'er 'tis spoke:
And all the great ones, they shall wonder,
  How they respect such little folk.

What tho', from fortune's lavish bounty,
    No mighty treasures we possess?
We'll find within our pittance plenty,
    And be content without excess.

Still shall each kind returning season
    Sufficient for our wishes give:
For we will live a life of reason,
    And that 's the only life to live.

Through youth and age in love excelling,
    We'll hand in hand together tread;
Sweet-smiling peace shall crown our dwelling,
    And babes, sweet-smiling babes, our bed.

How should I love the pretty creatures,
    While round my knees they fondly clung,
To see them look their mother's features,
    To hear them lisp their mother's tongue!

And, when with envy time transported
    Shall think to rob us of our joys,
You'll in your girls again be courted,
    And I'll go wooing in my boys.

THE SPANISH ARMADO

Some years of late, in eighty-eight,
    As I do well remember,
It was, some say, the middle of May,
    And some say in September,
        And some say in September.

The Spanish train launched forth amain,
    With many a fine bravado,
Their (as they thought, but it proved not)
    Invincible Armado,
        Invincible Armado.

There was a man that dwelt in Spain
   Who shot well with a gun a,
Don Pedro hight, as black a wight
   As the Knight of the Sun a,
     As the Knight of the Sun a.

King Philip made him Admiral,
   And bid him not to stay a,
But to destroy both man and boy
   And so to come away a,
     And so to come away a.

Their navy was well victualled
   With biscuit, pease, and bacon,
They brought two ships, well fraught with whips,
   But I think they were mistaken,
     But I think they were mistaken.

Their men were young, munition strong,
   And to do us more harm a,
They thought it meet to join their fleet
   All with the Prince of Parma,
     All with the Prince of Parma.

They coasted round about our land,
   And so came in by Dover:
But we had men set on 'em then,
   And threw the rascals over,
     And threw the rascals over.

The Queen was then at Tilbury,
   What could we more desire a?
Sir Francis Drake for her sweet sake
   Did set them all on fire a,
     Did set them all on fire a.

        hight] named.

Then straight they fled by sea and land,
    That one man killed threescore a,
And had not they all run away,
    In truth he had killed more a,
    In truth he had killed more a.

Then let them neither bray nor boast,
    But if they come again a,
Let them take heed they do not speed
    As they did you know when a,
    As they did you know when a.

ROBIN GOODFELLOW

FROM Oberon, in fairy land,
    The king of ghosts and shadows there,
Mad Robin I, at his command,
    Am sent to view the night-sports here.
        What revel rout
        Is kept about,
In every corner where I go,
        I will o'ersee,
        And merry be,
And make good sport, with ho, ho, ho!

More swift than lightning can I fly
    About this airy welkin soon,
And, in a minute's space, descry
    Each thing that's done below the moon.
        There's not a hag
        Or ghost shall wag,
Or cry, 'ware goblins! where I go;
        But Robin I
        Their feasts will spy,
And send them home with ho, ho, ho!

Whene'er such wanderers I meet,
  As from their night-sports they trudge home,
With counterfeiting voice I greet,
  And call them on with me to roam:
      Through woods, through lakes,
      Through bogs, through brakes;
  Or else, unseen, with them I go,
      All in the nick,
      To play some trick,
  And frolic it, with ho, ho, ho!

Sometimes I meet them like a man,
  Sometimes an ox, sometimes a hound;
And to a horse I turn me can,
  To trip and trot about them round.
      But if to ride
      My back they stride,
  More swift than wind away I go:
      O'er hedge and lands,
      Through pools and ponds
  I hurry, laughing, ho, ho, ho!

When lads and lasses merry be,
  With possets and with junkets fine;
Unseen of all the company,
  I eat their cakes and sip their wine!
      And, to make sport,
      I puff and snort:
  And out the candles I do blow:
      The maids I kiss,
      They shriek—Who's this?
  I answer nought but ho, ho, ho!

Yet now and then, the maids to please,
  At midnight I card up their wool;

And, while they sleep and take their ease,
  With wheel to threads their flax I pull.
      I grind at mill
      Their malt up still;
  I dress their hemp; I spin their tow;
      If any wake,
      And would me take,
  I wend me, laughing, ho, ho, ho!

When any need to borrow aught,
  We lend them what they do require:
And for the use demand we nought;
  Our own is all we do desire.
      If to repay
      They do delay,
  Abroad amongst them then I go,
      And night by night
      I them affright
  With pinchings, dreams, and ho, ho, ho!

When lazy queans have nought to do,
  But study how to cheat and lie:
To make debate and mischief too,
  'Twixt one another secretly:
      I mark their gloze,
      And it disclose
  To them whom they have wrongèd so:
      When I have done,
      I get me gone,
  And leave them scolding, ho, ho, ho!

When men do traps and engines set
  In loop-holes, where the vermin creep,
Who from their folds and houses get
  Their ducks and geese, and lambs and sheep;

I spy the gin,
And enter in,
And seem a vermin taken so;
But when they there
Approach me near,
I leap out laughing, ho, ho, ho!

By wells and rills, in meadows green,
We nightly dance our heyday guise;
And to our fairy king and queen
We chant our moonlight minstrelsies.
When larks 'gin sing,
Away we fling;
And babes newborn steal as we go;
And elf in bed
We leave instead,
And wend us laughing, ho, ho, ho!

From hag-bred Merlin's time, have I
Thus nightly revelled to and fro;
And for my pranks men call me by
The name of Robin Goodfellow.
Fiends, ghosts, and sprites,
Who haunt the nights,
The hags and goblins do me know
And beldames old
My feats have told,
So vale, vale; ho, ho, ho!

LATELY WRITTEN BY THOMAS, EARL OF
STRAFFORD

Go, empty joys,
With all your noise,
And leave me here alone,

In sweet sad silence, to bemoan
 Your vain and fleet delight,
Whose danger none can see aright;
Whilst your false splendour dims his sight.

  Go and ensnare
  With your false ware,
Some other easy wight,
And cheat him with your flattering light:
 Rain on his head a shower
Of honours, favour, wealth, and power;
Then snatch it from him in an hour!

  Fill his big mind
  With gallant wind
Of insolent applause:
Let him not fear all curbing laws,
 Nor king nor people's frown;
But dream of something like a crown,
And climbing towards it tumble down.

  Let him appear
  In his bright sphere,
Like Cynthia in her pride,
With star-like troops on every side;
 Such for their number and their light,
As may at last o'erwhelm him quite;
And blend us both in one dead night.

  Welcome, sad night,
  Grief's sole delight,
Your mourning best agrees
With honour's funeral obsequies!
 In Thetis' lap he lies,
Mantled with soft securities;
Whose too much sunshine blinds his eyes.

Was he too bold,
That needs would hold
With curbing reins, the day,
And make Sol's fiery steeds obey?
Then sure as rash was I,
Who with ambitious wings did fly
In Charles his Wain too loftily.

I fall, I fall;
Whom shall I call?
Alas, can he be heard,
Who now is neither loved nor feared?
You, who were wont to kiss the ground
Where'er my honoured steps were found,
Come catch me at my last rebound.

How each admires
Heaven's twinkling fires;
When from their glorious seat
Their influence gives light and heat.
But O! how few there are
(Though danger from that act be far)
Will stoop and catch a falling star.

Now 'tis too late
To imitate
Those lights, whose pallidness
Argues no inward guiltiness:
Their course one way is bent.
The reason is, there's no dissent
In Heaven's High Court of Parliament.

London. Printed 1641.

SONG: HERE'S A HEALTH UNTO HIS MAJESTY

HERE's a health unto his Majesty,
With a fal, lal, la, la, la, la, la!
Conversion to his enemies,
With a fal, lal, la, la, la, la, la!
And he that will not pledge his health,
I wish him neither wit nor wealth,
Nor yet a rope to hang himself,
With a fal, lal, la, la, la, la, la!

THE LIBERTY AND REQUIEM OF AN IMPRISONED ROYALIST

BEAT on, proud billows! Boreas, blow!
Swell, curled waves, high as Jove's roof!
Your incivility shall know,
That innocence is tempest-proof.
Though surly Nereus frown, my thoughts are calm,
Then strike, afflictions, for your wounds are balm.

That which the world miscalls a jail,
A private closet is to me,
Whilst a good conscience is my bail,
And innocence my liberty.
Locks, bars, walls, loneness, though together met,
Make me no prisoner, but an Anchoret.

I, whilst I wished to be retired,
Into this private room was turned
As if their wisdoms had conspired
A salamander should be burned:
And like those sophies who would drown a fish,
I am condemned to suffer what I wish.

The cynic hugs his poverty,
The pelican, her wilderness,

And 'tis the Indian's pride to lie
    Naked on frozen Caucasus.
And like to these, stoics severe we see
Make torments easy by their apathy.

These manacles upon my arm,
    I as my sweetheart's favours wear,
And then to keep my ankles warm,
    I have some iron shackles there:
These walls are but my garrison, this cell,
Which men call jail, doth prove my citadel.

So he that struck at Jason's life,
    Thinking he had his purpose sure,
By a malicious friendly knife,
    Did only wound him to a cure.
Malice I see wants wit, for what is meant
Mischief, ofttimes proves favour by th' event.

I'm in this cabinet locked up
    Like some high-prizèd margarite;
Or like some Great Mogul, or Pope,
    Am cloistered up from public sight:
Retiredness is a part of majesty,
And thus, proud sultan, I'm as great as thee.

Here sin for want of food doth starve,
    Where tempting objects are not seen,
And these [strong] walls do only serve
    To keep vice out, and keep me in.
Malice of late 's grown charitable, sure!
I'm not committed, but am kept secure.

When once my Prince affliction hath,
    Prosperity doth treason seem,

And then to smooth so rough a path
 I can learn patience too from him.
Now not to suffer shews no loyal heart:
When kings want ease, subjects must love **to**
 smart.

What though I cannot see my King
 Either in 's person or his coin,
Yet contemplation is a thing
 Which renders what I have not, mine.
My King from me no adamant can part,
Whom I do wear engraven in my heart.

My soul's free as th' ambient air,
 Although my baser part 's immured,
Whilst loyal thoughts do still repair
 T' accompany my solitude:
And though rebellion do my body bind,
My King can only captivate my mind.

Have you not seen the nightingale
 When turned a pilgrim to a cage,
How she doth sing her wonted tale
 In that her narrow hermitage;
Even there her chanting melody doth prove
That all her bars are trees, her cage a grove.

I am that bird, which they combine
 Thus to deprive of liberty,
Who though they do my corpse confine,
 Yet, maugre hate, my soul is free:
And though immured, yet can I chirp and sing
'Disgrace to rebels, glory to my King!'

THE QUEEN OF FAIRIES

Come follow, follow me,
    You, fairy elves that be,
    Which circle on the green;
    Come follow me, your queen.
Hand in hand, let's dance a round,
For this place is fairy ground.

When mortals are at rest,
    And snoring in their nest;
    Unheard and unespied,
    Through key-holes we do glide;
Over tables, stools, and shelves,
We trip it with our fairy elves.

And, if the house be foul,
    Or platter, dish, or bowl,
    Up stairs we nimbly creep,
    And find the sluts asleep:
There we pinch their arms and thighs—
None escapes; nor none espies.

But if the house be swept,
    And from uncleanness kept,
    We praise the household maid,
    And surely she is paid:
For we do use before we go,
To drop a tester in her shoe.

Upon a mushroom's head,
    Our table we do spread;
    A grain of rye, or wheat,
    Is manchet, which we eat;
Pearly drops of dew we drink
In acorn cups filled to the brink.

The brains of nightingales,
With unctuous dew of snails,
Between two nutshells stewed,
Is meat that 's easily chewed;
And the beards of little mice
Do make a feast of wondrous price.

On tops of dewy grass,
So nimbly do we pass,
The young and tender stalk
Ne'er bends when we do walk;
Yet in the morning may be seen
Where we, the night before, have been.

The grasshopper, gnat and fly,
Serve for our minstrelsy;
Grace said, we dance a while,
And so the time beguile:
And when the moon doth hide her head,
The glow-worm lights us home to bed.

IN PRAISE OF ALE

When the chill Charoko blows,
And Winter tells a heavy tale,
And pyes and daws and rooks and crows
Do sit and curse the frosts and snows;
Then give me ale.

Ale in a Saxon rumkin then,
Such as will make grim Malkin prate;
Bids valour burgeon in tall men,
Quickens the poet's wits and pen,
Despises fate.

Charoko] Sirocco.   burgeon] spring forth, bud.

Ale, that the absent battle fights,
   And forms the march of Swedish drum,
Disputes the princes' laws, and rights,
What 's past and done tells mortal wights,
      And what 's to come.

Ale, that the plowman's heart up-keeps
   And equals it to tyrants' thrones,
That wipes the eye that ever-weeps,
And lulls in sweet and dainty sleeps
      Their very bones.

Grandchild of Ceres, Bacchus' daughter,
   Wine's emulous neighbour, though but stale,
Ennobling all the nymphs of water,
And filling each man's heart with laughter—
      Ha! Ha! give me ale!

THE FAREWELL

It was a' for our rightfu' King
   We left fair Scotland's strand;
It was a' for our rightfu' King
   We e'er saw Irish land,
      My dear—
We e'er saw Irish land.

Now a' is done that men can do,
   And a' is done in vain;
My love and native land, farewell!
   For I maun cross the main,
      My dear—
For I maun cross the main.

He turn'd him right and round about
   Upon the Irish shore;

And gae his bridle-reins a shake,
  With Adieu for evermore,
      My dear—
  With Adieu for evermore!

The sodger frae the wars returns,
  The sailor frae the main;
But I hae parted frae my love,
  Never to meet again,
      My dear—
  Never to meet again.

When day is gane, and night is come,
  And a' folk bound to sleep,
I think on him that 's far awa',
  The lee-lang night, and weep,
      My dear—
  The lee-lang night, and weep.

TIME'S ALTERATION

When this old cap was new,
  'Tis since two hundred year;
No malice then we knew,
  But all things plenty were:
All friendship now decays
  (Believe me, this is true);
Which was not in those days,
  When this old cap was new.

The nobles of our land
  Were much delighted then,
To have at their command
  A crew of lusty men,
Which by their coats were known,
  Of tawny, red, or blue,
With crests on their sleeves shewn,
  When this old cap was new.

Now pride hath banished all,
  Unto our land's reproach,
When he whose means is small,
  Maintains both horse and coach:
Instead of a hundred men,
  The coach allows but two;
This was not thought on then,
  When this old cap was new.

Good hospitality
  Was cherished then of many;
Now poor men starve and die,
  And are not helped by any:
For charity waxeth cold,
  And love is found in few;
This was not in time of old,
  When this old cap was new.

Where'er you travelled then,
  You might meet on the way
Brave knights and gentlemen
  Clad in their country gray,
That courteous would appear,
  And kindly welcome you;
No puritans then were,
  When this old cap was new.

Our ladies in those days
  In civil habit went;
Broadcloth was then worth praise,
  And gave the best content:
French fashions then were scorned;
  Fond fangles then none knew;
Then modesty women adorned,
  When this old cap was new.

A man might then behold,
    At Christmas, in each hall,
Good fires to curb the cold,
    And meat for great and small:
The neighbours were friendly bidden,
    And all had welcome true;
The poor from the gates were not chidden
    When this old cap was new.

Black jacks to every man
    Were filled with wine and beer;
No pewter pot nor can
    In those days did appear:
Good cheer in a nobleman's house
    Was counted a seemly show;
We wanted no brawn nor souse,
    When this old cap was new.

We took not such delight
    In cups of silver fine;
None under the degree of a knight
    In plate drank beer or wine:
Now each mechanical man
    Hath a cupboard of plate for a show;
Which was a rare thing then,
    When this old cap was new.

Then bribery was unborn,
    No simony men did use;
Christians did usury scorn,
    Devised among the Jews.
The lawyers to be fee'd
    At that time hardly knew;
For man with man agreed,
    When this old cap was new.

No captain then caroused,
   Nor spent poor soldiers' pay;
They were not so abused
   As they are at this day:
Of seven days they make eight,
   To keep from them their due;
Poor soldiers had their right,
   When this old cap was new.

Which made them forward still
   To go, although not pressed;
And going with good-will,
   Their fortunes were the best.
Our English then in fight
   Did foreign foes subdue,
And forced them all to flight,
   When this old cap was new.

God save our gracious king,
   And send him long to live:
Lord, mischief on them bring
   That will not their alms give,
But seek to rob the poor
   Of that which is their due:
This was not in time of yore,
   When this old cap was new.

MADRIGAL

Love not me for comely grace,
For my pleasing eye or face;
Nor for any outward part,
No, nor for my constant heart:
    For those may fail or turn to ill,
      So thou and I shall sever.

Keep therefore a true woman's eye,
And love me still, but know not why;
    So hast thou the same reason still
      To doat upon me ever.

MY LADY GREENSLEEVES

ALAS! my love, you do me wrong
    To cast me off discourteously;
And I have lovèd you so long,
    Delighting in your company.

    Greensleeves was all my joy!
    Greensleeves was my delight!
    Greensleeves was my heart of gold!
      And who but my Lady Greensleeves!

I bought thee petticoats of the best,
    The cloth so fine as fine as might be;
I gave thee jewels for thy chest,
    And all this cost I spent on thee.
      Greensleeves, etc.

Thy smock of silk, both fair and white,
    With gold embroidered gorgeously;
Thy petticoat of sendal right:
    And these I bought thee gladly.
      Greensleeves, etc.

Thy gown was of the grassy green,
    The sleeves of satin hanging by;
Which made thee be our harvest queen:
    And yet thou wouldest not love me!
      Greensleeves, etc.

Greensleeves now farewell! adieu!
  God I pray to prosper thee!
For I am still thy lover true:
  Come once again and love me!
    Greensleeves was all my joy!
    Greensleeves was my delight!
    Greensleeves was my heart of gold!
      And who but Lady Greensleeves!

THE WEAVER'S SONG

WHEN Hercules did use to spin,
  And Pallas wrought upon the loom,
Our trade to flourish did begin,
  While conscience went not selling broom;
Then love and friendship did agree
  To keep the bands of amity.

When princes' sons kept sheep in field,
  And queens made cakes of wheaten flour,
The men to lucre did not yield,
  Which brought good cheer in every bower;
Then love and friendship, etc.

But when the Giants huge and high,
  Did fight with spears like weavers' beams,
Then they in iron beds did lie,
  And brought poor men to hard extremes:
Yet love and friendship, etc.

Then David took his sling and stone,
  Not fearing great Goliath's strength,
He pierced his brains, and broke the bone,
  Though he were fifty foot of length;
For love and friendship, etc.

But while the Greeks besiegèd Troy,
   Penelope apace did spin;
And weavers wrought with mickle joy,
   Though little gains were coming in;
For love and friendship, etc.

Had Helen then sate carding wool,
   (Whose beauteous face did breed such strife),
She had not been Sir Paris' trull,
   Nor caused so many to lose their life;
Yet we by love did still agree
To hold the bands of amity.

Or had King Priam's wanton son
   Been making quills with sweet content,
He had not then his friends undone,
   When he to Greece a-gadding went;
For love and friendship, etc.

The cedar-trees endure more storms
   Than little shrubs that sprout on high;
The weavers live more void of harms
   Than princes of great dignity;
While love and friendship doth agree, etc.

The shepherd sitting in the field
   Doth tune his pipe with heart's delight;
When princes watch with spear and shield,
   The poor man soundly sleeps all night;
While love and friendship doth agree, etc.

Yet this by proof is daily tried,
   For God's good gifts we are ingrate,
And no man through the world so wide
   Lives well contented with his state;
No love and friendship we can see
To hold the bands of amity.

CAROLS

I SING OF A MAIDEN

I SING of a maiden
  That is makeless
King of all kings
  To her son she ches.

He came all so still
  There his mother was,
As dew in April
  That falleth on the grass.

He came all so still
  To His mother's bower,
As dew in April
  That falleth on the flower.

He came all so still
  There His mother lay,
As dew in April
  That falleth on the spray.

Mother and maiden
  Was never none but she;
Well may such a lady
  God's mother be.

CHILD OF MARY

THIS endris night
I saw a sight,
A star as bright as day;
And ever among
A maiden sung
  Lullay, byby, lullay.

makeless] mateless.   ches] chose.   endris] last.
among] anon.

This lovely lady sat and sang, and to her child gan
    say
'My son, my brother, my father dear, why liest
    thou thus in hay?

> My sweetë brid,
> Thus it is betid
>   Though thou be King veray;
> But, nevertheless,
> I will not cease
>   To sing byby, lullay.'

The child then spake in his talking; and to his
    mother said—
'I am beknown for heaven's king, in crib though I
    be laid;

> For angels bright
> Down to me light,
>   Thou knowest it is no nay.
> And of that sight
> Thou mayest be light,
>   To sing byby, lullay.'

'Now, sweetë son, since thou art king, why art thou
    laid in stall?
Why ne thou ordainëd thy bedding in some great
    kingës hall?

> Methinketh it right
> That king or knight
>   Should lie in good array;
> And then among
> It were no wrong
>   To sing byby, lullay.'

brid] bird.   ne thou ordainëd] ordainëd thou not.

'Mary, mother, I am thy child, though I be laid in
    stall,
Lords and dukes shall worship me, and so shall
    kingës all.
> Ye shall well see,
> The kingës three,
> > Shall come the twelfthē day;
> For this behest
> Give me thy breast,
> > And sing byby, lullay.'

'Now tell me, sweet son, I thee pray, thou art me
    lief and dear,
How should I keep thee to thy pay, and make thee
    glad of cheer?
> For all thy will
> I would fulfil,
> > Thou weet'st full well in fay.
> And for all this
> I will thee kiss,
> > And sing byby, lullay.'

'My dear mother, when time it be, thou take me up
    aloft,
And settē me upon thy knee, and handle me full
    soft.
> And in thy arm
> Thou hile me warm,
> > And keepë night and day;
> If I weep
> And may not sleep,
> > Thou sing byby, lullay.'

fief] beloved.   pay] content, satisfaction.   fay]
faith.   hile] cover.

'Now, sweetë son, since it is so, that all is at thy
        will,
I pray thee grant to me a boon if it be right and
        skill,
            That child or man,
            That will or can,
                Be merry upon my day;
            To bliss them bring,
            And I shall sing
                Lullay, byby, lullay.'

CAN I NOT SING BUT HOY!

CAN I not sing but Hoy!
When the jolly shepherd made so much joy!

The shepherd upon a hill he sat,
He had on him his tabard and his hat,
His tar-box, his pipe, and his flagat.
His name was called Jolly, Jolly Wat;
            For he was a good herds-boy,
                Ut hoy!
        For in his pipe he made so much joy.
            Can I not sing but hoy.

The shepherd upon a hill was laid,
His dog to his girdle was tayd,
He had not slept but a little braid,
But *gloria in excelsis* was to him said;
                Ut hoy!
        For in his pipe he made so much joy!
            Can I not sing, &c.

The shepherd on a hill he stood,
Round about him his sheep they yode,

skill] fitting.   tabard] loose frock.   little braid]
little while.   yode] went.

He put his hand under his hood,
He saw a star as red as blood.
Ut hoy!
For in his pipe he made so much joy!
Can I not sing, &c.

Now farewell Mall, and also Will,
For my love go ye all still,
Unto I come again you till,
And ever more, Will, ring well thy bell.
Ut hoy!
For in his pipe he made so much joy!
Can I not sing, &c.

Now must I go where Christ was born,
Farewell, I come again to-morn;
Dog, keep well my sheep fro the corn,
And warn well Warroke when I blow my horn!
Ut hoy!
For in his pipe he made so much joy!
Can I not sing, &c.

When Wat to Bethlehem come was,
He sweat, he had gone faster than a pace.
He found Jesus in a simple place,
Between an ox and an ass.
Ut hoy!
For in his pipe he made so much joy!
Can I not sing, &c.

The shepherd said anon right:
'I will go see yon ferly sight,
Where as the angel singeth on-height,
And the star that shineth so bright!'

ferly] strange.

Ut hoy!
For in his pipe he made so much joy!
Can I not sing, &c.

'Jesus, I offer to thee here my pipe,
My skirt, my tar box, and my scrip,
Home to my fellows now will I skip,
And also look unto my sheep!'
Ut hoy!
For in his pipe he made so much joy!
Can I not sing, &c.

'Now farewell, mine own herds-man Wat!'
'Yea, 'fore God, Lady, even so I hat!
Lull well, Jesus, in thy lap,
And farewell, Joseph, with thy round cap!'
Ut hoy!
For in his pipe he made so much joy!
Can I not sing, &c.

'Now may I well both hop and sing
For I have been at Christ's bearing;
Home to my fellows now will I fling;
Christ of heaven to His bliss us bring!'
Ut hoy!
For in his pipe he made so much joy!
Can I not sing, &c.

GOD REST YOU MERRY, GENTLEMEN

GOD rest you merry, gentlemen,
  Let nothing you dismay,
For Jesus Christ, our Saviour,
  Was born upon this day,

To save us all from Satan's power
  When we were gone astray.
        O tidings of comfort and joy!
        For Jesus Christ, our Saviour,
        Was born on Christmas Day.

In Bethlehem, in Jewry,
  This blessèd babe was born,
And laid within a manger,
  Upon this blessèd morn;
The which His mother, Mary,
  Nothing did take in scorn.
        O tidings—

From God, our Heavenly Father,
  A blessèd angel came;
And unto certain shepherds
  Brought tidings of the same:
How that in Bethlehem was born
  The Son of God by name.
        O tidings—

'Fear not,' then said the angel,
  'Let nothing you affright,
This day is born a Saviour
  Of virtue, power, and might,
So frequently to vanquish all
  The friends of Satan quite.'
        O tidings—

The shepherds at those tidings
  Rejoicèd much in mind,
And left their flocks a-feeding
  In tempest, storm, and wind,
And went to Bethlehem straightway,
  This blessèd babe to find.
        O tidings—

But when to Bethlehem they came,
  Whereat this infant lay,
They found Him in a manger,
  Where oxen feed on hay,
His mother Mary kneeling
  Unto the Lord did pray.
        O tidings—

Now to the Lord sing praises,
  All you within this place,
And with true love and brotherhood
  Each other now embrace;
This holy tide of Christmas
  All others doth deface.
        O tidings of comfort and joy!
        For Jesus Christ, our Saviour,
        Was born on Christmas Day.

THE FIRST NOWELL

THE first Nowell the angels did say
Was to certain poor shepherds in fields as they lay,
In fields where they lay keeping their sheep,
On a cold winter's night that was so deep.
  Nowell, Nowell, Nowell, Nowell,
  Born is the King of Israel.

They lookèd up and saw a star
Shining in the East beyond them far,
And to the earth it gave great light,
And so it continued both day and night.
  Nowell, Nowell, Nowell, Nowell,
  Born is the King of Israel.

And by the light of that same star
Three wise men came from country far;
To seek for a King was their intent,
And to follow the star wherever it went.
    Nowell, Nowell, Nowell, Nowell,
    Born is the King of Israel.

The star drew nigh to the north-west,
O'er Bethlehem it took its rest,
And there it did both stop and stay
Right over the place where Jesus lay.
    Nowell, Nowell, Nowell, Nowell,
    Born is the King of Israel.

Then entered in those wise men three,
Most reverently upon their knee,
And offered there in His presence
Their gold and myrrh and frankincense.
    Nowell, Nowell, Nowell, Nowell,
    Born is the King of Israel.

Then let us all with one accord
Sing praises to our heavenly Lord,
That hath made heaven and earth of naught,
And with His blood mankind hath bought.
    Nowell, Nowell, Nowell, Nowell,
    Born is the King of Israel.

INDEX OF FIRST LINES

REPRINTED LITHOGRAPHiCALLY IN GREAT BRITAIN
AT THE UNIVERSITY PRESS, OXFORD
BY VIVIAN RIDLER
PRINTER TO THE UNIVERSITY